The CUDA Handbook

The CUDA Handbook

A Comprehensive Guide
to GPU Programming

Nicholas Wilt

✦✦ Addison-Wesley

Upper Saddle River, NJ • Boston • Indianapolis • San Francisco
New York • Toronto • Montreal • London • Munich • Paris • Madrid
Capetown • Sydney • Tokyo • Singapore • Mexico City

The publisher offers excellent discounts on this book when ordered in quantity for bulk purchases or special sales, which may include electronic versions and/or custom covers and content partic-ular to your business, training goals, marketing focus, and branding interests. For more informa-tion, please contact:

U.S. Corporate and Government Sales
(800) 382-3419
corpsales@pearsontechgroup.com

For sales outside the United States, please contact:

International Sales
international@pearsoned.com

Visit us on the Web: informit.com/aw

Cataloging in Publication Data is on file with the Library of Congress.

ISBN-13: 978-0-321-80946-9
ISBN-10:   0-321-80946-7
Text printed in the United States on recycled paper at RR Donnelley in Crawfordsville, Indiana.
First printing, June 2013.

For Robin

Contents

PART I   1

PART III   351

Preface

If you are reading this book, I probably don't have to sell you on CUDA. Readers of this book should already be familiar with CUDA from using NVIDIA's SDK materials and documentation, taking a course on parallel programming, or reading the excellent introductory book *CUDA by Example* (Addison-Wesley, 2011) by Jason Sanders and Edward Kandrot.

Reviewing *CUDA by Example*, I am still struck by how much ground the book covers. Assuming no special knowledge from the audience, the authors manage to describe everything from memory types and their applications to graphics interoperability and even atomic operations. It is an excellent introduction to CUDA, but it is just that: an introduction. When it came to giving more detailed descriptions of the workings of the platform, the GPU hardware, the compiler driver nvcc, and important "building block" parallel algorithms like parallel prefix sum ("scan"), Jason and Edward rightly left those tasks to others.

This book is intended to help novice to intermediate CUDA programmers continue to elevate their game, building on the foundation laid by earlier work. In addition, while introductory texts are best read from beginning to end, *The CUDA Handbook* can be sampled. If you're preparing to build or program a new CUDA-capable platform, a review of Chapter 2 ("Hardware Architecture") might be in order. If you are wondering whether your application would benefit from using CUDA streams for additional concurrency, take a look at Chapter 6 ("Streams and Events"). Other chapters give detailed descriptions of the software architecture, GPU subsystems such as texturing and the streaming multiprocessors, and applications chosen according to their data access pattern and their relative importance in the universe of parallel algorithms. The chapters are relatively self-contained, though they do reference one another when appropriate.

The latest innovations, up to and including CUDA 5.0, also are covered here. In the last few years, CUDA and its target platforms have significantly evolved.

When *CUDA by Example* was published, the GeForce GTX 280 (GT200) was new, but since then, two generations of CUDA-capable hardware have become available. So besides more detailed discussions of existing features such as mapped pinned memory, this book also covers new instructions like Fermi's "ballot" and Kepler's "shuffle" and features such as 64-bit and unified virtual addressing and dynamic parallelism. We also discuss recent platform innovations, such as the integration of the PCI Express bus controller into Intel's "Sandy Bridge" CPUs.

However you choose to read the book—whether you read it straight through or keep it by your keyboard and consult it periodically—it's my sincerest hope that you will enjoy reading it as much as I enjoyed writing it.

Acknowledgments

I would like to take this opportunity to thank the folks at NVIDIA who have been patient enough to answer my questions, review my work, and give constructive feedback. Mark Harris, Norbert Juffa, and Lars Nyland deserve special thanks.

My reviewers generously took the time to examine the work before submission, and their comments were invaluable in improving the quality, clarity, and correctness of this work. I am especially indebted to Andre Brodtkorb, Scott Le Grand, Allan MacKinnon, Romelia Salomon-Ferrer, and Patrik Tennberg for their feedback.

My editor, the inimitable Peter Gordon, has been extraordinarily patient and supportive during the course of this surprisingly difficult endeavor. Peter's assistant, Kim Boedigheimer, set the standard for timeliness and professionalism in helping to complete the project. Her efforts at soliciting and coordinating review feedback and facilitating uploads to the Safari Web site are especially appreciated.

My wife Robin and my sons Benjamin, Samuel, and Gregory have been patient and supportive while I brought this project across the finish line.

About the Author

Nicholas Wilt has been programming computers professionally for more than twenty-five years in a variety of areas, including industrial machine vision, graphics, and low-level multimedia software. While at Microsoft, he served as the development lead for Direct3D 5.0 and 6.0, built the prototype for the Windows Desktop Manager, and did early GPU computing work. At NVIDIA, he worked on CUDA from the beginning, designing and often implementing most of CUDA's low-level abstractions. Now at Amazon, Mr. Wilt is working in cloud computing technologies relating to GPUs.

PART I

Chapter 1

Background

Much ink has been spilled describing the GPU revolution in computing. I have read about it with interest because I got involved very early. I was at Microsoft in the mid-1990s as development lead for Direct3D when Intel and AMD were introducing the first multimedia instruction sets to accelerate floating point computation. Intel had already tried (unsuccessfully) to forestall the migration of clock cycles for 3D rasterization from their CPUs by working with Microsoft to ship rasterizers that used their MMX instruction set. I knew that effort was doomed when we found that the MMX rasterizer, running on a yet-to-be-released Pentium 2 processor, was half as fast as a humble S3 Virge GX rasterizer that was available for sale.

For Direct3D 6.0, we worked with CPU vendors to integrate their code into our geometry pipeline so developers could transparently benefit from vendor-optimized code paths that used new instruction sets from Intel and AMD. Game developers embraced the new geometry pipeline, but it did not forestall the continued migration of clock cycles from the CPU to the GPU, as the new instruction sets were used to generate vertex data for consumption by GPUs' hardware geometry pipelines.

About this time, the number of transistors on GPUs overtook the number of transistors on CPUs. The crossover was in 1997–1998, when the Pentium 2 and the NVIDIA RIVA TNT both had transistor counts of about 8M. Subsequently, the Geforce 256 (15M transistors), Geforce 2 (28M transistors), and Geforce3 (63M transistors) all had more transistors than contemporary CPUs. Additionally, the architectural differences between the two devices were becoming clear: Most of the die area for CPUs was dedicated to cache, while most of the die area for GPUs was dedicated to logic. Intel was able to add significant new instruction set extensions (MMX, SSE, SSE2, etc.) with negligible area cost because their CPUs were mostly cache. GPUs were designed for parallel throughput processing; their small caches were intended more for bandwidth aggregation than for reducing latency.

While companies like ATI and NVIDIA were building GPUs that were faster and increasingly capable, CPU vendors continued to drive clock rates higher as Moore's Law enabled both increased transistor budgets and increased clock speeds. The first Pentium (c. 1993) had a clock rate of 60MHz, while MMX-enabled Pentiums (c. 1997) had clock rates of 200MHz. By the end of the decade, clock rates had exceeded 1,000MHz. But shortly thereafter, an important event in the history of computing took place: Moore's Law hit a wall. The transistors would continue to shrink, but clock rates could not continue to increase.

The event was not unexpected. Pat Gelsinger of Intel delivered a keynote at the 2001 IEEE Solid-State Circuits Conference and stated that if chips continued on their current design path, they would be as hot as nuclear reactors by the end of the decade and as hot as the surface of the sun by 2015. In the future, performance would have to come from "simultaneous multithreading" (SMT), possibly supported by putting multiple CPU cores on a single chip. Indeed, that is exactly what CPU vendors have done; today, it is difficult to almost impossible to find a desktop PC with a single-core CPU. But the decades-long free ride enabled by Moore's Law, in which increased clock rates made it possible for applications to run faster with little to no effort on the part of software developers, was over. Multicore CPUs require multithreaded applications. Only applications that benefit from parallelism can expect increased performance from CPUs with a larger number of cores.

GPUs were well positioned to take advantage of this new trend in Moore's Law. While CPU applications that had not been authored with parallelism in mind would require extensive refactoring (if they could be made parallel at all), graphics applications were already formulated in a way that exploited the inherent parallelism between independent pixels. For GPUs, increasing performance by increasing the number of execution cores was a natural progression. In fact, GPU designers tend to prefer more cores over more capable cores. They eschew strategies that CPU manufacturers take for granted, like maximizing clock frequency (GPUs had never, and still do not, run at clock rates approaching the limits of transistor fabrication), speculative execution, branch prediction, and store forwarding. And to prevent this ever-more-capable processor from becoming I/O bound, GPU designers integrated memory controllers and worked with DRAM manufacturers to enable bandwidths that far exceeded the amount of bandwidth available to CPUs.

But that abundant horsepower was difficult for nongraphics developers to exploit. Some adventurous souls used graphics APIs such as Direct3D and OpenGL to subvert graphics hardware to perform nongraphics computations. The term *GPGPU* (general-purpose GPU programming) was invented to describe this approach, but for the most part, the computational potential of GPUs remained untapped until CUDA. Ian Buck, whose Brook project at Stanford enabled simplified development of GPGPU applications, came to NVIDIA and led development of a new set of development tools that would enable nongraphics applications to be authored for GPUs much more easily. The result is CUDA: a proprietary toolchain from NVIDIA that enables C programmers to write parallel code for GPUs using a few easy-to-use language extensions.

Since its introduction in 2007, CUDA has been well received. Tens of thousands of academic papers have been written that use the technology. It has been used in commercial software packages as varied as Adobe's CS5 to Manifold's GIS (geographic information system). For suitable workloads, CUDA-capable GPUs range from 5x to 400x faster than contemporary CPUs. The sources of these speedups vary. Sometimes the GPUs are faster because they have more cores; sometimes because they have higher memory bandwidth; and sometimes because the application can take advantage of specialized GPU hardware not present in CPUs, like the texture hardware or the SFU unit that can perform fast transcendentals. Not all applications can be implemented in CUDA. In fact, not all *parallel* applications can be implemented in CUDA. But it has been used in a wider variety of applications than any other GPU computing technology. I hope this book helps accomplished CUDA developers to get the most out of CUDA.

1.1 Our Approach

CUDA is a difficult topic to write about. Parallel programming is complicated even without operating system considerations (Windows, Linux, MacOS), platform considerations (Tesla and Fermi, integrated and discrete GPUs, multiple GPUs), CPU/GPU concurrency considerations, and CUDA-specific considerations, such as having to decide between using the CUDA runtime or the driver API. When you add in the complexities of how best to structure CUDA kernels, it may seem overwhelming.

To present this complexity in a manageable way, most topics are explained more than once from different perspectives. *What does the texture mapping hardware do?* is a different question than *How do I write a kernel that does texture mapping?* This book addresses both questions in separate sections. Asynchronous memory copy operations can be explained in several different contexts: the interactions between software abstractions (for example, that participating host memory must be pinned), different hardware implementations, API support for the feature, and optimization strategies. Readers sometimes may wish to consult the index and read all of the different presentations on a given topic.

Optimization guides are like advice columns: Too often, the guidance is offered without enough context to be applied meaningfully, and they often seem to contradict themselves. That observation isn't intended to be pejorative; it's just a symptom of the complexity of the problem. It has been at least 20 years since blanket generalizations could be made about CPU optimizations, and GPUs are more complicated to program, so it's unrealistic to expect CUDA optimization advice to be simple.

Additionally, GPU computing is so new that GPU architects, let alone developers, are still learning how best to program them. For CUDA developers, the ultimate arbiter is usually performance, and performance is usually measured in wall clock time! Recommendations on grid and block sizes, how and when to use shared memory, how many results to compute per thread, and the implications of occupancy on performance should be confirmed empirically by implementing different approaches and measuring the performance of each.

1.2 Code

Developers want CUDA code that is illustrative yet not a toy; useful but does not require a technical dive into a far-afield topic; and high performance but does not obscure the path taken by implementors from their initial port to the final version. To that end, this book presents three types of code examples designed to address each of those considerations: microbenchmarks, microdemos, and optimization journeys.

1.2.1 MICROBENCHMARKS

Microbenchmarks are designed to illustrate the performance implications of a very specific CUDA question, such as how uncoalesced memory transactions degrade device memory bandwidth or the amount of time it takes the WDDM driver to perform a kernel thunk. They are designed to be compiled standalone and will look familiar to many CUDA programmers who've already implemented microbenchmarks of their own. In a sense, I wrote a set of microbenchmarks to obviate the need for other people to do the same.

1.2.2 MICRODEMOS

Microdemos are small applications designed to shed light on specific questions of how the hardware or software behaves. Like microbenchmarks, they are small and self-contained, but instead of highlighting a performance question, they highlight a question of functionality. For example, the chapter on texturing includes microdemos that illustrate how to texture from 1D device memory, how the float→int conversion is performed, how different texture addressing modes work, and how the linear interpolation performed by texture is affected by the 9-bit weights.

Like the microbenchmarks, these microdemos are offered in the spirit in which developers probably wanted to write them, or at least have them available. I wrote them so you don't have to!

1.2.3 OPTIMIZATION JOURNEYS

Many papers on CUDA present their results as a *fait accompli*, perhaps with some side comments on tradeoffs between different approaches that were investigated before settling on the final approach presented in the paper. Authors often have length limits and deadlines that work against presenting more complete treatments of their work.

For some select topics central to the data parallel programming enabled by CUDA, this book includes *optimization journeys* in the spirit of Mark Harris's "Optimizing Parallel Reduction in CUDA" presentation that walks the reader through seven increasingly complex implementations of increasing performance.[1] The topics we've chosen to address this way include reduction, parallel prefix sum ("scan"), and the N-body problem.

1.3 Administrative Items

1.3.1 OPEN SOURCE

The source code that accompanies this book is available on www.cudahandbook. com, and it is open source, copyrighted with the 2-clause BSD license.[2]

---

1. http://bit.ly/Z2q37x
2. www.opensource.org/licenses/bsd-license.php

1.3.2 CUDA HANDBOOK LIBRARY (CHLIB)

The CUDA Handbook Library, located in the chLib/ directory of the source code, contains a portable library with support for timing, threading, driver API utilities, and more. They are described in more detail in Appendix A.

1.3.3 CODING STYLE

Arguments over brace placement aside, the main feature of the code in this book that will engender comment is the goto-based error handling mechanism. Functions that perform multiple resource allocations (or other operations that might fail, and where failure should be propagated to the caller) are structured around an Initialize / ErrorCheck / Cleanup idiom, similar to a pattern commonly used in Linux kernel code.

On failure, all cleanup is performed by the same body of code at the end of the function. It is important to initialize the resources to guaranteed-invalid values at the top of the function, so the cleanup code knows which resources must be freed. If a resource allocation or other function fails, the code performs a goto the cleanup code. chError.h, described in Section A.6, defines error-handling macros for the CUDA runtime and the driver API that implement this idiom.

1.3.4 CUDA SDK

The SDK is a shared experience for all CUDA developers, so we assume you've installed the CUDA SDK and that you can build CUDA programs with it. The SDK also includes the GLUT (GL Utility Library), a convenient library that enables OpenGL applications to target a variety of operating systems from the same code base. GLUT is designed to build demo-quality as opposed to produc-tion-quality applications, but it fits the bill for our needs.

1.4 Road Map

The remaining chapters in Part I provide architectural overviews of CUDA hard-ware and software.

• Chapter 2 details both the CUDA hardware platforms and the GPUs themselves.

- Chapter 3 similarly covers the CUDA software architecture.

- Chapter 4 covers the CUDA software environment, including descriptions of CUDA software tools and Amazon's EC2 environment.

In Part II, Chapters 5 to 10 cover various aspects of the CUDA programming model in great depth.

- Chapter 5 covers memory, including device memory, constant memory, shared memory, and texture memory.

- Chapter 6 covers streams and events—the mechanisms used for "coarse-grained" parallelism between the CPU and GPU, between hardware units of the GPU such as copy engines and the streaming multiprocessors, or between discrete GPUs.

- Chapter 7 covers kernel execution, including the dynamic parallelism feature that is new in SM 3.5 and CUDA 5.0.

- Chapter 8 covers every aspect of streaming multiprocessors.

- Chapter 9 covers multi-GPU applications, including peer-to-peer operations and embarrassingly parallel operations, with N-body as an example.

- Chapter 10 covers every aspect of CUDA texturing.

Finally, in Part III, Chapters 11 to 15 discuss various targeted CUDA applications.

- Chapter 11 describes bandwidth-bound, streaming workloads such as vector-vector multiplication.

- Chapters 12 and 13 describe reduction and parallel prefix sum (otherwise known as scan), both important building blocks in parallel programming.

- Chapter 14 describes N-body, an important family of applications with high computational density that derive a particular benefit from GPU computing.

- Chapter 15 takes an in-depth look at an image processing operation called *normalized cross-correlation* that is used for feature extraction. Chapter 15 features the only code in the book that uses texturing and shared memory together to deliver optimal performance.

Chapter 2

Hardware Architecture

This chapter provides more detailed descriptions of CUDA platforms, from the system level to the functional units within the GPUs. The first section discusses the many different ways that CUDA systems can be built. The second section discusses address spaces and how CUDA's memory model is implemented in hardware and software. The third section discusses CPU/GPU interactions, with special attention paid to how commands are submitted to the GPU and how CPU/GPU synchronization is performed. Finally, the chapter concludes with a high-level description of the GPUs themselves: functional units such as copy engines and streaming multiprocessors, with block diagrams of the different types of streaming multiprocessors over three generations of CUDA-capable hardware.

2.1 CPU Configurations

This section describes a variety of CPU/GPU architectures, with some comments on how a CUDA developer would approach programming the system differently. We examine a variety of CPU configurations, integrated GPUs, and multi-GPU configurations. We begin with Figure 2.1.

An important element that was omitted from Figure 2.1 is the "chipset" or "core logic" that connects the CPU to the outside world. Every bit of input and output of the system, including disk and network controllers, keyboards and mice, USB devices, and, yes, GPUs, goes through the chipset. Until recently, chipsets were

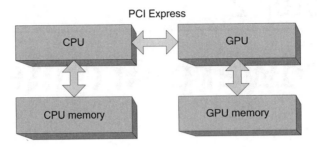

Figure 2.1 CPU/GPU architecture simplified.

divided into a "southbridge" that connected most peripherals to the system[1] and a "northbridge" that contained the graphics bus (the Accelerated Graphics Port, until the PCI Express [PCIe] bus displaced it) and a memory controller ("front side bus") connected to the CPU memory.

Each "lane" in PCI Express 2.0 can theoretically deliver about 500MB/s of bandwidth, and the number of lanes for a given peripheral can be 1, 4, 8, or 16. GPUs require the most bandwidth of any peripheral on the platform, so they generally are designed to be plugged into 16-lane PCIe slots. With packet overhead, the 8G/s of bandwidth for such a connection delivers about 6G/s in practice.[2]

2.1.1 FRONT-SIDE BUS

Figure 2.2 adds the northbridge and its memory controller to the original simplified diagram. For completeness, Figure 2.2 also shows the GPU's integrated memory controller, which is designed under a very different set of constraints than the CPU's memory controller. The GPU must accommodate so-called *isochronous* clients, such as video display(s), whose bandwidth requirements are fixed and nonnegotiable. The GPU's memory controller also is designed with the GPU's extreme latency-tolerance and vast memory bandwidth requirements in mind. As of this writing, high-end GPUs commonly deliver local GPU memory bandwidths well in excess of 100G/s. GPU memory controllers are always integrated with the GPU, so they are omitted from the rest of the diagrams in this chapter.

---

1. For simplicity, the southbridge is omitted from all diagrams in this section.
2. PCI 3.0 delivers about twice as much bandwidth as PCIe 2.0.

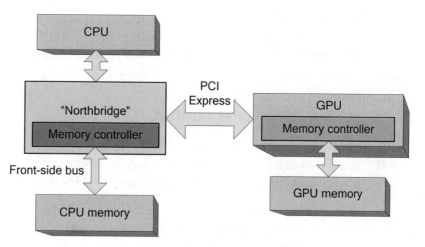

Figure 2.2 CPU/GPU architecture—northbridge.

2.1.2 SYMMETRIC MULTIPROCESSORS

Figure 2.3 shows a system with multiple CPUs in a traditional northbridge configuration.[3] Before multicore processors, applications had to use multiple threads to take full advantage of the additional power of multiple CPUs. The northbridge must ensure that each CPU sees the same coherent view of

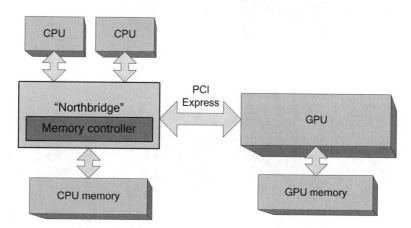

Figure 2.3 Multiple CPUs (SMP configuration).

---

3. For reasons that will soon become clear, we offer Figure 2.3 more for historical reference than because there are CUDA-capable computers with this configuration.

memory, even though every CPU and the northbridge itself all contain caches. Since these so-called "symmetric multiprocessor" (SMP) systems share a common path to CPU memory, memory accesses exhibit relatively uniform performance.

2.1.3 NONUNIFORM MEMORY ACCESS

Starting with AMD's Opteron and Intel's Nehalem (i7) processors, the memory controller in the northbridge was integrated directly into the CPU, as shown in Figure 2.4. This architectural change improves CPU memory performance.

For developers, the system in Figure 2.4 is only slightly different from the ones we've already discussed. For systems that contain multiple CPUs, as shown in Figure 2.5, things get more interesting.

For machine configurations with multiple CPUs,[4] this architecture implies that each CPU gets its own pool of memory bandwidth. At the same time, because multithreaded operating systems and applications rely on the cache coherency enforced by previous CPUs and northbridge configurations, the Opteron and

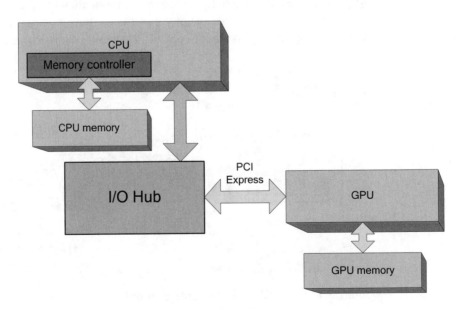

Figure 2.4 CPU with integrated memory controller.

---

4. On such systems, the CPUs also may be referred to as "nodes" or "sockets."

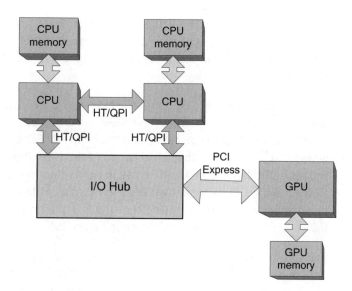

Figure 2.5 Multiple CPUs (NUMA).

Nehalem architectures also introduced HyperTransport (HT) and QuickPath Interconnect (QPI), respectively.

HT and QPI are point-to-point interconnects that connect CPUs to other CPUs, or CPUs to I/O hubs. On systems that incorporate HT/QPI, any CPU can access any memory location, but accesses are much faster to "local" memory locations whose physical address is in the memory directly attached to the CPU. Nonlocal accesses are resolved by using HT/QPI to snoop the caches of other CPUs, evict any cached copies of the requested data, and deliver the data to the CPU that performed the memory request. In general, the enormous on-chip caches on these CPUs mitigate the cost of these nonlocal memory accesses; the requesting CPU can keep the data in its own cache hierarchy until the memory is requested by another CPU.

To help developers work around these performance pitfalls, Windows and Linux have introduced APIs to enable applications to steer their allocations toward specific CPUs and to set CPU "thread affinities" so the operating system schedules threads onto CPUs so most or all of their memory accesses will be local.

A determined programmer can use these APIs to write contrived code that exposes the performance vulnerabilities of NUMA, but the more common (and insidious!) symptom is a slowdown due to "false sharing" where two threads running on different CPUs cause a plethora of HT/QPI transactions by accessing memory locations that are in the same cache line. So NUMA APIs must be used with caution: Although they give programmers the tools to improve performance, they also can make it easy for developers to inflict performance problems on themselves.

One approach to mitigating the performance impact of nonlocal memory accesses is to enable *memory interleaving*, in which physical memory is evenly split between all CPUs on cache line boundaries.[5] For CUDA, this approach works well on systems that are designed exactly as shown in Figure 2.5, with multiple CPUs in a NUMA configuration connected by a shared I/O hub to the GPU(s). Since PCI Express bandwidth is often a bottleneck to overall application performance, however, many systems have separate I/O hubs to service more than one PCI Express bus, as shown in Figure 2.6.

In order to run well on such "affinitized" systems, CUDA applications must take care to use NUMA APIs to match memory allocations and thread affinities to the PCI Express bus attached to a given GPU. Otherwise, memory copies initiated by the GPU(s) are nonlocal, and the memory transactions take an extra "hop" over the HT/QPI interconnect. Since GPUs demand a huge amount of bandwidth, these DMA operations reduce the ability of HT/QPI to serve its primary purpose. Compared to false sharing, the performance impact of nonlocal GPU memory copies is a much more plausible performance risk for CUDA applications.

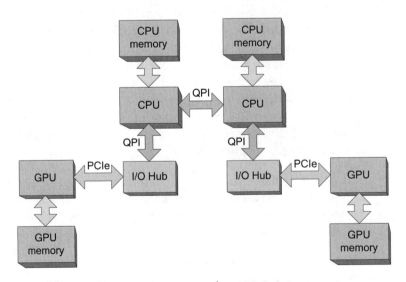

Figure 2.6 Multi-CPU (NUMA configuration), multiple buses.

---

5. A cynic would say this makes all memory accesses "equally bad."

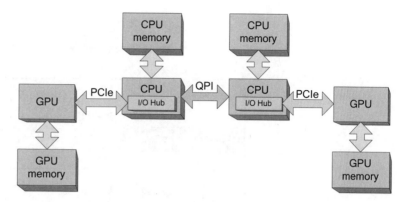

Figure 2.7 Multi-CPU with integrated PCI Express.

2.1.4 PCI EXPRESS INTEGRATION

Intel's Sandy Bridge class processors take another step toward full system integration by integrating the I/O hub into the CPU, as shown in Figure 2.7. A single Sandy Bridge CPU has up to 40 lanes of PCI Express bandwidth (remember that one GPU can use up to 16 lanes, so 40 are enough for more than two full-size GPUs).

For CUDA developers, PCI Express integration brings bad news and good news. The bad news is that PCI Express traffic is always affinitized. Designers cannot build systems like the system in Figure 2.5, where a single I/O hub serves multiple CPUs; all multi-CPU systems resemble Figure 2.6. As a result, GPUs associated with different CPUs cannot perform peer-to-peer operations. The good news is that the CPU cache can participate in PCI Express bus traffic: The CPU can service DMA read requests out of cache, and writes by the GPU are posted to the CPU cache.

2.2 Integrated GPUs

Here, the term *integrated* means "integrated into the chipset." As Figure 2.8 shows, the memory pool that previously belonged only to the CPU is now shared between the CPU and the GPU that is integrated into the chipset. Examples of NVIDIA chipsets with CUDA-capable GPUs include the MCP79 (for laptops and netbooks) and MCP89. MCP89 is the last and greatest CUDA-capable x86 chipset that NVIDIA will manufacture; besides an integrated L3 cache, it has 3x as many SMs as the MCP7x chipsets.

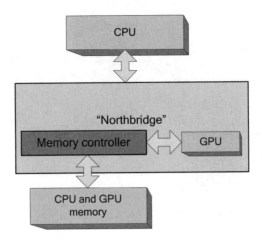

Figure 2.8 Integrated GPU.

CUDA's APIs for mapped pinned memory have special meaning on integrated GPUs. These APIs, which map host memory allocations into the address space of CUDA kernels so they can be accessed directly, also are known as "zero-copy," because the memory is shared and need not be copied over the bus. In fact, for transfer-bound workloads, an integrated GPU can outperform a much larger discrete GPU.

"Write-combined" memory allocations also have significance on integrated GPUs; cache snoops to the CPU are inhibited on this memory, which increases GPU performance when accessing the memory. Of course, if the CPU reads from the memory, the usual performance penalties for WC memory apply.

Integrated GPUs are not mutually exclusive with discrete ones; the MCP7x and MCP89 chipsets provide for PCI Express connections (Figure 2.9). On such systems, CUDA prefers to run on the discrete GPU(s) because most CUDA applications are authored with them in mind. For example, a CUDA application designed to run on a single GPU will automatically select the discrete one.

CUDA applications can query whether a GPU is integrated by examining `cudaDeviceProp.integrated` or by passing `CU_DEVICE_ATTRIBUTE_INTEGRATED` to `cuDeviceGetAttribute()`.

For CUDA, integrated GPUs are not exactly a rarity; millions of computers have integrated, CUDA-capable GPUs on board, but they are something of a curiosity, and in a few years, they will be an anachronism because NVIDIA has exited the

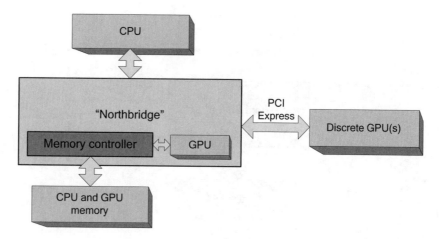

Figure 2.9 Integrated GPU with discrete GPU(s).

x86 chipset business. That said, NVIDIA has announced its intention to ship systems on a chip (SOCs) that integrate CUDA-capable GPUs with ARM CPUs, and it is a safe bet that zero-copy optimizations will work well on those systems.

2.3 Multiple GPUs

This section explores the different ways that multiple GPUs can be installed in a system and the implications for CUDA developers. For purposes of this discussion, we will omit GPU memory from our diagrams. Each GPU is assumed to be connected to its own dedicated memory.

Around 2004, NVIDIA introduced "SLI" (Scalable Link Interface) technology that enables multiple GPUs to deliver higher graphics performance by working in parallel. With motherboards that could accommodate multiple GPU boards, end users could nearly double their graphics performance by installing two GPUs in their system (Figure 2.10). By default, the NVIDIA driver software configures these boards to behave as if they were a single, very fast GPU to accelerate graphics APIs such as Direct3D and OpenGL. End users who intend to use CUDA must explicitly enable it in the Display Control panel on Windows.

It also is possible to build GPU boards that hold multiple GPUs (Figure 2.11). Examples of such boards include the GeForce 9800GX2 (dual-G92), the GeForce GTX 295 (dual-GT200), the GeForce GTX 590 (dual-GF110), and

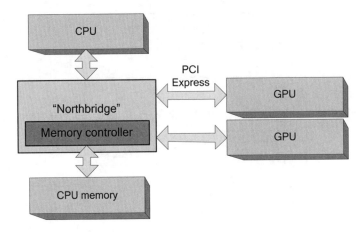

Figure 2.10 GPUs in multiple slots.

the GeForce GTX 690 (dual-GK104). The only thing shared by the GPUs on these boards is a bridge chip that enables both chips to communicate via PCI Express. They do not share memory resources; each GPU has an integrated memory controller that gives full-bandwidth performance to the memory connected to that GPU. The GPUs on the board can communicate via peer-to-peer memcpy, which will use the bridge chip to bypass the main PCIe fabric. In addition, if they are Fermi-class or later GPUs, each GPU can map memory belonging to the other GPU into its global address space.

SLI is an NVIDIA technology that makes multiple GPUs (usually on the same board, as in Figure 2.11) appear as a single, much faster GPU. When the graphics

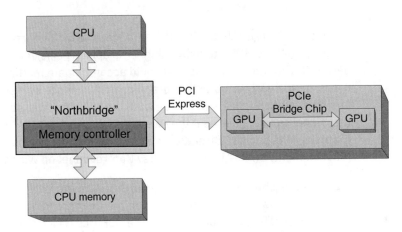

Figure 2.11 Multi-GPU board.

application downloads textures or other data, the NVIDIA graphics driver broadcasts the data to both GPUs; most rendering commands also are broadcast, with small changes to enable each GPU to render its part of the output buffer. Since SLI causes the multiple GPUs to appear as a single GPU, and since CUDA applications cannot be transparently accelerated like graphics applications, CUDA developers generally should disable SLI.

This board design oversubscribes the PCI Express bandwidth available to the GPUs. Since only one PCI Express slot's worth of bandwidth is available to both GPUs on the board, the performance of transfer-limited workloads can suffer. If multiple PCI Express slots are available, an end user can install multiple dual-GPU boards. Figure 2.12 shows a machine with four GPUs.

If there are multiple PCI Express I/O hubs, as with the system in Figure 2.6, the placement and thread affinity considerations for NUMA systems apply to the boards just as they would to single-GPU boards plugged into that configuration.

If the chipset, motherboard, operating system, and driver software can support it, even more GPUs can be crammed into the system. Researchers at the University of Antwerp caused a stir when they built an 8-GPU system called FASTRA by plugging four GeForce 9800GX2's into a single desktop computer. A similar system built on a dual-PCI Express chipset would look like the one in Figure 2.13.

As a side note, peer-to-peer memory access (the mapping of other GPUs' device memory, not memcpy) does not work across I/O hubs or, in the case of CPUs such as Sandy Bridge that integrate PCI Express, sockets.

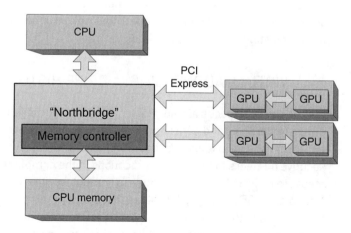

Figure 2.12 Multi-GPU boards in multiple slots.

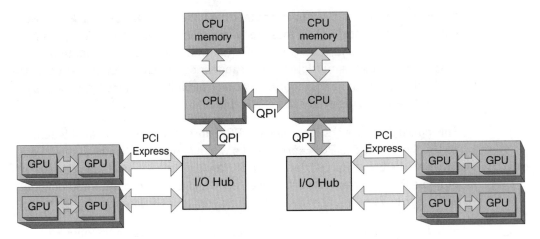

Figure 2.13 Multi-GPU boards, multiple I/O hubs.

2.4 Address Spaces in CUDA

As every beginning CUDA programmer knows, the address spaces for the CPU and GPU are separate. The CPU cannot read or write the GPU's device memory, and in turn, the GPU cannot read or write the CPU's memory. As a result, the application must explicitly copy data to and from the GPU's memory in order to process it.

The reality is a bit more complicated, and it has gotten even more so as CUDA has added new capabilities such as mapped pinned memory and peer-to-peer access. This section gives a detailed description of how address spaces work in CUDA, starting from first principles.

2.4.1 VIRTUAL ADDRESSING: A BRIEF HISTORY

Virtual address spaces are such a pervasive and successful abstraction that most programmers use and benefit from them every day without ever knowing they exist. They are an extension of the original insight that it was useful to assign consecutive numbers to the memory locations in the computer. The standard unit of measure is the *byte*, so, for example, a computer with 64K of memory had memory locations 0..65535. The 16-bit values that specify memory locations are known as *addresses*, and the process of computing addresses and operating on the corresponding memory locations is collectively known as *addressing*.

Early computers performed *physical addressing*. They would compute a memory location and then read or write the corresponding memory location, as shown in Figure 2.14. As software grew more complex and computers hosting multiple users or running multiple jobs grew more common, it became clear that allowing any program to read or write any physical memory location was unacceptable; software running on the machine could fatally corrupt other software by writing the wrong memory location. Besides the robustness concern, there were also security concerns: Software could spy on other software by reading memory locations it did not "own."

As a result, modern computers implement *virtual address spaces*. Each program (operating system designers call it a *process*) gets a view of memory similar to Figure 2.14, but each process gets its own address space. They cannot read or write memory belonging to other processes without special permission from the operating system. Instead of specifying a physical address, the machine instruction specifies a *virtual address* to be translated into a physical address by performing a series of lookups into tables that were set up by the operating system.

In most systems, the virtual address space is divided into *pages*, which are units of addressing that are at least 4096 bytes in size. Instead of referencing physical memory directly from the address, the hardware looks up a *page table entry* (PTE) that specifies the physical address where the page's memory resides.

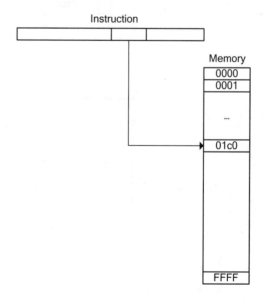

Figure 2.14 Simple 16-bit address space.

It should be clear from Figure 2.15 that virtual addressing enables a contiguous virtual address space to map to discontiguous pages in physical memory. Also, when an application attempts to read or write a memory location whose page has not been mapped to physical memory, the hardware signals a fault that must be handled by the operating system.

Just a side note: In practice, no hardware implements a single-level page table as shown in Figure 2.15. At minimum, the address is split into at least two indices: an index into a "page directory" of page tables, and an index into the page table selected by the first index. The hierarchical design reduces the amount of memory needed for the page tables and enables inactive page tables to be marked nonresident and swapped to disk, much like inactive pages.

Besides a physical memory location, the PTEs contain permissions bits that the hardware can validate while doing the address translation. For example,

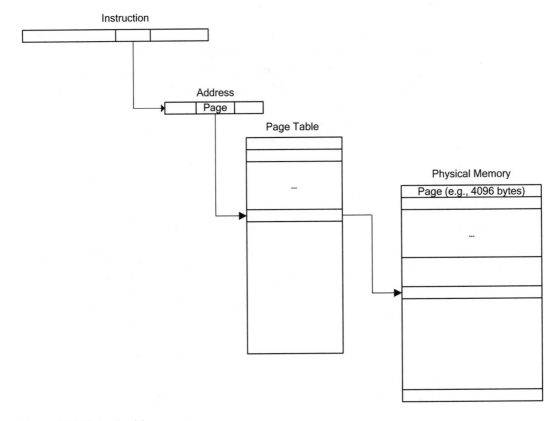

Figure 2.15 Virtual address space.

the operating system can make pages read-only, and the hardware will signal a fault if the application attempts to write the page.

Operating systems use virtual memory hardware to implement many features.

- *Lazy allocation*: Large amounts of memory can be "allocated" by setting aside PTEs with no physical memory backing them. If the application that requested the memory happens to access one of those pages, the OS resolves the fault by finding a page of physical memory at that time.

- *Demand paging*: Memory can be copied to disk and the page marked nonresident. If the memory is referenced again, the hardware signals a "page fault," and the OS resolves the fault by copying the data to a physical page, fixing up the PTE to point there, and resuming execution.

- *Copy-on-write*: Virtual memory can be "copied" by creating a second set of PTEs that map to the same physical pages, then marking both sets of PTEs read-only. If the hardware catches an attempt to write to one of those pages, the OS can copy it to another physical page, mark both PTEs writeable again, and resume execution. If the application only writes to a small percentage of pages that were "copied," copy-on-write is a big performance win.

- *Mapped file I/O*: Files can be mapped into the address space, and page faults can be resolved by accessing the file. For applications that perform random access on the file, it may be advantageous to delegate the memory management to the highly optimized VMM code in the operating system, especially since it is tightly coupled to the mass storage drivers.

It is important to understand that address translation is performed on *every* memory access performed by the CPU. To make this operation fast, the CPU contains special hardware: caches called translation lookaside buffers (TLBs) that hold recently translated address ranges, and "page walkers" that resolve cache misses in the TLBs by reading the page tables.[6] Modern CPUs also include hardware support for "unified address spaces," where multiple CPUs can access one another's memory efficiently via AMD's HT (HyperTransport) and Intel's QuickPath Interconnect (QPI). Since these hardware facilities enable CPUs to access any memory location in the system using a unified address space, this section refers to "the CPU" and the "CPU address space" regardless of how many CPUs are in the system.

---

6. It is possible to write programs (for both CPUs and CUDA) that expose the size and structure of the TLBs and/or the memory overhead of the page walkers if they stride through enough memory in a short enough period of time.

Sidebar: Kernel Mode and User Mode

A final point about memory management on CPUs is that the operating system code must use memory protections to prevent applications from corrupting the operating system's own data structures—for example, the page tables that control address translation. To aid with this memory protection, operating systems have a "privileged" mode of execution that they use when performing critical system functions. In order to manage low-level hardware resources such as page tables or to program hardware registers on peripherals such as the disk or network controller or the CUDA GPU, the CPU must be running in *kernel mode*. The unprivileged execution mode used by application code is called *user mode*.[7] Besides code written by the operating system provider, low-level driver code to control hardware peripherals also runs in kernel mode. Since mistakes in kernel mode code can lead to system stability or security problems, kernel mode code is held to a higher quality standard. Also, many operating system services, such as mapped file I/O or other memory management facilities listed above, are not available in kernel mode.

To ensure system stability and security, the interface between user mode and kernel mode is carefully regulated. The user mode code must set up a data structure in memory and make a special system call that validates the memory and the request that is being made. This transition from user mode to kernel mode is known as a *kernel thunk*. Kernel thunks are expensive, and their cost sometimes must be taken into account by CUDA developers.

Every interaction with CUDA hardware by the user mode driver is arbitrated by kernel mode code. Often this means having resources allocated on its behalf—not only memory but also hardware resources such as the hardware register used by the user mode driver to submit work to the hardware.

The bulk of CUDA's driver runs in user mode. For example, in order to allocate page-locked system memory (e.g., with the `cudaHostAlloc()` function), the CUDA application calls into the user mode CUDA driver, which composes a request to the kernel mode CUDA driver and performs a kernel thunk. The kernel mode CUDA driver uses a mix of low-level OS services (for example, it may call a system service to map GPU hardware registers) and hardware-specific code (for example, to program the GPU's memory management hardware) to satisfy the request.

2.4.2 DISJOINT ADDRESS SPACES

On the GPU, CUDA also uses virtual address spaces, although the hardware does not support as rich a feature set as do the CPUs. GPUs do enforce memory

---

7. The x86-specific terms for *kernel mode* and *user mode* are "Ring 0" and "Ring 3," respectively.

protections, so CUDA programs cannot accidentally read or corrupt other CUDA programs' memory or access memory that hasn't been mapped for them by the kernel mode driver. But GPUs do not support demand paging, so every byte of virtual memory allocated by CUDA must be backed by a byte of physical memory. Also, demand paging is the underlying hardware mechanism used by operating systems to implement most of the features outlined above.

Since each GPU has its own memory and address translation hardware, the CUDA address space is separate from the CPU address space where the host code in a CUDA application runs. Figure 2.16 shows the address space architecture for CUDA as of version 1.0, before mapped pinned memory became available. The CPU and GPU each had its own address space, mapped with each device's own page tables. The two devices exchanged data via explicit memcpy commands. The GPU could allocate *pinned memory*—page-locked memory that had been mapped for DMA by the GPU—but pinned memory only made DMA faster; it did not enable CUDA kernels to access host memory.[8]

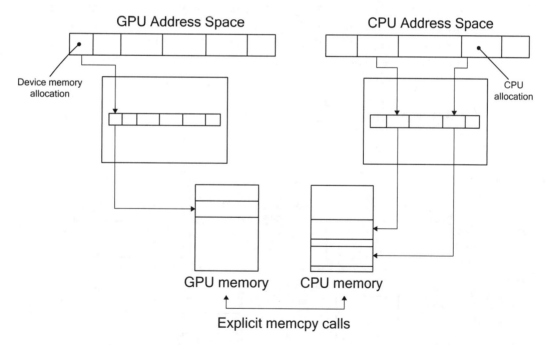

Figure 2.16 Disjoint address spaces.

---

8. On 32-bit operating systems, CUDA-capable GPUs can map pinned memory for memcpy in a 40-bit address space that is outside the CUDA address space used by kernels.

The CUDA driver tracks pinned memory ranges and automatically accelerates memcpy operations that reference them. Asynchronous memcpy calls require pinned memory ranges to ensure that the operating system does not unmap or move the physical memory before the memcpy is performed.

Not all CUDA applications can allocate the host memory they wish to process using CUDA. For example, a CUDA-aware plugin to a large, extensible application may want to operate on host memory that was allocated by non-CUDA-aware code. To accommodate that use case, CUDA 4.0 added the ability to *register* existing host address ranges, which page-locks a virtual address range, maps it for the GPU, and adds the address range to the tracking data structure so CUDA knows it is pinned. The memory then can be passed to asynchronous memcpy calls or otherwise treated as if it were allocated by CUDA.

2.4.3 MAPPED PINNED MEMORY

CUDA 2.2 added a feature called *mapped pinned memory*, shown in Figure 2.17. Mapped pinned memory is page-locked host memory that has been mapped into the CUDA address space, where CUDA kernels can read or write it directly. The page tables of both the CPU and the GPU are updated so that both the CPU and the GPU have address ranges that point to the same host

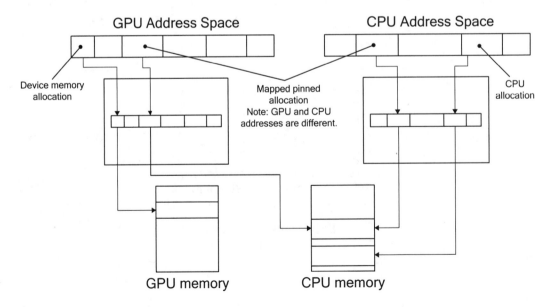

Figure 2.17 Mapped pinned memory.

memory buffer. Since the address spaces are different, the GPU pointer(s) to the buffer must be queried using `cuMemHostGetDevicePointer()` / `cudaHostGetDevicePointer()`.[9]

2.4.4 PORTABLE PINNED MEMORY

CUDA 2.2 also enabled a feature called *portable pinned memory*, shown in Figure 2.18. Making pinned memory "portable" causes the CUDA driver to map it for *all* GPUs in the system, not just the one whose context is current. A separate set of page table entries is created for the CPU and every GPU in the system, enabling the corresponding device to translate virtual addresses to the underlying physical memory. The host memory range also is added to every

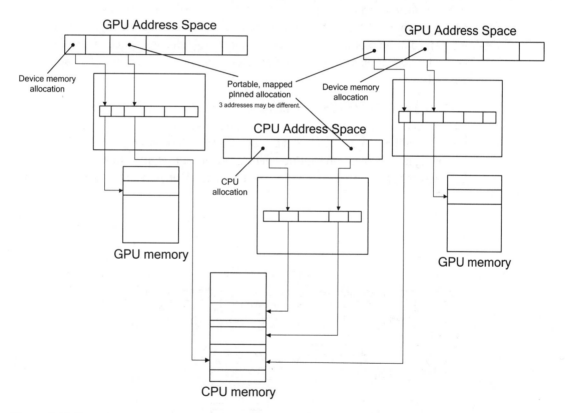

Figure 2.18 Portable, mapped pinned memory.

---

9. For multi-GPU configurations, CUDA 2.2 also added a feature called "portable" pinned memory that causes the allocation to be mapped into every GPU's address space. But there is no guarantee that `cu(da)HostGetDevicePointer()` will return the same value for different GPUs!

active CUDA context's tracking mechanism, so every GPU will recognize the portable allocation as pinned.

Figure 2.18 likely represents the limit of developer tolerance for multiple address spaces. Here, a 2-GPU system has 3 addresses for an allocation; a 4-GPU system would have 5 addresses. Although CUDA has fast APIs to look up a given CPU address range and pass back the corresponding GPU address range, having N+1 addresses on an N-GPU system, all for the same allocation, is inconvenient to say the least.

2.4.5 UNIFIED ADDRESSING

Multiple address spaces are required for 32-bit CUDA GPUs, which can only map 2^{32}=4GiB of address space; since some high-end GPUs have up to 4GiB of device memory, they are hard-pressed to address all of device memory and also map any pinned memory, let alone use the same address space as the CPU. But on 64-bit operating systems with Fermi or later GPUs, a simpler abstraction is possible.

CUDA 4.0 added a feature called *unified virtual addressing* (UVA), shown in Figure 2.19. When UVA is in force, CUDA allocates memory for both CPUs and GPUs from the same virtual address space. The CUDA driver accomplishes this by having its initialization routine perform large virtual allocations from the CPU address space—allocations that are not backed by physical memory—and then

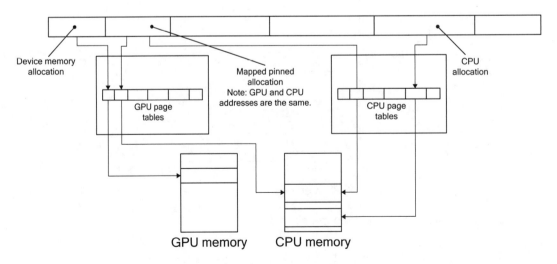

Figure 2.19 Unified virtual addressing (UVA).

mapping GPU allocations into those address ranges. Since x64 CPUs support 48-bit virtual address spaces,[10] while CUDA GPUs only support 40 bits, applications using UVA should make sure CUDA gets initialized early to guard against CPU code using virtual address needed by CUDA.

For mapped pinned allocations, the GPU and CPU pointers are the same. For other types of allocation, CUDA can infer the device for which a given allocation was performed from the address. As a result, the family of linear memcpy functions (cudaMemcpy() with a direction specified, cuMemcpyHtoD(), cuMemcpyDtoH(), etc.) have been replaced by simplified cuMemcpy() and cudaMemcpy() functions that do not take a memory direction.

UVA is enabled automatically on UVA-capable systems. At the time of this writing, UVA is enabled on 64-bit Linux, 64-bit MacOS, and 64-bit Windows when using the TCC driver; the WDDM driver does not yet support UVA. When UVA is in effect, all pinned allocations performed by CUDA are both mapped and portable. Note that for system memory that has been pinned using cuMemRegisterHost(), the device pointers still must be queried using cu(da)HostGetDevicePointer(). Even when UVA is in effect, the CPU(s) cannot access device memory. In addition, by default, the GPU(s) cannot access one another's memory.

2.4.6 PEER-TO-PEER MAPPINGS

In the final stage of our journey through CUDA's virtual memory abstractions, we discuss peer-to-peer mapping of device memory, shown in Figure 2.20. Peer-to-peer enables a Fermi-class GPU to read or write memory that resides in another Fermi-class GPU. Peer-to-peer mapping is supported only on UVA-enabled platforms, and it only works on GPUs that are connected to the same I/O hub. Because UVA is always in force when using peer-to-peer, the address ranges for different devices do not overlap, and the driver (and runtime) can infer the owning device from a pointer value.

Peer-to-peer memory addressing is asymmetric; note that Figure 2.20 shows an asymmetric mapping in which GPU 1's allocations are visible to GPU 0, but not vice versa. In order for GPUs to see each other's memory, each GPU must explicitly map the other's memory. The API functions to manage peer-to-peer mappings are discussed in Section 9.2.

---

10. 48 bits of virtual address space = 256 terabytes. Future x64 CPUs will support even larger address spaces.

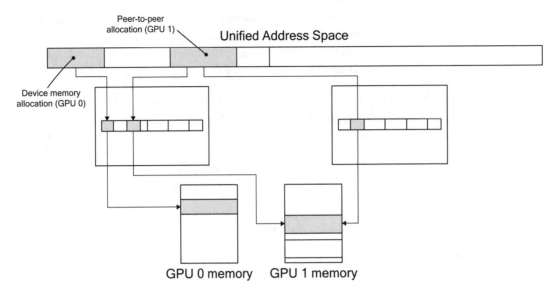

Figure 2.20 Peer-to-peer.

2.5 CPU/GPU Interactions

This section describes key elements of CPU-GPU interactions.

- *Pinned host memory:* CPU memory that the GPU can directly access

- *Command buffers:* the buffers written by the CUDA driver and read by the GPU to control its execution

- *CPU/GPU synchronization:* how the GPU's progress is tracked by the CPU

This section describes these facilities at the hardware level, citing APIs only as necessary to help the reader understand how they pertain to CUDA development. For simplicity, this section uses the CPU/GPU model in Figure 2.1, setting aside the complexities of multi-CPU or multi-GPU programming.

2.5.1 PINNED HOST MEMORY AND COMMAND BUFFERS

For obvious reasons, the CPU and GPU are each best at accessing its own memory, but the GPU can directly access page-locked CPU memory via direct memory access (DMA). Page-locking is a facility used by operating systems to enable hardware peripherals to directly access CPU memory, avoiding extraneous copies. The "locked" pages have been marked as ineligible for eviction by the operating system, so device drivers can program these peripherals to use the pages' physical addresses to access the memory directly. The CPU still can access the memory in question, but the memory cannot be moved or paged out to disk.

Since the GPU is a distinct device from the CPU, direct memory access also enables the GPU to read and write CPU memory independently of, and in parallel with, the CPU's execution. Care must be taken to synchronize between the CPU and GPU to avoid race conditions, but for applications that can make productive use of CPU clock cycles while the GPU is processing, the performance benefits of concurrent execution can be significant.

Figure 2.21 depicts a "pinned" buffer that has been mapped by the GPU[11] for direct access. CUDA programmers are familiar with pinned buffers because CUDA has always given them the ability to allocate pinned memory via APIs such as cudaMallocHost(). But under the hood, one of the main applications for such buffers is to submit commands to the GPU. The CPU writes commands into a "command buffer" that the GPU can consume, and the GPU simultaneously reads and executes previously written commands. Figure 2.22 shows how the CPU and GPU share this buffer. This diagram is simplified because the commands may be hundreds of bytes long, and the buffer is big enough to hold several thousand such commands. The "leading edge" of the buffer is under construction by the CPU and not yet ready to be read by the GPU. The "trailing edge" of the buffer is being read by the GPU. The commands in between are ready for the GPU to process when it is ready.

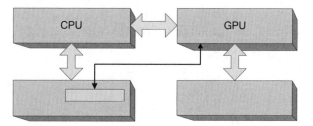

Figure 2.21 Pinned buffer.

---

11. Important note: In this context, "mapping" for the GPU involves setting up hardware tables that refer to the CPU memory's physical addresses. The memory may or may not be mapped into the address space where it can be accessed by CUDA kernels.

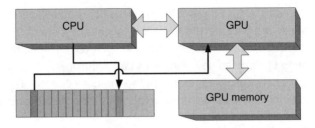

Figure 2.22 CPU/GPU command buffer.

Typically, the CUDA driver will reuse command buffer memory because once the GPU has finished processing a command, the memory becomes eligible to be written again by the CPU. Figure 2.23 shows how the CPU can "wrap around" the command buffer.

Since it takes several thousand CPU clock cycles to launch a CUDA kernel, a key use case for CPU/GPU concurrency is simply to prepare more GPU commands while the GPU is processing. Applications that are not balanced to keep both the CPU and GPU busy may become "CPU bound" or "GPU bound," as shown in Figures 2.24 and 2.25, respectively. In a CPU-bound application, the GPU is poised and ready to process the next command as soon as it becomes available; in a GPU-bound application, the CPU has completely filled the command buffer and

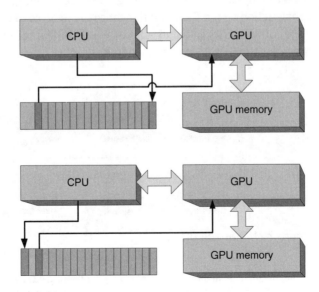

Figure 2.23 Command buffer wrap-around.

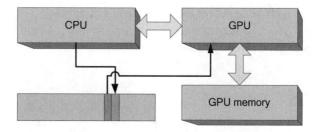

Figure 2.24 GPU-bound application.

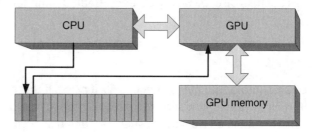

Figure 2.25 CPU-bound application.

must wait for the GPU before writing the next GPU command. Some applications are intrinsically CPU-bound or GPU-bound, so CPU- and GPU-boundedness does not necessarily indicate a fundamental problem with an application's structure. Nevertheless, knowing whether an application is CPU-bound or GPU-bound can help highlight performance opportunities.

2.5.2 CPU/GPU CONCURRENCY

The previous section introduced the coarsest-grained parallelism available in CUDA systems: *CPU/GPU concurrency*. All launches of CUDA kernels are asynchronous: the CPU requests the launch by writing commands into the command buffer, then returns without checking the GPU's progress. Memory copies optionally also may be asynchronous, enabling CPU/GPU concurrency and possibly enabling memory copies to be done concurrently with kernel processing.

Amdahl's Law

When CUDA programs are written correctly, the CPU and GPU can fully operate in parallel, potentially doubling performance. CPU- or GPU-bound programs do not benefit much from CPU/GPU concurrency because the CPU or GPU will limit performance even if the other device is operating in parallel. This vague observation can be concretely characterized using *Amdahl's Law*, first articulated in a paper by Gene Amdahl in 1967.[12] Amdahl's Law is often summarized as follows.

$$Speedup = \frac{1}{r_s + \frac{r_p}{N}}$$

where $r_s + r_p = 1$ and r_s represents the ratio of the sequential portion. This formulation seems awkward when examining small-scale performance opportunities such as CPU/GPU concurrency. Rearranging the equation as follows

$$Speedup = \frac{N}{N\left(1 - r_p\right) + r_p}$$

clearly shows that the speedup is Nx if $r_p = 1$. If there is one CPU and one GPU ($N = 2$), the maximum speedup from full concurrency is 2x; this is almost achievable for balanced workloads such as video transcoding, where the CPU can perform serial operations (such as variable-length decoding) in parallel with the GPU's performing parallel operations (such as pixel processing). But for more CPU- or GPU-bound applications, this type of concurrency offers limited benefits.

Amdahl's paper was intended as a cautionary tale for those who believed that parallelism would be a panacea for performance problems, and we use it elsewhere in this book when discussing intra-GPU concurrency, multi-GPU concurrency, and the speedups achievable from porting to CUDA kernels. It can be empowering, though, to know which forms of concurrency will not confer any benefit to a given application, so developers can spend their time exploring other avenues for increased performance.

Error Handling

CPU/GPU concurrency also has implications for error handling. If the CPU launches a dozen kernels and one of them causes a memory fault, the CPU cannot discover the fault until it has performed CPU/GPU synchronization (described in the next section). Developers can manually perform CPU/GPU synchronization by calling `cudaThreadSynchronize()` or `cuCtxSynchronize()`, and other functions such as `cudaFree()` or `cuMemFree()` may cause CPU/GPU synchronization to occur as a side effect. The *CUDA C Programming Guide* references this behavior by calling out functions that may cause CPU/GPU synchronization:

---

12. http://bit.ly/13UqBm0

"Note that this function may also return error codes from previous, asynchronous launches."

As CUDA is currently implemented, if a fault does occur, there is no way to know which kernel caused the fault. For debug code, if it's difficult to isolate faults with synchronization, developers can set the `CUDA_LAUNCH_BLOCKING` environment variable to force all launches to be synchronous.

CPU/GPU Synchronization

Although most GPU commands used by CUDA involve performing memory copies or kernel launches, an important subclass of commands helps the CUDA driver track the GPU's progress in processing the command buffer. Because the application cannot know how long a given CUDA kernel may run, the GPU itself must report progress to the CPU. Figure 2.26 shows both the command buffer and the "sync location" (which also resides in pinned host memory) used by the driver and GPU to track progress. A monotonically increasing integer value (the "progress value") is maintained by the driver, and every major GPU operation is followed by a command to write the new progress value to the shared sync location. In the case of Figure 2.26, the progress value is 3 until the GPU finishes executing the command and writes the value 4 to the sync location.

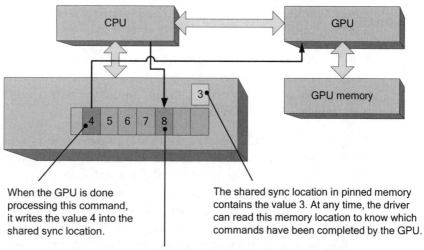

When the GPU is done processing this command, it writes the value 4 into the shared sync location.

The shared sync location in pinned memory contains the value 3. At any time, the driver can read this memory location to know which commands have been completed by the GPU.

The driver keeps track of a monotonically increasing value to track the GPU's progress. Every major operation, such as a memcpy or kernel launch, is followed by a command to the GPU to write this new value to the shared sync location.

Figure 2.26 Shared sync value—before.

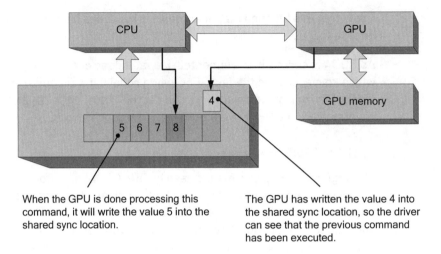

When the GPU is done processing this command, it will write the value 5 into the shared sync location.

The GPU has written the value 4 into the shared sync location, so the driver can see that the previous command has been executed.

Figure 2.27 Shared sync value—after.

CUDA exposes these hardware capabilities both implicitly and explicitly. Context-wide synchronization calls such as `cuCtxSynchronize()` or `cudaThreadSynchronize()` simply examine the last sync value requested of the GPU and wait until the sync location attains that value. For example, if the command 8 being written by the CPU in Figure 2.27 were followed by `cuCtxSynchronize()` or `cudaThreadSynchronize()`, the driver would wait until the shared sync value became greater than or equal to 8.

CUDA events expose these hardware capabilities more explicitly. `cuEvent-Record()` enqueues a command to write a new sync value to a shared sync location, and `cuEventQuery()` and `cuEventSynchronize()` examine and wait on the event's sync value, respectively.

Early versions of CUDA simply polled shared sync locations, repeatedly reading the memory until the wait criterion had been achieved, but this approach is expensive and only works well when the application doesn't have to wait long (i.e., the sync location doesn't have to be read many times before exiting because the wait criterion has been satisfied). For most applications, interrupt-based schemes (exposed by CUDA as "blocking syncs") are better because they enable the CPU to suspend the waiting thread until the GPU signals an interrupt. The driver maps the GPU interrupt to a platform-specific thread synchronization primitive, such as Win32 events or Linux signals, that can be used to suspend the CPU thread if the wait condition is not true when the application starts to wait.

Applications can force the context-wide synchronization to be blocking by specifying `CU_CTX_BLOCKING_SYNC` to `cuCtxCreate()` or `cudaDeviceBlockingSync` to `cudaSetDeviceFlags()`. It is preferable, however, to use blocking CUDA events (specify `CU_EVENT_BLOCKING_SYNC` to `cuEventCreate()` or `cudaEvent-BlockingSync` to `cudaEventCreate()`), since they are more fine-grained and interoperate seamlessly with any type of CUDA context.

Astute readers may be concerned that the CPU and GPU read and write this shared memory location without using atomic operations or other synchronization primitives. But since the CPU only reads the shared location, race conditions are not a concern. The worst that can happen is the CPU reads a "stale" value that causes it to wait a little longer than it would otherwise.

Events and Timestamps

The host interface has an onboard high-resolution timer, and it can write a timestamp at the same time it writes a 32-bit sync value. CUDA uses this hardware facility to implement the asynchronous timing features in CUDA events.

2.5.3 THE HOST INTERFACE AND INTRA-GPU SYNCHRONIZATION

The GPU may contain multiple engines to enable concurrent kernel processing and memory copying. In this case, the driver will write commands that are dispatched to different engines that run concurrently. Each engine has its own command buffer and shared sync value, and the engine's progress is tracked as described in Figures 2.26 and 2.27. Figure 2.28 shows this situation, with two copy engines and a compute engine operating in parallel. The host interface is responsible for reading the commands and dispatching them to the appropriate engine. In Figure 2.28, a host→device memcpy and two dependent operations—a kernel launch and a device→host memcpy—have been submitted to the hardware. In terms of CUDA programming abstractions, these operations are within the same stream. The stream is like a CPU thread, and the kernel launch was submitted to the stream after the memcpy, so the CUDA driver must insert GPU commands for intra-GPU synchronization into the command streams for the host interface.

As Figure 2.28 shows, the host interface plays a central role in coordinating the needed synchronization for streams. When, for example, a kernel must not be launched until a needed memcpy is completed, the DMA unit can stop giving commands to a given engine until a shared sync location attains a certain value.

After the initial H→D memcpy, Copy Engine 1 will write 7 to this sync location…

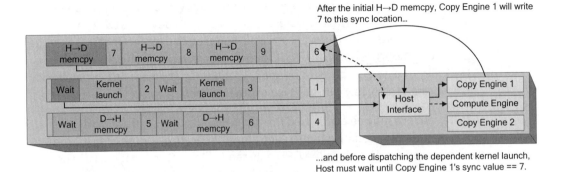

…and before dispatching the dependent kernel launch, Host must wait until Copy Engine 1's sync value == 7.

When the kernel launch is done, the SM will write 2 to this sync location…

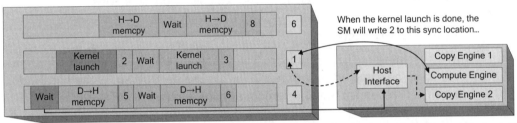

…while Host Interface waits for the sync value to equal 2 before dispatching this D→H memcpy.

Figure 2.28 Intra-GPU synchronization.

This operation is similar to CPU/GPU synchronization, but the GPU is synchronizing different engines within itself.

The software abstraction layered on this hardware mechanism is a CUDA stream. CUDA streams are like CPU threads in that operations within a stream are sequential and multiple streams are needed for concurrency. Because the command buffer is shared between engines, applications must "software-pipeline" their requests in different streams. So instead of

```
foreach stream
    Memcpy device←host
    Launch kernel
    Memcpy host←device
```

they must implement

```
foreach stream
        Memcpy device←host
foreach stream
        Launch kernel
foreach stream
        Memcpy host←device
```

Without the software pipelining, the DMA engine will "break concurrency" by synchronizing the engines to preserve each stream's model of sequential execution.

Multiple DMA Engines on Kepler

The latest Kepler-class hardware from NVIDIA implements a DMA unit per engine, obviating the need for applications to software-pipeline their streamed operations.

2.5.4 INTER-GPU SYNCHRONIZATION

Since the sync location in Figures 2.26 through 2.28 is in host memory, it can be accessed by any of the GPUs in the system. As a result, in CUDA 4.0, NVIDIA was able to add inter-GPU synchronization in the form of `cudaStreamWait-Event()` and `cuStreamWaitEvent()`. These API calls cause the driver to insert wait commands for the host interface into the current GPU's command buffer, causing the GPU to wait until the given event's sync value has been written. Starting with CUDA 4.0, the event may or may not be signaled by the same GPU that is doing the wait. Streams have been promoted from being able to synchronize execution between hardware units on a single GPU to being able to synchronize execution between GPUs.

2.6 GPU Architecture

Three distinct GPU architectures can run CUDA.

- Tesla hardware debuted in 2006, in the GeForce 8800 GTX (G80).

- Fermi hardware debuted in 2010, in the GeForce GTX 480 (GF100).

- Kepler hardware debuted in 2012, in the GeForce GTX 680 (GK104).

The GF100/GK104 nomenclature refers to the ASIC that implements the GPU. The "K" and "F" in GK104 and GF100 refer to Kepler and Fermi, respectively.

The Tesla and Fermi families followed an NVIDIA tradition in which they would first ship the huge, high-end flagship chip that would win benchmarks. These chips were expensive because NVIDIA's manufacturing costs are closely related to the number of transistors (and thus the amount of die area) required to build the ASIC. The first large "win" chips would then be followed by smaller chips: half-size for the mid-range, quarter-size for the low end, and so on.

In a departure from that tradition, NVIDIA's first Kepler-class chip is targeted at the midrange; their "win" chip shipped months after the first Kepler-class chips became available. GK104 has 3.5B transistors, while GK110 has 7.1B transistors.

2.6.1 OVERVIEW

CUDA's simplified view of the GPU includes the following.

- A host interface that connects the GPU to the PCI Express bus

- 0 to 2 copy engines

- A DRAM interface that connects the GPU to its device memory

- Some number of TPCs or GPCs (texture processing clusters or graphics processing clusters), each of which contains caches and some number of streaming multiprocessors (SMs)

The architectural papers cited at the end of this chapter give the full story on GPU functionality in CUDA-capable GPUs, including graphics-specific function-ality like antialiased rendering support.

Host Interface

The host interface implements the functionality described in the previous sec-tion. It reads GPU commands (such as memcpy and kernel launch commands) and dispatches them to the appropriate hardware units, and it also implements the facilities for synchronization between the CPU and GPU, between different engines on the GPU, and between different GPUs. In CUDA, the host interface's functionality primarily is exposed via the Stream and Event APIs (see Chapter 6).

Copy Engine(s)

Copy engines can perform host↔device memory transfers while the SMs are doing computations. The earliest CUDA hardware did not have any copy engines; subsequent versions of the hardware included a copy engine that could transfer linear device memory (but not CUDA arrays), and the most recent CUDA hard-ware includes up to two copy engines that can convert between CUDA arrays and linear memory while saturating the PCI Express bus.[13]

---

13. More than two copy engines doesn't really make sense, since each engine can saturate one of the two directions of PCI Express.

DRAM Interface

The GPU-wide DRAM interface, which supports bandwidths in excess of 100 GB/s, includes hardware to coalesce memory requests. More recent CUDA hardware has more sophisticated DRAM interfaces. The earliest (SM 1.x) hardware had onerous coalescing requirements, requiring addresses to be contiguous and 64-, 128-, or 256-byte aligned (depending on the operand size). Starting with SM 1.2 (the GT200 or GeForce GTX 280), addresses could be coalesced based on locality, regardless of address alignment. Fermi-class hardware (SM 2.0 and higher) has a write-through L2 cache that provides the benefits of the SM 1.2 coalescing hardware and additionally improves performance when data is reused.

TPCs and GPCs

TPCs and GPCs are units of hardware that exist between the full GPU and the streaming multiprocessors that perform CUDA computation. Tesla-class hardware groups the SMs in "TPCs" (texture processing clusters) that contain texturing hardware support (in particular, a texture cache) and two or three streaming multiprocessors, described below. Fermi-class hardware groups the SMs in "GPCs" (graphics processing clusters) that each contain a raster unit and four SMs.

For the most part, CUDA developers need not concern themselves with TPCs or GPCs because streaming multiprocessors are the most important unit of abstraction for computational hardware.

Contrasting Tesla and Fermi

The first generation of CUDA-capable GPUs was code-named Tesla, and the second, Fermi. These were confidential code names during development, but NVIDIA decided to use them as external product names to describe the first two generations of CUDA-capable GPU. To add to the confusion, NVIDIA chose the name "Tesla" to describe the server-class boards used to build compute clusters out of CUDA machines.[14] To distinguish between the expensive server-class Tesla boards and the architectural families, this book refers to the architectural families as "Tesla-class hardware," "Fermi-class hardware," and "Kepler-class hardware."

---

14. Of course, when the Tesla brand name was chosen, Fermi-class hardware did not exist. The marketing department told us engineers that it was just a coincidence that the architectural codename and the brand name were both "Tesla"!

> All of the differences between Tesla-class hardware and Fermi-class hardware also apply to Kepler.

Early Tesla-class hardware is subject to onerous performance penalties (up to 6x) when running code that performs uncoalesced memory transactions. Later implementations of Tesla-class hardware, starting with the GeForce GTX 280, decreased the penalty for uncoalesced transactions to about 2x. Tesla-class hardware also has performance counters that enable developers to measure how many memory transactions are uncoalesced.

Tesla-class hardware only included a 24-bit integer multiplier, so developers must use intrinsics such as __mul24() for best performance. Full 32-bit multiplication (i.e., the native operator * in CUDA) is emulated with a small instruction sequence.

Tesla-class hardware initialized shared memory to zero, while Fermi-class hardware leaves it uninitialized. For applications using the driver API, one subtle side effect of this behavior change is that applications that used cuParamSeti() to pass pointer parameters on 64-bit platforms do not work correctly on Fermi. Since parameters were passed in shared memory on Tesla class hardware, the uninitialized top half of the parameter would become the most significant 32 bits of the 64-bit pointer.

Double-precision support was introduced with SM 1.3 on the GT200, the second-generation "win" chip of the Tesla family.[15] At the time, the feature was considered speculative, so it was implemented in an area-efficient manner that could be added and subtracted from the hardware with whatever ratio of double-to-single performance NVIDIA desired (in the case of GT200, this ratio was 1:8). Fermi integrated double-precision support much more tightly and at higher performance.[16] Finally, for graphics applications, Tesla-class hardware was the first DirectX 10-capable hardware.

Fermi-class hardware is much more capable than Tesla-class hardware. It supports 64-bit addressing; it added L1 and L2 cache hardware; it added a full 32-bit integer multiply instruction and new instructions specifically to support the Scan primitive; it added surface load/store operations so CUDA kernels could read and write CUDA arrays without using the texture hardware; it was

---

15. In fact, the only difference between SM 1.2 and SM 1.3 is that SM 1.3 supports double precision.
16. In SM 3.x, NVIDIA has decoupled double precision floating-point performance from the SM version, so GK104 has poor double precision performance and GK110 has excellent double precision performance.

the first family of GPUs to feature multiple copy engines; and it improved support for C++ code, such as virtual functions.

Fermi-class hardware does not include the performance counters needed to track uncoalesced memory transactions. Also, because it does not include a 24-bit multiplier, Fermi-class hardware may incur a small performance penalty when running code that uses the 24-bit multiplication intrinsics. On Fermi, using operator * for multiplication is the fast path.

For graphics applications, Fermi-class hardware can run DirectX 11. Table 2.1 summarizes the differences between Tesla- and Fermi-class hardware.

Texturing Niceties

A subtle difference between Tesla- and Fermi-class hardware is that on Tesla-class hardware, the instructions to perform texturing overwrite the input register vector with the output. On Fermi-class hardware, the input and output register vectors can be different. As a result, Tesla-class hardware may have extra instructions to move the texture coordinates into the input registers where they will be overwritten.

Table 2.1 Differences between Tesla- and Fermi-Class Hardware

CHARACTERISTIC	TESLA	FERMI
Penalty for uncoalesced memory transactions	Up to 8x[*]	Up to 10%[**]
24-bit IMUL	✔	
32-bit IMUL		✔
Shared memory RAM	✔	
L1 cache		✔
L2 cache		✔
Concurrent kernels		✔
Surface load/store		✔

[*] Up to 2x for Tesla2 hardware.

[**] Up to 2x if ECC is enabled.

Another subtle difference between Tesla- and Fermi-class hardware is that when texturing from 1D CUDA arrays, Fermi-class hardware emulates this functionality using 2D textures with the second coordinate always set to 0.0. Since this emulation only costs an extra register and very few extra instructions, the difference will be noticed by very few applications.

2.6.2 STREAMING MULTIPROCESSORS

The workhorse of the GPU is the streaming multiprocessor, or SM. As mentioned in the previous section, each TPC in SM 1.x hardware contains 2 or 3 SMs, and each GPC in SM 2.x hardware contains 4 SMs. The very first CUDA-capable GPU, the G80 or GeForce 8800 GTX, contained 8 TPCs; at 2 SMs per TPC, that is a total of 16 SMs. The next big CUDA-capable GPU, the GT200 or GeForce GTX 280, increased the number of SMs/TPC to 3 and contained 10 TPCs, for a total of 30 SMs.

The number of SMs in a CUDA GPU may range from 2 to several dozen, and each SM contains

- Execution units to perform 32-bit integer and single- and double-precision floating-point arithmetic

- Special function units (SFUs) to compute single-precision approximations of log/exp, sin/cos, and rcp/rsqrt

- A warp scheduler to coordinate instruction dispatch to the execution units

- A constant cache to broadcast data to the SMs

- Shared memory for data interchange between threads

- Dedicated hardware for texture mapping

Figure 2.29 shows a Tesla-class streaming multiprocessor (SM 1.x). It contains 8 streaming processors that support 32-bit integer and single-precision floating-point arithmetic. The first CUDA hardware did not support double precision at all, but starting with GT200, the SMs may include one double-precision floating-point unit.[17]

---

17. GT200 added a few instructions as well as double precision (such as shared memory atomics), so the GT200 instruction set without double precision is SM 1.2 and with double precision is SM 1.3.

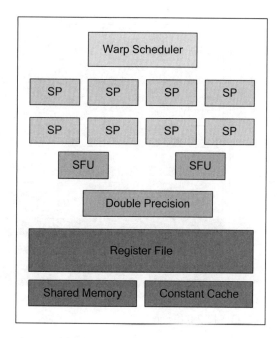

Figure 2.29 Streaming multiprocessor 1.x.

Figure 2.30 shows a Fermi-class streaming multiprocessor (SM 2.0). Unlike Tesla-class hardware, which implemented double-precision floating-point support separately, each Fermi-class SM has full double-precision support. The double-precision instructions execute slower than single precision, but since the ratio is more favorable than the 8:1 ratio of Tesla-class hardware, overall double-precision performance is much higher.[18]

Figure 2.31 shows an updated Fermi-class streaming multiprocessor (SM 2.1) that may be found in, for example, the GF104 chip. For higher performance, NVIDIA chose to increase the number of streaming processors per SM to 48. The SFU-to-SM ratio is increased from 1:8 to 1:6.

Figure 2.32 shows the most recent (as of this writing) streaming multiprocessor design, featured in the newest Kepler-class hardware from NVIDIA. This design is so different from previous generations that NVIDIA calls it "SMX" (next-generation SM). The number of cores is increased by a factor of 6 to 192,

18. For Kepler-class hardware, NVIDIA can tune floating-point performance to the target market of the GPU.

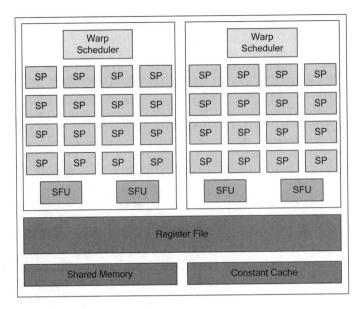

Figure 2.30 SM 2.0 (Fermi).

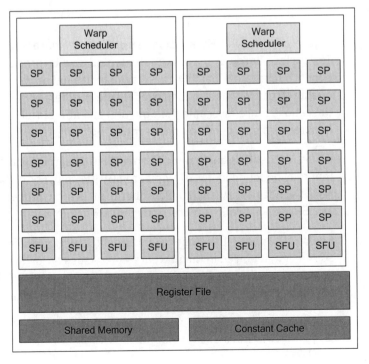

Figure 2.31 SM 2.1 (Fermi).

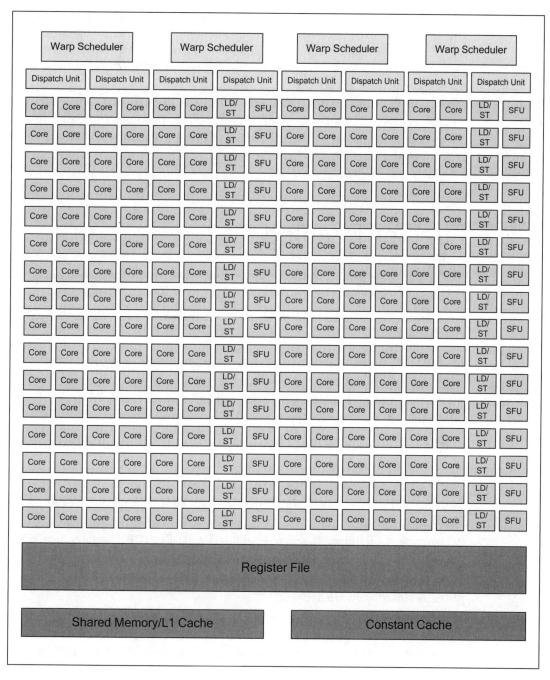

Figure 2.32 SM 3.0 (SMX).

and each SMX is much larger than analogous SMs in previous-generation GPUs. The largest Fermi GPU, GF110, had about 3 billion transistors containing 16 SMs; the GK104 has 3.5 billion transistors and much higher performance but only 8 SMX's. For area savings and power efficiency reasons, NVIDIA greatly increased the resources per SM, with the conspicuous exception of the shared memory/L1 cache. Like Fermi's SMs, each Kepler SMX has 64K of cache that can be partitioned as 48K L1/16K shared or 48K shared/16K L1. The main implication for CUDA developers is that on Kepler, developers have even more incentive to keep data in registers (as opposed to L1 cache or shared memory) than on previous architectures.

2.7 Further Reading

NVIDIA has white papers on their Web site that describe the Fermi and Kepler architectures in detail. The following white paper describes Fermi.

The Next Generation of NVIDIA GeForce GPU www.nvidia.com/object/GTX_400_architecture.html

The following white paper describes the Kepler architecture and its implementation in the NVIDIA GeForce GTX 680 (GK104).

www.geforce.com/Active/en_US/en_US/pdf/GeForce-GTX-680-Whitepaper-FINAL.pdf

NVIDIA engineers also have published several architectural papers that give more detailed descriptions of the various CUDA-capable GPUs.

Lindholm, E., J. Nickolls, S. Oberman, and J. Montrym. NVIDIA Tesla: A unified graphics and computing architecture. *IEEE Micro* 28 (2), March–April 2008, pp. 39–55.

Wittenbrink, C., E. Kilgariff, and A. Prabhu. Fermi GF100 GPU architecture. *IEEE Micro* 31 (2), March–April 2011, pp. 50–59.

Wong et al. used CUDA to develop microbenchmarks and clarify some aspects of Tesla-class hardware architecture.

Wong, H., M. Papadopoulou, M. Sadooghi-Alvandi, and A. Moshovos. Demystifying GPU microarchitecture through microbenchmarking. 2010 IEEE International Symposium on Performance Analysis of Systems and Software (IPSASS), March 28–30, 2010, pp. 235–246.

Chapter 3

Software Architecture

This chapter provides an overview of the CUDA software architecture. Chapter 2 gave an overview of the hardware platform and how it interacts with CUDA, and we'll start this chapter with a description of the software platforms and operating environments supported by CUDA. Next, each software abstraction in CUDA is briefly described, from devices and contexts to modules and kernels to memory. This section may refer back to Chapter 2 when describing how certain software abstractions are supported by the hardware. Finally, we spend some time contrasting the CUDA runtime and driver API and examining how CUDA source code is translated into microcode that operates on the GPU. Please remember that this chapter is just an overview. Most of the topics covered are described in more detail in later chapters.

3.1 Software Layers

Figure 3.1 shows the different layers of software in a CUDA application, from the application itself to the CUDA driver that operates the GPU hardware. All of the software except the kernel mode driver operate in the target operating system's unprivileged user mode. Under the security models of modern multitasking operating systems, user mode is "untrusted," and the hardware and operating system software must take measures to strictly partition applications from one another. In the case of CUDA, that means host and device memory allocated by one CUDA program cannot be accessed by other CUDA programs. The only exceptions happen when these programs specifically request memory sharing, which must be provided by the kernel mode driver.

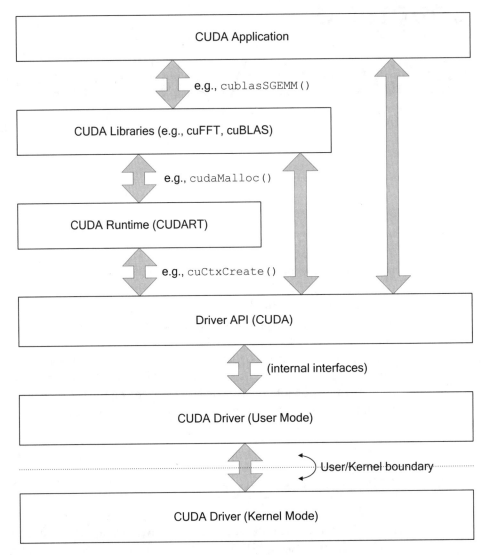

Figure 3.1 Software layers in CUDA.

CUDA libraries, such as cuBLAS, are built on top of the CUDA runtime or driver API. The CUDA runtime is the library targeted by CUDA's integrated C++/GPU toolchain. When the nvcc compiler splits .cu files into host and device portions, the host portion contains automatically generated calls to the CUDA runtime to facilitate operations such as the kernel launches invoked by nvcc's special triple-angle bracket <<< >>> syntax.

The CUDA driver API, exported directly by CUDA's user mode driver, is the lowest-level API available to CUDA apps. The driver API calls into the user mode driver, which may in turn call the kernel mode driver to perform operations such as memory allocation. Functions in the driver API and CUDA runtime generally start with `cu*()` and `cuda*()`, respectively. Many functions, such as `cudaEventElapsedTime()`, are essentially identical, with the only difference being in the prefix.

3.1.1 CUDA RUNTIME AND DRIVER

The CUDA runtime (often abbreviated CUDART) is the library used by the language integration features of CUDA. Each version of the CUDA toolchain has its own specific version of the CUDA runtime, and programs built with that toolchain will automatically link against the corresponding version of the runtime. A program will not run correctly unless the correct version of CUDART is available in the path.

The CUDA driver is designed to be backward compatible, supporting all programs written against its version of CUDA, or older ones. It exports a low-level "driver API" (in `cuda.h`) that enables developers to closely manage resources and the timing of initialization. The driver version may be queried by calling `cuDriverGetVersion()`.

```
CUresult CUDAAPI cuDriverGetVersion(int *driverVersion);
```

This function passes back a decimal value that gives the version of CUDA supported by the driver—for example, 3010 for CUDA 3.1 and 5000 for CUDA 5.0.

Table 3.1 summarizes the features that correspond to the version number passed back by `cuDriverGetVersion()`. For CUDA runtime applications, this information is given by the `major` and `minor` members of the `cudaDeviceProp` structure as described in Section 3.2.2.

The CUDA runtime requires that the installed driver have a version greater than or equal to the version of CUDA supported by the runtime. If the driver version is older than the runtime version, the CUDA application will fail to initialize with the error `cudaErrorInsufficientDriver` (35). CUDA 5.0 introduced the *device runtime*, a subset of the CUDA runtime that can be invoked from CUDA kernels. A detailed description of the device runtime is given in Chapter 7.

Table 3.1. CUDA Driver Features

CUDA VERSION	DRIVER FEATURES INTRODUCED
1.0	CUDA
1.1	Streams and events; concurrent 1D memcpy and kernel execution
2.0	3D texturing
2.1	Improved OpenGL interoperability
2.2	Portable, mapped and write-combined pinned memory; texturing from pitch memory
3.0	Fermi; multiple copy engines; concurrent kernel execution
3.1	GPUDirect
3.2	64-bit addressing; `malloc()`/`free()` in CUDA kernels
4.0	Unified virtual addressing; improved threading support; host memory registration; GPUDirect 2.0 (peer-to-peer memcpy and mapping); layered textures
4.1	Cubemap textures; interprocess peer-to-peer mappings
4.2	Kepler
5.0	Dynamic parallelism; GPUDirect RDMA

3.1.2 DRIVER MODELS

Other than Windows Vista and subsequent releases of Windows, all of the operating systems that CUDA runs—Linux, MacOS, and Windows XP—access the hardware with *user mode client drivers*. These drivers sidestep the require-ment, common to all modern operating systems, that hardware resources be manipulated by kernel code. Modern hardware such as GPUs can finesse that requirement by mapping certain hardware registers—such as the hardware register used to submit work to the hardware—into user mode. Since user mode code is not trusted by the operating system, the hardware must contain protec-tions against rogue writes to the user mode hardware registers. The goal is to prevent user mode code from prompting the hardware to use its direct memory access (DMA) facilities to read or write memory that it should not (such as the operating system's kernel code!).

Hardware designers protect against memory corruption by introducing a level of indirection into the command stream available to user mode software so DMA operations can only be initiated on memory that previously was validated and mapped by kernel code; in turn, driver developers must carefully validate their kernel code to ensure that it only gives access to memory that should be made available. The end result is a driver that can operate at peak efficiency by submitting work to the hardware without having to incur the expense of a kernel transition.

Many operations, such as memory allocation, still require kernel mode transitions because editing the GPU's page tables can only be done in kernel mode. In this case, the user mode driver may take steps to reduce the number of kernel mode transitions—for example, the CUDA memory allocator tries to satisfy memory allocation requests out of a pool.

Unified Virtual Addressing

Unified virtual addressing, described in detail in Section 2.4.5, is available on 64-bit Linux, 64-bit XPDDM, and MacOS. On these platforms, it is made available transparently. As of this writing, UVA is not available on WDDM.

Windows Display Driver Model

For Windows Vista, Microsoft introduced a new desktop presentation model in which the screen output was composed in a back buffer and page-flipped, like a video game. The new "Windows Desktop Manager" (WDM) made more extensive use of GPUs than Windows had previously, so Microsoft decided it would be best to revise the GPU driver model in conjunction with the presentation model. The resulting Windows Display Driver Model (WDDM) is now the default driver model on Windows Vista and subsequent versions. The term XPDDM was created to refer to the driver model used for GPUs on previous versions of Windows.[1]

As far as CUDA is concerned, these are the two major changes made by WDDM.

1. WDDM does not permit hardware registers to be mapped into user mode. Hardware commands—even commands to kick off DMA operations—must be

---

1. Tesla boards (CUDA-capable boards that do not have a display output) can use XPDDM on Windows, called the Tesla Compute Cluster (TCC) driver, and can be toggled with the `nvidia-smi` tool.

invoked by kernel code. The user→kernel transition is too expensive for the user mode driver to submit each command as it arrives, so instead the user mode driver buffers commands for later submission.

2. Since WDDM was built to enable many applications to use a GPU concurrently, and GPUs do not support demand paging, WDDM includes facilities to emulate paging on a "memory object" basis. For graphics applications, memory objects may be render targets, Z buffers, or textures; for CUDA, memory objects include global memory and CUDA arrays. Since the driver must set up access to CUDA arrays before each kernel invocation, CUDA arrays can be swapped by WDDM. For global memory, which resides in a linear address space (where pointers can be stored), every memory object for a given CUDA context must be resident in order for a CUDA kernel to launch.

The main effect of WDDM due to number 1 above is that work requested of CUDA, such as kernel launches or asynchronous memcpy operations, generally is not submitted to the hardware immediately.

The accepted idiom to force pending work to be submitted is to query the NULL stream: `cudaStreamQuery(0)` or `cuStreamQuery(NULL)`. If there is no pending work, these calls will return quickly. If any work is pending, it will be submitted, and since the call is asynchronous, execution may be returned to the caller before the hardware has finished processing. On non-WDDM platforms, querying the NULL stream is always fast.

The main effect of WDDM due to number 2 above is that CUDA's control of memory allocation is much less concrete. On user mode client drivers, successful memory allocations mean that the memory has been allocated and is no longer available to any other operating system client (such as a game or other CUDA application that may be running). On WDDM, if there are applications competing for time on the same GPU, Windows can and will swap memory objects out in order to enable each application to run. The Windows operating system tries to make this as efficient as possible, but as with all paging, having it *never* happen is much faster than having it *ever* happen.

Timeout Detection and Recovery

Because Windows uses the GPU to interact with users, it is important that compute applications not take inordinate amounts of GPU time. Under WDDM, Windows enforces a timeout (default of 2 seconds) that, if it should elapse, will cause a dialog box that says "Display driver stopped responding and has recovered," and the display driver is restarted. If this happens, all work in the CUDA context is lost. See http://bit.ly/16mG0dX.

Tesla Compute Cluster Driver

For compute applications that do not need WDDM, NVIDIA provides the Tesla Compute Cluster (TCC) driver, available only for Tesla-class boards. The TCC driver is a user mode client driver, so it does not require a kernel thunk to submit work to the hardware. The TCC driver may be enabled and disabled using the nvidia-smi tool.

3.1.3 NVCC, PTX, AND MICROCODE

nvcc is the compiler driver used by CUDA developers to turn source code into functional CUDA applications. It can perform many functions, from as complex as compiling, linking, and executing a sample program in one command (a usage encouraged by many of the sample programs in this book) to a simple targeted compilation of a GPU-only .cu file.

Figure 3.2 shows the two recommended workflows for using nvcc for CUDA runtime and driver API applications, respectively. For applications larger than the most trivial size, nvcc is best used strictly for purposes of compiling CUDA code and wrapping CUDA functionality into code that is callable from other tools. This is due to nvcc's limitations.

- nvcc only works with a specific set of compilers. Many CUDA developers never notice because their compiler of choice happens to be in the set of supported compilers. But in production software development, the amount of CUDA code tends to be minuscule compared to the amount of other code, and the presence or absence of CUDA support may not be the dominant factor in deciding which compiler to use.

- nvcc makes changes to the compile environment that may not be compatible with the build environment for the bulk of the application.

- nvcc "pollutes" the namespace with nonstandard built-in types (e.g., int2) and intrinsic names (e.g., __popc()). Only in recent versions of CUDA have the intrinsics symbols become optional and can be used by including the appropriate sm_*_intrinsics.h header.

For CUDA runtime applications, nvcc embeds GPU code into string literals in the output executable. If the --fatbin option is specified, the executable will automatically load suitable microcode for the target GPU or, if no microcode is available, have the driver automatically compile the PTX into microcode.

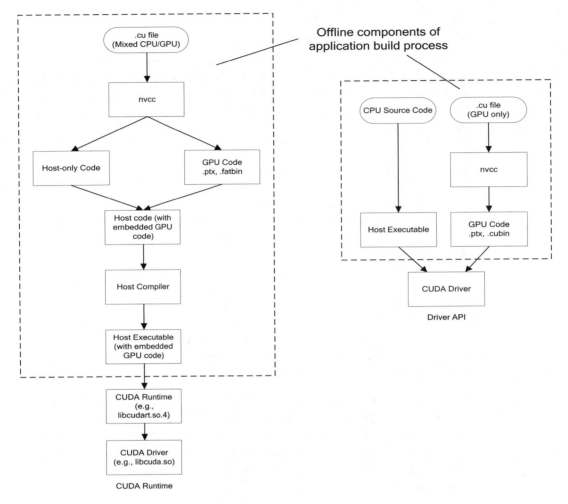

Figure 3.2 nvcc workflows.

nvcc and PTX

PTX ("Parallel Thread eXecution") is the intermediate representation of compiled GPU code that can be compiled into native GPU microcode. It is the mechanism that enables CUDA applications to be "future-proof" against instruction set innovations by NVIDIA—as long as the PTX for a given CUDA kernel is available, the CUDA driver can translate it into microcode for whichever GPU the application happens to be running on (even if the GPU was not available when the code was written).

PTX can be compiled into GPU microcode both "offline" and "online." Offline compilation refers to building software that will be executed by some computer in the future. For example, Figure 3.2 highlights the offline portions of the CUDA compilation process. Online compilation, otherwise known as "just-in-time" compilation, refers to compiling intermediate code (such as PTX) for the computer running the application for immediate execution.

`nvcc` can compile PTX offline by invoking the PTX assembler `ptxas`, which compiles PTX into the native microcode for a specific version of GPU. The resulting microcode is emitted into a CUDA binary called a "cubin" (pronounced like "Cuban"). Cubin files can be disassembled with `cuobjdump --dump-sass`; this will dump the SASS mnemonics for the GPU-specific microcode.[2]

PTX also can be compiled online (JITted) by the CUDA driver. Online compilation happens automatically when running CUDART applications that were built with the `--fatbin` option (which is the default). `.cubin` and PTX representations of every kernel are included in the executable, and if it is run on hardware that doesn't support any of the .cubin representations, the driver compiles the PTX version. The driver caches these compiled kernels on disk, since compiling PTX can be time consuming.

Finally, PTX can be generated at runtime and compiled explicitly by the driver by calling `cuModuleLoadEx()`. The driver API does not automate any of the embedding or loading of GPU microcode. Both `.cubin` and `.ptx` files can be given to `cuModuleLoadEx()`; if a `.cubin` is not suitable for the target GPU architecture, an error will be returned. A reasonable strategy for driver API developers is to compile and embed PTX, and they should always JIT-compile it onto the GPU with `cuModuleLoadEx()`, relying on the driver to cache the compiled microcode.

3.2 Devices and Initialization

Devices correspond to physical GPUs. When CUDA is initialized (either explicitly by calling the driver API's `cuInit()` function or implicitly by calling a CUDA runtime function), the CUDA driver enumerates the available devices and creates a global data structure that contains their names and immutable capabilities such as the amount of device memory and maximum clock rate.

For some platforms, NVIDIA includes a tool that can set policies with respect to specific devices. The `nvidia-smi` tool sets the policy with respect to a

---

2. Examining the SASS code is a key strategy to help drive optimization.

given GPU. For example, nvidia-smi can be used to enable and disable ECC (error correction) on a given GPU. nvidia-smi also can be used to control the number of CUDA contexts that can be created on a given device. These are the possible modes.

- Default: Multiple CUDA contexts may be created on the device.

- "Exclusive" mode: One CUDA context may be created on the device.

- "Prohibited": No CUDA context may be created on the device.

If a device is enumerated but you are not able to create a context on that device, it is likely the device is in "prohibited" mode or in "exclusive" mode and another CUDA context already has been created on that device.

3.2.1 DEVICE COUNT

The application can discover how many CUDA devices are available by calling cuDeviceGetCount() or cudaGetDeviceCount(). Devices can then be referenced by an index in the range [0..*DeviceCount*-1]. The driver API requires applications to call cuDeviceGet() to map the device index to a device handle (CUdevice).

3.2.2 DEVICE ATTRIBUTES

Driver API applications can query the name of a device by calling cuDevice-GetName() and query the amount of global memory by calling cuDevice-TotalMem(). The major and minor compute capabilities of the device (i.e., the SM version, such as 2.0 for the first Fermi-capable GPUs) can be queried by calling cuDeviceComputeCapability().

CUDA runtime applications can call cudaGetDeviceProperties(), which will pass back a structure containing the name and properties of the device. Table 3.2 gives the descriptions of the members of cudaDeviceProp, the structure passed back by cudaGetDeviceProperties().

The driver API's function for querying device attributes, cuDeviceGetAttribute(), can pass back one attribute at a time, depending on the CUdevice_attribute parameter. In CUDA 5.0, the CUDA runtime added the same function in the form of cudaDeviceGetAttribute(), presumably because the structure-based interface was too cumbersome to run on the device.

Table 3.2 `cudaDeviceProp` Members

CUDADEVICEPROP MEMBER	DESCRIPTION
`char name[256];`	ASCII string identifying device
`size_t totalGlobalMem;`	Global memory available on device in bytes
`size_t sharedMemPerBlock;`	Shared memory available per block in bytes
`int regsPerBlock;`	32-bit registers available per block
`int warpSize;`	Warp size in threads
`size_t memPitch;`	Maximum pitch in bytes allowed by memory copies
`int maxThreadsPerBlock;`	Maximum number of threads per block
`int maxThreadsDim[3];`	Maximum size of each dimension of a block
`int maxGridSize[3];`	Maximum size of each dimension of a grid
`int clockRate;`	Clock frequency in kilohertz
`size_t totalConstMem;`	Constant memory available on device in bytes
`int major;`	Major compute capability
`int minor;`	Minor compute capability
`size_t textureAlignment;`	Alignment requirement for textures
`size_t texturePitchAlignment;`	Pitch alignment requirement for texture references bound to pitched memory
`int deviceOverlap;`	Device can concurrently copy memory and execute a kernel. Deprecated. Use `asyncEngineCount` instead.
`int multiProcessorCount;`	Number of multiprocessors on device
`int kernelExecTimeoutEnabled;`	Specified whether there is a runtime limit on kernels
`int integrated;`	Device is integrated as opposed to discrete

continues

Table 3.2 cudaDeviceProp Members *(Continued)*

CUDADEVICEPROP MEMBER	DESCRIPTION
`int canMapHostMemory;`	Device can map host memory with `cudaHostAlloc/cudaHostGetDevicePointer`
`int computeMode;`	Compute mode (see `::cudaComputeMode`)
`int maxTexture1D;`	Maximum 1D texture size
`int maxTexture1DMipmap;`	Maximum 1D mipmapped texture size
`int maxTexture1DLinear;`	Maximum size for 1D textures bound to linear memory
`int maxTexture2D[2];`	Maximum 2D texture dimensions
`int maxTexture2DMipmap[2];`	Maximum 2D mipmapped texture dimensions
`int maxTexture2DLinear[3];`	Maximum dimensions (width)
`int maxTexture2DGather[2];`	Maximum 2D texture dimensions if texture gather operations have to be performed
`int maxTexture3D[3];`	Maximum 3D texture dimensions
`int maxTextureCubemap;`	Maximum Cubemap texture dimensions
`int maxTexture1DLayered[2];`	Maximum 1D layered texture dimensions
`int maxTexture2DLayered[3];`	Maximum 2D layered texture dimensions
`int maxTextureCubemapLayered[2];`	Maximum Cubemap layered texture dimensions
`int maxSurface1D;`	Maximum 1D surface size
`int maxSurface2D[2];`	Maximum 2D surface dimensions
`int maxSurface3D[3];`	Maximum 3D surface dimensions
`int maxSurface1DLayered[2];`	Maximum 1D layered surface dimensions
`int maxSurface2DLayered[3];`	Maximum 2D layered surface dimensions

Table 3.2 `cudaDeviceProp` Members *(Continued)*

CUDADEVICEPROP MEMBER	DESCRIPTION
`int maxSurfaceCubemap;`	Maximum Cubemap surface dimensions
`int maxSurfaceCubemapLayered[2];`	Maximum Cubemap layered surface dimensions
`size_t surfaceAlignment;`	Alignment requirements for surfaces
`int concurrentKernels;`	Device can possibly execute multiple kernels concurrently
`int ECCEnabled;`	Device has ECC support enabled
`int pciBusID;`	PCI bus ID of the device
`int pciDeviceID;`	PCI device ID of the device
`int pciDomainID;`	PCI domain ID of the device
`int tccDriver;`	1 if device is a Tesla device using TCC driver
`int asyncEngineCount;`	Number of asynchronous engines
`int unifiedAddressing;`	Device shares a unified address space with the host
`int memoryClockRate;`	Peak memory clock frequency in kilohertz
`int memoryBusWidth;`	Global memory bus width in bits
`int l2CacheSize;`	Size of L2 cache in bytes
`int maxThreadsPerMultiProcessor;`	Maximum resident threads per multiprocessor

3.2.3 WHEN CUDA IS NOT PRESENT

The CUDA runtime can run on machines that cannot run CUDA or that do not have CUDA installed; if `cudaGetDeviceCount()` returns `cudaSuccess` and a nonzero device count, CUDA is available.

When using the driver API, executables that link directly against `nvcuda.dll` (Windows) or `libcuda.so` (Linux) will not load unless the driver binary

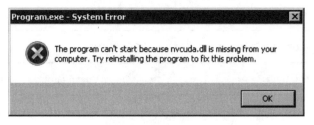

Figure 3.3 Error when CUDA is not present (Windows).

is available. For driver API applications that require CUDA, trying to launch an application that was linked directly against the driver will result in an error such as in Figure 3.3.

For those applications that must run with or without CUDA, the CUDA SDK provides a set of header files and a C source file that wrap the driver API such that the application can check for CUDA without having the operating system signal an exception. These files, in the `dynlink` subdirectory `<SDKRoot>/C/common/inc/dynlink`, can be included in lieu of the core CUDA files. They interpose an intermediate set of functions that lazily load the CUDA libraries if CUDA is available.

As an example, let's compare two programs that use the driver API to initialize CUDA and write the name of each device in the system. Listing 3.1 gives `init_hardcoded.cpp`, a file that can be compiled against the CUDA SDK with the following command line.

```
nvcc -oinit_hardcoded -I ../chLib init_hardcoded.cpp -lcuda
```

Using `nvcc` to compile a C++ file that doesn't include any GPU code is just a convenient way to pick up the CUDA headers. The `-oinit_hardcoded` at the beginning specifies the root name of the output executable. The `-lcuda` at the end causes `nvcc` to link against the driver API's library; without it, the build will fail with link errors. This program hard-links against the CUDA driver API, so it will fail on systems that don't have CUDA installed.

Listing 3.1 Initialization (hard-coded).

```
/*
 * init_hardcoded.cpp
 *
 */
```

```
#include <stdio.h>

#include <cuda.h>
#include <chError.h>

int
main()
{
    CUresult status;
    int numDevices;

    CUDA_CHECK( cuInit( 0 ) );
    CUDA_CHECK( cuDeviceGetCount( &numDevices ) );

    printf( "%d devices detected:\n", numDevices );
    for ( int i = 0; i < numDevices; i++ ) {
        char szName[256];
        CUdevice device;
        CUDA_CHECK( cuDeviceGet( &device, i ) );
        CUDA_CHECK( cuDeviceGetName( szName, 255, device ) );
        printf( "\t%s\n", szName );
    }

    return 0;
Error:
    fprintf( stderr, "CUDA failure code: 0x%x\n", status );
    return 1;

}
```

Listing 3.2 gives a program that will work on systems without CUDA. As you can see, the source code is identical except for a few lines of code.

```
#include <cuda.h>
```

is replaced by

```
#include "cuda_drvapi_dynlink.c"
#include "dynlink/cuda_drvapi_dynlink.h"
```

and the cuInit() call has been changed to specify a CUDA version.

```
 CUDA_CHECK( cuInit(0) );
```

is replaced by

```
 CUDA_CHECK( cuInit( 0, 4010 ) );
```

Here, passing 4010 as the second parameter requests CUDA 4.1 , and the function will fail if the system doesn't include that level of functionality.

Note that you could compile and link `cuda_drvapi_dynlink.c` into the application separately instead of #include'ing it into a single source file. The header file and C file work together to interpose a set of wrapper functions onto the driver API. The header uses the preprocessor to rename the driver API functions to wrapper functions declared in `cuda_drvapi_dynlink.h` (e.g., calls to `cuCtxCreate()` become calls to `tcuCtxCreate()`). On CUDA-capable systems, the driver DLL is loaded dynamically, and the wrapper functions call pointers-to-function that are obtained from the driver DLL during initialization. On non-CUDA-capable systems, or if the driver does not support the request CUDA version, the initialization function returns an error.

Listing 3.2 Initialization (dynlink).

```
/*
 * init_dynlink.cpp
 *
 */

#include <stdio.h>

#include "dynlink/cuda_drvapi_dynlink.h"
#include <chError.h>

int
main()
{
    CUresult status;
    int numDevices;

    CUDA_CHECK( cuInit( 0, 4010 ) );
    CUDA_CHECK( cuDeviceGetCount( &numDevices ) );

    printf( "%d devices detected:\n", numDevices );
    for ( int i = 0; i < numDevices; i++ ) {
        char szName[256];
        CUdevice device;
        CUDA_CHECK( cuDeviceGet( &device, i ) );
        CUDA_CHECK( cuDeviceGetName( szName, 255, device ) );
        printf( "\t%s\n", szName );
    }

    return 0;
Error:
    fprintf( stderr, "CUDA failure code: 0x%x\n", status );
    return 1;

}
```

CUDA-Only DLLs

For Windows developers, another way to build CUDA applications that can run on non-CUDA-capable systems is as follows.

1. Move the CUDA-specific code into a DLL.

2. Call `LoadLibrary()` explicitly to load the DLL.

3. Enclose the `LoadLibrary()` call in a `__try/__except` clause to catch the exception if CUDA is not present.

3.3 Contexts

Contexts are analogous to processes on CPUs. With few exceptions, they are containers that manage the lifetimes of all other objects in CUDA, including the following.

- All memory allocations (including linear device memory, host memory, and CUDA arrays)

- Modules

- CUDA streams

- CUDA events

- Texture and surface references

- Device memory for kernels that use local memory

- Internal resources for debugging, profiling, and synchronization

- The pinned staging buffers used for pageable memcpy

The CUDA runtime does not provide direct access to CUDA contexts. It performs context creation through *deferred initialization.* Every CUDART library call or kernel invocation checks whether a CUDA context is current and, if necessary, creates a CUDA context (using the state previously set by calls such as `cudaSetDevice()`, `cudaSetDeviceFlags()`, `cudaGLSetGLDevice()`, etc.).

Many applications prefer to explicitly control the timing of this deferred initialization. To force CUDART to initialize without any other side effects, call

`cudaFree(0);`

CUDA runtime applications can access the current-context stack (described below) via the driver API.

For functions that specify per-context state in the driver API, the CUDA runtime conflates contexts and devices. Instead of `cuCtxSynchronize()`, the CUDA runtime has `cudaDeviceSynchronize()`; instead of `cuCtxSetCacheConfig()`, the CUDA runtime has `cudaDeviceSetCacheConfig()`.

Current Context

Instead of the current-context stack, the CUDA runtime provides the `cudaSetDevice()` function, which sets the current context for the calling thread. A device can be current to more than one CPU thread at a time.[3]

3.3.1 LIFETIME AND SCOPING

All of the resources allocated in association with a CUDA context are destroyed when the context is destroyed. With few exceptions, the resources created for a given CUDA context may not be used with any other CUDA context. This restriction applies not only to memory but also to objects such as CUDA streams and CUDA events.

3.3.2 PREALLOCATION OF RESOURCES

CUDA tries to avoid "lazy allocation," where resources are allocated as needed to avoid failing operations for lack of resources. For example, pageable memory copies cannot fail with an out-of-memory condition because the pinned staging buffers needed to perform pageable memory copies are allocated at context creation time. If CUDA is not able to allocate these buffers, the context creation fails.

There are some isolated cases where CUDA does not preallocate all the resources that it might need for a given operation. The amount of memory needed to hold local memory for a kernel launch can be prohibitive, so CUDA does not preallocate the maximum theoretical amount needed. As a result, a kernel launch may fail if it needs more local memory than the default allocated by CUDA for the context.

---

3. Early versions of CUDA prohibited contexts from being current to more than one thread at a time because the driver was not thread-safe. Now the driver implements the needed synchronization—even when applications call synchronous functions such as `cudaDeviceSynchronize()`.

3.3.3 ADDRESS SPACE

Besides objects that are automatically destroyed ("cleaned up") when the context is destroyed, the key abstraction embodied in a context is its *address space*: the private set of virtual memory addresses that it can use to allocate linear device memory or to map pinned host memory. These addresses are unique per context. The same address for different contexts may or may not be valid and certainly will not resolve to the same memory location unless special provisions are made. The address space of a CUDA context is separate and distinct from the CPU address space used by CUDA host code. In fact, unlike shared-memory multi-CPU systems, CUDA contexts on multi-GPU configurations do not share an address space. When UVA (unified virtual addressing) is in effect, the CPU and GPU(s) share the same address space, in that any given allocation has a unique address within the process, but the CPUs and GPUs can only read or write each other's memory under special circumstances, such as mapped pinned memory (see Section 5.1.3) or peer-to-peer memory (see Section 9.2.2).

3.3.4 CURRENT CONTEXT STACK

Most CUDA entry points do not take a context parameter. Instead, they operate on the "current context," which is stored in a thread-local storage (TLS) handle in the CPU thread. In the driver API, each CPU thread has a stack of current contexts; creating a context pushes the new context onto the stack.

The current-context stack has three main applications.

- Single-threaded applications can drive multiple GPU contexts.

- Libraries can create and manage their own CUDA contexts without interfering with their callers' CUDA contexts.

- Libraries can be agnostic with respect to which CPU thread calls into the CUDA-aware library.

The original motivation for the current-context stack to CUDA was to enable a single-threaded CUDA application to drive multiple CUDA contexts. After creating and initializing each CUDA context, the application can pop it off the current-context stack, making it a "floating" context. Since only one CUDA context at a time may be current to a CPU thread, a single-threaded CUDA application drives multiple contexts by pushing and popping the contexts in turn, keeping all but one of the contexts "floating" at any given time.

On most driver architectures, pushing and popping a CUDA context is inexpensive enough that a single-threaded application can keep multiple GPUs busy. On WDDM (Windows Display Driver Model) drivers, which run only on Windows Vista and later, popping the current context is only fast if there are no GPU commands pending. If there are commands pending, the driver will incur a kernel thunk to submit the commands before popping the CUDA context.[4]

Another benefit of the current-context stack is the ability to drive a given CUDA context from different CPU threads. Applications using the driver API can "migrate" a CUDA context to other CPU threads by popping the context with `cuCtxPopCurrent()`, then calling `cuCtxPushCurrent()` from another thread. Libraries can use this functionality to create CUDA contexts without the knowledge or involvement of their callers. For example, a CUDA-aware plugin library could create its own CUDA context on initialization, then pop it and keep it floating except when called by the main application. The floating context enables the library to be completely agnostic about which CPU thread is used to call into it. When used in this way, the containment enforced by CUDA contexts is a mixed blessing. On the one hand, the floating context's memory cannot be polluted by spurious writes by third-party CUDA kernels, but on the other hand, the library can only operate on CUDA resources that it allocated.

Attaching and Detaching Contexts

Until CUDA 4.0, every CUDA context had a "usage count" set to 1 when the context was created. The functions `cuCtxAttach()` and `cuCtxDetach()` incremented and decremented the usage count, respectively.[5] The usage count was intended to enable libraries to "attach" to CUDA contexts created by the application into which the library was linked. This way, the application and its libraries could interoperate via a CUDA context that was created by the application.[6]

If a CUDA context is already current when CUDART is first invoked, it attaches the CUDA context instead of creating a new one. The CUDA runtime did not provide access to the usage count of a context. As of CUDA 4.0, the usage count is deprecated, and `cuCtxAttach()`/`cuCtxDetach()` do not have any side effects.

---

4. This expense isn't unique to the driver API or the current-context stack. Calling `cudaSetDevice()` to switch devices when commands are pending also will cause a kernel thunk on WDDM.
5. Until the `cuCtxDestroy()` function was added in CUDA 2.2, CUDA contexts were destroyed by calling `cuCtxDetach()`.
6. In retrospect, it would have been wiser for NVIDIA to leave reference-counting to higher-level software layers than the driver API.

3.3.5 CONTEXT STATE

The `cuCtxSetLimit()` and `cuCtxGetLimit()` functions configure limits related to CPU-like functionality: in-kernel `malloc()` and `printf()`. The `cuCtxSetCacheConfig()` specifies the preferred cache configuration to use when launching kernels (whether to allocate 16K or 48K to shared memory and L1 cache). This is a hint, since any kernel that uses more than 16K of shared memory needs the configuration setting with 48K of shared memory. Additionally, the context state can be overridden by a kernel-specific state (`cuFuncSetCache-Config()`). These states have context scope (in other words, they are not specified for each kernel launch) because they are expensive to change.

3.4 Modules and Functions

Modules are collections of code and related data that are loaded together, analogous to DLLs on Windows or DSOs on Linux. Like CUDA contexts, the CUDA runtime does not explicitly support modules; they are available only in the CUDA driver API.[7]

CUDA does not have an intermediate structure analogous to object files that can be synthesized into a CUDA module. Instead, `nvcc` directly emits files that can be loaded as CUDA modules.

- `.cubin` files that target specific SM versions

- `.ptx` files that can be compiled onto the hardware by the driver

This data needn't be sent to end users in the form of these files. CUDA includes APIs to load modules as NULL-terminated strings that can be embedded in executable resources or elsewhere.[8]

Once a CUDA module is loaded, the application can query for the resources contained in it.

- Globals

- Functions (kernels)

- Texture references

---

7. If CUDA adds the oft-requested ability to JIT from source code (as OpenCL can), NVIDIA may see fit to expose modules to the CUDA runtime.
8. The `cuModuleLoadDataEx()` function is described in detail in Section 4.2.

One important note: All of these resources are created when the module is loaded, so the query functions cannot fail due to a lack of resources.

Like contexts, the CUDA runtime hides the existence and management of modules. All modules are loaded at the same time CUDART is initialized. For applications with large amounts of GPU code, the ability to explicitly manage residency by loading and unloading modules is one of the principal reasons to use the driver API instead of the CUDA runtime.

Modules are built by invoking nvcc, which can emit different types of modules, depending on the command line parameters, as summarized in Table 3.3. Since cubins have been compiled to a specific GPU architecture, they do not have to be compiled "just in time" and are faster to load. But they are neither backward compatible (e.g., cubins compiled onto SM 2.x cannot run on SM 1.x architectures) nor forward compatible (e.g., cubins compiled onto SM 2.x architectures will not run on SM 3.x architectures). As a result, only applications with *a priori* knowledge of their target GPU architectures (and thus cubin versions) can use cubins without also embedding PTX versions of the same modules to use as backup.

PTX is the intermediate language used as a source for the driver's just-in-time compilation. Because this compilation can take a significant amount of time, the driver saves compiled modules and reuses them for a given PTX module, provided the hardware and driver have not changed. If the driver or hardware changes, all PTX modules must be recompiled.

With fatbins, the CUDA runtime automates the process of using a suitable cubin, if available, and compiling PTX otherwise. The different versions are embedded as strings in the host C++ code emitted by nvcc. Applications using the driver

Table 3.3 **nvcc** Module Types

NVCC PARAMETER	DESCRIPTION
-cubin	Compiled onto a specific GPU architecture
-ptx	Intermediate representation used as a source for the driver's just-in-time compilation
-fatbin	Combination of cubin and PTX. Loads the suitable cubin if available; otherwise, compiles PTX onto the GPU. CUDART only

Table 3.4 Module Query Functions

FUNCTION	DESCRIPTION
cuModuleGetGlobal()	Passes back the pointer and size of a symbol in a module.
cuModuleGetTexRef()	Passes back a texture reference declared in a module
cuModuleGetFunction()	Passes back a kernel declared in a module

API have the advantage of finer-grained control over modules. For example, they can be embedded as resources in the executable, encrypted, or generated at runtime, but the process of using cubins if available and compiling PTX otherwise must be implemented explicitly.

Once a module is loaded, the application can query for the resources contained in it: globals, functions (kernels), and texture references. One important note: All of these resources are created when the module is loaded, so the query functions (summarized in Table 3.4) cannot fail due to a lack of resources.

3.5 Kernels (Functions)

Kernels are highlighted by the __global__ keyword in .cu files. When using the CUDA runtime, they can be invoked in-line with the triple-angle-bracket <<< >>> syntax. Chapter 7 gives a detailed description of how kernels can be invoked and how they execute on the GPU.

The GPU executable code of the module comes in the form of kernels that are invoked with the language integration features of the CUDA runtime (<<< >>> syntax) or the cuLaunchKernel() function in the driver API. At the time of this writing, CUDA does not do any dynamic residency management of the executable code in CUDA modules. When a module is loaded, *all* of the kernels are loaded into device memory.

Once a module is loaded, kernels may be queried with cuModuleGetFunction(); the kernel's attributes can be queried with cuFuncGetAttribute(); and the kernel may be launched with cuLaunchKernel(). cuLaunchKernel()

rendered a whole slew of API entry points obsolete: Functions such as `cuFuncSetBlockShape()` specified the block size to use the next time a given kernel was launched; functions such as `cuParamSetv()` specified the parameters to pass the next time a given kernel was launched; and `cuLaunch()`, `cuLaunchGrid()`, and `cuLaunchGridAsync()` launched a kernel using the previously set state. These APIs were inefficient because it took so many calls to set up a kernel launch and because parameters such as block size are best specified atomically with the request to launch the kernel.

The `cuFuncGetAttribute()` function may be used to query specific attributes of a function, such as

- The maximum number of threads per block

- The amount of statically allocated shared memory

- The size of user-allocated constant memory

- The amount of local memory used by each function

- The number of registers used by each thread of the function

- The virtual (PTX) and binary architecture versions for which the function was compiled

When using the driver API, it is usually a good idea to use `extern "C"` to inhibit the default name-mangling behavior of C++. Otherwise, you have to specify the mangled name to `cuModuleGetFunction()`.

CUDA Runtime

As executables that were built with the CUDA runtime are loaded, they create global data structures in host memory that describe the CUDA resources to be allocated when a CUDA device is created. Once a CUDA device is initialized, these globals are used to create the CUDA resources all at once. Because these globals are shared process-wide by the CUDA runtime, it is not possible to incrementally load and unload CUDA modules using the CUDA runtime.

Because of the way the CUDA runtime is integrated with the C++ language, kernels and symbols should be specified by name (i.e., not with a string literal) to API functions such as `cudaFuncGetAttributes()` and `cudaMemcpyToSymbol()`.

Cache Configuration

In Fermi-class architectures, the streaming multiprocessors have L1 caches that can be split as 16K shared/48K L1 cache or 48K shared/16K L1 cache.[9] Initially, CUDA allowed the cache configuration to be specified on a per-kernel basis, using `cudaFuncSetCacheConfig()` in the CUDA runtime or `cuFuncSetCacheConfig()` in the driver API. Later, this state was moved to be more global: `cuCtxSetCacheConfig()`/`cudaDeviceSetCacheConfig()` specifies the default cache configuration.

3.6 Device Memory

Device memory (or linear device memory) resides in the CUDA address space and may be accessed by CUDA kernels via normal C/C++ pointer and array dereferencing operations. Most GPUs have a dedicated pool of device memory that is directly attached to the GPU and accessed by an integrated memory controller.

CUDA hardware does not support demand paging, so all memory allocations are backed by actual physical memory. Unlike CPU applications, which can allocate more virtual memory than there is physical memory in the system, CUDA's memory allocation facilities fail when the physical memory is exhausted. The details of how to allocate, free, and access device memory are given in Section 5.2.

CUDA Runtime

CUDA runtime applications may query the total amount of device memory available on a given device by calling `cudaGetDeviceProperties()` and examining `cudaDeviceProp::totalGlobalMem`. `cudaMalloc()` and `cudaFree()` allocate and free device memory, respectively. `cudaMallocPitch()` allocates pitched memory; `cudaFree()` may be used to free it. `cudaMalloc3D()` performs a 3D allocation of pitched memory.

Driver API

Driver API applications may query the total amount of device memory available on a given device by calling `cuDeviceTotalMem()`. Alternatively, the

---

9. SM 3.x added the ability to split the cache evenly (32K/32K) between L1 and shared memory.

`cuMemGetInfo()` function may be used to query the amount of free device memory as well as the total. `cuMemGetInfo()` can only be called when a CUDA context is current to the CPU thread. `cuMemAlloc()` and `cuMemFree()` allocate and free device memory, respectively. `cuMemAllocPitch()` allocates pitched memory; `cuMemFree()` may be used to free it.

3.7 Streams and Events

In CUDA, streams and events were added to enable host↔device memory copies to be performed concurrently with kernel execution. Later versions of CUDA expanded streams' capabilities to support execution of multiple kernels concurrently on the same GPU and to support concurrent execution between multiple GPUs.

CUDA streams are used to manage concurrency between execution units with coarse granularity.

* The GPU and the CPU

* The copy engine(s) that can perform DMA while the SMs are processing

* The streaming multiprocessors (SMs)

* Kernels that are intended to run concurrently

* Separate GPUs that are executing concurrently

The operations requested in a given stream are performed sequentially. In a sense, CUDA streams are like CPU threads in that operations within a CUDA stream are performed in order.

3.7.1 SOFTWARE PIPELINING

Because there is only one DMA engine serving the various coarse-grained hardware resources in the GPU, applications must "software-pipeline" the operations performed on multiple streams. Otherwise, the DMA engine will "break concurrency" by enforcing synchronization within the stream between different engines. A detailed description of how to take full advantage of CUDA streams using software pipelining is given in Section 6.5, and more examples are given in Chapter 11.

The Kepler architecture reduced the need to software-pipeline streamed operations and, with NVIDIA's Hyper-Q technology (first available with SM 3.5), virtually eliminated the need for software pipelining.

3.7.2 STREAM CALLBACKS

CUDA 5.0 introduced another mechanism for CPU/GPU synchronization that complements the existing mechanisms, which focus on enabling CPU threads to wait until streams are idle or events have been recorded. Stream callbacks are functions provided by the application, registered with CUDA, and later called by CUDA when the stream has reached the point at which cuStreamAddCallback() was called.

Stream execution is suspended for the duration of the stream callback, so for performance reasons, developers should be careful to make sure other streams are available to process during the callback.

3.7.3 THE NULL STREAM

Any of the asynchronous memcpy functions may be called with NULL as the stream parameter, and the memcpy will not be initiated until all preceding operations on the GPU have been completed; in effect, the NULL stream is a join of all the engines on the GPU. Additionally, all streamed memcpy functions are *asynchronous*, potentially returning control to the application before the memcpy has been performed. The NULL stream is most useful for facilitating CPU/GPU concurrency in applications that have no need for the intra-GPU concurrency facilitated by multiple streams. Once a streamed operation has been initiated with the NULL stream, the application must use synchronization functions such as cuCtxSynchronize() or cudaThreadSynchronize() to ensure that the operation has been completed before proceeding. But the application may request many such operations before performing the synchronization. For example, the application may perform

- an asynchronous host→device memcpy

- one or more kernel launches

- an asynchronous device→host memcpy

before synchronizing with the context. The cuCtxSynchronize() or cudaThreadSynchronize() call returns after the GPU has performed the last-requested operation. This idiom is especially useful when performing smaller memcpy's or launching kernels that will not run for long. The CUDA driver takes valuable CPU time to write commands to the GPU, and overlapping that CPU execution with the GPU's processing of the commands can improve performance.

Note: Even in CUDA 1.0, kernel launches were asynchronous; the NULL stream is implicitly specified to any kernel launch in which no stream is explicitly specified.

3.7.4 EVENTS

CUDA events present another mechanism for synchronization. Introduced at the same time as CUDA streams, "recording" CUDA events is a way for applications to track progress within a CUDA stream. All CUDA events work by writing a shared sync memory location when all preceding operations in the CUDA stream have been performed.[10] *Querying* the CUDA event causes the driver to peek at this memory location and report whether the event has been recorded; *synchronizing* with the CUDA event causes the driver to wait until the event has been recorded.

Optionally, CUDA events also can write a timestamp derived from a high-resolution timer in the hardware. Event-based timing can be more robust than CPU-based timing, especially for smaller operations, because it is not subject to spurious unrelated events (such as page faults or network traffic) that may affect wall-clock timing by the CPU. Wall-clock times are definitive because they are a better approximation of what the end users sees, so CUDA events are best used for performance tuning during product development.[11]

Timing using CUDA events is best performed in conjunction with the NULL stream. This rule of thumb is motivated by reasons similar to the reasons RDTSC (Read TimeStamp Counter) is a serializing instruction on the CPU: Just as the CPU is a superscalar processor that can execute many instructions at once, the GPU can be operating on multiple streams at the same time. Without explicit serialization, a timing operation may inadvertently include operations that were not intended to be timed or may exclude operations that were supposed to be timed. As with RDTSC, the trick is to bracket the CUDA event

---

10. Specifying the NULL stream to `cuEventRecord()` or `cudaEventRecord()` means the event will not be recorded until the GPU has processed *all* preceding operations.
11. Additionally, CUDA events that can be used for timing cannot be used for certain other operations; more recent versions of CUDA allow developers to opt out of the timing feature to enable the CUDA event to be used, for example, for interdevice synchronization.

recordings with enough work that the overhead of performing the timing itself is negligible.

CUDA events optionally can cause an interrupt to be signaled by the hardware, enabling the driver to perform a so-called "blocking" wait. Blocking waits suspend the waiting CPU thread, saving CPU clock cycles and power while the driver waits for the GPU. Before blocking waits became available, CUDA developers commonly complained that the CUDA driver burned a whole CPU core waiting for the GPU by polling a memory location. At the same time, blocking waits may take longer due to the overhead of handling the interrupt, so latency-sensitive applications may still wish to use the default polling behavior.

3.8 Host Memory

"Host" memory is CPU memory—the stuff we all were managing with `malloc()`/`free()` and `new[]`/`delete[]` for years before anyone had heard of CUDA. On all operating systems that run CUDA, host memory is *virtualized*; memory protections enforced by hardware are in place to protect CPU processes from reading or writing each other's memory without special provisions.[12] "Pages" of memory, usually 4K or 8K in size, can be relocated without changing their virtual address; in particular, they can be swapped to disk, effectively enabling the computer to have more virtual memory than physical memory. When a page is marked "nonresident," an attempt to access the page will signal a "page fault" to the operating system, which will prompt the operating system to find a physical page available to copy the data from disk and resume execution with the virtual page pointing to the new physical location.

The operating system component that manages virtual memory is called the "virtual memory manager" or VMM. Among other things, the VMM monitors memory activity and uses heuristics to decide when to "evict" pages to disk and resolves the page faults that happen when evicted pages are referenced.

The VMM provides services to hardware drivers to facilitate direct access of host memory by hardware. In modern computers, many peripherals, including disk controllers, network controllers, and GPUs, can read or write host memory using a facility known as "direct memory access" or DMA. DMA gives two

---

12. Examples of APIs that facilitate interprocess sharing include `MapViewOfFile()` on Windows or `mmap()` on Linux.

performance benefits: It avoids a data copy[13] and enables the hardware to operate concurrently with the CPU. A tertiary benefit is that hardware may achieve better bus performance over DMA.

To facilitate DMA, operating system VMMs provide a service called "page-locking." Memory that is page-locked has been marked by the VMM as ineligible for eviction, so its physical address cannot change. Once memory is page-locked, drivers can program their DMA hardware to reference the physical addresses of the memory. This hardware setup is a separate and distinct operation from the page-locking itself. Because page-locking makes the underlying physical memory unavailable for other uses by the operating system, page-locking too much memory can adversely affect performance.

Memory that is not page-locked is known as "pageable." Memory that is page-locked is sometimes known as "pinned" memory, since its physical address cannot be changed by the operating system (it has been pinned in place).

3.8.1 PINNED HOST MEMORY

"Pinned" host memory is allocated by CUDA with the functions cuMemHostAlloc() / cudaHostAlloc(). This memory is page-locked and set up for DMA by the current CUDA context.[14]

CUDA tracks the memory ranges allocated in this way and automatically accelerates memcpy operations that reference pinned memory. Asynchronous memcpy operations only work on pinned memory. Applications can determine whether a given host memory address range is pinned using the cuMemHostGetFlags() function.

In the context of operating system documentation, the terms *page-locked* and *pinned* are synonymous, but for CUDA purposes, it may be easier to think of "pinned" memory as host memory that has been page-locked and mapped for access by the hardware. "Page-locking" refers only to the operating system mechanism for marking host memory pages as ineligible for eviction.

---

13. This extra copy is more obvious to developers using GPUs, whose target peripheral can consume much more bandwidth than more pedestrian devices like those for disk or network controllers. Whatever the type of peripheral, without DMA, the driver must use the CPU to copy data to or from special hardware buffers.
14. CUDA developers often ask if there is any difference between page-locked memory and CUDA's "pinned" memory. There is! Pinned memory allocated or registered by CUDA is mapped for direct access by the GPU(s); ordinary page-locked memory is not.

3.8.2 PORTABLE PINNED MEMORY

Portable pinned memory is mapped for all CUDA contexts after being page-locked. The underlying mechanism for this operation is complicated: When a portable pinned allocation is performed, it is mapped into all CUDA contexts before returning. Additionally, whenever a CUDA context is created, all portable pinned memory allocations are mapped into the new CUDA context before returning. For either portable memory allocation or context creation, any failure to perform these mappings will cause the allocation or context creation to fail. Happily, as of CUDA 4.0, if UVA (unified virtual addressing) is in force, *all* pinned allocations are portable.

3.8.3 MAPPED PINNED MEMORY

Mapped pinned memory is mapped into the address space of the CUDA context, so kernels may read or write the memory. By default, pinned memory is not mapped into the CUDA address space, so it cannot be corrupted by spurious writes by a kernel. For integrated GPUs, mapped pinned memory enables "zero copy": Since the host (CPU) and device (GPU) share the same memory pool, they can exchange data without explicit copies.

For discrete GPUs, mapped pinned memory enables host memory to be read or written directly by kernels. For small amounts of data, this has the benefit of eliminating the overhead of explicit memory copy commands. Mapped pinned memory can be especially beneficial for writes, since there is no latency to cover. As of CUDA 4.0, if UVA (unified virtual addressing) is in effect, *all* pinned allocations are mapped.

3.8.4 HOST MEMORY REGISTRATION

Since developers (especially library developers) don't always get to allocate memory they want to access, CUDA 4.0 added the ability to "register" existing virtual address ranges for use by CUDA. The cuMemHostRegister()/cudaHostRegister() functions take a virtual address range and page-locks and maps it for the current GPU (or for all GPUs, if CU_MEMHOSTREGISTER_PORTABLE or cudaHostRegisterPortable is specified). Host memory registration has a perverse relationship with UVA (unified virtual addressing), in that any address range eligible for registration must not have been included in the virtual address ranges reserved for UVA purposes when the CUDA driver was initialized.

3.9 CUDA Arrays and Texturing

CUDA arrays are allocated from the same pool of physical memory as device memory, but they have an opaque layout that is optimized for 2D and 3D locality. The graphics drivers use these layouts to hold textures; by decoupling the indexing from the addressing, the hardware can operate on 2D or 3D blocks of elements instead of 1D rows. For applications that exhibit sparse access patterns, especially patterns with dimensional locality (for example, computer vision applications), CUDA arrays are a clear win. For applications with regular access patterns, especially those with little to no reuse or whose reuse can be explicitly managed by the application in shared memory, device pointers are the obvious choice.

Some applications, such as image processing applications, fall into a gray area where the choice between device pointers and CUDA arrays is not obvious. All other things being equal, device memory is probably preferable to CUDA arrays, but the following considerations may be used to help in the decision-making process.

- CUDA arrays do not consume CUDA address space.

- On WDDM drivers (Windows Vista and later), the system can automatically manage the residence of CUDA arrays.

- CUDA arrays can reside only in device memory, and the GPU can convert between the two representations while transferring the data across the bus. For some applications, keeping a pitch representation in host memory and a CUDA array representation in device memory is the best approach.

3.9.1 TEXTURE REFERENCES

Texture references are objects that CUDA uses to set up the texturing hardware to "interpret" the contents of underlying memory.[15] Part of the reason this level of indirection exists is because it is valid to have multiple texture references referencing the same memory with different attributes.

A texture reference's attributes may be *immutable*—that is, specified at compile time and not subject to change without causing the application to behave

---

15. Before CUDA 3.2, texture references were the only way to read from CUDA arrays, other than explicit memcpy. Today, surface references may be used to write to CUDA arrays as well as to read from them.

incorrectly—or *mutable*—that is, where the application may change the texture's behavior in ways that are not visible to the compiler (Table 3.5). For example, the dimensionality of the texture (1D, 2D, or 3D) is immutable, since it must be known by the compiler to take the correct number of input parameters and emit the correct machine instruction. In contrast, the filtering and addressing modes are mutable, since they implicitly change the application's behavior without any knowledge or involvement from the compiler.

The CUDA runtime (language integration) and the CUDA driver API deal with texture references very differently. In both cases, a texture reference is declared by invoking a template called `texture`.

```
texture<Type, Dimension, ReadMode> Name;
```

where *Type* is the type of the elements in the memory being read by the texture, *Dimension* is the dimension of the texture (1, 2, or 3), and *ReadMode* specifies whether integer-valued texture types should be converted to normalized floating point when read by the texture reference.

The texture reference must be *bound* to underlying memory before it can be used. The hardware is better optimized to texture from CUDA arrays, but in the following cases, applications benefit from texturing from device memory.

- It enlists the texture cache, which serves as a bandwidth aggregator.

- It enables applications to work around coalescing restrictions.

- It avoids superfluous copies when reading from memory that is otherwise best written via device memory. For example, a video codec may wish to emit frames into device memory, yet read from them via texture.

Table 3.5 Mutable and Immutable Texture Attributes

IMMUTABLE ATTRIBUTES	MUTABLE ATTRIBUTES
Dimensionality	Filtering mode
Type (format)	Addressing modes
Return type	Normalized coordinates
	sRGB conversion

Table 3.6 Texture Intrinsics

TEXTURE TYPE	INTRINSIC
Device memory	`tex1Dfetch(int)`
1D	`tex1D(float x, float y)`
2D	`tex2D(float x, float y)`
3D	`tex3D(float x, float y, float z)`
Cubemap	`texCubemap(float x, float y, float z)`
Layered (1D)	`tex1DLayered(float x, int layer)`
Layered (2D)	`tex2DLayered(float x, float y, int layer)`
Layered (Cubemap)	`texCubemapLayered(float x, float y, float z, int layer)`

Once the texture reference is bound to underlying memory, CUDA kernels may read the memory by invoking `tex*` intrinsics, such as `tex1D()`, given in Table 3.6.

Note: There are no coherency guarantees between texture reads and writes performed via global load/store or surface load/store. As a result, CUDA kernels must take care not to texture from memory that also is being accessed by other means.

CUDA Runtime

To bind memory to a texture, applications must call one of the functions in Table 3.7. CUDA runtime applications can modify mutable attributes of the texture reference by directly assigning structure members.

```
texture<float, 1, cudaReadModeElementType> tex1;
...
tex1.filterMode = cudaFilterModeLinear; // enable linear filtering
tex1.normalized = true; // texture coordinates will be normalized
```

Assigning to these structure members has an immediate effect; there is no need to rebind the texture.

Table 3.7 Functions to Bind Device Memory to Textures

MEMORY	FUNCTION
1D device memory	cudaBindTexture()
2D device memory	cudaBindTexture2D()
CUDA array	cudaBindTextureToArray()

Driver API

Since there is a stricter partition between CPU code and GPU code when using the driver API, any texture references declared in a CUDA module must be queried via cuModuleGetTexRef(), which passes back a CUtexref. Unlike the CUDA runtime, the texture reference then must be initialized with *all* of the correct attributes—both mutable and immutable—because the compiler does not encode the immutable attributes of the texture reference into the CUDA module. Table 3.8 summarizes the driver API functions that can be used to bind a texture reference to memory.

3.9.2 SURFACE REFERENCES

Surface references, a more recent addition to CUDA not available on Tesla-class GPUs, enable CUDA kernels to read and write CUDA arrays via the surface load/store intrinsics. Their primary purpose is to enable CUDA kernels to write CUDA arrays directly. Before surface load/store became available, kernels had to write to device memory and then perform a device→array memcpy to copy and convert the output into a CUDA array.

Table 3.8 Driver API Functions to Bind Memory to Textures

MEMORY	FUNCTION
1D device memory	cuTexRefSetAddress()
2D device memory	cuTexRefSetAddress2D()
CUDA array	cuTexRefSetArray()

Compared to texture references, which can transform everything from the input coordinates to the output format, depending on how they are set up, surface references expose a vanilla, bitwise interface to read and write the contents of the CUDA array.

You might wonder why CUDA did not implement surface load/store intrinsics that operated directly on CUDA arrays (as OpenCL did). The reason is to be future-proof to surface load/store operations that convert to the underlying representation in a more sophisticated way, such as enabling samples to be "splatted" into the CUDA array with fractional coordinates, or interoperating with an antialiased graphics surface. For now, CUDA developers will have to make do implementing such operations in software.

3.10 Graphics Interoperability

The graphics interoperability (or "graphics interop") family of functions enables CUDA to read and write memory belonging to the OpenGL or Direct3D APIs. If applications could attain acceptable performance by sharing data via host memory, there would be no need for these APIs. But with local memory bandwidth that can exceed 140G/s and PCI Express bandwidth that rarely exceeds 6G/s in practice, it is important to give applications the opportunity to keep data on the GPU when possible. Using the graphics interop APIs, CUDA kernels can write data into images and textures that are then incorporated into graphical output to be performed by OpenGL or Direct3D.

Because the graphics and CUDA drivers must coordinate under the hood to enable interoperability, applications must signal their intention to perform graphics interop early. In particular, the CUDA context must be notified that it will be interoperating with a given API by calling special context creation APIs such as `cuD3D10CtxCreate()` or `cudaGLSetDevice()`.

The coordination between drivers also motivated resource-sharing between graphics APIs and CUDA to occur in two steps.

1. *Registration:* a potentially expensive operation that signals the developer's intent to share the resources to the underlying drivers, possibly prompting them to move and/or lock down the resources in question

2. *Mapping:* a lightweight operation that is expected to occur at high frequency

In early versions of CUDA, the APIs for graphics interoperability with all four graphics APIs (OpenGL, Direct3D 9, Direct3D 10, and Direct3D 11) were strictly separate. For example, for Direct3D 9 interoperability, the following functions would be used in conjunction with one another.

- `cuD3D9RegisterResource()`/`cudaD3D9RegisterResource()`

- `cuD3D9MapResources()`/`cudaD3D9MapResources()`

- `cuD3D9UnmapResources()`/`cudaD3D9UnmapResources()`

- `cuD3D9UnregisterResource()`/`cudaD3D9UnregisterResource()`

Because the underlying hardware capabilities are the same, regardless of the API used to access them, many of these functions were merged in CUDA 3.2. The registration functions remain API-specific, since they require API-specific bindings, but the functions to map, unmap, and unregister resources were made common. The CUDA 3.2 APIs corresponding to the above are as follows.

- `cuD3D9RegisterResource()`/`cudaD3D9RegisterResource()`

- `cuGraphicsMapResources()`/`cudaGraphicsMapResources()`

- `cuGraphicsUnmapResources()`/`cudaGraphicsUnmapResources()`

- `cuGraphicsUnregisterResource()`/
  `cudaGraphicsUnregisterResource()`

The interoperability APIs for Direct3D 10 are the same, except the developer must use `cuD3D10RegisterResource()`/`cudaD3D10RegisterResource()` instead of the `cuD3D9*` variants.

CUDA 3.2 also added the ability to access textures from graphics APIs in the form of CUDA arrays. In Direct3D, textures are just a different type of "resource" and may be referenced by `IDirect3DResource9 *` (or `IDirect3DResource10 *`, etc.). In OpenGL, a separate function `cuGraphicsGLRegisterImage()` is provided.

3.11 The CUDA Runtime and CUDA Driver API

The CUDA runtime ("CUDART") facilitates the language integration that makes CUDA so easy to program out of the gate. By automatically taking care of tasks such as initializing contexts and loading modules, and especially by enabling kernel invocation to be done in-line with other C++ code, CUDART lets developers focus on getting their code working quickly. A handful of CUDA abstractions, such as CUDA modules, are not accessible via CUDART.

In contrast, the driver API exposes all CUDA abstractions and enables them to be manipulated by developers as needed for the application. The driver API does not provide any performance benefit. Instead, it enables explicit resource management for applications that need it, like large-scale commercial applications with plug-in architectures.

> The driver API is not noticeably faster than the CUDA runtime. If you are looking to improve performance in your CUDA application, look elsewhere.

Most CUDA features are available to both CUDART and the driver API, but a few are exclusive to one or the other. Table 3.9 summarizes the differences.

Table 3.9 CUDA Runtime versus Driver API Features

FEATURE	CUDART	DRIVER API
Device memory allocation	*	*
Pinned host memory allocation	*	*
Memory copies	*	*
CUDA streams	*	*
CUDA events	*	*
Graphics interoperability	*	*
Texture support	*	*
Surface support	*	*
cuMemGetAddressRange		*
Language integration	*	
"Fat binary"	*	
Explicit JIT options		*

Table 3.9 CUDA Runtime versus Driver API Features *(Continued)*

FEATURE	CUDART	DRIVER API
Simplified kernel invocation	*	
Explicit context and module management		*
Context migration		*
Float16 textures		*
Memset of 16- and 32-bit values		*
Compiler independence		*

Between the two APIs, operations like memcpy tend to be functionally identical, but the interfaces can be quite different. The stream APIs are almost identical.

CUDART	DRIVER API
`cudaStream_t stream;`	`CUstream stream;`
`cudaError_t status =` `    cudaStreamCreate( &stream );`	`CUresult status =` `    cuStreamCreate( &stream, 0 );`
`. . .`	`. . .`
`status = cudaStreamSynchronize(` `    stream );`	`status = cuStreamSynchronize(` `    stream );`

The event APIs have minor differences, with CUDART providing a separate `cudaEventCreateWithFlags()` function if the developer wants to specify a flags word (needed to create a blocking event).

CUDART	DRIVER API
`cudaEvent_t eventPolling;`	`CUevent eventPolling;`
`cudaEvent_t eventBlocking;`	`CUevent eventBlocking;`

continues

CUDART	DRIVER API

`cudaError_t status = `
`    cudaEventCreate(`
`    &eventPolling );`
	`CUresult status = cuEventCreate(`
	`    &eventPolling, 0);`

`cudaError_t status = `
`    cudaEventCreateWithFlags(`
`    &eventBlocking,`
`    cudaEventBlockingSync );`
	`CUresult status = cuEventCreate(`
	`    &eventBlocking,`
	`    CU_EVENT_BLOCKING_SYNC );`

`. . .`	`. . .`
`status = cudaEventSynchronize(` `    event );`	`status = cuEventSynchronize(` `    event );`

The memcpy functions are the family where the interfaces are the most different, despite identical underlying functionality. CUDA supports three variants of memory—host, device, and CUDA array—which are all permutations of participating memory types, and 1D, 2D, or 3D memcpy. So the memcpy functions must contain either a large family of different functions or a small number of functions that support many types of memcpy.

The simplest memcpy's in CUDA copy between host and device memory, but even those function interfaces are different: CUDART uses `void *` for the types of both host and device pointers and a single memcpy function with a direction parameter, while the driver API uses `void *` for host memory, `CUdeviceptr` for device memory, and three separate functions (`cuMemcpyHtoD()`, `cuMemcpyDtoH()`, and `cuMemcpyDtoD()`) for the different memcpy directions. Here are equivalent CUDART and driver API formulations of the three permutations of host↔device memcpy.

CUDART	DRIVER API

`void *dptr;`
`void *hptr;`
`void *dptr2;`
`status = cudaMemcpy( dptr, hptr,`
`  size, cudaMemcpyHostToDevice );`
	`CUdeviceptr dptr;`
	`void *hptr;`
	`Cudeviceptr dptr2;`
	`status = cuMemcpyHtoD( dptr,`
	`  hptr, size );`

`status = cudaMemcpy( hptr, dptr,` `   size, cudaMemcpyDeviceToHost );`	`status = cuMemcpyDtoH( hptr,` `   dptr, size );`
`status = cudaMemcpy( dptr, dptr2,` `   size, cudaMemcpyDeviceToDevice );`	`status = cuMemcpyDtoD( dptr,` `   dptr2, size );`

For 2D and 3D memcpy's, the driver API implements a handful of functions that take a descriptor struct and support all permutations of memcpy, including lower-dimension memcpy's. For example, if desired, cuMemcpy3D() can be used to perform a 1D host→device memcpy instead of cuMemcpyHtoD().

```
CUDA_MEMCPY3D cp = {0};
cp.dstMemoryType = CU_MEMORYTYPE_DEVICE;
cp.dstDevice = dptr;
cp.srcMemoryType = CU_MEMORYTYPE_HOST;
cp.srcHost = host;
cp.WidthInBytes = bytes;
cp.Height = cp.Depth = 1;
status = cuMemcpy3D( &cp );
```

CUDART uses a combination of descriptor structs for more complicated memcpy's (e.g., cudaMemcpy3D()), while using different functions to cover the different memory types. Like cuMemcpy3D(), CUDART's cudaMemcpy3D() function takes a descriptor struct that can describe any permutation of memcpy, including inter-dimensional memcpy's (e.g., performing a 1D copy to or from the row of a 2D CUDA array, or copying 2D CUDA arrays to or from slices of 3D CUDA arrays). Its descriptor struct is slightly different in that it embeds other structures; the two APIs' 3D memcpy structures are compared side-by-side in Table 3.10.

Usage of both 3D memcpy functions is similar. They are designed to be zero-initialized, and developers set the members needed for a given operation. For example, performing a host→3D array copy may be done as follows.

```
struct cudaMemcpy3DParms cp = {0};        CUDA_MEMCPY3D cp = {0};
cp.srcPtr.ptr = host;                     cp.srcMemoryType = CU_MEMORYTYPE_HOST;
cp.srcPtr.pitch = pitch;                  cp.srcHost = host;
cp.dstArray = hArray;                      cp.srcPitch = pitch;
cp.extent.width = Width;                   cp.srcHeight = Height;
cp.extent.height = Height;                 cp.dstMemoryType = CU_MEMORYTYPE_ARRAY;
cp.extent.depth = Depth;                   cp.dstArray = hArray;
cp.kind = cudaMemcpyHostToDevice;          cp.WidthInBytes = Width;
                                           cp.Height = Height;
status = cudaMemcpy3D( &cp );             cp.Depth = Depth;
                                           status = cuMemcpy3D( &cp );
```

For a 3D copy that covers the entire CUDA array, the source and destination offsets are set to 0 by the first line and don't have to be referenced again. Unlike parameters to a function, the code only needs to reference the parameters needed by the copy, and if the program must perform more than one similar copy (e.g., to populate more than one CUDA array or device memory region), the descriptor struct can be reused.

Table 3.10 3D Memcpy Structures

```
struct cudaMemcpy3DParms              typedef struct CUDA_MEMCPY3D_st {
{                                         size_t srcXInBytes;
    struct cudaArray *srcArray;           size_t srcY;
    struct cudaPos srcPos;                size_t srcZ;
    struct cudaPitchedPtr                 size_t srcLOD;
srcPtr;                                   CUmemorytype srcMemoryType;
                                          const void *srcHost;
    struct cudaArray *dstArray;           CUdeviceptr srcDevice;
    struct cudaPos dstPos;                CUarray srcArray;
    struct cudaPitchedPtr                 void *reserved0;
dstPtr;                                   size_t srcPitch;
                                          size_t srcHeight;
    struct cudaExtent extent;
    enum cudaMemcpyKind kind;             size_t dstXInBytes;
};                                        size_t dstY;
                                          size_t dstZ;
struct cudaPos                            size_t dstLOD;
{                                         CUmemorytype dstMemoryType;
    size_t x;                             void *dstHost;
    size_t y;                             CUdeviceptr dstDevice;
    size_t z;                             CUarray dstArray;
};                                        void *reserved1;
                                          size_t dstPitch;
struct cudaPitchedPtr                     size_t dstHeight;
{
    void *ptr;                            size_t WidthInBytes;
    size_t pitch;                         size_t Height;
    size_t xsize;                         size_t Depth;
    size_t ysize;                     } CUDA_MEMCPY3D;
};

struct cudaExtent
{
    size_t width;
    size_t height;
    size_t depth;
};
```

Chapter 4

Software Environment

This chapter gives an overview of the CUDA development tools and the software environments that can host CUDA applications. Sections are devoted to the various tools in the NVIDIA toolkit.

- `nvcc`: the CUDA compiler driver

- `ptxas`: the PTX assembler

- `cuobjdump`: the CUDA object file dump utility

- `nvidia-smi`: the NVIDIA System Management Interface

Section 4.5 describes Amazon's EC2 (Elastic Compute Cloud) service and how to use it to access GPU-capable servers over the Internet. This chapter is intended more as a reference than as a tutorial. Example usages are given in Part III of this book.

4.1 `nvcc`—CUDA Compiler Driver

`nvcc` is the compiler driver CUDA developers use to translate source code into functional CUDA applications. It can perform many functions, from as simple as a targeted compilation of a GPU-only `.cu` file to as complex as compiling, linking, and executing a sample program in one command (a usage encouraged by many of the sample programs in this book).

As a compiler driver, `nvcc` does nothing more than set up a build environment and spawn a combination of native tools (such as the C compiler installed on the system) and CUDA-specific command-line tools (such as ptxas) to build the CUDA code. It implements many sensible default behaviors that can be over-ridden by command-line options; its exact behavior depends on which "compile trajectory" is requested by the main command-line option.

Table 4.1 lists the file extensions understood by nvcc and the default behavior implemented for them. (*Note:* Some intermediate file types, like the .i/.ii files that contain host code generated by CUDA's front end, are omitted here.) Table 4.2 lists the compilation stage options and corresponding compile trajec-tory. Table 4.3 lists nvcc options that affect the environment, such as paths to include directories. Table 4.4 lists nvcc options that affect the output, such as whether to include debugging information. Table 4.5 lists "passthrough" options that enable nvcc to pass options to the tools that it invokes, such as ptxas. Table 4.6 lists nvcc options that aren't easily categorized, such as the –keep option that instructs nvcc not to delete the temporary files it created.

Table 4.1 Extensions for nvcc Input Files

FILE EXTENSION	DEFAULT BEHAVIOR
.c/.cc/.cpp/.cxx	Preprocess, compile, link
.cu	Split host and device cost, compile them separately
.o(bj)	Link
..ptx	PTX-assemble into cubin

Table 4.2 Compilation Trajectories

OPTION	TRAJECTORY
--cuda	Compile all .cu input files to .cu.cpp.ii output.
--cubin	Compile all .cu/.ptx/.gpu files to .cubin files.*
--fatbin	Compile all .cu/.ptx/.gpu files to PTX and/or device-only bina-ries, as specified by --arch and/or --code, and output the result into the fat binary file specified with the –o option.*

Table 4.2 Compilation Trajectories *(Continued)*

OPTION	TRAJECTORY
`--ptx`	Compile all `.cu`/`.gpu` files to device-only `.ptx` files.*
`--gpu`	Compile all `.cu` files to device-only `.gpu` files.*
`--preprocess (-E)`	Preprocess all `.c`/`.cc`/`.cpp`/`.cxx`/`.cu` input files.
`--generate-dependencies (-M)`	Generate for the one `.c`/`.cc`/`.cpp`/`.cxx`/`.cu` input file (more than one input file is not allowed in this mode) a dependency file that can be included in a makefile.
`--compile (-c)`	Compile each `.c`/`.cc`/`.cpp`/`.cxx`/`.cu` input file into an object file.
`--link (-link)`	Compile and link all inputs (this is the default trajectory).
`--lib (-lib)`	Compile all inputs into object files (if necessary) and add the results to the specified output library file.
`--x (-x)`	Explicitly specify the language for the input files rather than letting the compiler choose a default based on the file name suffix. Allowed values: c, c++, cu.
`--run (-run)`	Compiles and links all inputs into an executable, then runs it. If the input is an executable, runs it without any compiling or linking.

* These command-line options discard any host code in the input file.

Table 4.3 nvcc Options (Environment)

OPTION	DESCRIPTION
`--output-file <file>` `(-o)`	Specify name and location of the output file. Only a single input file is allowed when this option is present in nvcc non-linking/archiving mode.
`--pre-include <include-file>` `(-include)`	Specify header files that must be preincluded during preprocessing.
`--library <library>` `(-l)`	Specify libraries to be used in the linking stage. The libraries are searched for on the library search paths that have been specified using –L.

continues

Table 4.3 `nvcc` Options (Environment) *(Continued)*

OPTION	DESCRIPTION
`--define-macro <macrodef>` `(-D)`	Specify macro definitions to define during preprocessing or compilation.
`--undefine-macro` `(-U)`	Specify macro definitions to undefine during preprocessing or compilation.
`--include-path <include-path>` `(-I)`	Specify include search paths.
`--system-include <include-path>` `-isystem`	Specify system include search paths.
`--library-path` `(-L)`	Specify library search paths.
`--output-directory` `(-odir)`	Specify the directory of the output file. This option is intended to enable the dependency generation step (`--generate-dependencies`) to generate a rule that defines the target object file in the proper directory.
`--compiler-bindir <path>` `(--ccbin)`	Specify the directory in which the compiler executable (Microsoft Visual Studio cl, or a gcc derivative) resides. By default, this executable is expected in the current executable search path. For a different compiler, or to specify these compilers with a different executable name, specify the path to the compiler including the executable name.
`--cl-version <cl-version-number>` `(-cl-version)`	Specify the version of Microsoft Visual Studio installation. Allowed values for this option: 2005, 2008, 2010. This option is required if `--use-local-env` is specified.

Table 4.4 Options for Specifying Behavior of Compiler/Linker

OPTION	DESCRIPTION
`--profile` `(-pg)`	Instrument-generated code/executable for use by gprof (Linux only).
`--debug` `(-g)`	Generate debug information for host code.

Table 4.4 Options for Specifying Behavior of Compiler/Linker *(Continued)*

OPTION	DESCRIPTION
`--device-debug<level>` `(-G)`	Generate debug information for device code, plus also specify the optimization level (0–3) for the device code in order to control its "debuggability."
`--optimize <level>` `-O`	Specify optimization level for host code.
`--shared` `-shared`	Generate a shared library during linking.
`--machine <bits>` `-m`	Specify 32- vs. 64-bit architecture. Allowed values for this option: 32, 64.

Table 4.5 `nvcc` Options for Passthrough

OPTION	DESCRIPTION
`--compiler-options <options>` `(-Xcompiler)`	Specify options directly to the compiler/preprocessor.
`--linker-options <options>` `-Xlinker`	Specify options directly to the linker.
`--archive-options <options>` `(-Xarchive)`	Specify options directly to library manager.
`--cudafe-options <options>` `-Xcudafe`	Specify options directly to `cudafe`.
`--ptx-options <options>` `-Xptxas`	Specify options directly to the PTX optimizing assembler.

Table 4.6 Miscellaneous `nvcc` Options

OPTION	DESCRIPTION
`--dont-use-profile` `(-noprof)`	Do not use `nvcc.profiles` file for compilation.
`--dryrun` `(-dryrun)`	Suppresses execution of the compilation commands.

continues

Table 4.6 Miscellaneous nvcc Options *(Continued)*

OPTION	DESCRIPTION
--verbose (-v)	List the commands generated by nvcc.
--keep (-keep)	Keep all the intermediate files generated during internal compilation steps.
--keep-dir (-keep-dir)	Specifies the directory where files specified by --keep should be written.
--save-temps (-save-temps)	(Same as --keep)
--clean-targets (-clean)	Causes nvcc to delete all the nontemporary files that otherwise would be created by nvcc.
--run-args <arguments> (-run-args)	If --run is specified, this option specifies command-line arguments to pass to the executable.
--input-drive-prefix <prefix> (-idp)	Windows specific: specifies prefix for absolute paths of input files. For Cygwin users, specify "-idp /cygwin/"; for Mingw, specify "-idp /"
--dependency-drive-prefix <prefix> (-ddp)	Windows specific: specifies prefix for absolute paths when generating dependency files (--generate-dependencies). For Cygwin users, specify "-idp /cygwin/"; for Mingw, specify "-idp /"
--drive-prefix <prefix> (-dp)	Specifies prefix to use for both input files and dependency files.
--no-align-double	Specifies that –malign-double should not be passed as a compiler argument on 32-bit platforms. *Note:* For certain 64-bit types, this option makes the ABI incompatible with CUDA's kernel ABI.

Table 4.7 lists nvcc options related to code generation. The --gpu-architecture and --gpu-code options are especially confusing. The former controls which *virtual* GPU architecture to compile for (i.e., which version of PTX to emit), while the latter controls which *actual* GPU architecture to compile for (i.e., which version of SM microcode to emit). The --gpu-code option must specify SM versions that are at least as high as the versions specified to --gpu-architecture.

Table 4.7 `nvcc` Options for Code Generation

OPTION	DESCRIPTION

`--gpu-architecture`
  `<gpu architecture name>`
`-arch`
	Specify the virtual NVIDIA GPU architectures to compile for. This option specifies which version of PTX to target. Valid options include: `compute_10`, `compute_11`, `compute_12`, `compute_13`, `compute_20`, `compute_30`, `compute_35`, `sm_10`, `sm_11`, `sm_12`, `sm_13`, `sm_20`, `sm_21`, `sm_30`, `sm_35`.

`--gpu-code`
  `<gpu architecture name>`
`-code`
	Specify the actual GPU architecture to compile for. This option specifies which SM versions to compile for. If left unspecified, this option is inferred to be the SM version corresponding to the PTX version specified by `--gpu-architecture`. Valid options include: `compute_10`, `compute_11`, `compute_12`, `compute_13`, `compute_20`, `compute_30`, `compute_35`, `sm_10`, `sm_11`, `sm_12`, `sm_13`, `sm_20`, `sm_21`, `sm_30`, `sm_35`.

`--generate-code` `(-gencode)`	Specifies a tuple of virtual and actual GPU architectures to target. `--generate-code arch=<arch>,code=<code>` is equivalent to `--gpu-architecture <arch> --gpu-code <code>`.
`--export-dir`	Specify the name of the directory to which all device code images will be copied.
`--maxregcount <N>` `(-maxregcount)`	Specify the maximum number of registers that GPU functions can use.
`--ftz [true,false]` `(-ftz)`	Flush-to-zero: when performing single-precision floating-point operations, denormals are flushed to zero. `--use-fast-math` implies `--ftz=true`. The default is `false`.
`--prec-div [true, false]` `(-prec-div)`	Precise division: if `true`, single-precision floating-point division and reciprocals are performed to full precision (round-to-nearest-even with 0 ulps in error). `--use-fast-math` implies `--prec-div=false`. The default value is true.
`--prec-sqrt [true, false]`	Precise square root: if `true`, single-precision floating-point square root is performed to full precision (round-to-nearest-even with 0 ulps in error). `--use-fast-math` implies `--prec-sqrt=false`. The default value is true.

continues

Table 4.7 `nvcc` Options for Code Generation *(Continued)*

OPTION	DESCRIPTION
`--fmad [true, false]`	Enables or disables the contraction of floating-point multiplies and adds/subtracts into floating-point multiply-add (FMAD) instructions. This option is supported only when `--gpu-architecture` is compute_20, sm_20, or higher. For other architecture classes, the contraction is always enabled. `--use-fast-math` implies `--fmad=true`.
`--use-fast-math`	Use fast math library. Besides implying `--prec-div false`, `--prec-sqrt false`, `--fmad true`, the single-precision runtime math functions are compiled directly to SFU intrinsics.

The `--export-dir` option specifies a directory where all device code images will be copied. It is intended as a device code repository that can be inspected by the CUDA driver when the application is running (in which case the directory should be in the `CUDA_DEVCODE_PATH` environment variable). The repository can be either a directory or a ZIP file. In either case, CUDA will maintain a directory structure to facilitate code lookup by the CUDA driver. If a filename is specified but does not exist, a directory structure (not a ZIP file) will be created at that location.

4.2 `ptxas`—the PTX Assembler

`ptxas`, the tool that compiles PTX into GPU-specific microcode, occupies a unique place in the CUDA ecosystem in that NVIDIA makes it available both in the offline tools (which developers compile into applications) and as part of the driver, enabling so-called "online" or "just-in-time" (JIT) compilation (which occurs at runtime).

When compiling offline, `ptxas` generally is invoked by `nvcc` if any actual GPU architectures are specified with the `--gpu-code` command-line option. In that case, command-line options (summarized in Table 4.8) can be passed to `ptxas` via the `-Xptxas` command-line option to `nvcc`.

Table 4.8 Command-Line Options for `ptxas`

OPTION	DESCRIPTION
`--abi-compile <yes|no>` `(-abi)`	Enable or disable the compiling of functions using the Application Binary Interface (ABI). The default is `yes`.

`--allow-expensive-optimizations`
   `<true|false>`
`(-allow-expensive-optimizations)`
	Enable or disable expensive compile-time optimizations that use maximum available resources (memory and compile time). If unspecified, the default behavior is to enable this feature for optimization level ≥O2.

`--compile-only` `(-c)`	Generate a relocatable object.
`--def-load-cache [ca|cg|cs|lu|cv]` `-dlcm`	Default cache modifier on global load. Default value: ca.
`--device-debug` `(-g)`	Generate debug information for device code.

`--device-function-maxregcount`
   `<archmax/archmin/N>`
`(-func-maxregcount)`
	When compiling with `--compile-only`, specify the maximum number of registers that device functions can use. This option is ignored for whole-program compilation and does not affect the number of registers used by entry functions. For device functions, this option overrides the value specified by `--maxrregcount`. If neither `--device-function-maxregcount` nor `--maxrregcount` is specified, then no maximum is assumed.

`--dont-merge-basicblocks` `(-no-bb-merge)`	Normally, ptxas attempts to merge consecutive basic blocks as part of its optimization process. This option inhibits basic block merging, improving the debuggability of generated code at a slight performance cost.
`--entry <entry function>` `(-e)`	Entry function name.
`--fmad <true|false>` `(-fmad)`	Enables or disables the contraction of floating-point multiplies and adds/subtracts into floating-point multiply-add operations (FMAD, FFMA, or DFMA). Default value: `true`.
`--generate-line-info` `(-lineinfo)`	Generate line-number information for device code.

continues

Table 4.8 Command-Line Options for `ptxas` *(Continued)*

OPTION	DESCRIPTION
`--gpu-name <gpu name>` `(-arch)`	Specify the SM version for which to generate code. This option also takes virtual compute architectures, in which case code generation is suppressed. This can be used for parsing only. Allowed values for this option: `compute_10`, `compute_11`, `compute_12`, `compute_13`, `compute_20`, `compute_30`, `compute_35`, `sm_10`, `sm_11`, `sm_12`, `sm_13`, `sm_20`, `sm_21`, `sm_30`, `sm_35`. Default value: `sm_10`.
`--input-as-string <ptx-string>` `(-ias)`	Specifies the string containing the PTX module to compile on the command line.
`--machine [32|34]` `(-m)`	Compile for 32-bit versus 64-bit architecture.
`--maxrregcount <archmax/archmin/N>` `-maxrregcount`	Specify the maximum amount of registers that GPU functions can use.
`--opt-level <N>` `(-O)`	Specifies the optimization level (0–3).
`--options-file <filename>` `(-optf)`	Include command-line options from the specified file.
`--output-file <filename>` `(-o)`	Specify name of output file. (Default: `elf.o`)
`--return-at-end` `-ret-end`	Suppresses the default `ptxas` behavior of optimizing out return instructions at the end of the program for improved debuggability.
`--sp-bounds-check` `(-sp-bounds-check)`	Generate a stack-pointer bounds-checking code sequence. Automatically enabled when `--device-debug` (`-g`) or `--generate-line-info` (`-lineinfo`) is specified.
`--suppress-double-demote-warning` `-suppress-double-demote-warning`	Suppress the warning when a double precision instruction is encountered in PTX being compiled for an SM version that does not include double precision support.
`--verbose` `-v`	Enable verbose mode.

Table 4.8 Command-Line Options for `ptxas` *(Continued)*

OPTION	DESCRIPTION
`--version`	Print version information.
`--warning-as-error` `-Werror`	Make all warnings into errors.

Developers also can load PTX code dynamically by invoking `cuModuleLoadDataEx()`, as follows.

```
CUresult cuModuleLoadDataEx (
    CUmodule *module,
    const void *image,
    unsigned int numOptions,
    CUjit_option *options,
    void **optionValues
);
```

`cuModuleLoadDataEx()` takes a pointer image and loads the corresponding module into the current context. The pointer may be obtained by mapping a `cubin` or PTX or `fatbin` file, passing a `cubin` or PTX or `fatbin` file as a NULL-terminated text string, or incorporating a `cubin` or `fatbin` object into the executable resources and using operating system calls such as Windows `FindResource()` to obtain the pointer. Options are passed as an array via options, and any corresponding parameters are passed in `optionValues`. The number of total options is specified by `numOptions`. Any outputs will be returned via `optionValues`. Supported options are given in Table 4.9.

Table 4.9 Options for `cuModuleLoadDataEx()`

OPTION	DESCRIPTION
`CU_JIT_MAX_REGISTERS`	Specifies the maximum number of registers per thread.
`CU_JIT_THREADS_PER_BLOCK`	Input is the minimum number of threads per block for which to target compilation. Output is the number of threads used by the compiler. This parameter enables the caller to restrict the number of registers such that a block with the given number of threads should be able to launch based on register limitations. Note that this option does not account for resources other than registers (such as shared memory).

Table 4.9 Options for `cuModuleLoadDataEx()` *(Continued)*

OPTION	DESCRIPTION
CU_JIT_WALL_TIME	Passes back a float containing the wall clock time (in milli-seconds) spent compiling the PTX code.
CU_JIT_INFO_LOG_BUFFER	Input is a pointer to a buffer in which to print any informational log messages from PTX assembly (the buffer size is specified via option CU_JIT_INFO_LOG_BUFFER_SIZE_BYTES).
CU_JIT_INFO_LOG_BUFFER_SIZE_BYTES	Input buffer size in bytes; passes back the number of bytes filled with messages.
CU_JIT_ERROR_LOG_BUFFER	Input is a pointer to a buffer in which to print any error log messages from PTX assembly (the buffer size is specified via option CU_JIT_ERROR_LOG_BUFFER_SIZE_BYTES).
CU_JIT_ERROR_LOG_BUFFER_BYTES	Input is the size in bytes of the buffer; output is the number of bytes filled with messages.
CU_JIT_OPTIMIZATION_LEVEL	Level of optimization to apply to generated code (0–4), with 4 being the default.
CU_JIT_TARGET_FROM_CUCONTEXT	Infers compilation target from the current CUDA context. This is the default behavior if CU_JIT_TARGET is not specified.
CU_JIT_TARGET	CUjit_target_enum: specifies the compilation target. May be any of: CU_TARGET_COMPUTE_10, CU_TARGET_COMPUTE_11, CU_TARGET_COMPUTE_12, CU_TARGET_COMPUTE_13, CU_TARGET_COMPUTE_20, CU_TARGET_COMPUTE_21, CU_TARGET_COMPUTE_30, CU_TARGET_COMPUTE_35.
CU_JIT_TARGET_FALLBACK_STRATEGY	CUjit_fallback_enum: specifies fallback strategy of matching cubin is not found; possibly values are CU_PREFER_PTX or CU_PREFER_BINARY.

4.3 cuobjdump

cuobjdump is the utility that may be used to examine the binaries generated by CUDA. In particular, it is useful for examining the microcode generated by nvcc. Specify the --cubin parameter to nvcc to generate a .cubin file, and then use

```
cuobjdump --dump-sass <filename.cubin>
```

to dump the disassembled microcode from the .cubin file. The complete list of command-line options for cuobjdump is given in Table 4.10.

Table 4.10 cuobjdump Command-Line Options

OPTION	DESCRIPTION
--all-fatbin (-all)	Dump all fatbin sections. By default, will only dump the contents of executable fatbin; if there is no executable fatbin, dumps the contents of the relocatable fatbin.
--dump-cubin (-cubin)	Dump cubin for all listed device functions.
--dump-elf (-elf)	Dump ELF Object sections.
--dump-elf-symbols (-symbols)	Dump ELF symbol names.
--dump-function-names (-fnam)	Dump names of device functions. This option is implied if options --dump-sass, --dump-cubin, or --dump-ptx are given.
--dump-ptx (-ptx)	Dump PTX for all listed device functions.
--dump-sass (-sass)	Dump disassembly for all listed device functions.
--file <filename> (-f)	Specify names of source files whose fat binary structures must be dumped. Source files may be specified by the full path by which they were compiled with nvcc, by filename only, or by base filename (with no file extension).
--function <function name> (-fun)	Specify names of device functions whose fat binary structures must be dumped.

continues

Table 4.10 `cuobjdump` Command-Line Options *(Continued)*

OPTION	DESCRIPTION
`--help` `(-h)`	Print this help information on this tool.
`--options-file <file>` `(-optf)`	Include command-line options from specified file.
`--sort-functions` `(-sort)`	Sort functions when dumping SASS.
`--version` `(-V)`	Print version information on this tool.

4.4 `nvidia-smi`

`nvidia-smi`, the NVIDIA System Management Interface, is used to manage the environment in which Tesla-class NVIDIA GPU boards operate. It can report GPU status and control aspects of GPU execution, such as whether ECC is enabled and how many CUDA contexts can be created on a given GPU.

When `nvidia-smi` is invoked with the `--help` `(-h)` option, it generates a usage message that, besides giving a brief description of its purpose and command-line options, also gives a list of supported products. Tesla- and Quadro-branded GPUs are fully supported, while GeForce-branded GPUs get limited support.

Many of the GPU boards supported by `nvidia-smi` include multiple GPUs; `nvidia-smi` refers to these boards as *units*. Some operations, such as toggling the status of an LED (light emitting diode), are available only on a per-unit basis.

`nvidia-smi` has several modes of operation. If no other command-line parameters are given, it lists a summary of available GPUs that can be refined by the command-line options in Table 4.11. Otherwise, the other command-line options that are available include the following.

- List: The `--list-gpus` `(-L)` option displays a list of available GPUs and their UUIDs. Additional options to refine the listing are summarized in Table 4.11.

- Query: The `--query` (`-q`) option displays GPU or unit information. Additional options to refine the query are summarized in Table 4.12.

- Document Type Definition (DTD): The `--dtd` option produces the Document Type Definition for the XML-formatted output of `nvidia-smi`. The `--filename` (`-f`) option optionally specifies an output file; the `--unit` (`-u`) option causes the DTD for GPU boards (as opposed to GPUs) to be written.

- Device modification: The options specified in Table 4.13 may be used to set the persistent state of the GPU, such as whether ECC (error correction) is enabled.

- Unit modification: The `--toggle-led` option (`-t`) may be set to `0`/`GREEN` or `1`/`AMBER`. The `--id` (`-i`) option can be used to target a specific unit.

Table 4.11 `nvidia-smi` List Options

OPTION	DESCRIPTION
`--list-gpus` (`-L`)	Display a list of available GPUs.
`--id=<GPU>` (`-i`)	Target a specific GPU.
`--filename=<name>` (`-f`)	Log to a given file rather than to stdout.
`--loop=<interval>` (`-l`)	Probe at specified interval (in seconds) until Ctrl+C.

Table 4.12 `nvidia-smi` Query Options

OPTION	DESCRIPTION
`--query` (`-q`)	Display GPU or unit information.
`--unit` (`-u`)	Show unit attributes rather than GPU attributes.
`--id=<GPU>` (`-i`)	Target a specific GPU.
`--filename=<name>` (`-f`)	Log to a given file rather than to stdout.

continues

Table 4.12 `nvidia-smi` Query Options *(Continued)*

OPTION	DESCRIPTION
`--xml-format (-x)`	Produce XML output.
`--display=<list> (-d)`	Display only selected information. The following options may be selected with a comma-delimited list: MEMORY, UTILIZATION, ECC, TEMPERATURE, POWER, CLOCK, COMPUTER, PIDS, PERFORMNACE, SUPPORTED_CLOCKS.
`--loop=<interval> (-l)`	Probe at specified interval (in seconds) until Ctrl+C.

Table 4.13 `nvidia-smi` Device Modification Options

OPTION	DESCRIPTION
`--application-clocks=<clocks> (-ac)`	Specifies GPU clock speeds as a tuple: <memory, graphics> (e.g., 2000,800).
`--compute-mode=<mode> (-c)`	Set compute mode: `0/DEFAULT`, `1/EXCLUSIVE_THREAD`, `2/PROHIBITED`, or `3/EXCLUSIVE_PROCESS`.
`--driver-model=<model> (-dm)`	Windows only: Enable or disable TCC (Tesla Compute Cluster) driver: `0/WDDM`, `1/TCC`. See also `--force-driver-model` (-fdm).
`--ecc-config=<config> (-e)`	Set ECC mode: `0/DISABLED` or `1/ENABLED`.
`--force-driver-model=<model> (-fdm)`	Windows only: Enable or disable TCC (Tesla Compute Cluster) driver: `0/WDDM`, `1/TCC`. This option causes TCC to be enabled even if a display is connected to the GPU, which otherwise would cause `nvidia-smi` to report an error.
`--gom=<mode>`	Set GPU operation mode: `0/ALL_ON`, `1/COMPUTE`, `2/LOW_DP`.
`--gpu-reset (-r)`	Trigger secondary bus reset of GPU. This operation can be used to reset GPU hardware state when a machine reboot might otherwise be required. Requires `--id`.

Table 4.13 `nvidia-smi` Device Modification Options *(Continued)*

OPTION	DESCRIPTION
`--id=<GPU> (-i)`	Target a specific GPU.
`--persistence-mode=<mode> (-pm)`	Set persistence mode: `0/DISABLED` or `1/ENABLED`.
`--power-limit (-pl)`	Specifies maximum power management limit in watts.
`--reset-application-clocks (-rac)`	Reset the application clocks to the default.
`--reset-ecc-errors=<type> (-p)`	Reset ECC error counts: `0/VOLATILE` or `1/AGGREGATE`.

4.5 Amazon Web Services

Amazon Web Services is the preeminent vendor of "infrastructure as a service" (IAAS) cloud computing services. Their Web services enable customers to allocate storage, transfer data to and from their data centers, and run servers in their data centers. In turn, customers are charged for the privilege on an a la carte basis: per byte of storage, per byte transferred, or per instance-hour of server time. On the one hand, customers can access potentially unlimited compute resources without having to invest in their own infrastructure, and on the other hand, they need only pay for the resources they use. Due to the flexibility and the cloud's ability to accommodate rapidly increasing demand (say, if an independent game developer's game "goes viral"), cloud computing is rapidly increasing in popularity.

A full description of the features of AWS and how to use them is outside the scope of this book. Here we cover some salient features for those who are interested in test-driving CUDA-capable virtual machines.

- S3 (Simple Storage Service) objects can be uploaded and downloaded.

- EC2 (Elastic Compute Cloud) instances can be launched, rebooted, and terminated.

- EBS (Elastic Block Storage) volumes can be created, copied, attached to EC2 instances, and destroyed.

- It features security groups, which are analogous to firewalls for EC2 instances.

- It features key pairs, which are used for authentication.

All of the functionality of Amazon Web Services is accessible via the AWS Management Console, accessible via aws.amazon.com. The AWS Management Console can do many tasks not listed above, but the preceding handful of operations are all we'll need in this book.

4.5.1 COMMAND-LINE TOOLS

The AWS command-line tools can be downloaded from `http://aws.amazon. com/developertools`. Look for "Amazon EC2 API Tools." These tools can be used out of the box on Linux machines; Windows users can install Cygwin. Once installed, you can use commands such as `ec2-run-instances` to launch EC2 instances, `ec2-describe-instances` to give a list of running instances, or `ec2-terminate-instances` to terminate a list of instances. Anything that can be done in the Management Console also can be done using a command-line tool.

4.5.2 EC2 AND VIRTUALIZATION

EC2, the "Elastic Compute Cloud," is the member of the AWS family that enables customers to "rent" a CUDA-capable server for a period of time and be charged only for the time the server was in use. These virtual computers, which look to the customer like standalone servers, are called *instances*. Customers can use EC2's Web services to launch, reboot, and terminate instances according to their need for the instances' computing resources.

One of the enabling technologies for EC2 is *virtualization*, which enables a single server to host multiple "guest" operating systems concurrently. A single server in the EC2 fleet potentially can host several customers' running instances, improving the economies of scale and driving down costs. Different instance types have different characteristics and pricing. They may have different amounts of RAM, CPU power,[1] local storage, and I/O performance, and the on-demand pricing may range from $0.085 to $2.40 per instance-hour. As of this writing, the CUDA-capable `cg1.4xlarge` instance type costs $2.10 per instance-hour and has the following characteristics.

---

1. The CPU capabilities are measured in EC2 Compute Units (ECUs). As of this writing, the ECUs available from a given instance range from 1 (in the `m1.small` instance type) to 88.5 (in the `cc2.8xlarge` instance type).

- 23 GB of RAM

- 33.5 ECUs (two quad-core Intel Xeon X5570 "Nehalem" CPUs)

- 1690 GB of instance storage

- 64-bit platform

Since `cg1.4xlarge` is a member of the "cluster" instance family, only a single instance will run on a given server; also, it is plugged into a much higher band-width network than other EC2 instance types to enable cluster computing for parallel workloads.

4.5.3 KEY PAIRS

Access to EC2 instances is facilitated by *key pairs*. The term refers to the central concept in public key cryptography that the authentication is performed using a private key (available only to those who are authorized) and a public key that can be freely shared.

When a key pair is created, the private key is downloaded in the form of a `.pem` file. There are two reasons to keep careful track of a `.pem` file after creating a key pair: First, anyone with access to the `.pem` file can use it to gain access to your EC2 computing resources, and second, there is no way to obtain new copies of the private key! Amazon is not in the key retention business, so once the private key is downloaded, it is yours to keep track of.

Listing 4.1 gives an example `.pem` file. The format is convenient because it has anchor lines (the "BEGIN RSA PRIVATE KEY" / "END RSA PRIVATE KEY") and is "7-bit clean" (i.e., only uses ASCII text characters), so it can be emailed, copied-and-pasted into text fields, appended to files such as `~/.ssh/authorized_keys` to enable password-less login, or published in books. The name for a given key pair is specified when launching an EC2 instance; in turn, the corresponding private key file is used to gain access to that instance. To see more specifically how the `.pem` file is used to access EC2 instances, see the sections on Linux and Windows below.

Listing 4.1 Example `.pem` file.

```
-----BEGIN RSA PRIVATE KEY-----
MIIEowIBAAKCAQEA2mHaXk9tTZqN7ZiUWoxhcSHjVCbHmn1SKamXqOKdLDfmqducvVkAlB1cjIz/
NcwIHk0TxbnEPEDyPPHg8RYGya34evswzBUCOIcilbVIpVCyaTyzo4k0WKPW8znXJzQpxr/OHzzu
```

```
tAvlq95HGoBobuGM5kaDSlkugOmTUXFKxZ4ZN1rm2kUo21N2m9jrkDDq4qTMFxuYW0H0AXeHOfNF
ImroUCN2udTWOjpdgIPCgYEzz3Cssd9QIzDyadw+wbkTYq7eeqTNKULs4/gmLIAw+EXKE2/seyBL
leQeK11j1TFhDCjYRfghp0ecv4UnpAtiO6nNzod7aTAR1bXqJXbSqwIDAQABAoIBAAh2umvlUCst
zkpjG3zW6//ifFkKl7nZGZIbzJDzF3xbPklfBZghFvCmoquf21ROcBIckqObK4vaSIksJrexTtoK
MBM0IRQHzGo8co6y0/n0QrXpcFzqOGknEHGk0D3ou6XEUUzMo8O+okwi9UaFq4aAn2FdYkFDa5X7
d4Y0id1WzPcVurOSrnFNkWl4GRu+pluD2bmSmb7RUxQWGbP7bf98EyhpdugOdO7R3yOCcdaaGg0L
hdTlwJ3jCP9dmnk7NqApRzkv7R1sXzOnU2v3b9+WpF0g6wCeM2eUuK1IY3BPl0Pg+Q4xU0jpRSr0
vLDt8fUcIdH4PXTKua1NxsBA1uECgYEA72wC3BmL7HMIgf33yvK+/yA1z6AsAvIIAlCHJOi9sihT
XF6dnfaJ6d12oCj1RUqG9e9Y3cW1YjgcdqQBk5F8M6bPuIfzOctM/urd1ryWZ3ddSxgBaLEO1h4c
3/cQWGGvaMPpDSAihs2d/CnnlVoQGiQrlWxDGzIHzu8RRV43fKcCgYEA6YDkj6kzlx4cuQwwsPVb
IfdtP6WrHe+Ro724ka3Ry+4xFPcarXj5yl5/aPHNpdPPCfR+uYNjBiTD90w+duV8LtBxJoF+i/lt
Mui4116xXMBaMGQfFMS0u2+z3aZI8MXZF8gGDIrI9VVfpDCi2RNKaT7KhfraZ8VzZsdAqDO8Zl0C
gYEAvVq3iEvMFl2ERQsPhzslQ7G93U/Yfxvcqbf2qoJIRTcPduZ90gjCWmwE/fZmxT6ELs31grBz
HBM0r8BWXteZW2B6uH8NJpBbfOFUQhk0+u+0oUeDFcGy8jUusRM9oijgCgOntfHMXMESSfT6a2yn
f4VL0wmkqUWQV2FMT4iMadECgYATFUGYrA9XTlKynNht3d9wyzPWe8ecTrPsWdj3rujybaj9OaSo
gLaJX2eyP/C6mLDW83BX4PD6045ga46/UMnxWX+l0fdxoRTXkEVq9IYyOlYklkoj/F944gwlFS3o
34J6exJjfAQoaK3EUWU9sGHocAVFJdcrm+tufuI93NyM0QKBgB+koBIkJG8u0f19oW1dhUWERsuo
poXZ9Kh/GvJ9u5DUwv6F+hCGRotdBFhjuwKNTbutdzElxDMNHKoy/rhiqgcneMUmyHh/F0U4sOWl
XqqMD2QfKXBAU0ttviPbsmm0dbjzTTd3FO1qx2K90T3u9GEUdWYqMxOyZjUoLyNr+Tar
-----END RSA PRIVATE KEY-----
```

4.5.4 AVAILABILITY ZONES (AZS) AND REGIONS

AWS provides its services in separate Availability Zones (AZs) that are carefully segregated from one another, with the intention of preventing outages affecting one Availability Zone from affecting any other Availability Zone. For CUDA developers, the main consideration to bear in mind is that instances, EBS volumes, and other resources must be in the same AZ to interoperate.

4.5.5 S3

S3 (Simple Storage Service) is designed to be a reliable way to store data for later retrieval. The "objects" (basically files) are stored in a hierarchical layout consisting of "buckets" at the top of the hierarchy, with optional intervening "folders."

Besides storage and retrieval ("PUT" and "GET," respectively), S3 includes the following features.

- Permissions control. By default, S3 objects are accessible only to the owner of the S3 account, but they may be made public or permissions can be granted to specific AWS accounts.

- Objects may be encrypted.

- Metadata may be associated with an S3 object, such as the language of a text file or whether the object is an image.

- Logging: Operations performed on S3 objects can be logged (and the logs are stored as more S3 objects).

- Reduced Redundancy: S3 objects can be stored with a lower reliability factor, for a lower price.

- Notifications: Automatic notifications can be set up, to, for example, let the customer know if loss of a Reduced Redundancy object is detected.

- Object lifetime management: Objects can be scheduled to be deleted automatically after a specified period of time.

Many other AWS services use S3 as a persistent data store; for example, snapshots of AMIs and EBS volumes are stored in S3.

4.5.6 EBS

EBS (Elastic Block Storage) consists of network-based storage that can be allocated and attached and detached to running instances. AWS customers also can "snapshot" EBS volumes, creating templates for new EBS volumes.

EC2 instances often have a root EBS volume that contains the operating system and driver software. If more storage is desired, you can create and attach an EBS volume and mount it within the guest operating system.[2]

4.5.7 AMIS

Amazon Machine Images (AMIs) are descriptions of what an EC2 instance would "look like" once launched, including the operating system and the number and contents of attached EBS volumes. Most EC2 customers start with a "stock" AMI provided by Amazon, modify it to their satisfaction, and then take a snapshot of the AMI so they can launch more instances with the same setup.

When an instance is launched, EC2 will take a few minutes to muster the requested resources and boot the virtual machine. Once the instance is running,

---

2. You may have to change the OS configuration if you want the EBS volume to be available to instances launched from a derivative AMI; see the "Linux on EC2" or "Windows on EC2" sections in this chapter.

you can query its IP address and access it over the Internet using the private key whose name was specified at instance launch time.

The external IP address of the instance is incorporated into the DNS name. For example, a `cg1.4xlarge` instance might be named

```
ec2-70-17-16-35.compute-1.amazonaws.com
```

and the external IP address of that machine is `70.17.16.35`.[3]

EC2 instances also have internal IP addresses that can be used for intracluster communication. If, for example, you launch a cluster of instances that need to communicate using software such as the Message Passing Interface (MPI), use the internal IP addresses.

4.5.8 LINUX ON EC2

EC2 supports many different flavors of Linux, including an Amazon-branded flavor ("Amazon Linux") that is derived from Red Hat. Once an instance is launched, it may be accessed via `ssh` using the key pair that was used to launch the instance. Using the IP address above and the `Example.pem` file in Listing 4.1, we might type

```
ssh -i Example.pem ec2-user@70.17.16.35
```

(The root username varies with the flavor of Linux: `ec2-user` is the root username for Amazon Linux, while CentOS uses `root` and Ubuntu uses `ubuntu`.)

Once logged in, the machine is all yours! You can add users and set their passwords, set up SSH for password-less login, install needed software (such as the CUDA toolchain), attach more EBS volumes, and set up the ephemeral disks. You can then snapshot an AMI to be able to launch more instances that look exactly like the one you've set up.

EBS

EBS (Elastic Block Storage) volumes are easy to create, either from a blank volume or by making a live copy of a snapshot. Once created, the EBS volume may be attached to an instance, where it will appear as a device (such as `/dev/sdf` or, on more recent Linux kernels, `/dev/xvdf`). When the EBS volume is first attached, it is just a raw block storage device that must be formatted before

---

3. IP addresses have been changed to protect the innocent.

use using a command such as `mkfs.ext3`. Once formatted, the drive may be mounted to a directory.

```
mount <Device> <Directory>
```

Finally, if you want to snapshot an AMI and for the drive to be visible on instances launched using the derivative AMI, edit `/etc/fstab` to include the volume. When creating an EBS volume to attach to a running instance, make sure to create it in the same Availability Zone (e.g., us-east-1b) as the instance.

Ephemeral Storage

Many EC2 instance types, including `cg1.4xlarge`, have local hard disks associated with them. These disks, when available, are used strictly for scratch local storage; unlike EBS or S3, no erasure encoding or other technologies are employed to make the disks appear more reliable. To emphasize this reduced reliability, the disks are referred to as *ephemeral storage*.

To make ephemeral disks available, specify the "-b" option to ec2-run-instances—for example,

```
ec2-run-instances -t cg1.4xlarge -k nwiltEC2 -b /dev/sdb=ephemeral0
/dev/sdc=ephemeral1
```

Like EBS volumes, ephemerals must be formatted (e.g., mkfs.ext3) and mounted before they can be used, and they must have `fstab` entries in order to reappear when the instance is rebooted.

User Data

User data may be specified to an instance, either at launch time or while an instance is running (in which case the instance must be rebooted). The user data then may be queried at

http://169.254.169.254/latest/user-data

4.5.9 WINDOWS ON EC2

Windows instances are accessed in a slightly different way than Linux instances. Once launched, customers must use their private key file to retrieve the password for the EC2 instance's Administrator account. You can either specify your .pem file or copy-and-paste its contents into the AWS Management Console (shown in Figure 4.1).

Figure 4.1 AWS Windows password retrieval.

By default, this password-generation behavior is only in force on "stock" AMIs from AWS. If you "snapshot" one of these AMIs, they will retain whatever passwords were present on the machine when the snapshot was taken. To create a new Windows AMI that generates a random password upon launch, run the "EC2 Config Service" tool (available in the Start menu), click the "Bundle" tab, and click the button that says "Run Sysprep and Shutdown Now" (Figure 4.2). After clicking this button, any AMI created against it will generate a random password, like the stock Windows AMIs.

Ephemeral Storage

In order for ephemeral storage to be useable by a Windows instance, you must specify the –b option to ec2-run-instances, as follows.

```
ec2-run-instances -t cg1.4xlarge -k nwiltEC2 -b /dev/sdb=ephemeral0
/dev/sdc=ephemeral1
```

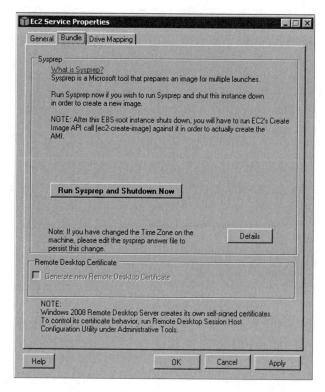

Figure 4.2 Sysprep for Windows on EC2.

User Data

User data may be specified to an instance, either at launch time or while an instance is running (in which case the instance must be rebooted). The user data then may be queried at

http://169.254.169.254/latest/user-data

PART II

Chapter 5

Memory

To maximize performance, CUDA uses different types of memory, depending on the expected usage. *Host memory* refers to the memory attached to the CPU(s) in the system. CUDA provides APIs that enable faster access to host memory by page-locking and mapping it for the GPU(s). *Device memory* is attached to the GPU and accessed by a dedicated memory controller, and, as every beginning CUDA developer knows, data must be copied explicitly between host and device memory in order to be processed by the GPU.

Device memory can be allocated and accessed in a variety of ways.

- *Global memory* may be allocated statically or dynamically and accessed via pointers in CUDA kernels, which translate to global load/store instructions.

- *Constant memory* is read-only memory accessed via different instructions that cause the read requests to be serviced by a cache hierarchy optimized for broadcast to multiple threads.

- *Local memory* contains the stack: local variables that cannot be held in registers, parameters, and return addresses for subroutines.

- *Texture memory* (in the form of CUDA arrays) is accessed via texture and surface load/store instructions. Like constant memory, read requests from texture memory are serviced by a separate cache that is optimized for read-only access.

Shared memory is an important type of memory in CUDA that is *not* backed by device memory. Instead, it is an abstraction for an on-chip "scratchpad" memory that can be used for fast data interchange between threads within a block. Physically, shared memory comes in the form of built-in memory on the SM: On

SM 1.x hardware, shared memory is implemented with a 16K RAM; on SM 2.x and more recent hardware, shared memory is implemented using a 64K cache that may be partitioned as 48K L1/16K shared, or 48K shared/16K L1.

5.1 Host Memory

In CUDA, *host memory* refers to memory accessible to the CPU(s) in the system. By default, this memory is *pageable*, meaning the operating system may move the memory or evict it out to disk. Because the physical location of pageable memory may change without notice, it cannot be accessed by peripherals like GPUs. To enable "direct memory access" (DMA) by hardware, operating systems allow host memory to be "page-locked," and for performance reasons, CUDA includes APIs that make these operating system facilities available to application developers. So-called *pinned memory* that has been page-locked and mapped for direct access by CUDA GPU(s) enables

- Faster transfer performance

- Asynchronous memory copies (i.e., memory copies that return control to the caller before the memory copy necessarily has finished; the GPU does the copy in parallel with the CPU)

- Mapped pinned memory that can be accessed directly by CUDA kernels

Because the virtual→physical mapping for pageable memory can change unpredictably, GPUs cannot access pageable memory at all. CUDA copies pageable memory using a pair of *staging buffers* of pinned memory that are allocated by the driver when a CUDA context is allocated. Chapter 6 includes hand crafted pageable memcpy routines that use CUDA events to do the synchronization needed to manage this double-buffering.

5.1.1 ALLOCATING PINNED MEMORY

Pinned memory is allocated and freed using special functions provided by CUDA: `cudaHostAlloc()`/`cudaFreeHost()` for the CUDA runtime, and `cuMemHostAlloc()`/`cuMemFreeHost()` for the driver API. These functions work with the host operating system to allocate page-locked memory and map it for DMA by the GPU(s).

CUDA keeps track of memory it has allocated and transparently accelerates memory copies that involve host pointers allocated with `cuMemHostAlloc()` / `cudaHostAlloc()`. Additionally, some functions (notably the asynchronous memcpy functions) require pinned memory.

The `bandwidthTest` SDK sample enables developers to easily compare the performance of pinned memory versus normal pageable memory. The `--memory=pinned` option causes the test to use pinned memory instead of pageable memory. Table 5.1 lists the `bandwidthTest` numbers for a `cg1.4xlarge` instance in Amazon EC2, running Windows 7-x64 (numbers in MB/s). Because it involves a significant amount of work for the host, including a kernel transition, allocating pinned memory is expensive.

CUDA 2.2 added several features to pinned memory. *Portable pinned memory* can be accessed by any GPU; *mapped pinned memory* is mapped into the CUDA address space for direct access by CUDA kernels; and *write-combined pinned memory* enables faster bus transfers on some systems. CUDA 4.0 added two important features that pertain to host memory: Existing host memory ranges can be page-locked in place using *host memory registration*, and Unified Virtual Addressing (UVA) enables all pointers to be unique process-wide, including host and device pointers. When UVA is in effect, the system can infer from the address range whether memory is device memory or host memory.

5.1.2 PORTABLE PINNED MEMORY

By default, pinned memory allocations are only accessible to the GPU that is current when `cudaHostAlloc()` or `cuMemHostAlloc()` is called. By specifying the `cudaHostAllocPortable` flag to `cudaHostAlloc()`, or the `CU_MEMHOSTALLOC_PORTABLE` flag to `cuHostMemAlloc()`, applications can request that the pinned allocation be mapped for *all* GPUs instead. Portable pinned allocations benefit from the transparent acceleration of memcpy described earlier and can participate in asynchronous memcpys for any GPU in

Table 5.1 Pinned versus Pageable Bandwidth

	HOST→DEVICE	DEVICE→HOST
Pinned	5523	5820
Pageable	2951	2705

the system. For applications that intend to use multiple GPUs, it is good practice to specify all pinned allocations as portable.

NOTE

When UVA is in effect, all pinned memory allocations are portable.

5.1.3 MAPPED PINNED MEMORY

By default, pinned memory allocations are mapped for the GPU outside the CUDA address space. They can be directly accessed by the GPU, but only through memcpy functions. CUDA kernels cannot read or write the host memory directly. On GPUs of SM 1.2 capability and higher, however, CUDA kernels are able to read and write host memory directly; they just need allocations to be mapped into the device memory address space.

To enable mapped pinned allocations, applications using the CUDA runtime must call cudaSetDeviceFlags() with the cudaDeviceMapHost flag before any initialization has been performed. Driver API applications specify the CU_CTX_MAP_HOST flag to cuCtxCreate().

Once mapped pinned memory has been enabled, it may be allocated by calling cudaHostAlloc() with the cudaHostAllocMapped flag, or cuMemHostAlloc() with the CU_MEMALLOCHOST_DEVICEMAP flag. Unless UVA is in effect, the application then must query the device pointer corresponding to the allocation with cudaHostGetDevicePointer() or cuMemHostGetDevicePointer(). The resulting device pointer then can be passed to CUDA kernels. Best practices with mapped pinned memory are described in the section "Mapped Pinned Memory Usage."

NOTE

When UVA is in effect, all pinned memory allocations are mapped.[1]

5.1.4 WRITE-COMBINED PINNED MEMORY

Write-combined memory, also known as write-combining or Uncacheable Write Combining (USWC) memory, was created to enable the CPU to write

---

1. Except those marked as write combining.

to GPU frame buffers quickly and without polluting the CPU cache.[2] To that end, Intel added a new page table kind that steered writes into special write-combining buffers instead of the main processor cache hierarchy. Later, Intel also added "nontemporal" store instructions (e.g., MOVNTPS and MOVNTI) that enabled applications to steer writes into the write-combining buffers on a per-instruction basis. In general, memory fence instructions (such as MFENCE) are needed to maintain coherence with WC memory. These operations are not needed for CUDA applications because they are done automatically when the CUDA driver submits work to the hardware.

For CUDA, write-combining memory can be requested by calling cudaHost-Alloc() with the cudaHostWriteCombined flag, or cuMemHostAlloc() with the CU_MEMHOSTALLOC_WRITECOMBINED flag. Besides setting the page table entries to bypass the CPU caches, this memory also is not snooped during PCI Express bus transfers. On systems with front side buses (pre-Opteron and pre-Nehalem), avoiding the snoops improves PCI Express transfer performance. There is little, if any, performance advantage to WC memory on NUMA systems.

Reading WC memory with the CPU is very slow (about 6x slower), unless the reads are done with the MOVNTDQA instruction (new with SSE4). On NVIDIA's integrated GPUs, write-combined memory is as fast as the system memory carveout—system memory that was set aside at boot time for use by the GPU and is not available to the CPU.

Despite the purported benefits, as of this writing, there is little reason for CUDA developers to use write-combined memory. It's just too easy for a host memory pointer to WC memory to "leak" into some part of the application that would try to read the memory. In the absence of empirical evidence to the contrary, it should be avoided.

NOTE

When UVA is in effect, write-combined pinned allocations are *not* mapped into the unified address space.

5.1.5 REGISTERING PINNED MEMORY

CUDA developers don't always get the opportunity to allocate host memory they want the GPU(s) to access directly. For example, a large, extensible application

---

2. WC memory originally was announced by Intel in 1997, at the same time as the Accelerated Graphics Port (AGP). AGP was used for graphics boards before PCI Express.

may have an interface that passes pointers to CUDA-aware plugins, or the application may be using an API for some other peripheral (notably high-speed networking) that has its own dedicated allocation function for much the same reason CUDA does. To accommodate these usage scenarios, CUDA 4.0 added the ability to *register* pinned memory.

Pinned memory registration decouples allocation from the page-locking and mapping of host memory. It takes an *already-allocated* virtual address range, page-locks it, and maps it for the GPU. Just as with cudaHostAlloc(), the memory optionally may be mapped into the CUDA address space or made portable (accessible to all GPUs).

The cuMemHostRegister()/cudaHostRegister() and cuMemHost-Unregister()/ cudaHostUnregister() functions register and unregister host memory for access by the GPU(s), respectively. The memory range to register must be page-aligned: In other words, both the base address and the size must be evenly divisible by the page size of the operating system. Applications can allocate page-aligned address ranges in two ways.

- Allocate the memory with operating system facilities that traffic in whole pages, such as VirtualAlloc() on Windows or valloc() or mmap()[3] on other platforms.

- Given an arbitrary address range (say, memory allocated with malloc() or operator new[]), clamp the address range to the next-lower page boundary and pad to the next page size.

NOTE

Even when UVA is in effect, registered pinned memory that has been mapped into the CUDA address space has a different device pointer than the host pointer. Applications must call cudaHostGetDevicePointer()/ cuMemHostGetDevicePointer() in order to obtain the device pointer.

5.1.6 PINNED MEMORY AND UVA

When UVA (Unified Virtual Addressing) is in effect, all pinned memory allocations are both mapped and portable. The exceptions to this rule are write-combined memory and registered memory. For those, the device pointer

---

3. Or posix_memalign() in conjunction with getpagesize().

may differ from the host pointer, and applications still must query it with `cudaHostGetDevicePointer()`/`cuMemHostGetDevicePointer()`.

UVA is supported on all 64-bit platforms except Windows Vista and Windows 7. On Windows Vista and Windows 7, only the TCC driver (which may be enabled or disabled using `nvidia-smi`) supports UVA. Applications can query whether UVA is in effect by calling `cudaGetDeviceProperties()` and examining the `cudaDeviceProp::unifiedAddressing` structure member, or by calling `cuDeviceGetAttribute()` with `CU_DEVICE_ATTRIBUTE_UNIFIED_ADDRESSING`.

5.1.7 MAPPED PINNED MEMORY USAGE

For applications whose performance relies on PCI Express transfer performance, mapped pinned memory can be a boon. Since the GPU can read or write host memory directly from kernels, it eliminates the need to perform some memory copies, reducing overhead. Here are some common idioms for using mapped pinned memory.

- Posting writes to host memory: Multi-GPU applications often must stage results back to system memory for interchange with other GPUs; writing these results via mapped pinned memory avoids an extraneous device→host memory copy. Write-only access patterns to host memory are appealing because there is no latency to cover.

- Streaming: These workloads otherwise would use CUDA streams to coordinate concurrent memcpys to and from device memory, while kernels do their processing on device memory.

- "Copy with panache": Some workloads benefit from performing computations as data is transferred across PCI Express. For example, the GPU may compute subarray reductions while transferring data for Scan.

Caveats

Mapped pinned memory is not a panacea. Here are some caveats to consider when using it.

- Texturing from mapped pinned memory is possible, but very slow.

- It is important that mapped pinned memory be accessed with coalesced memory transactions (see Section 5.2.9). The performance penalty for uncoalesced memory transactions ranges from 6x to 2x. But even on SM 2.x and later GPUs, whose caches were supposed to make coalescing an obsolete consideration, the penalty is significant.

- Polling host memory with a kernel (e.g., for CPU/GPU synchronization) is not recommended.

- Do not try to use atomics on mapped pinned host memory, either for the host (locked compare-exchange) or the device (atomicAdd()). On the CPU side, the facilities to enforce mutual exclusion for locked operations are not visible to peripherals on the PCI Express bus. Conversely, on the GPU side, atomic operations only work on local device memory locations because they are implemented using the GPU's local memory controller.

5.1.8 NUMA, THREAD AFFINITY, AND PINNED MEMORY

Beginning with the AMD Opteron and Intel Nehalem, CPU memory controllers were integrated directly into CPUs. Previously, the memory had been attached to the so-called "front-side bus" (FSB) of the "northbridge" of the chipset. In multi-CPU systems, the northbridge could service memory requests from any CPU, and memory access performance was reasonably uniform from one CPU to another. With the introduction of integrated memory controllers, each CPU has its own dedicated pool of "local" physical memory that is directly attached to that CPU. Although any CPU can access any other CPU's memory, "nonlocal" accesses—accesses by one CPU to memory attached to another CPU—are performed across the AMD HyperTransport (HT) or Intel QuickPath Interconnect (QPI), incurring latency penalties and bandwidth limitations. To contrast with the uniform memory access times exhibited by systems with FSBs, these system architectures are known as NUMA for *nonuniform memory access*.

As you can imagine, performance of multithreaded applications can be heavily dependent on whether memory references are local to the CPU that is running the current thread. For most applications, however, the higher cost of a nonlocal access is offset by the CPUs' on-board caches. Once nonlocal memory is fetched into a CPU, it remains in-cache until evicted or needed by a memory access to the same page by another CPU. In fact, it is common for NUMA systems to include a System BIOS option to "interleave" memory physically between CPUs. When this BIOS option is enabled, the memory is evenly divided between CPUs on a per-cache line (typically 64 bytes) basis, so, for example, on a 2-CPU system, about 50% of memory accesses will be nonlocal on average.

For CUDA applications, PCI Express transfer performance can be dependent on whether memory references are local. If there is more than one I/O hub (IOH) in the system, the GPU(s) attached to a given IOH have better performance and reduce demand for QPI bandwidth when the pinned memory is local. Because some high-end NUMA systems are hierarchical but don't associate the pools of memory bandwidth strictly with CPUs, NUMA APIs refer to *nodes* that may or may not strictly correspond with CPUs in the system.

If NUMA is enabled on the system, it is good practice to allocate host memory on the same node as a given GPU. Unfortunately, there is no official CUDA API to affiliate a GPU with a given CPU. Developers with a priori knowledge of the system design may know which node to associate with which GPU. Then platform-specific, NUMA-aware APIs may be used to perform these memory allocations, and host memory registration (see Section 5.1.5) can be used to pin those virtual allocations and map them for the GPU(s).

Listing 5.1 gives a code fragment to perform NUMA-aware allocations on Linux,[4] and Listing 5.2 gives a code fragment to perform NUMA-aware allocations on Windows.[5]

Listing 5.1 NUMA-aware allocation (Linux).

```
bool
numNodes( int *p )
{
    if ( numa_available() >= 0 ) {
        *p = numa_max_node() + 1;
        return true;
    }
    return false;
}

void *
pageAlignedNumaAlloc( size_t bytes, int node )
{
    void *ret;
    printf( "Allocating on node %d\n", node ); fflush(stdout);
    ret = numa_alloc_onnode( bytes, node );
    return ret;
}

void
pageAlignedNumaFree( void *p, size_t bytes )
{
    numa_free( p, bytes );
}
```

---

4. http://bit.ly/USy4e7
5. http://bit.ly/XY1g8m

Listing 5.2 NUMA-aware allocation (Windows).

```
bool
numNodes( int *p )
{
    ULONG maxNode;
    if ( GetNumaHighestNodeNumber( &maxNode ) ) {
        *p = (int) maxNode+1;
        return true;
    }
    return false;
}

void *
pageAlignedNumaAlloc( size_t bytes, int node )
{
    void *ret;
    printf( "Allocating on node %d\n", node ); fflush(stdout);
    ret = VirtualAllocExNuma( GetCurrentProcess(),
                              NULL,
                              bytes,
                              MEM_COMMIT | MEM_RESERVE,
                              PAGE_READWRITE,
                              node );
    return ret;
}

void
pageAlignedNumaFree( void *p )
{
    VirtualFreeEx( GetCurrentProcess(), p, 0, MEM_RELEASE );
}
```

5.2 Global Memory

Global memory is the main abstraction by which CUDA kernels read or write device memory.[6] Since device memory is directly attached to the GPU and read and written using a memory controller integrated into the GPU, the peak bandwidth is extremely high: typically more than 100G/s for high-end CUDA cards.

Device memory can be accessed by CUDA kernels using *device pointers*. The following simple memset kernel gives an example.

```
template<class T>
__global__ void
```

---

6. For maximum developer confusion, CUDA uses the term *device pointer* to refer to pointers that reside in *global memory* (device memory addressable by CUDA kernels).

```
GPUmemset ( int *base, int value, size_t N )
{
    for ( size_t i = blockIdx.x*blockDim.x + threadIdx.x;
        i < N;
        i += gridDim.x*blockDim.x )
    {
        base[i] = value;
    }
}
```

The device pointer base resides in the *device address space*, separate from the CPU address space used by the host code in the CUDA program. As a result, host code in the CUDA program can perform pointer arithmetic on device pointers, but they may not dereference them.[7]

This kernel writes the integer value into the address range given by base and N. The references to blockIdx, blockDim, and gridDim enable the kernel to operate correctly, using whatever block and grid parameters were specified to the kernel launch.

5.2.1 POINTERS

When using the CUDA runtime, device pointers and host pointers both are typed as void *. The driver API uses an integer-valued typedef called CUdeviceptr that is the same width as host pointers (i.e., 32 bits on 32-bit operating systems and 64 bits on 64-bit operating systems), as follows.

```
#if defined(__x86_64) || defined(AMD64) || defined(_M_AMD64)
typedef unsigned long long CUdeviceptr;
#else
typedef unsigned int CUdeviceptr;
#endif
```

The uintptr_t type, available in <stdint.h> and introduced in C++0x, may be used to portably convert between host pointers (void *) and device pointers (CUdeviceptr), as follows.

```
CUdeviceptr devicePtr;
void *p;
p = (void *) (uintptr_t) devicePtr;
devicePtr = (CUdeviceptr) (uintptr_t) p;
```

---

7. Mapped pinned pointers represent an exception to this rule. They are located in system memory but can be accessed by the GPU. On non-UVA systems, the host and device pointers to this memory are different: The application must call cuMemHostGetDevicePointer() or cudaHostGetDevicePointer() to map the host pointer to the corresponding device pointer. But when UVA is in effect, the pointers are the same.

The host can do pointer arithmetic on device pointers to pass to a kernel or memcpy call, but the host cannot read or write device memory with these pointers.

32- and 64-Bit Pointers in the Driver API

Because the original driver API definition for a pointer was 32-bit, the addition of 64-bit support to CUDA required the definition of CUdeviceptr and, in turn, all driver API functions that took CUdeviceptr as a parameter, to change.[8] cuMemAlloc(), for example, changed from

```
CUresult CUDAAPI cuMemAlloc(CUdeviceptr *dptr, unsigned int bytesize);
```

to

```
CUresult CUDAAPI cuMemAlloc(CUdeviceptr *dptr, size_t bytesize);
```

To accommodate both old applications (which linked against a cuMemAlloc() with 32-bit CUdeviceptr and size) and new ones, cuda.h includes two blocks of code that use the preprocessor to change the bindings without requiring function names to be changed as developers update to the new API.

First, a block of code surreptitiously changes function names to map to newer functions that have different semantics.

```
#if defined(__CUDA_API_VERSION_INTERNAL) || __CUDA_API_VERSION
>= 3020

 #define cuDeviceTotalMem cuDeviceTotalMem_v2
...
 #define cuTexRefGetAddress cuTexRefGetAddress_v2
#endif /* __CUDA_API_VERSION_INTERNAL || __CUDA_API_VERSION >= 3020 */
```

This way, the client code uses the same old function names, but the compiled code generates references to the new function names with _v2 appended.

Later in the header, the old functions are defined as they were. As a result, developers compiling for the latest version of CUDA get the latest function definitions and semantics. cuda.h uses a similar strategy for functions whose semantics changed from one version to the next, such as cuStreamDestroy().

5.2.2 DYNAMIC ALLOCATIONS

Most global memory in CUDA is obtained through dynamic allocation. Using the CUDA runtime, the functions

---

8. The old functions had to stay for compatibility reasons.

```
cudaError_t cudaMalloc( void **, size_t );
cudaError_t cudaFree( void );
```

allocate and free global memory, respectively. The corresponding driver API functions are

```
CUresult CUDAAPI cuMemAlloc(CUdeviceptr *dptr, size_t bytesize);
CUresult CUDAAPI cuMemFree(CUdeviceptr dptr);
```

Allocating global memory is expensive. The CUDA driver implements a sub-allocator to satisfy small allocation requests, but if the suballocator must create a new memory block, that requires an expensive operating system call to the kernel mode driver. If that happens, the CUDA driver also must synchronize with the GPU, which may break CPU/GPU concurrency. As a result, it's good practice to avoid allocating or freeing global memory in performance-sensitive code.

Pitched Allocations

The coalescing constraints, coupled with alignment restrictions for texturing and 2D memory copy, motivated the creation of *pitched* memory allocations. The idea is that when creating a 2D array, a pointer into the array should have the same alignment characteristics when updated to point to a different row. The *pitch* of the array is the number of bytes per row of the array.[9] The pitch allocations take a width (in bytes) and height, pad the width to a suitable hard-ware-specific pitch, and pass back the base pointer and pitch of the allocation. By using these allocation functions to delegate selection of the pitch to the driver, developers can future-proof their code against architectures that widen alignment requirements.[10]

CUDA programs often must adhere to alignment constraints enforced by the hardware, not only on base addresses but also on the widths (in bytes) of memory copies and linear memory bound to textures. Because the alignment constraints are hardware-specific, CUDA provides APIs that enable developers to delegate the selection of the appropriate alignment to the driver. Using these APIs enables CUDA applications to implement hardware-independent code and to be "future-proof" against CUDA architectures that have not yet shipped.

---

9. The idea of padding 2D allocations is much older than CUDA. Graphics APIs such as Apple QuickDraw and Microsoft DirectX exposed "rowBytes" and "pitch," respectively. At one time, the padding simplified addressing computations by replacing a multiplication by a shift, or even replacing a multiplication by two shifts and an add with "two powers of 2" such as 640 (512 + 128). But these days, integer multiplication is so fast that pitch allocations have other motiva-tions, such as avoiding negative performance interactions with caches.

10. Not an unexpected trend. Fermi widened several alignment requirements over Tesla.

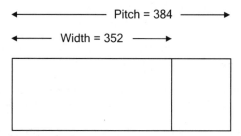

Figure 5.1 Pitch versus width.

Figure 5.1 shows a pitch allocation being performed on an array that is 352 bytes wide. The pitch is padded to the next multiple of 64 bytes before allocating the memory. Given the pitch of the array in addition to the row and column, the address of an array element can be computed as follows.

```
inline T *
getElement( T *base, size_t Pitch, int row, int col )
{
    return (T *) ((char *) base + row*Pitch) + col;
}
```

The CUDA runtime function to perform a pitched allocation is as follows.

```
template<class T>
__inline__ __host__ cudaError_t cudaMallocPitch(
T **devPtr,
size_t *pitch,
size_t widthInBytes,
size_t height
);
```

The CUDA runtime also includes the function cudaMalloc3D(), which allocates 3D memory regions using the cudaPitchedPtr and cudaExtent structures.

```
extern __host__ cudaError_t CUDARTAPI cudaMalloc3D(struct
cudaPitchedPtr* pitchedDevPtr, struct cudaExtent extent);
```

cudaPitchedPtr, which receives the allocated memory, is defined as follows.

```
struct cudaPitchedPtr
{
    void *ptr;
    size_t pitch;
    size_t xsize;
    size_t ysize;
};
```

cudaPitchedPtr::ptr specifies the pointer; cudaPitchedPtr::pitch specifies the pitch (width in bytes) of the allocation; and cudaPitchedPtr::xsize and cudaPitchedPtr::ysize are the logical width and height of the allocation, respectively. cudaExtent is defined as follows.

```
struct cudaExtent
{
    size_t width;
    size_t height;
    size_t depth;
};
```

cudaExtent::width is treated differently for arrays and linear device memory. For arrays, it specifies the width in array elements; for linear device memory, it specifies the pitch (width in bytes).

The driver API function to allocate memory with a pitch is as follows.

```
CUresult CUDAAPI cuMemAllocPitch(CUdeviceptr *dptr, size_t *pPitch,
size_t WidthInBytes, size_t Height, unsigned int ElementSizeBytes);
```

The ElementSizeBytes parameter may be 4, 8, or 16 bytes, and it causes the allocation pitch to be padded to 64-, 128-, or 256-byte boundaries. Those are the alignment requirements for coalescing of 4-, 8-, and 16-byte memory transactions on SM 1.0 and SM 1.1 hardware. Applications that are not concerned with running well on that hardware can specify 4.

The pitch returned by cudaMallocPitch()/cuMemAllocPitch() is the width-in-bytes passed in by the caller, padded to an alignment that meets the alignment constraints for both coalescing of global load/store operations, and texture bind APIs. The amount of memory allocated is height*pitch.

For 3D arrays, developers can multiply the height by the depth before performing the allocation. This consideration only applies to arrays that will be accessed via global loads and stores, since 3D textures cannot be bound to global memory.

Allocations within Kernels

Fermi-class hardware can dynamically allocate global memory using malloc(). Since this may require the GPU to interrupt the CPU, it is potentially slow. The sample program mallocSpeed.cu measures the performance of malloc() and free() in kernels.

Listing 5.3 shows the key kernels and timing routine in mallocSpeed.cu. As an important note, the cudaSetDeviceLimit() function must be called with cudaLimitMallocHeapSize before malloc() may be called in kernels. The invocation in mallocSpeed.cu requests a full gigabyte (2^{30} bytes).

```
CUDART_CHECK( cudaDeviceSetLimit(cudaLimitMallocHeapSize, 1<<30) );
```

When cudaDeviceSetLimit() is called, the requested amount of memory is allocated and may not be used for any other purpose.

Listing 5.3 MallocSpeed function and kernels.

```
__global__ void
AllocateBuffers( void **out, size_t N )
{
    size_t i = blockIdx.x*blockDim.x + threadIdx.x;
    out[i] = malloc( N );
}

__global__ void
FreeBuffers( void **in )
{
    size_t i = blockIdx.x*blockDim.x + threadIdx.x;
    free( in[i] );
}

cudaError_t
MallocSpeed( double *msPerAlloc, double *msPerFree,
             void **devicePointers, size_t N,
             cudaEvent_t evStart, cudaEvent_t evStop,
             int cBlocks, int cThreads )
{
    float etAlloc, etFree;
    cudaError_t status;

    CUDART_CHECK( cudaEventRecord( evStart ) );
    AllocateBuffers<<<cBlocks,cThreads>>>( devicePointers, N );
    CUDART_CHECK( cudaEventRecord( evStop ) );
    CUDART_CHECK( cudaThreadSynchronize() );
    CUDART_CHECK( cudaGetLastError() );
    CUDART_CHECK( cudaEventElapsedTime( &etAlloc, evStart, evStop ) );

    CUDART_CHECK( cudaEventRecord( evStart ) );
    FreeBuffers<<<cBlocks,cThreads>>>( devicePointers );
    CUDART_CHECK( cudaEventRecord( evStop ) );
    CUDART_CHECK( cudaThreadSynchronize() );
    CUDART_CHECK( cudaGetLastError() );
    CUDART_CHECK( cudaEventElapsedTime( &etFree, evStart, evStop ) );

    *msPerAlloc = etAlloc / (double) (cBlocks*cThreads);
    *msPerFree = etFree / (double) (cBlocks*cThreads);
```

```
Error:
    return status;
}
```

Listing 5.4 shows the output from a sample run of `mallocSpeed.cu` on Amazon's `cg1.4xlarge` instance type. It is clear that the allocator is optimized for small allocations: The 64-byte allocations take an average of 0.39 microseconds to perform, while allocations of 12K take at least 3 to 5 microseconds. The first result (155 microseconds per allocation) is having 1 thread per each of 500 blocks allocate a 1MB buffer.

Listing 5.4 Sample `mallocSpeed.cu` output.

```
Microseconds per alloc/free (1 thread per block):
alloc       free
154.93      4.57

Microseconds per alloc/free (32-512 threads per block, 12K
allocations):
32              64              128             256             512
alloc  free     alloc  free     alloc  free     alloc  free     alloc   free
3.53   1.18     4.27   1.17     4.89   1.14     5.48   1.14     10.38   1.11

Microseconds per alloc/free (32-512 threads per block, 64-byte
allocations):
32              64              128             256             512
alloc  free     alloc  free     alloc  free     alloc  free     alloc   free
0.35   0.27     0.37   0.29     0.34   0.27     0.37   0.22     0.53    0.27
```

IMPORTANT NOTE

Memory allocated by invoking `malloc()` in a kernel must be freed by a *kernel* calling `free()`. Calling `cudaFree()` on the host will not work.

5.2.3 QUERYING THE AMOUNT OF GLOBAL MEMORY

The amount of global memory in a system may be queried even before CUDA has been initialized.

CUDA Runtime

Call `cudaGetDeviceProperties()` and examine `cudaDeviceProp.totalGlobalMem`:

```
size_t totalGlobalMem; /**< Global memory on device in bytes */.
```

Driver API

Call this driver API function.

```
CUresult CUDAAPI cuDeviceTotalMem(size_t *bytes, CUdevice dev);
```

WDDM and Available Memory

The Windows Display Driver Model (WDDM) introduced with Windows Vista changed the model for memory management by display drivers to enable chunks of video memory to be swapped in and out of host memory as needed to perform rendering. As a result, the amount of memory reported by cuDeviceTotalMem() / cudaDeviceProp::totalGlobalMem will not exactly reflect the amount of physical memory on the card.

5.2.4 STATIC ALLOCATIONS

Applications can statically allocate global memory by annotating a memory declaration with the __device__ keyword. This memory is allocated by the CUDA driver when the module is loaded.

CUDA Runtime

Memory copies to and from statically allocated memory can be performed by cudaMemcpyToSymbol() and cudaMemcpyFromSymbol().

```
cudaError_t cudaMemcpyToSymbol(
    char *symbol,
    const void *src,
    size_t count,
    size_t offset = 0,
    enum cudaMemcpyKind kind = cudaMemcpyHostToDevice
);
cudaError_t cudaMemcpyFromSymbol(
    void *dst,
    char *symbol,
    size_t count,
    size_t offset = 0,
    enum cudaMemcpyKind kind = cudaMemcpyDeviceToHost
);
```

When calling cudaMemcpyToSymbol() or cudaMemcpyFromSymbol(), do not enclose the symbol name in quotation marks. In other words, use

```
cudaMemcpyToSymbol(g_xOffset, poffsetx, Width*Height*sizeof(int));
```

not

```
cudaMemcpyToSymbol("g_xOffset", poffsetx, ... );
```

Both formulations work, but the latter formulation will compile for any symbol name (even undefined symbols). If you want the compiler to report errors for invalid symbols, avoid the quotation marks.

CUDA runtime applications can query the pointer corresponding to a static allocation by calling `cudaGetSymbolAddress()`.

```
cudaError_t cudaGetSymbolAddress( void **devPtr, char *symbol );
```

Beware: It is all too easy to pass the symbol for a statically declared device memory allocation to a CUDA kernel, but this does not work. You must call `cudaGetSymbolAddress()` and use the resulting pointer.

Driver API

Developers using the driver API can obtain pointers to statically allocated memory by calling `cuModuleGetGlobal()`.

```
CUresult CUDAAPI cuModuleGetGlobal(CUdeviceptr *dptr, size_t *bytes,
CUmodule hmod, const char *name);
```

Note that `cuModuleGetGlobal()` passes back both the base pointer and the size of the object. If the size is not needed, developers can pass `NULL` for the `bytes` parameter. Once this pointer has been obtained, the memory can be accessed by passing the `CUdeviceptr` to memory copy calls or CUDA kernel invocations.

5.2.5 MEMSET APIS

For developer convenience, CUDA provides 1D and 2D memset functions. Since they are implemented using kernels, they are asynchronous even when no stream parameter is specified. For applications that must serialize the execution of a memset within a stream, however, there are `*Async()` variants that take a stream parameter.

CUDA Runtime

The CUDA runtime supports byte-sized memset only:

```
cudaError_t cudaMemset(void *devPtr, int value, size_t count);
cudaError_t cudaMemset2D(void *devPtr, size_t pitch, int value,
size_t width, size_t height);
```

The pitch parameter specifies the bytes per row of the memset operation.

Table 5.2 Memset Variations

OPERAND SIZE	1D	2D
8-bit	cuMemsetD8	cuMemsetD2D8
16-bit	cuMemsetD16	cuMemsetD2D16
32-bit	cuMemset32	cuMemsetD2D32

Driver API

The driver API supports 1D and 2D memset of a variety of sizes, shown in Table 5.2. These memset functions take the destination pointer, value to set, and number of values to write starting at the base address. The pitch parameter is the bytes per row (not elements per row!).

```
CUresult CUDAAPI cuMemsetD8(CUdeviceptr dstDevice, unsigned char uc,
size_t N);
CUresult CUDAAPI cuMemsetD16(CUdeviceptr dstDevice, unsigned short
us, size_t N);
CUresult CUDAAPI cuMemsetD32(CUdeviceptr dstDevice, unsigned int ui,
size_t N);
CUresult CUDAAPI cuMemsetD2D8(CUdeviceptr dstDevice, size_t dstPitch,
unsigned char uc, size_t Width, size_t Height);
CUresult CUDAAPI cuMemsetD2D16(CUdeviceptr dstDevice, size_t
dstPitch, unsigned short us, size_t Width, size_t Height);
CUresult CUDAAPI cuMemsetD2D32(CUdeviceptr dstDevice, size_t
dstPitch, unsigned int ui, size_t Width, size_t Height);
```

Now that CUDA runtime and driver API functions can peacefully coexist in the same application, CUDA runtime developers can use these functions as needed. The unsigned char, unsigned short, and unsigned int parameters just specify a bit pattern; to fill a global memory range with some other type, such as float, use a volatile union to coerce the float to unsigned int.

5.2.6 POINTER QUERIES

CUDA tracks all of its memory allocations, and provides APIs that enable applications to query CUDA about pointers that were passed in from some other party. Libraries or plugins may wish to pursue different strategies based on this information.

CUDA Runtime

The `cudaPointerGetAttributes()` function takes a pointer as input and passes back a `cudaPointerAttributes` structure containing information about the pointer.

```
struct cudaPointerAttributes {
    enum cudaMemoryType memoryType;
    int device;
    void *devicePointer;
    void *hostPointer;
}
```

When UVA is in effect, pointers are unique process-wide, so there is no ambiguity as to the input pointer's address space. When UVA is not in effect, the input pointer is assumed to be in the current device's address space (Table 5.3).

Driver API

Developers can query the address range where a given device pointer resides using the `cuMemGetAddressRange()` function.

```
CUresult CUDAAPI cuMemGetAddressRange(CUdeviceptr *pbase, size_t
*psize, CUdeviceptr dptr);
```

This function takes a device pointer as input and passes back the base and size of the allocation containing that device pointer.

Table 5.3 `cudaPointerAttributes` Members

STRUCTURE MEMBER	DESCRIPTION
`enum cudaMemoryType memoryType;`	Type of memory referenced by the input pointer.
`int device;`	If `memoryType== cudaMemoryTypeDevice`, the device where the memory resides. If `memoryType== cudaMemoryTypeHost`, the device whose context was used to allocate the memory.
`void *devicePointer;`	Device pointer corresponding to the allocation. If the memory cannot be accessed by the current device, this structure member is set to NULL.
`void *hostPointer;`	Host pointer corresponding to the allocation. If the allocation is not mapped pinned memory, this structure member is set to NULL.

With the addition of UVA in CUDA 4.0, developers can query CUDA to get even more information about an address using cuPointerGetAttribute().

```
CUresult CUDAAPI cuPointerGetAttribute(void *data, CUpointer_
attribute attribute, CUdeviceptr ptr);
```

This function takes a device pointer as input and passes back the information corresponding to the attribute parameter, as shown in Table 5.4. Note that for unified addresses, using CU_POINTER_ATTRIBUTE_DEVICE_POINTER or CU_POINTER_ATTRIBUTE_HOST_POINTER will cause the same pointer value to be returned as the one passed in.

Kernel Queries

On SM 2.x (Fermi) hardware and later, developers can query whether a given pointer points into global space. The __isGlobal() intrinsic

```
unsigned int __isGlobal( const void *p );
```

returns 1 if the input pointer refers to global memory and 0 otherwise.

Table 5.4 cuPointerAttribute Usage

ENUM VALUE	PASSBACK
CU_POINTER_ATTRIBUTE_CONTEXT	CUcontext in which the pointer was allocated or registered.
CU_POINTER_ATTRIBUTE_MEMORY_TYPE	cuMemoryType corresponding to the pointer's memory type: CU_MEMORYTYPE_HOST if host memory, CU_MEM-ORYTYPE_DEVICE if device memory, or CU_MEMORY-TYPE_UNIFIED if unified.
CU_POINTER_ATTRIBUTE_DEVICE_POINTER	ptr is assumed to be a mapped host pointer; data points to a void * and receives the device pointer corresponding to the allocation. If the memory cannot be accessed by the current device, this structure member is set to NULL.
CU_POINTER_ATTRIBUTE_HOST_POINTER	ptr is assumed to be device memory; data points to a void * and receives the host pointer corresponding to the allocation. If the allocation is not mapped pinned memory, this structure member is set to NULL.

5.2.7 PEER-TO-PEER ACCESS

Under certain circumstances, SM 2.0-class and later hardware can map memory belonging to other, similarly capable GPUs. The following conditions apply.

- UVA must be in effect.

- Both GPUs must be Fermi-class and be based on the same chip.

- The GPUs must be on the same I/O hub.

Since peer-to-peer mapping is intrinsically a multi-GPU feature, it is described in detail in the multi-GPU chapter (see Section 9.2).

5.2.8 READING AND WRITING GLOBAL MEMORY

CUDA kernels can read or write global memory using standard C semantics such as pointer indirection (operator*, operator->) or array subscripting (operator[]). Here is a simple templatized kernel to write a constant into a memory range.

```
template<class T>
__global__ void
GlobalWrites( T *out, T value, size_t N )
{
    for ( size_t i = blockIdx.x*blockDim.x+threadIdx.x;
                 i < N;
                 i += blockDim.x*gridDim.x ) {
        out[i] = value;
    }
}
```

This kernel works correctly for any inputs: any component size, any block size, any grid size. Its code is intended more for illustrative purposes than maximum performance. CUDA kernels that use more registers and operate on multiple values in the inner loop go faster, but for some block and grid configurations, its performance is perfectly acceptable. In particular, provided the base address and block size are specified correctly, it performs coalesced memory transactions that maximize memory bandwidth.

5.2.9 COALESCING CONSTRAINTS

For best performance when reading and writing data, CUDA kernels must perform *coalesced* memory transactions. Any memory transaction that does not meet the full set of criteria needed for coalescing is "uncoalesced." The penalty for uncoalesced memory transactions varies from 2x to 8x, depending on the chip implementation. Coalesced memory transactions have a much less dramatic impact on performance on more recent hardware, as shown in Table 5.5.

Transactions are coalesced on a per-warp basis. A simplified set of criteria must be met in order for the memory read or write being performed by the warp to be coalesced.

- The words must be at least 32 bits in size. Reading or writing bytes or 16-bit words is always uncoalesced.

- The addresses being accessed by the threads of the warp must be contiguous and increasing (i.e., offset by the thread ID).

- The base address of the warp (the address being accessed by the first thread in the warp) must be aligned as shown in Table 5.6.

Table 5.5 Bandwidth Penalties for Uncoalesced Memory Access

CHIP	PENALTY
SM 1.0-1.1	6x
SM 1.2	2x
SM 2.x (ECC off)	20%
SM 2.x (ECC on)	2x

Table 5.6 Alignment Criteria for Coalescing

WORD SIZE	ALIGNMENT
8-bit	*
16-bit	*
32-bit	64-byte
64-bit	128-byte
128-bit	256-byte

* 8- and 16-bit memory accesses are always uncoalesced.

The `ElementSizeBytes` parameter to `cuMemAllocPitch()` is intended to accommodate the size restriction. It specifies the size in bytes of the memory accesses intended by the application, so the pitch guarantees that a set of coalesced memory transactions for a given row of the allocation also will be coalesced for other rows.

Most kernels in this book perform coalesced memory transactions, provided the input addresses are properly aligned. NVIDIA has provided more detailed, architecture-specific information on how global memory transactions are handled, as detailed below.

SM 1.x (Tesla)

SM 1.0 and SM 1.1 hardware require that each thread in a warp access adjacent memory locations in sequence, as described above. SM 1.2 and 1.3 hardware relaxed the coalescing constraints somewhat. To issue a coalesced memory request, divide each 32-thread warp into two "half warps," lanes 0–15 and lanes 16–31. To service the memory request from each half-warp, the hardware performs the following algorithm.

1. Find the active thread with the lowest thread ID and locate the memory segment that contains that thread's requested address. The segment size depends on the word size: 1-byte requests result in 32-byte segments; 2-byte requests result in 64-byte segments; and all other requests result in 128-byte segments.

2. Find all other active threads whose requested address lies in the same segment.

3. If possible, reduce the segment transaction size to 64 or 32 bytes.

4. Carry out the transaction and mark the services threads as inactive.

5. Repeat steps 1–4 until all threads in the half-warp have been serviced.

Although these requirements are somewhat relaxed compared to the SM 1.0–1.1 constraints, a great deal of locality is still required for effective coalescing. In practice, the relaxed coalescing means the threads within a warp can permute the inputs within small segments of memory, if desired.

SM 2.x (Fermi)

SM 2.x and later hardware includes L1 and L2 caches. The L2 cache services the entire chip; the L1 caches are per-SM and may be configured to be 16K or 48K in size. The cache lines are 128 bytes and map to 128-byte aligned segments in device memory. Memory accesses that are cached in both L1 and L2 are serviced with 128-byte memory transactions, whereas memory accesses that are cached in L2 only are serviced with 32-byte memory transactions. Caching in L2 only can therefore reduce overfetch, for example, in the case of scattered memory accesses.

The hardware can specify the cacheability of global memory accesses on a per-instruction basis. By default, the compiler emits instructions that cache memory accesses in both L1 and L2 (-Xptxas -dlcm=ca). This can be changed to cache in L2 only by specifying -Xptxas -dlcm=cg. Memory accesses that are not present in L1 but cached in L2 only are serviced with 32-byte memory transactions, which may improve cache utilization for applications that are performing scattered memory accesses.

Reading via pointers that are declared volatile causes any cached results to be discarded and for the data to be refetched. This idiom is mainly useful for polling host memory locations. Table 5.7 summarizes how memory requests by a warp are broken down into 128-byte cache line requests.

NOTE

On SM 2.x and higher architectures, threads within a warp can access any words in any order, including the same words.

Table 5.7 SM 2.x Cache Line Requests

WORD SIZE	128-BYTE REQUESTS	PER...
8-bit	1	Warp
16-bit	1	Warp
32-bit	1	Warp
64-bit	2	Half-warp
128-bit	4	Quarter-warp

SM 3.x (Kepler)

The L2 cache architecture is the same as SM 2.x. SM 3.x does not cache global memory accesses in L1. In SM 3.5, global memory may be accessed via the texture cache (which is 48K per SM in size) by accessing memory via `const restricted` pointers or by using the `__ldg()` intrinsics in `sm_35_intrinsics.h`. As when texturing directly from device memory, it is important not to access memory that might be accessed concurrently by other means, since this cache is not kept coherent with respect to the L2.

5.2.10 MICROBENCHMARKS: PEAK MEMORY BANDWIDTH

The source code accompanying this book includes microbenchmarks that determine which combination of operand size, loop unroll factor, and block size maximizes bandwidth for a given GPU. Rewriting the earlier `GlobalWrites` code as a template that takes an additional parameter `n` (the number of writes to perform in the inner loop) yields the kernel in Listing 5.5.

Listing 5.5 `GlobalWrites` kernel.

```
template<class T, const int n>
__global__ void
GlobalWrites( T *out, T value, size_t N )
{
    size_t i;
    for ( i = n*blockIdx.x*blockDim.x+threadIdx.x;
          i < N-n*blockDim.x*gridDim.x;
          i += n*blockDim.x*gridDim.x ) {
        for ( int j = 0; j < n; j++ ) {
            size_t index = i+j*blockDim.x;
            out[index] = value;
        }
    }
    // to avoid the (index<N) conditional in the inner loop,
    // we left off some work at the end
    for ( int j = 0; j < n; j++ ) {
        size_t index = i+j*blockDim.x;
        if ( index<N ) out[index] = value;
    }
}
```

`ReportRow()`, the function given in Listing 5.6 that writes one row of output calls by calling a template function `BandwidthWrites` (not shown), reports the bandwidth for a given type, grid, and block size.

Listing 5.6 ReportRow function.

```
template<class T, const int n, bool bOffset>
double
ReportRow( size_t N,
           size_t threadStart,
           size_t threadStop,
           size_t cBlocks )
{
    int maxThreads = 0;
    double maxBW = 0.0;
    printf( "%d\t", n );
    for ( int cThreads = threadStart;
              cThreads <= threadStop;
              cThreads *= 2 ) {
        double bw;
        bw = BandwidthWrites<T,n,bOffset>( N, cBlocks, cThreads );
        if ( bw > maxBW ) {
            maxBW = bw;
            maxThreads = cThreads;
        }
        printf( "%.2f\t", bw );
    }
    printf( "%.2f\t%d\n", maxBW, maxThreads );
    return maxBW;
}
```

The threadStart and threadStop parameters typically are 32 and 512, 32 being the warp size and the minimum number of threads per block that can occupy the machine. The bOffset template parameter specifies whether BandwidthWrites should offset the base pointer, causing all memory transactions to become uncoalesced. If the program is invoked with the --uncoalesced command line option, it will perform the bandwidth measurements with the offset pointer.

Note that depending on sizeof(T), kernels with n above a certain level will fall off a performance cliff as the number of temporary variables in the inner loop grows too high to hold in registers.

The five applications summarized in Table 5.8 implement this strategy. They measure the memory bandwidth delivered for different operand sizes (8-, 16-, 32-, 64-, and 128-bit), threadblock sizes (32, 64, 128, 256, and 512), and loop unroll factors (1–16). CUDA hardware isn't necessarily sensitive to all of these parameters. For example, many parameter settings enable a GK104 to deliver 140GB/s of bandwidth via texturing, but only if the operand size is at least 32-bit. For a given workload and hardware, however, the microbenchmarks highlight

Table 5.8 Memory Bandwidth Microbenchmarks

MICROBENCHMARK FILENAME	MEMORY TRANSACTIONS
`globalCopy.cu`	One read, one write
`globalCopy2.cu`	Two reads, one write
`globalRead.cu`	One read
`globalReadTex.cu`	One read via texture
`globalWrite.cu`	One write

which parameters matter. Also, for small operand sizes, they highlight how loop unrolling can help increase performance (not all applications can be refactored to read larger operands).

Listing 5.7 gives example output from `globalRead.cu`, run on a GeForce GTX 680 GPU. The output is grouped by operand size, from bytes to 16-byte quads; the leftmost column of each group gives the loop unroll factor. The bandwidth delivered for blocks of sizes 32 to 512 is given in each column, and the `maxBW` and `maxThreads` columns give the highest bandwidth and the block size that delivered the highest bandwidth, respectively.

The GeForce GTX 680 can deliver up to 140GB/s, so Listing 5.7 makes it clear that when reading 8- and 16-bit words on SM 3.0, global loads are not the way to go. Bytes deliver at most 60GB/s, and 16-bit words deliver at most 101GB/s.[11] For 32-bit operands, a 2x loop unroll and at least 256 threads per block are needed to get maximum bandwidth.

These microbenchmarks can help developers optimize their bandwidth-bound applications. Choose the one whose memory access pattern most closely resembles your application, and either run the microbenchmark on the target GPU or, if possible, modify the microbenchmark to resemble the actual workload more closely and run it to determine the optimal parameters.

11. Texturing works better. Readers can run `globalReadTex.cu` to confirm.

Listing 5.7 Sample output, `globalRead.cu`.

```
Running globalRead.cu microbenchmark on GeForce GTX 680
Using coalesced memory transactions
Operand size: 1 byte
Input size: 16M operands
                       Block Size
Unroll  32       64       128      256      512      maxBW    maxThreads
1       9.12     17.39    30.78    30.78    28.78    30.78    128
2       18.37    34.54    56.36    53.53    49.33    56.36    128
3       23.55    42.32    61.56    60.15    52.91    61.56    128
4       21.25    38.26    58.99    58.09    51.26    58.99    128
5       25.29    42.17    60.13    58.49    52.57    60.13    128
6       25.68    42.15    59.93    55.42    47.46    59.93    128
7       28.84    47.03    56.20    51.41    41.41    56.20    128
8       29.88    48.55    55.75    50.68    39.96    55.75    128
9       28.65    47.75    56.84    51.17    37.56    56.84    128
10      27.35    45.16    52.99    46.30    32.94    52.99    128
11      22.27    38.51    48.17    42.74    32.81    48.17    128
12      23.39    40.51    49.78    42.42    31.89    49.78    128
13      21.62    37.49    40.89    34.98    21.43    40.89    128
14      18.55    32.12    36.04    31.41    19.96    36.04    128
15      21.47    36.87    39.94    33.36    19.98    39.94    128
16      21.59    36.79    39.49    32.71    19.42    39.49    128
Operand size: 2 bytes
Input size: 16M operands
                       Block Size
Unroll  32       64       128      256      512      maxBW    maxThreads
1       18.29    35.07    60.30    59.16    56.06    60.30    128
2       34.94    64.39    94.28    92.65    85.99    94.28    128
3       45.02    72.90    101.38   99.02    90.07    101.38   128
4       38.54    68.35    100.30   98.29    90.28    100.30   128
5       45.49    75.73    98.68    98.11    90.05    98.68    128
6       47.58    77.50    100.35   97.15    86.17    100.35   128
7       53.64    81.04    92.89    87.39    74.14    92.89    128
8       44.79    74.02    89.19    83.96    69.65    89.19    128
9       47.63    76.63    91.60    83.52    68.06    91.60    128
10      51.02    79.82    93.85    84.69    66.62    93.85    128
11      42.00    72.11    88.23    79.24    62.27    88.23    128
12      40.53    69.27    85.75    76.32    59.73    85.75    128
13      44.90    73.44    78.08    66.96    41.27    78.08    128
14      39.18    68.43    74.46    63.27    39.27    74.46    128
15      37.60    64.11    69.93    60.22    37.09    69.93    128
16      40.36    67.90    73.07    60.79    36.66    73.07    128
Operand size: 4 bytes
Input size: 16M operands
                       Block Size
Unroll  32       64       128      256      512      maxBW    maxThreads
1       36.37    67.89    108.04   105.99   104.09   108.04   128
2       73.85    120.90   139.91   139.93   136.04   139.93   256
3       62.62    109.24   140.07   139.66   138.38   140.07   128
4       56.02    101.73   138.70   137.42   135.10   138.70   128
5       87.34    133.65   140.64   140.33   139.00   140.64   128
```

6	100.64	137.47	140.61	139.53	127.18	140.61	128
7	89.08	133.99	139.60	138.23	124.28	139.60	128
8	58.46	103.09	129.24	122.28	110.58	129.24	128
9	68.99	116.59	134.17	128.64	114.80	134.17	128
10	54.64	97.90	123.91	118.84	106.96	123.91	128
11	64.35	110.30	131.43	123.90	109.31	131.43	128
12	68.03	113.89	130.95	125.40	108.02	130.95	128
13	71.34	117.88	123.85	113.08	76.98	123.85	128
14	54.72	97.31	109.41	101.28	71.13	109.41	128
15	67.28	111.24	118.88	108.35	72.30	118.88	128
16	63.32	108.56	117.77	103.24	69.76	117.77	128

Operand size: 8 bytes
Input size: 16M operands

			Block Size				
Unroll	32	64	128	256	512	maxBW	maxThreads
1	74.64	127.73	140.91	142.08	142.16	142.16	512
2	123.70	140.35	141.31	141.99	142.42	142.42	512
3	137.28	141.15	140.86	141.94	142.63	142.63	512
4	128.38	141.39	141.85	142.56	142.00	142.56	256
5	117.57	140.95	141.17	142.08	141.78	142.08	256
6	112.10	140.62	141.48	141.86	141.95	141.95	512
7	85.02	134.82	141.59	141.50	141.09	141.59	128
8	94.44	138.71	140.86	140.25	128.91	140.86	128
9	100.69	139.83	141.09	141.45	127.82	141.45	256
10	92.51	137.76	140.74	140.93	126.50	140.93	256
11	104.87	140.38	140.67	136.70	128.48	140.67	128
12	97.71	138.62	140.12	135.74	125.37	140.12	128
13	95.87	138.28	139.90	134.18	123.41	139.90	128
14	85.69	134.18	133.84	131.16	120.95	134.18	64
15	94.43	135.43	135.30	133.47	120.52	135.43	64
16	91.62	136.69	133.59	129.95	117.99	136.69	64

Operand size: 16 bytes
Input size: 16M operands

			Block Size				
Unroll	32	64	128	256	512	maxBW	maxThreads
1	125.37	140.67	141.15	142.06	142.59	142.59	512
2	131.26	141.95	141.72	142.32	142.49	142.49	512
3	141.03	141.65	141.63	142.43	138.44	142.43	256
4	139.90	142.70	142.62	142.20	142.84	142.84	512
5	138.24	142.08	142.18	142.79	140.94	142.79	256
6	131.41	142.45	142.32	142.51	142.08	142.51	256
7	131.98	142.26	142.27	142.11	142.26	142.27	128
8	132.70	142.47	142.10	142.67	142.19	142.67	256
9	136.58	142.28	141.89	142.42	142.09	142.42	256
10	135.61	142.67	141.85	142.86	142.36	142.86	256
11	136.27	142.48	142.45	142.14	142.41	142.48	64
12	130.62	141.79	142.06	142.39	142.16	142.39	256
13	107.98	103.07	105.54	106.51	107.35	107.98	32
14	103.53	95.38	96.38	98.34	102.92	103.53	32
15	89.47	84.86	85.31	87.01	90.26	90.26	512
16	81.53	75.49	75.82	74.36	76.91	81.53	32

5.2.11 ATOMIC OPERATIONS

Support for atomic operations was added in SM 1.x, but they were prohibitively slow; atomics on global memory were improved on SM 2.x (Fermi-class) hardware and vastly improved on SM 3.x (Kepler-class) hardware.

Most atomic operations, such as `atomicAdd()`, enable code to be simplified by replacing reductions (which often require shared memory and synchronization) with "fire and forget" semantics. Until SM 3.x hardware arrived, however, that type of programming idiom incurred huge performance degradations because pre-Kepler hardware was not efficient at dealing with "contended" memory locations (i.e., when many GPU threads are performing atomics on the same memory location).

NOTE

Because atomic operations are implemented in the GPU memory controller, they only work on local device memory locations. As of this writing, trying to perform atomic operations on remote GPUs (via peer-to-peer addresses) or host memory (via mapped pinned memory) will not work.

Atomics and Synchronization

Besides "fire and forget" semantics, atomics also may be used for synchronization between blocks. CUDA hardware supports the workhorse base abstraction for synchronization, "compare and swap" (or CAS). On CUDA, compare-and-swap (also known as compare-and-exchange—e.g., the `CMPXCHG` instruction in x86) is defined as follows.

```
int atomicCAS( int *address, int expected, int value);
```
[12]

This function reads the word `old` at `address`, computes `(old == expected ? value : old)`, stores the result back to `address`, and returns `old`. In other words, the memory location is left alone *unless it was equal to the expected value specified by the caller*, in which case it is updated with the new value.

A simple critical section called a "spin lock" can be built out of CAS, as follows.

```
void enter_spinlock( int *address )
{
    while atomicCAS( address, 0, 1 );
}
```

---

12. Unsigned and 64-bit variants of `atomicCAS()` also are available.

Assuming the spin lock's value is initialized to 0, the while loop iterates until the spin lock value is 0 when the atomicCAS() is executed. When that happens, *address atomically becomes 1 (the third parameter to atomicCAS()) and any other threads trying to acquire the critical section spin waiting for the critical section value to become 0 again.

The thread owning the spin lock can give it up by atomically swapping the 0 back in

```
void leave_spinlock( int *address )
{
    atomicExch( m_p, 0 );
}
```

On CPUs, compare-and-swap instructions are used to implement all manner of synchronization. Operating systems use them (sometimes in conjunction with the kernel-level thread context switching code) to implement higher-level synchronization primitives. CAS also may be used directly to implement "lock-free" queues and other data structures.

The CUDA execution model, however, imposes restrictions on the use of global memory atomics for synchronization. Unlike CPU threads, some CUDA threads within a kernel launch may not begin execution until other threads in the same kernel have exited. On CUDA hardware, each SM can context switch a limited number of thread blocks, so any kernel launch with more than *MaxThreadBlocksPerSM*NumSMs* requires the first thread blocks to exit before more thread blocks can begin execution. As a result, it is important that developers not assume all of the threads in a given kernel launch are active.

Additionally, the enter_spinlock() routine above is prone to deadlock if used for intrablock synchronization,[13] for which it is unsuitable in any case, since the hardware supports so many better ways for threads within the same block to communicate and synchronize with one another (shared memory and __syncthreads(), respectively).

Listing 5.8 shows the implementation of the cudaSpinlock class, which uses the algorithm listed above and is subject to the just-described limitations.

---

13. Expected usage is for one thread in each block to attempt to acquire the spinlock. Otherwise, the divergent code execution tends to deadlock.

Listing 5.8 cudaSpinlock class.

```
class cudaSpinlock {
public:
    cudaSpinlock( int *p );
    void acquire();
    void release();
private:
    int *m_p;
};

inline __device__
cudaSpinlock::cudaSpinlock( int *p )
{
    m_p = p;
}

inline __device__ void
cudaSpinlock::acquire( )
{
    while ( atomicCAS( m_p, 0, 1 ) );
}

inline __device__ void
cudaSpinlock::release( )
{
    atomicExch( m_p, 0 );
}
```

Use of cudaSpinlock is illustrated in the spinlockReduction.cu sample, which computes the sum of an array of double values by having each block perform a reduction in shared memory, then using the spin lock to synchronize for the summation. Listing 5.9 gives the SumDoubles function from this sample. Note how adding the partial sum is performed only by thread 0 of each block.

Listing 5.9 SumDoubles function.

```
__global__ void
SumDoubles(
    double *pSum,
    int *spinlock,
    const double *in,
    size_t N,
    int *acquireCount )
{
    SharedMemory<double> shared;
    cudaSpinlock globalSpinlock( spinlock );

    for ( size_t i = blockIdx.x*blockDim.x+threadIdx.x;
                  i < N;
                  i += blockDim.x*gridDim.x ) {
```

```
        shared[threadIdx.x] = in[i];
        __syncthreads();
        double blockSum = Reduce_block<double,double>( );
        __syncthreads();

        if ( threadIdx.x == 0 ) {
            globalSpinlock.acquire( );
            *pSum += blockSum;
            __threadfence();
            globalSpinlock.release( );
        }
    }
}
```

5.2.12 TEXTURING FROM GLOBAL MEMORY

For applications that cannot conveniently adhere to the coalescing constraints, the texture mapping hardware presents a satisfactory alternative. The hardware supports texturing from global memory (via cudaBindTexture() / cuTexRefSetAddress(), which has lower peak performance than coalesced global reads but higher performance for less-regular access. The texture cache resources are also separate from other cache resources on the chip. A software coherency scheme is enforced by the driver invalidating the texture cache before kernel invocations that contain TEX instructions.[14] See Chapter 10 for details.

SM 3.x hardware added the ability to read global memory through the texture cache hierarchy without setting up and binding a texture reference. This functionality may be accessed with a standard C++ language constructs: the const restrict keywords. Alternatively, you can use the __ldg() intrinsics defined in sm_35_intrinsics.h.

5.2.13 ECC (ERROR CORRECTING CODES)

SM 2.x and later GPUs in the Tesla (i.e., server GPU) product line come with the ability to run with error correction. In exchange for a smaller amount of memory (since some memory is used to record some redundancy) and lower bandwidth, GPUs with ECC enabled can silently correct single-bit errors and report double-bit errors.

---

14. TEX is the SASS mnemonic for microcode instructions that perform texture fetches.

ECC has the following characteristics.

- It reduces the amount of available memory by 12.5%. On a `cg1.4xlarge` instance in Amazon EC2, for example, it reduces the amount of memory from 3071MB to 2687MB.

- It makes context synchronization more expensive.

- Uncoalesced memory transactions are more expensive when ECC is enabled than otherwise.

ECC can be enabled and disabled using the `nvidia-smi` command-line tool (described in Section 4.4) or by using the NVML (NVIDIA Management Library).

When an uncorrectable ECC error is detected, synchronous error-reporting mechanisms will return `cudaErrorECCUncorrectable` (for the CUDA runtime) and `CUDA_ERROR_ECC_UNCORRECTABLE` (for the driver API).

5.3 Constant Memory

Constant memory is optimized for read-only broadcast to multiple threads. As the name implies, the compiler uses constant memory to hold constants that couldn't be easily computed or otherwise compiled directly into the machine code. Constant memory resides in device memory but is accessed using different instructions that cause the GPU to access it using a special "constant cache."

The compiler for constants has 64K of memory available to use at its discretion. The developer has another 64K of memory available that can be declared with the `__constant__` keyword. These limits are per-module (for driver API applications) or per-file (for CUDA runtime applications).

Naïvely, one might expect `__constant__` memory to be analogous to the `const` keyword in C/C++, where it cannot be changed after initialization. But `__constant__` memory can be changed, either by memory copies or by querying the pointer to `__constant__` memory and writing to it with a kernel. CUDA kernels must not write to `__constant__` memory ranges that they may be accessing because the constant cache is not kept coherent with respect to the rest of the memory hierarchy during kernel execution.

5.3.1 HOST AND DEVICE __CONSTANT__ MEMORY

Mark Harris describes the following idiom that uses the predefined macro
__CUDA_ARCH__ to maintain host and device copies of __constant__
memory that are conveniently accessed by both the CPU and GPU.[15]

```
__constant__ double dc_vals[2] = { 0.0, 1000.0 };
      const double hc_vals[2] = { 0.0, 1000.0 };

__device__ __host__ double f(size_t i)
{
#ifdef __CUDA_ARCH__
    return dc_vals[i];
#else
    return hc_vals[i];
#endif
}
```

5.3.2 ACCESSING __CONSTANT__ MEMORY

Besides the accesses to constant memory implicitly caused by C/C++ operators,
developers can copy to and from constant memory, and even query the pointer
to a constant memory allocation.

CUDA Runtime

CUDA runtime applications can copy to and from __constant__ memory using cudaMemcpyToSymbol() and cudaMemcpyFromSymbol(),
respectively. The pointer to __constant__ memory can be queried with
cudaGetSymbolAddress().

```
cudaError_t cudaGetSymbolAddress( void **devPtr, char *symbol );
```

This pointer may be used to write to constant memory with a kernel, though
developers must take care not to write to the constant memory while another
kernel is reading it.

Driver API

Driver API applications can query the device pointer of constant memory using
cuModuleGetGlobal(). The driver API does not include a special memory
copy function like cudaMemcpyToSymbol(), since it does not have the language integration of the CUDA runtime. Applications must query the address with
cuModuleGetGlobal() and then call cuMemcpyHtoD() or cuMemcpyDtoH().

---

15. http://bit.ly/OpMdN5

The amount of constant memory used by a kernel may be queried with
`cuFuncGetAttribute(CU_FUNC_ATTRIBUTE_CONSTANT_SIZE_BYTES)`.

5.4 Local Memory

Local memory contains the stack for every thread in a CUDA kernel. It is used as follows.

- To implement the application binary interface (ABI)—that is, the calling convention

- To spill data out of registers

- To hold arrays whose indices cannot be resolved by the compiler

In early implementations of CUDA hardware, *any* use of local memory was the "kiss of death." It slowed things down so much that developers were encouraged to take whatever measure was needed to get rid of the local memory usage. With the advent of an L1 cache in Fermi, these performance concerns are less urgent, provided the local memory traffic is confined to L1.[16]

Developers can make the compiler report the amount of local memory needed by a given kernel with the `nvcc` options: `-Xptxas -v,abi=no`. At runtime, the amount of local memory used by a kernel may be queried with

`cuFuncGetAttribute(CU_FUNC_ATTRIBUTE_LOCAL_SIZE_BYTES)`.

Paulius Micikevicius of NVIDIA gave a good presentation on how to determine whether local memory usage was impacting performance and what to do about it.[17] Register spilling can incur two costs: an increased number of instructions and an increase in the amount of memory traffic.

The L1 and L2 performance counters can be used to determine if the memory traffic is impacting performance. Here are some strategies to improve performance in this case.

- At compile time, specify a higher limit in `-maxregcount`. By increasing the number of registers available to the thread, both the instruction count and

---

16. The L1 cache is per-SM and is physically implemented in the same hardware as shared memory.
17. http://bit.ly/ZAeHc5

the memory traffic will decrease. The __launch_bounds__ directive may be used to tune this parameter when the kernel is being compiled online by PTXAS.

- Use noncaching loads for global memory, such as nvcc -Xptxas -dlcm=cg.

- Increase the L1 size to 48K. (Call cudaFuncSetCacheConfig() or cudaDeviceSetCacheconfig().)

When launching a kernel that uses more than the default amount of memory allocated for local memory, the CUDA driver must allocate a new local memory buffer before the kernel can launch. As a result, the kernel launch may take extra time; may cause unexpected CPU/GPU synchronization; and, if the driver is unable to allocate the buffer for local memory, may fail.[18] By default, the CUDA driver will free these larger local memory allocations after the kernel has launched. This behavior can be inhibited by specifying the CU_CTX_RESIZE_ LMEM_TO_MAX flag to cuCtxCreate() or calling cudaSetDeviceFlags() with the cudaDeviceLmemResizeToMax flag set.

It is not difficult to build a templated function that illustrates the "performance cliff" when register spills occur. The templated GlobalCopy kernel in Listing 5.10 implements a simple memcpy routine that uses a local array temp to stage global memory references. The template parameter n specifies the number of elements in temp and thus the number of loads and stores to perform in the inner loop of the memory copy.

As a quick review of the SASS microcode emitted by the compiler will confirm, the compiler can keep temp in registers until n becomes too large.

Listing 5.10 GlobalCopy kernel.

```
template<class T, const int n>
__global__ void
GlobalCopy( T *out, const T *in, size_t N )
{
    T temp[n];
    size_t i;
    for ( i = n*blockIdx.x*blockDim.x+threadIdx.x;
          i < N-n*blockDim.x*gridDim.x;
          i += n*blockDim.x*gridDim.x ) {
        for ( int j = 0; j < n; j++ ) {
            size_t index = i+j*blockDim.x;
            temp[j] = in[index];
        }
```

---

18. Since most resources are preallocated, an inability to allocate local memory is one of the few circumstances that can cause a kernel launch to fail at runtime.

```
        for ( int j = 0; j < n; j++ ) {
            size_t index = i+j*blockDim.x;
            out[index] = temp[j];
        }
    }
    // to avoid the (index<N) conditional in the inner loop,
    // we left off some work at the end
    for ( int j = 0; j < n; j++ ) {
        for ( int j = 0; j < n; j++ ) {
            size_t index = i+j*blockDim.x;
            if ( index<N ) temp[j] = in[index];
        }
        for ( int j = 0; j < n; j++ ) {
            size_t index = i+j*blockDim.x;
            if ( index<N ) out[index] = temp[j];
        }
    }
}
```

Listing 5.11 shows an excerpt of the output from `globalCopy.cu` on a GK104 GPU: the copy performance of 64-bit operands only. The degradation in performance due to register spilling becomes obvious in the row corresponding to a loop unroll of 12, where the delivered bandwidth decreases from 117GB/s to less than 90GB/s, and degrades further to under 30GB/s as the loop unroll increases to 16.

Table 5.9 summarizes the register and local memory usage for the kernels corresponding to the unrolled loops. The performance degradation of the copy corresponds to the local memory usage. In this case, every thread always spills in the inner loop; presumably, the performance wouldn't degrade so much if only some of the threads were spilling (for example, when executing a divergent code path).

Listing 5.11 `globalCopy.cu` output (64-bit only).

```
Operand size: 8 bytes
Input size: 16M operands
                        Block Size
Unroll   32      64      128     256     512     maxBW    maxThreads
1        75.57   102.57  116.03  124.51  126.21  126.21   512
2        105.73  117.09  121.84  123.07  124.00  124.00   512
3        112.49  120.88  121.56  123.09  123.44  123.44   512
4        115.54  122.89  122.38  122.15  121.22  122.89   64
5        113.81  121.29  120.11  119.69  116.02  121.29   64
6        114.84  119.49  120.56  118.09  117.88  120.56   128
7        117.53  122.94  118.74  116.52  110.99  122.94   64
8        116.89  121.68  119.00  113.49  105.69  121.68   64
9        116.10  120.73  115.96  109.48  99.60   120.73   64
10       115.02  116.70  115.30  106.31  93.56   116.70   64
11       113.67  117.36  111.48  102.84  88.31   117.36   64
```

```
12    88.16    86.91    83.68    73.78    58.55    88.16    32
13    85.27    85.58    80.09    68.51    52.66    85.58    64
14    78.60    76.30    69.50    56.59    41.29    78.60    32
15    69.00    65.78    59.82    48.41    34.65    69.00    32
16    65.68    62.16    54.71    43.02    29.92    65.68    32
```

Table 5.9 globalCopy Register and Local Memory Usage

UNROLL FACTOR	REGISTERS	LOCAL MEMORY (BYTES)
1	20	None
2	19	None
3	26	None
4	33	None
5	39	None
6	46	None
7	53	None
8	58	None
9	62	None
10	63	None
11	63	None
12	63	16
13	63	32
14	63	60
15	63	96
16	63	116

5.5 Texture Memory

In CUDA, the concept of texture memory is realized in two parts: a *CUDA array* contains the physical memory allocation, and a *texture reference* or *surface reference*[19] contains a "view" that can be used to read or write a CUDA array. The CUDA array is just an untyped "bag of bits" with a memory layout optimized for 1D, 2D, or 3D access. A texture reference contains information on how the CUDA array should be addressed and how its contents should be interpreted.

When using a texture reference to read from a CUDA array, the hardware uses a separate, read-only cache to resolve the memory references. While the kernel is executing, the texture cache is not kept coherent with respect to the rest of the memory subsystem, so it is important not to use texture references to alias memory that will be operated on by the kernel. (The cache is invalidated between kernel launches.)

On SM 3.5 hardware, reads via texture can be explicitly requested by the developer using the `const restricted` keywords. The `restricted` keyword does nothing more than make the just-described "no aliasing" guarantee that the memory in question won't be referenced by the kernel in any other way. When reading or writing a CUDA array with a surface reference, the memory traffic goes through the same memory hierarchy as global loads and stores. Chapter 10 contains a detailed discussion of how to allocate and use textures in CUDA.

5.6 Shared Memory

Shared memory is used to exchange data between CUDA threads within a block. Physically, it is implemented with a per-SM memory that can be accessed very quickly. In terms of speed, shared memory is perhaps 10x slower than register accesses but 10x faster than accesses to global memory. As a result, shared memory is often a critical resource to reduce the external bandwidth needed by CUDA kernels.

Since developers explicitly allocate and reference shared memory, it can be thought of as a "manually managed" cache or "scratchpad" memory. Developers can request different cache configurations at both the kernel and the device level: `cudaDeviceSetCacheConfig()`/`cuCtxSetCacheConfig()`

---

19. Surface references can be used only on SM 2.x and later hardware.

specify the preferred cache configuration for a CUDA device, while `cudaFuncSetCacheConfig()`/`cuFuncSetCacheConfig()` specify the preferred cache configuration for a given kernel. If both are specified, the per-kernel request takes precedence, but in any case, the requirements of the kernel may override the developer's preference.

Kernels that use shared memory typically are written in three phases.

- Load shared memory and `__syncthreads()`

- Process shared memory and `__syncthreads()`

- Write results

Developers can make the compiler report the amount of shared memory used by a given kernel with the `nvcc` options: `-Xptxas -v,abi=no`. At runtime, the amount of shared memory used by a kernel may be queried with `cuFuncGetAttribute(CU_FUNC_ATTRIBUTE_SHARED_SIZE_BYTES)`.

5.6.1 UNSIZED SHARED MEMORY DECLARATIONS

Any shared memory declared in the kernel itself is automatically allocated for each block when the kernel is launched. If the kernel also includes an unsized declaration of shared memory, the amount of memory needed by that declaration must be specified when the kernel is launched.

If there is more than one `extern __shared__` memory declaration, they are aliased with respect to one another, so the declaration

```
extern __shared__ char sharedChars[];
extern __shared__ int sharedInts[];
```

enables the same shared memory to be addressed as 8- or 32-bit integers, as needed. One motivation for using this type of aliasing is to use wider types when possible to read and write global memory, while using the narrow ones for kernel computations.

NOTE

If you have more than one kernel that uses unsized shared memory, they must be compiled in separate files.

5.6.2 WARP-SYNCHRONOUS CODING

Shared memory variables that will be participating in warp-synchronous programming must be declared as `volatile` to prevent the compiler from applying optimizations that will render the code incorrect.

5.6.3 POINTERS TO SHARED MEMORY

It is valid—and often convenient—to use pointers to refer to shared memory. Example kernels that use this idiom include the reduction kernels in Chapter 12 (Listing 12.3) and the `scanBlock` kernel in Chapter 13 (Listing 13.3).

5.7 Memory Copy

CUDA has three different memory types—host memory, device memory, and CUDA arrays—and a full complement of functions to copy between them. For host↔device memcpy, an additional set of functions provide *asynchronous* memcpy between pinned host memory and device memory or CUDA arrays. Additionally, a set of peer-to-peer memcpy functions enable memory to be copied between GPUs.

The CUDA runtime and the driver API take very different approaches. For 1D memcpy, the driver API defined a family of functions with type-strong parameters. The host-to-device, device-to-host, and device-to-device memcpy functions are separate.

```
CUresult cuMemcpyHtoD(CUdeviceptr dstDevice, const void *srcHost,
size_t ByteCount);
CUresult cuMemcpyDtoH(void *dstHost, CUdeviceptr srcDevice, size_t
ByteCount);
CUresult cuMemcpyDtoD(CUdeviceptr dstDevice, CUdeviceptr srcDevice,
size_t ByteCount);
```

In contrast, the CUDA runtime tends to define functions that take an extra "memcpy kind" parameter that depends on the memory types of the host and destination pointers.

```
enum cudaMemcpyKind
{
 cudaMemcpyHostToHost = 0,
 cudaMemcpyHostToDevice = 1,
 cudaMemcpyDeviceToHost = 2,
 cudaMemcpyDeviceToDevice = 3,
 cudaMemcpyDefault = 4
};
```

For more complex memcpy operations, both APIs use descriptor structures to specify the memcpy.

5.7.1 SYNCHRONOUS VERSUS ASYNCHRONOUS MEMCPY

Because most aspects of memcpy (dimensionality, memory type) are independent of whether the memory copy is asynchronous, this section examines the difference in detail, and later sections include minimal coverage of asynchronous memcpy.

By default, any memcpy involving host memory is *synchronous*: The function does not return until after the operation has been performed.[20] Even when operating on pinned memory, such as memory allocated with cudaMallocHost(), synchronous memcpy routines must wait until the operation is completed because the application may rely on that behavior.[21]

When possible, synchronous memcpy should be avoided for performance reasons. Even when streams are not being used, keeping all operations asynchronous improves performance by enabling the CPU and GPU to run concurrently. If nothing else, the CPU can set up more GPU operations such as kernel launches and other memcpys while the GPU is running! If CPU/GPU concurrency is the only goal, there is no need to create any CUDA streams; calling an asynchronous memcpy with the NULL stream will suffice.

While memcpys involving host memory are synchronous by default, any memory copy not involving host memory (device↔device or device↔array) is asynchronous. The GPU hardware internally enforces serialization on these operations, so there is no need for the functions to wait until the GPU has finished before returning.

Asynchronous memcpy functions have the suffix Async(). For example, the driver API function for asynchronous host→device memcpy is cuMemcpyHtoDAsync() and the CUDA runtime function is cudaMemcpyAsync().

The hardware that implements asynchronous memcpy has evolved over time. The very first CUDA-capable GPU (the GeForce 8800 GTX) did not have any copy engines, so asynchronous memcpy only enabled CPU/GPU concurrency. Later GPUs added copy engines that could perform 1D transfers while the SMs were running, and still

---

20. This is because the hardware cannot directly access host memory unless it has been page-locked and mapped for the GPU. An asynchronous memory copy for pageable memory could be implemented by spawning another CPU thread, but so far, the CUDA team has chosen to avoid that additional complexity.
21. When pinned memory is specified to a synchronous memcpy routine, the driver does take advantage by having the hardware use DMA, which is generally faster.

later, fully capable copy engines were added that could accelerate 2D and 3D transfers, even if the copy involved converting between pitch layouts and the block-linear layouts used by CUDA arrays. Additionally, early CUDA hardware only had one copy engine, whereas today, it sometimes has two. More than two copy engines wouldn't necessarily make sense. Because a single copy engine can saturate the PCI Express bus in one direction, only two copy engines are needed to maximize both bus performance and concurrency between bus transfers and GPU computation.

The number of copy engines can be queried by calling `cuDeviceGetAttribute()` with `CU_DEVICE_ATTRIBUTE_ASYNC_ENGINE_COUNT`, or by examining the `cudaDeviceProp::asyncEngineCount`.

5.7.2 UNIFIED VIRTUAL ADDRESSING

Unified Virtual Addressing enables CUDA to make inferences about memory types based on address ranges. Because CUDA tracks which address ranges contain device addresses versus host addresses, there is no need to specify `cudaMemcpyKind` parameter to the `cudaMemcpy()` function. The driver API added a `cuMemcpy()` function that similarly infers the memory types from the addresses.

```
CUresult cuMemcpy(CUdeviceptr dst, CUdeviceptr src, size_t ByteCount);
```

The CUDA runtime equivalent, not surprisingly, is called `cudaMemcpy()`:

```
cudaError_t cudaMemcpy( void *dst, const void *src, size_t bytes );.
```

5.7.3 CUDA RUNTIME

Table 5.10 summarizes the memcpy functions available in the CUDA runtime.

Table 5.10 Memcpy Functions (CUDA Runtime)

DEST TYPE	SOURCE TYPE	DIM	FUNCTION
Host	Device	1D	`cudaMemcpy( , ...cudaMemcpyHostToDevice);`
Host	Array	1D	`cudaMemcpyFromArray( , ...cudaMemcpyDeviceToHost);`
Device	Host	1D	`cudaMemcpy(..., cudaMemcpyDeviceToHost);`
Device	Device	1D	`cudaMemcpy(..., cudaMemcpyDeviceToDevice);`

Table 5.10 Memcpy Functions (CUDA Runtime) *(Continued)*

DEST TYPE	SOURCE TYPE	DIM	FUNCTION
Device	Array	1D	`cudaMemcpyFromArray`
Array	Host	1D	`cudaMemcpyToArray`
Array	Device	1D	`cudaMemcpyToArray`
Array	Array	1D	`cudaMemcpyArrayToArray`
Host	Device	2D	`cudaMemcpy2D(..., cudaMemcpyHostToDevice);`
Host	Array	2D	`cudaMemcpy2DToArray(..., cudaMemcpyHostToDevice);`
Device	Host	2D	`cudaMemcpy2D(..., cudaMemcpyDeviceToHost);`
Device	Device	2D	`cudaMemcpy2D(..., cudaMemcpyDeviceToDevice);`
Device	Array	2D	`cudaMemcpy2DToArray(..., cudaMemcpyDeviceToDevice);`
Array	Host	2D	`cudaMemcpy2DToArray( , ...cudaMemcpyHostToDevice );`
Array	Device	2D	`cudaMemcpy2DToArray( , ...cudaMemcpyHostToDevice );`
Array	Array	2D	`cudaMemcpy2DArrayToArray( );`
Host	Device	3D	`cudaMemcpy3D`
Host	Array	3D	`cudaMemcpy3D`
Device	Host	3D	`cudaMemcpy3D`
Device	Device	3D	`cudaMemcpy3D`
Device	Array	3D	`cudaMemcpy3D`
Array	Host	3D	`cudaMemcpy3D`
Array	Device	3D	`cudaMemcpy3D`
Array	Array	3D	`cudaMemcpy3D`

Table 5.11 cudaMemcpy3DParms Structure Members

STRUCTURE MEMBER	DESCRIPTION
srcArray	Source array, if needed by kind
srcPos	Offset of the source
srcPtr	Source pointer, if needed by kind
dstArray	Destination array, if needed by kind
dstPos	Offset into the destination
dstPtr	Destination pointer, if needed by kind
extent	Width, height, and depth of the memcpy
kind	"Kind" of the memcpy: cudaMemcpyHostToDevice, cudaMemcpyDeviceToHost, cudaMemcpyDeviceToDevice, or cudaMemcpyDefault

1D and 2D memcpy functions take base pointers, pitches, and sizes as required. The 3D memcpy routines take a descriptor structure cudaMemcpy3Dparms, defined as follows.

```
struct cudaMemcpy3DParms
{
    struct cudaArray *srcArray;
    struct cudaPos srcPos;
    struct cudaPitchedPtr srcPtr;

    struct cudaArray *dstArray;
    struct cudaPos dstPos;
    struct cudaPitchedPtr dstPtr;

    struct cudaExtent extent;
    enum cudaMemcpyKind kind;
};
```

Table 5.11 summarizes the meaning of each member of the cudaMemcpy3D-Parms structure. The cudaPos and cudaExtent structures are defined as follows.

```
struct cudaExtent {
    size_t width;
    size_t height;
```

```
    size_t depth;
};

struct cudaPos {
    size_t x;
    size_t y;
    size_t z;
};
```

5.7.4 DRIVER API

Table 5.12 summarizes the driver API's memcpy functions.

Table 5.12 Memcpy Functions (Driver API)

DEST TYPE	SOURCE TYPE	DIM	FUNCTION
Host	Device	1D	cuMemcpyDtoH
Host	Array	1D	cuMemcpyAtoH
Device	Host	1D	cuMemcpyHtoD
Device	Device	1D	cuMemcpyDtoD
Device	Array	1D	cuMemcpyAtoD
Array	Host	1D	cuMemcpyHtoA
Array	Device	1D	cuMemcpyDtoA
Array	Array	1D	cuMemcpyAtoA
Host	Device	2D	cuMemcpy2D
Host	Array	2D	cuMemcpy2D
Device	Host	2D	cuMemcpy2D
Device	Device	2D	cuMemcpy2D
Device	Array	2D	cuMemcpy2D

continues

Table 5.12 Memcpy Functions (Driver API) *(Continued)*

DEST TYPE	SOURCE TYPE	DIM	FUNCTION
Array	Host	2D	cuMemcpy2D
Array	Device	2D	cuMemcpy2D
Array	Array	2D	cuMemcpy2D
Host	Device	3D	cuMemcpy3D
Host	Array	3D	cuMemcpy3D
Device	Host	3D	cuMemcpy3D
Device	Device	3D	cuMemcpy3D
Device	Array	3D	cuMemcpy3D
Array	Host	3D	cuMemcpy3D
Array	Device	3D	cuMemcpy3D
Array	Array	3D	cuMemcpy3D

cuMemcpy3D() is designed to implement a strict superset of all previous memcpy functionality. Any 1D, 2D, or 3D memcpy may be performed between any host, device, or CUDA array memory, and any offset into either the source or destination may be applied. The WidthInBytes, Height, and Depth members of the input structure, CUDA_MEMCPY_3D, define the dimensionality of the memcpy: Height==0 implies a 1D memcpy, and Depth==0 implies a 2D memcpy. The source and destination memory types are given by the srcMemoryType and dstMemoryType structure elements, respectively.

Structure elements that are not needed by cuMemcpy3D() are defined to be ignored. For example, if a 1D host→device memcpy is requested, the srcPitch, srcHeight, dstPitch, and dstHeight elements are ignored. If srcMemoryType is CU_MEMORYTYPE_HOST, the srcDevice and srcArray elements are ignored. This API semantic, coupled with the C idiom that assigning {0} to a structure zero-initializes it, enables memory copies to be described very concisely. Most other memcpy functions can be implemented in a few lines of code, such as the following.

```
CUresult
my_cuMemcpyHtoD( CUdevice dst, const void *src, size_t N )
{
    CUDA_MEMCPY_3D cp = {0};
    cp.srcMemoryType = CU_MEMORYTYPE_HOST;
    cp.srcHost = srcHost;
    cp.dstMemoryType = CU_MEMORYTYPE_DEVICE;
    cp.dstDevice = dst;
    cp.WidthInBytes = N;
    return cuMemcpy3D( &cp );
}
```

Chapter 6

Streams and Events

CUDA is best known for enabling fine-grained concurrency, with hardware facilities that enable threads to closely collaborate within blocks using a combination of shared memory and thread synchronization. But it also has hardware and software facilities that enable more coarse-grained concurrency:

- **CPU/GPU concurrency:** Since they are separate devices, the CPU and GPU can operate independently of each other.

- **Memcpy/kernel processing concurrency:** For GPUs that have one or more copy engines, host↔device memcpy can be performed while the SMs are processing kernels.

- **Kernel concurrency:** SM 2.x-class and later hardware can run up to 4 kernels in parallel.

- **Multi-GPU concurrency:** For problems with enough computational density, multiple GPUs can operate in parallel. (Chapter 9 is dedicated to multi-GPU programming.)

CUDA streams enable these types of concurrency. Within a given stream, operations are performed in sequential order, but operations in different streams may be performed in parallel. CUDA events complement CUDA streams by providing the synchronization mechanisms needed to coordinate the parallel execution enabled by streams. CUDA events may be asynchronously "recorded" into a stream, and the CUDA event becomes signaled when the operations preceding the CUDA event have been completed.

CUDA events may be used for CPU/GPU synchronization, for synchronization between the engines on the GPU, and for synchronization between GPUs. They also provide a GPU-based timing mechanism that cannot be perturbed by system events such as page faults or interrupts from disk or network controllers. Wall clock timers are best for overall timing, but CUDA events are useful for optimizing kernels or figuring out which of a series of pipelined GPU operations is taking the longest. All of the performance results reported in this chapter were gathered on a `cg1.4xlarge` cloud-based server from Amazon's EC2 service, as described in Section 4.5.

6.1 CPU/GPU Concurrency: Covering Driver Overhead

CPU/GPU concurrency refers to the CPU's ability to continue processing after having sent some request to the GPU. Arguably, the most important use of CPU/GPU concurrency is hiding the overhead of requesting work from the GPU.

6.1.1 KERNEL LAUNCHES

Kernel launches have always been asynchronous. A series of kernel launches, with no intervening CUDA operations in between, cause the CPU to submit the kernel launch to the GPU and return control to the caller before the GPU has finished processing.

We can measure the driver overhead by bracketing a series of NULL kernel launches with timing operations. Listing 6.1 shows `nullKernelAsync.cu`, a small program that measures the amount of time needed to perform a kernel launch.

Listing 6.1 `nullKernelAsync.cu`.

```
#include <stdio.h>

#include "chTimer.h"

__global__
void
NullKernel()
{
}

int
main( int argc, char *argv[] )
```

```
{
    const int cIterations = 1000000;
    printf( "Launches... " ); fflush( stdout );

    chTimerTimestamp start, stop;

    chTimerGetTime( &start );
    for ( int i = 0; i < cIterations; i++ ) {
        NullKernel<<<1,1>>>();
    }
    cudaThreadSynchronize();
    chTimerGetTime( &stop );

    double microseconds = 1e6*chTimerElapsedTime( &start, &stop );
    double usPerLaunch = microseconds / (float) cIterations;

    printf( "%.2f us\n", usPerLaunch );

    return 0;
}
```

The chTimerGetTime() calls, described in Appendix A, use the host operating system's high-resolution timing facilities, such as QueryPerformance-Counter() or gettimeofday(). The cudaThreadSynchronize() call in line 23 is needed for accurate timing. Without it, the GPU would still be processing the last kernel invocations when the end top is recorded with the following function call.

```
chTimerGetTime( &stop );
```

If you run this program, you will see that invoking a kernel—even a kernel that does nothing—costs anywhere from 2.0 to 8.0 microseconds. Most of that time is spent in the driver. The CPU/GPU concurrency enabled by kernel launches only helps if the kernel runs for longer than it takes the driver to invoke it! To underscore the importance of CPU/GPU concurrency for small kernel launches, let's move the cudaThreadSynchronize() call into the inner loop.[1]

```
chTimerGetTime( &start );
for ( int i = 0; i < cIterations; i++ ) {
    NullKernel<<<1,1>>>();
    cudaThreadSynchronize();
}
chTimerGetTime( &stop );
```

---

1. This program is in the source code as nullKernelSync.cu and is not reproduced here because it is almost identical to Listing 6.1.

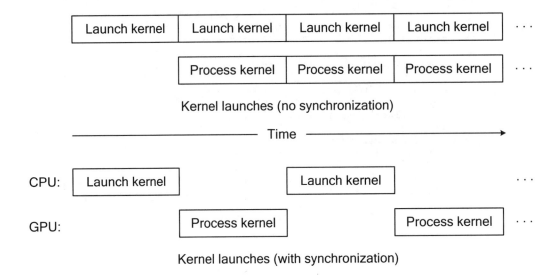

| Launch kernel | Launch kernel | Launch kernel | Launch kernel | · · · |
| | Process kernel | Process kernel | Process kernel | · · · |

Kernel launches (no synchronization)

————————————————— Time —————————————————▶

CPU: | Launch kernel | | Launch kernel | · · ·

GPU: | Process kernel | | Process kernel | · · ·

Kernel launches (with synchronization)

Figure 6.1 CPU/GPU concurrency.

The only difference here is that the CPU is waiting until the GPU has finished processing each NULL kernel launch before launching the next kernel, as shown in Figure 6.1. As an example, on an Amazon EC2 instance with ECC disabled, nullKernelNoSync reports a time of 3.4 ms per launch and nullKernelSync reports a time of 100 ms per launch. So besides giving up CPU/GPU concurrency, the synchronization itself is worth avoiding.

Even without synchronizations, if the kernel doesn't run for longer than the amount of time it took to launch the kernel (3.4 ms), the GPU may go idle before the CPU has submitted more work. To explore just how much work a kernel might need to do to make the launch worthwhile, let's switch to a kernel that busy-waits until a certain number of clock cycles (according to the clock() intrinsic) has completed.

```
__device__ int deviceTime;

__global__
void
WaitKernel( int cycles, bool bWrite )
{
    int start = clock();
    int stop;
    do {
        stop = clock();
    } while ( stop - start < cycles );
```

```
    if ( bWrite && threadIdx.x==0 && blockIdx.x==0 ) {
        deviceTime = stop - start;
    }
}
```

By conditionally writing the result to `deviceTime`, this kernel prevents the compiler from optimizing out the busy wait. The compiler does not know that we are just going to pass `false` as the second parameter.[2] The code in our `main()` function then checks the launch time for various values of cycles, from 0 to 2500.

```
for ( int cycles = 0; cycles < 2500; cycles += 100 ) {
    printf( "Cycles: %d - ", cycles ); fflush( stdout );
    chTimerGetTime( &start );
    for ( int i = 0; i < cIterations; i++ ) {
        WaitKernel<<<1,1>>>( cycles, false );
    }
    cudaThreadSynchronize();
    chTimerGetTime( &stop );
    double microseconds = 1e6*chTimerElapsedTime( &start, &stop );
    double usPerLaunch = microseconds / (float) cIterations;

    printf( "%.2f us\n", usPerLaunch );
}
```

This program may be found in `waitKernelAsync.cu`. On our EC2 instance, the output is as in Figure 6.2. On this host platform, the breakeven mark where the kernel launch time crosses over 2x that of a NULL kernel launch (4.90 µs) is at 4500 GPU clock cycles.

These performance characteristics can vary widely and depend on many factors, including the following.

• Performance of the host CPU

• Host operating system

• Driver version

• Driver model (TCC versus WDDM on Windows)

• Whether ECC is enabled on the GPU[3]

---

2. The compiler could still invalidate our timing results by branching around the loop if `bWrite` is `false`. If the timing results looked suspicious, we could see if this is happening by looking at the microcode with `cuobjdump`.
3. When ECC is enabled, the driver must perform a kernel thunk to check whether any memory errors have occurred. As a result, `cudaThreadSynchronize()` is expensive even on platforms with user-mode client drivers.

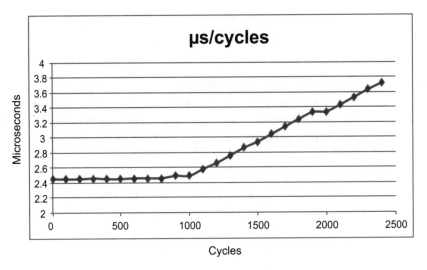

Figure 6.2 Microseconds/cycles plot for `waitKernelAsync.cu`.

But the common underlying theme is that for most CUDA applications, developers should do their best to avoid breaking CPU/GPU concurrency. Only applications that are very compute-intensive and only perform large data transfers can afford to ignore this overhead. To take advantage of CPU/GPU concurrency when performing memory copies as well as kernel launches, developers must use *asynchronous memcpy*.

6.2 Asynchronous Memcpy

Like kernel launches, asynchronous memcpy calls return before the GPU has performed the memcpy in question. Because the GPU operates autonomously and can read or write the host memory without any operating system involvement, only pinned memory is eligible for asynchronous memcpy.

The earliest application for asynchronous memcpy in CUDA was hidden inside the CUDA 1.0 driver. The GPU cannot access pageable memory directly, so the driver implements pageable memcpy using a pair of pinned "staging buffers" that are allocated with the CUDA context. Figure 6.3 shows how this process works.

To perform a host→device memcpy, the driver first "primes the pump" by copying to one staging buffer, then kicks off a DMA operation to read that data with the GPU. While the GPU begins processing that request, the driver copies more

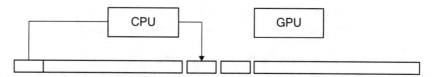

1. "Prime the pump": CPU copies to first staging buffer

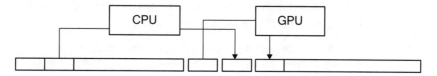

2. GPU pulls from first, while CPU copies to second

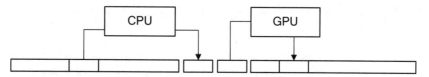

3. GPU pulls from second, while CPU copies to first

. . .

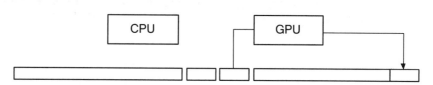

4. Final memcpy by GPU

Figure 6.3 Pageable memcpy.

data into the other staging buffer. The CPU and GPU keep ping-ponging between staging buffers, with appropriate synchronization, until it is time for the GPU to perform the final memcpy. Besides copying data, the CPU also naturally pages in any nonresident pages while the data is being copied.

6.2.1 ASYNCHRONOUS MEMCPY: HOST→DEVICE

As with kernel launches, asynchronous memcpys incur fixed CPU overhead in the driver. In the case of host→device memcpy, *all* memcpys below a certain size are asynchronous, because the driver copies the source data directly into the command buffer that it uses to control the hardware.

We can write an application that measures asynchronous memcpy overhead, much as we measured kernel launch overhead earlier. The following code, in a program called nullHtoDMemcpyAsync.cu, reports that on a cg1.4xlarge instance in Amazon EC2, each memcpy takes 3.3 ms. Since PCI Express can transfer almost 2K in that time, it makes sense to examine how the time needed to perform a small memcpy grows with the size.

```
CUDART_CHECK( cudaMalloc( &deviceInt, sizeof(int) ) );
CUDART_CHECK( cudaHostAlloc( &hostInt, sizeof(int), 0 ) );

chTimerGetTime( &start );
    for ( int i = 0; i < cIterations; i++ ) {
        CUDART_CHECK( cudaMemcpyAsync( deviceInt, hostInt, sizeof(int),
        cudaMemcpyHostToDevice, NULL ) );
    }
CUDART_CHECK( cudaThreadSynchronize() );
chTimerGetTime( &stop );
```

The breakevenHtoDMemcpy.cu program measures memcpy performance for sizes from 4K to 64K. On a cg1.4xlarge instance in Amazon EC2, it generates Figure 6.4. The data generated by this program is clean enough to fit to a linear regression curve—in this case, with intercept 3.3 μs and slope 0.000170 μs/byte. The slope corresponds to 5.9GB/s, about the expected bandwidth from PCI Express 2.0.

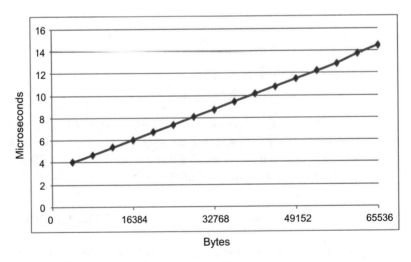

Figure 6.4 Small host→device memcpy performance.

6.2.2 ASYNCHRONOUS MEMCPY: DEVICE→HOST

The `nullDtoHMemcpyNoSync.cu` and `breakevenDtoHMemcpy.cu` programs perform the same measurements for small device→host memcpys. On our trusty Amazon EC2 instance, the minimum time for a memcpy is 4.00 µs (Figure 6.5).

6.2.3 THE NULL STREAM AND CONCURRENCY BREAKS

Any streamed operation may be called with NULL as the stream parameter, and the operation will not be initiated until all the preceding operations on the GPU have been completed.[4] Applications that have no need for copy engines to overlap memcpy operations with kernel processing can use the NULL stream to facilitate CPU/GPU concurrency.

Once a streamed operation has been initiated with the NULL stream, the application must use synchronization functions such as `cuCtxSynchronize()` or `cudaThreadSynchronize()` to ensure that the operation has been completed before proceeding. But the application may request many such operations before performing the synchronization. For example, the application may

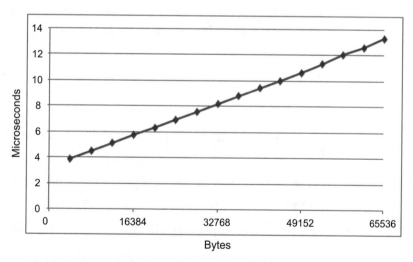

Figure 6.5 Small device→host memcpy performance.

---

4. When CUDA streams were added in CUDA 1.1, the designers had a choice between making the NULL stream "its own" stream, separate from other streams and serialized only with itself, or making it synchronize with ("join") all engines on the GPU. They opted for the latter, in part because CUDA did not yet have facilities for interstream synchronization.

perform an asynchronous host→device memcpy, one or more kernel launches, and an asynchronous device→host memcpy before synchronizing with the context. The cuCtxSynchronize() or cudaThreadSynchronize() call returns once the GPU has performed the most recently requested operation. This idiom is especially useful when performing smaller memcpys or launching kernels that will not run for long. The CUDA driver takes valuable CPU time to write commands to the GPU, and overlapping that CPU execution with the GPU's processing of the commands can improve performance.

Note: Even in CUDA 1.0, kernel launches were asynchronous. As a result, the NULL stream is implicitly specified to all kernel launches if no stream is given.

Breaking Concurrency

Whenever an application performs a full CPU/GPU synchronization (having the CPU wait until the GPU is completely idle), performance suffers. We can measure this performance impact by switching our NULL-memcpy calls from asynchronous ones to synchronous ones just by changing the cudaMemcpyAsync() calls to cudaMemcpy() calls. The nullDtoHMemcpySync.cu program does just that for device→host memcpy.

On our trusty Amazon cg1.4xlarge instance, nullDtoHMemcpySync.cu reports about 7.9 μs per memcpy. If a Windows driver has to perform a kernel thunk, or the driver on an ECC-enabled GPU must check for ECC errors, full GPU synchronization is much costlier.

Explicit ways to perform this synchronization include the following.

- cuCtxSynchronize()/cudaDeviceSynchronize()

- cuStreamSynchronize()/cudaStreamSynchronize() on the NULL stream

- Unstreamed memcpy between host and device—for example, cuMemcpyHtoD(), cuMemcpyDtoH(), cudaMemcpy()

Other, more subtle ways to break CPU/GPU concurrency include the following.

- Running with the CUDA_LAUNCH_BLOCKING environment variable set

- Launching kernels that require local memory to be reallocated

- Performing large memory allocations or host memory allocations

- Destroying objects such as CUDA streams and CUDA events

Nonblocking Streams

To create a stream that is exempt from the requirement to synchronize with the NULL stream (and therefore less likely to suffer a "concurrency break" as described above), specify the `CUDA_STREAM_NON_BLOCKING` flag to `cuStreamCreate()` or the `cudaStreamNonBlocking` flag to `cudaStreamCreateWithFlags()`.

6.3 CUDA Events: CPU/GPU Synchronization

One of the key features of CUDA events is that they can enable "partial" CPU/GPU synchronization. Instead of full CPU/GPU synchronization where the CPU waits until the GPU is idle, introducing a bubble into the GPU's work pipeline, CUDA events may be *recorded* into the asynchronous stream of GPU commands. The CPU then can wait until all of the work preceding the event has been done. The GPU can continue doing whatever work was submitted after the `cuEventRecord()`/`cudaEventRecord()`.

As an example of CPU/GPU concurrency, Listing 6.2 gives a memcpy routine for pageable memory. The code for this program implements the algorithm described in Figure 6.3 and is located in `pageableMemcpyHtoD.cu`. It uses two pinned memory buffers, stored in global variables declared as follows.

```
void *g_hostBuffers[2];
```

and two CUDA events declared as

```
cudaEvent_t g_events[2];
```

Listing 6.2 `chMemcpyHtoD()` —pageable memcpy.

```
void
chMemcpyHtoD( void *device, const void *host, size_t N )
{
    cudaError_t status;
    char *dst = (char *) device;
    const char *src = (const char *) host;
    int stagingIndex = 0;
    while ( N ) {
        size_t thisCopySize = min( N, STAGING_BUFFER_SIZE );
```

```
        cudaEventSynchronize( g_events[stagingIndex] );
        memcpy( g_hostBuffers[stagingIndex], src, thisCopySize );
        cudaMemcpyAsync( dst, g_hostBuffers[stagingIndex],
            thisCopySize, cudaMemcpyHostToDevice, NULL );
        cudaEventRecord( g_events[1-stagingIndex], NULL );
        dst += thisCopySize;
        src += thisCopySize;
        N -= thisCopySize;
        stagingIndex = 1 - stagingIndex;
    }
Error:
    return;
}
```

chMemcpyHtoD() is designed to maximize CPU/GPU concurrency by "ping-ponging" between the two host buffers. The CPU copies into one buffer, while the GPU pulls from the other. There is some "overhang" where no CPU/GPU concurrency is possible at the beginning and end of the operation when the CPU is copying the first and last buffers, respectively.

In this program, the only synchronization needed—the cudaEventSynchronize() in line 11—ensures that the GPU has finished with a buffer before starting to copy into it. cudaMemcpyAsync() returns as soon as the GPU commands have been enqueued. It does not wait until the operation is complete. The cudaEventRecord() is also asynchronous. It causes the event to be signaled when the just-requested asynchronous memcpy has been completed.

The CUDA events are recorded immediately after creation so the first cudaEventSynchronize() calls in line 11 work correctly.

```
CUDART_CHECK( cudaEventCreate( &g_events[0] ) );
CUDART_CHECK( cudaEventCreate( &g_events[1] ) );
// record events so they are signaled on first synchronize
CUDART_CHECK( cudaEventRecord( g_events[0], 0 ) );
CUDART_CHECK( cudaEventRecord( g_events[1], 0 ) );
```

If you run pageableMemcpyHtoD.cu, it will report a bandwidth number much smaller than the pageable memcpy bandwidth delivered by the CUDA driver. That's because the C runtime's memcpy() implementation is not optimized to move memory as fast as the CPU can. For best performance, the memory must be copied using SSE instructions that can move data 16 bytes at a time. Writing a general-purpose memcpy using these instructions is complicated by their alignment restrictions, but a simple version that requires the source, destination, and byte count to be 16-byte aligned is not difficult.[5]

```
#include <xmmintrin.h>
bool
memcpy16( void *_dst, const void *_src, size_t N )
{
    if ( N & 0xf ) {
        return false;
    }

    float *dst = (float *) _dst;
    const float *src = (const float *) _src;
    while ( N ) {
    _mm_store_ps( dst, _mm_load_ps( src ) );
        src += 4;
        dst += 4;
        N -= 16;
    }
    return true;
}
```

When the C runtime `memcpy()` is replaced by this one, performance on an Amazon EC2 `cg1.4xlarge` instance increases from 2155MB/s to 3267MB/s. More complicated memcpy routines can deal with relaxed alignment constraints, and slightly higher performance is possible by unrolling the inner loop. On `cg1.4xlarge`, the CUDA driver's more optimized SSE memcpy achieves about 100MB/s higher performance than `pageableMemcpyHtoD16.cu`.

How important is the CPU/GPU concurrency for performance of pageable memcpy? If we move the event synchronization, we can make the host→device memcpy synchronous, as follows.

```
while ( N ) {
size_t thisCopySize = min( N, STAGING_BUFFER_SIZE );

< CUDART_CHECK( cudaEventSynchronize( g_events[stagingIndex] ) );
 memcpy( g_hostBuffers[stagingIndex], src, thisCopySize );
 CUDART_CHECK( cudaMemcpyAsync( dst, g_hostBuffers[stagingIndex],
 thisCopySize, cudaMemcpyHostToDevice, NULL ) );
 CUDART_CHECK( cudaEventRecord( g_events[1-stagingIndex], NULL ) );
> CUDART_CHECK( cudaEventSynchronize( g_events[1-stagingIndex] ) );
 dst += thisCopySize;
 src += thisCopySize;
 N -= thisCopySize;
 stagingIndex = 1 - stagingIndex;
 }
```

---

5. On some platforms, nvcc does not compile this code seamlessly. In the code accompanying this book, memcpy16() is in a separate file called memcpy16.cpp.

This code is available in `pageableMemcpyHtoD16Synchronous.cu`, and it is about 70% as fast (2334MB/s instead of 3267MB/s) on the same `cg1.4xlarge` instance.

6.3.1 BLOCKING EVENTS

CUDA events also optionally can be made "blocking," in which they use an interrupt-based mechanism for CPU synchronization. The CUDA driver then implements `cu(da)EventSynchronize()` calls using thread synchronization primitives that suspend the CPU thread instead of polling the event's 32-bit tracking value.

For latency-sensitive applications, blocking events may impose a performance penalty. In the case of our pageable memcpy routine, using blocking events causes a slight slowdown (about 100MB/s) on our `cg1.4xlarge` instance. But for more GPU-intensive applications, or for applications with "mixed workloads" that need significant amounts of processing from both CPU and GPU, the benefits of having the CPU thread idle outweigh the costs of handling the interrupt that occurs when the wait is over. An example of a mixed workload is video transcoding, which features divergent code suitable for the CPU and signal and pixel processing suitable for the GPU.

6.3.2 QUERIES

Both CUDA streams and CUDA events may be queried with `cu(da)StreamQuery()` and `cu(da)EventQuery()`, respectively. If `cu(da)StreamQuery()` returns success, all of the operations pending in a given stream have been completed. If `cu(da)EventQuery()` returns success, the event has been recorded.

Although these queries are intended to be lightweight, if ECC is enabled, they do perform kernel thunks to check the current error status of the GPU. Additionally, on Windows, any pending commands will be submitted to the GPU, which also requires a kernel thunk.

6.4 CUDA Events: Timing

CUDA events work by submitting a command to the GPU that, when the preceding commands have been completed, causes the GPU to write a 32-bit memory location with a known value. The CUDA driver implements `cuEventQuery()` and `cuEventSynchronize()` by examining that 32-bit value. But besides the 32-bit "tracking" value, the GPU also can write a 64-bit timer value that is sourced from a high-resolution, GPU-based clock.

Because they use a GPU-based clock, timing using CUDA events is less subject to perturbations from system events such as page faults or interrupts, and the function to compute elapsed times from timestamps is portable across all operating systems. That said, the so-called "wall clock" times of operations are ultimately what users see, so CUDA events are best used in a targeted fashion to tune kernels or other GPU-intensive operations, not to report absolute times to the user.

The stream parameter to `cuEventRecord()` is for interstream synchronization, not for timing. When using CUDA events for timing, it is best to record them in the NULL stream. The rationale is similar to the reason the machine instructions in superscalar CPUs to read time stamp counters (e.g., `RDTSC` on x86) are serializing instructions that flush the pipeline: Forcing a "join" on all the GPU engines eliminates any possible ambiguity on the operations being timed.[6] Just make sure the `cu(da)EventRecord()` calls bracket enough work so that the timing delivers meaningful results.

Finally, note that CUDA events are intended to time GPU operations. Any synchronous CUDA operations will result in the GPU being used to time the resulting CPU/GPU synchronization operations.

```
CUDART_CHECK( cudaEventRecord( startEvent, NULL ) );
// synchronous memcpy - invalidates CUDA event timing
CUDART_CHECK( cudaMemcpy( deviceIn, hostIn, N*sizeof(int) ) );
CUDART_CHECK( cudaEventRecord( stopEvent, NULL ) );
```

The example explored in the next section illustrates how to use CUDA events for timing.

6.5 Concurrent Copying and Kernel Processing

Since CUDA applications must transfer data across the PCI Express bus in order for the GPU to operate on it, another performance opportunity presents itself in the form of performing those host↔device memory transfers concurrently with

---

6. An additional consideration: On CUDA hardware with SM 1.1, timing events could only be recorded by the hardware unit that performed kernel computation.

kernel processing. According to Amdahl's Law,[7] the maximum speedup achievable by using multiple processors is

$$Speedup = \frac{1}{r_s + \dfrac{r_p}{N}}$$

where $r_s + r_p = 1$ and N is the number of processors. In the case of concurrent copying and kernel processing, the "number of processors" is the number of autonomous hardware units in the GPU: one or two copy engines, plus the SMs that execute the kernels. For $N = 2$, Figure 6.6 shows the idealized speedup curve as r_s and r_p vary.

So in theory, a 2x performance improvement is possible on a GPU with one copy engine, but only if the program gets perfect overlap between the SMs and the copy engine, and only if the program spends equal time transferring and processing the data.

Before undertaking this endeavor, you should take a close look at whether it will benefit your application. Applications that are extremely transfer-bound (i.e., they spend most of their time transferring data to and from the GPU) or extremely compute-bound (i.e., they spend most of their time processing data on the GPU) will derive little benefit from overlapping transfer and compute.

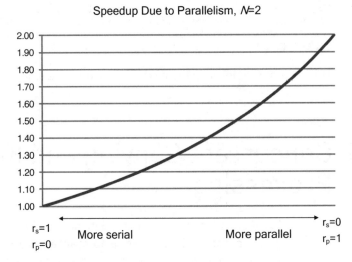

Speedup Due to Parallelism, $N=2$

Figure 6.6 Idealized Amdahl's Law curve.

---

7. http://bit.ly/13UqBm0

6.5.1 CONCURRENCYMEMCPYKERNEL.CU

The program concurrencyMemcpyKernel.cu is designed to illustrate not only how to implement concurrent memcpy and kernel execution but also how to determine whether it is worth doing at all. Listing 6.3 gives a AddKernel(), a "makework" kernel that has a parameter cycles to control how long it runs.

Listing 6.3 AddKernel(), a makework kernel with parameterized computational density.

```
__global__ void
AddKernel( int *out, const int *in, size_t N, int addValue, int
cycles )
{
    for ( size_t i = blockIdx.x*blockDim.x+threadIdx.x;
                 i < N;
                 i += blockDim.x*gridDim.x )
    {
        volatile int value = in[i];
        for ( int j = 0; j < cycles; j++ ) {
            value += addValue;
        }
        out[i] = value;
    }
}
```

AddKernel() streams an array of integers from in to out, looping over each input value cycles times. By varying the value of cycles, we can make the kernel range from a trivial streaming kernel that pushes the memory bandwidth limits of the machine to a totally compute-bound kernel.

These two routines in the program measure the performance of AddKernel().

- TimeSequentialMemcpyKernel() copies the input data to the GPU, invokes AddKernel(), and copies the output back from the GPU in separate, sequential steps.

- TimeConcurrentOperations() allocates a number of CUDA streams and performs the host→device memcpys, kernel processing, and device→host memcpys in parallel.

TimeSequentialMemcpyKernel(), given in Listing 6.4, uses four CUDA events to separately time the host→device memcpy, kernel processing, and device→host memcpy. It also reports back the total time, as measured by the CUDA events.

Listing 6.4 `TimeSequentialMemcpyKernel()` function.

```
bool
TimeSequentialMemcpyKernel(
    float *timesHtoD,
    float *timesKernel,
    float *timesDtoH,
    float *timesTotal,
    size_t N,
    const chShmooRange& cyclesRange,
    int numBlocks )
{
    cudaError_t status;
    bool ret = false;
    int *hostIn = 0;
    int *hostOut = 0;
    int *deviceIn = 0;
    int *deviceOut = 0;
    const int numEvents = 4;
    cudaEvent_t events[numEvents];

    for ( int i = 0; i < numEvents; i++ ) {
        events[i] = NULL;
        CUDART_CHECK( cudaEventCreate( &events[i] ) );
    }
    cudaMallocHost( &hostIn, N*sizeof(int) );
    cudaMallocHost( &hostOut, N*sizeof(int) );
    cudaMalloc( &deviceIn, N*sizeof(int) );
    cudaMalloc( &deviceOut, N*sizeof(int) );

    for ( size_t i = 0; i < N; i++ ) {
        hostIn[i] = rand();
    }

    cudaDeviceSynchronize();

    for ( chShmooIterator cycles(cyclesRange); cycles; cycles++ ) {

        printf( "." ); fflush( stdout );

        cudaEventRecord( events[0], NULL );
        cudaMemcpyAsync( deviceIn, hostIn, N*sizeof(int),
            cudaMemcpyHostToDevice, NULL );
        cudaEventRecord( events[1], NULL );
        AddKernel<<<numBlocks, 256>>>(
            deviceOut, deviceIn, N, 0xcc, *cycles );
        cudaEventRecord( events[2], NULL );
        cudaMemcpyAsync( hostOut, deviceOut, N*sizeof(int),
            cudaMemcpyDeviceToHost, NULL );
        cudaEventRecord( events[3], NULL );
```

```
        cudaDeviceSynchronize();

        cudaEventElapsedTime( timesHtoD, events[0], events[1] );
        cudaEventElapsedTime( timesKernel, events[1], events[2] );
        cudaEventElapsedTime( timesDtoH, events[2], events[3] );
        cudaEventElapsedTime( timesTotal, events[0], events[3] );

        timesHtoD += 1;
        timesKernel += 1;
        timesDtoH += 1;
        timesTotal += 1;
    }

    ret = true;

Error:
    for ( int i = 0; i < numEvents; i++ ) {
        cudaEventDestroy( events[i] );
    }
    cudaFree( deviceIn );
    cudaFree( deviceOut );
    cudaFreeHost( hostOut );
    cudaFreeHost( hostIn );
    return ret;
}
```

The cyclesRange parameter, which uses the "shmoo" functionality described in Section A.4, specifies the range of cycles values to use when invoking AddKernel(). On a cg1.4xlarge instance in EC2, the times (in ms) for cycles values from 4..64 are as follows.

CYCLES	HTOD	KERNEL	DTOH	TOTAL
4	89.19	11.03	82.03	182.25
8	89.16	17.58	82.03	188.76
12	89.15	24.10	82.03	195.28
16	89.15	30.57	82.03	201.74
20	89.14	37.03	82.03	208.21
24	89.16	43.46	82.03	214.65
28	89.16	49.90	82.03	221.10

continues

CYCLES	HTOD	KERNEL	DTOH	TOTAL
32	89.16	56.35	82.03	227.54
36	89.13	62.78	82.03	233.94
40	89.14	69.21	82.03	240.38
44	89.16	75.64	82.03	246.83
48	**89.16**	**82.08**	**82.03**	**253.27**
52	89.14	88.52	82.03	259.69
56	89.14	94.96	82.03	266.14
60	89.14	105.98	82.03	277.15
64	89.17	112.70	82.03	283.90

For values of `*cycles` around 48 (highlighted), where the kernel takes about the same amount of time as the memcpy operations, we presume there would be a benefit in performing the operations concurrently.

The routine `TimeConcurrentMemcpyKernel()` divides the computation performed by `AddKernel()` evenly into segments of size `streamIncrement` and uses a separate CUDA stream to compute each. The code fragment in Listing 6.5, from `TimeConcurrentMemcpyKernel()`, highlights the complexity of programming with streams.

Listing 6.5 `TimeConcurrentMemcpyKernel()` fragment.

```
intsLeft = N;
for ( int stream = 0; stream < numStreams; stream++ ) {
    size_t intsToDo = (intsLeft < intsPerStream) ?
        intsLeft : intsPerStream;
    CUDART_CHECK( cudaMemcpyAsync(
        deviceIn+stream*intsPerStream,
        hostIn+stream*intsPerStream,
        intsToDo*sizeof(int),
        cudaMemcpyHostToDevice, streams[stream] ) );
    intsLeft -= intsToDo;
}
```

```
intsLeft = N;
for ( int stream = 0; stream < numStreams; stream++ ) {
    size_t intsToDo = (intsLeft < intsPerStream) ?
        intsLeft : intsPerStream;
    AddKernel<<<numBlocks, 256, 0, streams[stream]>>>(
        deviceOut+stream*intsPerStream,
        deviceIn+stream*intsPerStream,
        intsToDo, 0xcc, *cycles );
    intsLeft -= intsToDo;
}

intsLeft = N;
for ( int stream = 0; stream < numStreams; stream++ ) {
    size_t intsToDo = (intsLeft < intsPerStream) ?
        intsLeft : intsPerStream;
    CUDART_CHECK( cudaMemcpyAsync(
        hostOut+stream*intsPerStream,
        deviceOut+stream*intsPerStream,
        intsToDo*sizeof(int),
        cudaMemcpyDeviceToHost, streams[stream] ) );
    intsLeft -= intsToDo;
}
```

Besides requiring the application to create and destroy CUDA streams, the streams must be looped over separately for each of the host→device memcpy, kernel processing, and device→host memcpy operations. Without this "software-pipelining," there would be no concurrent execution of the different streams' work, as each streamed operation is preceded by an "interlock" operation that prevents the operation from proceeding until the previous operation in that stream has completed. The result would be not only a failure to get parallel execution between the engines but also an additional performance degradation due to the slight overhead of managing stream concurrency.

The computation cannot be made fully concurrent, since no kernel processing can be overlapped with the first or last memcpys, and there is some overhead in synchronizing between CUDA streams and, as we saw in the previous section, in invoking the memcpy and kernel operations themselves. As a result, the optimal number of streams depends on the application and should be determined empirically. The concurrencyMemcpyKernel.cu program enables the number of streams to be specified on the command line using the --numStreams parameter.

6.5.2 PERFORMANCE RESULTS

The `concurrencyMemcpyKernel.cu` program generates a report on performance characteristics over a variety of `cycles` values, with a fixed buffer size and number of streams. On a `cg1.4xlarge` instance in Amazon EC2, with a buffer size of 128M integers and 8 streams, the report is as follows for cycles values from 4..64.

CYCLES	HTOD	KERNEL	DTOH	TOTAL	CONCURRENT	SPEEDUP
4	89.19	11.03	82.03	182.25	173.09	1.05
8	89.16	17.58	82.03	188.76	173.41	1.09
12	89.15	24.1	82.03	195.28	173.74	1.12
16	89.15	30.57	82.03	201.74	174.09	1.16
20	89.14	37.03	82.03	208.21	174.41	1.19
24	89.16	43.46	82.03	214.65	174.76	1.23
28	89.16	49.9	82.03	221.10	175.08	1.26
32	89.16	56.35	82.03	227.54	175.43	1.30
36	89.13	62.78	82.03	233.94	175.76	1.33
40	89.14	69.21	82.03	240.38	176.08	1.37
44	89.16	75.64	82.03	246.83	176.41	1.40
48	89.16	82.08	82.03	253.27	176.75	1.43
52	89.14	88.52	82.03	259.69	177.08	1.47
56	89.14	94.96	82.03	266.14	179.89	1.48
60	89.14	105.98	82.03	277.15	186.31	1.49
64	89.17	112.7	82.03	283.90	192.86	1.47

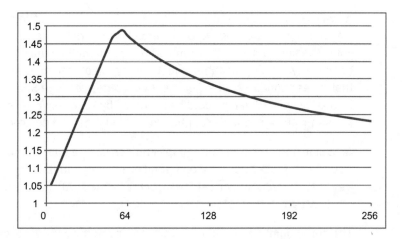

Figure 6.7 Speedup due memcpy/kernel concurrency (Tesla M2050).

The full graph for `cycles` values from 4..256 is given in Figure 6.7. Unfortunately, for these settings, the 50% speedup shown here falls well short of the 3x speedup that theoretically could be obtained.

The benefit on a GeForce GTX 280, which contains only one copy engine, is more pronounced. Here, the results from varying `cycles` up to 512 are shown. The maximum speedup, shown in Figure 6.8, is much closer to the theoretical maximum of 2x.

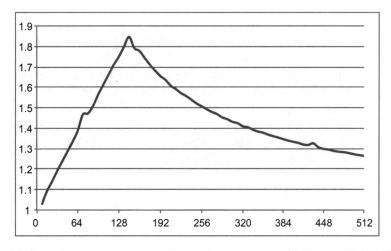

Figure 6.8 Speedup due to memcpy/kernel concurrency (GeForce GTX 280).

As written, `concurrencyMemcpyKernel.cu` serves little more than an illustrative purpose, because `AddValues()` is just make-work. But you can plug your own kernel(s) into this application to help determine whether the additional complexity of using streams is justified by the performance improvement. Note that unless concurrent kernel execution is desired (see Section 6.7), the kernel invocation in Listing 6.5 could be replaced by successive kernel invocations in the same stream, and the application will still get the desired concurrency.

As a side note, the number of copy engines can be queried by calling-`cudaGetDeviceProperties()` and examining `cudaDeviceProp::asyncEngineCount`, or calling `cuDeviceQueryAttribute()` with `CU_DEVICE_ATTRIBUTE_ASYNC_ENGINE_COUNT`.

The copy engines accompanying SM 1.1 and some SM 1.2 hardware could copy linear memory only, but more recent copy engines offer full support for 2D memcpy, including 2D and 3D CUDA arrays.

6.5.3 BREAKING INTERENGINE CONCURRENCY

Using CUDA streams for concurrent memcpy and kernel execution introduces many more opportunities to "break concurrency." In the previous section, CPU/GPU concurrency could be broken by unintentionally doing something that caused CUDA to perform a full CPU/GPU synchronization. Here, CPU/GPU concurrency can be broken by unintentionally performing an unstreamed CUDA operation. Recall that the NULL stream performs a "join" on all GPU engines, so even an asynchronous memcpy operation will stall interengine concurrency if the NULL stream is specified.

Besides specifying the NULL stream explicitly, the main avenue for these unintentional "concurrency breaks" is calling functions that run in the NULL stream implicitly because they do not take a stream parameter. When streams were first introduced in CUDA 1.1, functions such as `cudaMemset()` and `cuMemcpyDtoD()`, and the interfaces for libraries such as CUFFT and CUBLAS, did not have any way for applications to specify stream parameters. The Thrust library still does not include support. The CUDA Visual Profiler will call out concurrency breaks in its reporting.

6.6 Mapped Pinned Memory

Mapped pinned memory can be used to overlap PCI Express transfers and kernel processing, especially for device→host copies, where there is no need to cover the long latency to host memory. Mapped pinned memory has stricter alignment requirements than the native GPU memcpy, since they must be coalesced. Uncoalesced memory transactions run two to six times slower when using mapped pinned memory.

A naïve port of our `concurrencyMemcpyKernelMapped.cu` program yields an interesting result: On a `cg1.4xlarge` instance in Amazon EC2, mapped pinned memory runs very slowly for values of `cycles` below 64.

CYCLES	MAPPED	STREAMED	SPEEDUP
8	95.15	43.61	0.46
16	96.70	43.95	0.45
24	95.45	44.27	0.46
32	97.54	44.61	0.46
40	94.09	44.93	0.48
48	94.25	45.26	0.48
56	95.18	46.19	0.49
64	28.22	49.29	1.75
72	31.58	52.38	1.66
. . .			
208	92.59	104.60	1.13
216	96.11	107.68	1.12

For small values of `cycles`, the kernel takes a long time to run, as if `cycles` were greater than 200! Only NVIDIA can discover the reason for this performance anomaly for certain, but it is not difficult to work around: By unrolling the inner loop of the kernel, we create more work per thread, and performance improves.

Listing 6.6 `AddKernel()` with loop unrolling.

```
template<const int unrollFactor>
__device__ void
AddKernel_helper( int *out, const int *in, size_t N, int increment, int cycles )
{
    for ( size_t i = unrollFactor*blockIdx.x*blockDim.x+threadIdx.x;
                  i < N;
                  i += unrollFactor*blockDim.x*gridDim.x )
    {
        int values[unrollFactor];

        for ( int iUnroll = 0; iUnroll < unrollFactor; iUnroll++ ) {
            size_t index = i+iUnroll*blockDim.x;
            values[iUnroll] = in[index];
        }
        for ( int iUnroll = 0; iUnroll < unrollFactor; iUnroll++ ) {
            for ( int k = 0; k < cycles; k++ ) {
                values[iUnroll] += increment;
            }
        }
        for ( int iUnroll = 0; iUnroll < unrollFactor; iUnroll++ ) {
            size_t index = i+iUnroll*blockDim.x;
            out[index] = values[iUnroll];
        }
    }
}

__device__ void
AddKernel( int *out, const int *in, size_t N, int increment, int cycles, int
unrollFactor )
{
    switch ( unrollFactor ) {
        case 1: return AddKernel_helper<1>( out, in, N, increment, cycles );
        case 2: return AddKernel_helper<2>( out, in, N, increment, cycles );
        case 4: return AddKernel_helper<4>( out, in, N, increment, cycles );
    }
}
```

Note that this version of `AddKernel()` in Listing 6.6 is functionally identical to the one in Listing 6.3.[8] It just computes `unrollFactor` outputs per loop iteration. Since the unroll factor is a template parameter, the compiler can use

---

8. Except that, as written, N must be divisible by `unrollFactor`. This is easily fixed, of course, with a small change to the for loop and a bit of cleanup code afterward.

registers to hold the `values` array, and the innermost for loops can be unrolled completely.

For `unrollFactor==1`, this implementation is identical to that of Listing 6.3. For `unrollFactor==2`, mapped pinned formulation shows some improvement over the streamed formulation. The tipping point drops from `cycles==64` to `cycles==48`. For `unrollFactor==4`, performance is uniformly better than the streamed version.

CYCLES	MAPPED	STREAMED	SPEEDUP
8	36.73	43.77	1.19
16	34.09	44.23	1.30
24	32.21	44.72	1.39
32	30.67	45.21	1.47
40	29.61	45.90	1.55
48	26.62	49.04	1.84
56	32.26	53.11	1.65
64	36.75	57.23	1.56
72	41.24	61.36	1.49

These values are given for 32M integers, so the program reads and writes 128MB of data. For `cycles==48`, the program runs in 26ms. To achieve that effective bandwidth rate (more than 9GB/s over PCI Express 2.0), the GPU is concurrently reading and writing over PCI Express while performing the kernel processing!

6.7 Concurrent Kernel Processing

SM 2.x-class and later GPUs are capable of concurrently running multiple kernels, provided they are launched in different streams and have block sizes that are small enough so a single kernel will not fill the whole GPU. The code in Listing 6.5 (lines 9–14) will cause kernels to run concurrently, provided the number of blocks in each kernel launch is small enough. Since the kernels can only communicate through global memory, we can add some instrumentation to AddKernel() to track how many kernels are running concurrently. Using the following "kernel concurrency tracking" structure

```
static const int g_maxStreams = 8;
typedef struct KernelConcurrencyData_st {
    int mask; // mask of active kernels
    int maskMax; // atomic max of mask popcount
    int masks[g_maxStreams];
    int count; // number of active kernels
    int countMax; // atomic max of kernel count
    int counts[g_maxStreams];
} KernelConcurrencyData;
```

we can add code to AddKernel() to "check in" and "check out" at the beginning and end of the function, respectively. The "check in" takes the "kernel id" parameter kid (a value in the range 0..NumStreams-1 passed to the kernel), computes a mask 1<<kid corresponding to the kernel ID into a global, and atomically OR's that value into the global. Note that atomicOR() returns the value that was in the memory location before the OR was performed. As a result, the return value has one bit set for every kernel that was active when the atomic OR operation was performed.

Similarly, this code tracks the number of active kernels by incrementing kernelData->count and calling atomicMax() on a shared global.

```
// check in, and record active kernel mask and count
// as seen by this kernel.
if ( kernelData && blockIdx.x==0 && threadIdx.x == 0 ) {
    int myMask = atomicOr( &kernelData->mask, 1<<kid );
    kernelData->masks[kid] = myMask | (1<<kid);
    int myCount = atomicAdd( &kernelData->count, 1 );
    atomicMax( &kernelData->countMax, myCount+1 );
    kernelData->counts[kid] = myCount+1;
}
```

At the bottom of the kernel, similar code clears the mask and decrements the active-kernel count.

```
// check out
if ( kernelData && blockIdx.x==0 && threadIdx.x==0 ) {
    atomicAnd( &kernelData->mask, ~(1<<kid) );
    atomicAdd( &kernelData->count, -1 );
}
```

The kernelData parameter refers to a __device__ variable declared at file scope.

```
__device__ KernelConcurrencyData g_kernelData;
```

Remember that the pointer to g_kernelData must be obtained by calling cudaGetSymbolAddress(). It is possible to write code that references &g_kernelData, but CUDA's language integration will not correctly resolve the address.

The concurrencyKernelKernel.cu program adds support for a command line option blocksPerSM to specify the number of blocks with which to launch these kernels. It will generate a report on the number of kernels that were active. Two sample invocations of concurrencyKernelKernel are as follows.

```
$ ./concurrencyKernelKernel -blocksPerSM 2
Using 2 blocks per SM on GPU with 14 SMs = 28 blocks
Timing sequential operations... Kernel data:
 Masks: ( 0x1 0x0 0x0 0x0 0x0 0x0 0x0 0x0 )
 Up to 1 kernels were active: (0x1 0x0 0x0 0x0 0x0 0x0 0x0 0x0 )

Timing concurrent operations...
Kernel data:
 Masks: ( 0x1 0x3 0x7 0xe 0x1c 0x38 0x60 0xe0 )
 Up to 3 kernels were active: (0x1 0x2 0x3 0x3 0x3 0x3 0x2 0x3 )

$ ./concurrencyKernelKernel -blocksPerSM 3
Using 3 blocks per SM on GPU with 14 SMs = 42 blocks
Timing sequential operations... Kernel data:
 Masks: ( 0x1 0x0 0x0 0x0 0x0 0x0 0x0 0x0 )
 Up to 1 kernels were active: (0x1 0x0 0x0 0x0 0x0 0x0 0x0 0x0 )

Timing concurrent operations... Kernel data:
 Masks: ( 0x1 0x3 0x6 0xc 0x10 0x30 0x60 0x80 )
 Up to 2 kernels were active: (0x1 0x2 0x2 0x2 0x1 0x2 0x2 0x1 )
```

Note that blocksPerSM is the number of blocks specified to each kernel launch, so a total of numStreams*blocksPerSM blocks are launched in numStreams separate kernels. You can see that the hardware can run more kernels concurrently when the kernel grids are smaller, but there is no performance benefit to concurrent kernel processing for the workload discussed in this chapter.

6.8 GPU/GPU Synchronization: `cudaStreamWaitEvent()`

Up to this point, all of the synchronization functions described in this chapter have pertained to CPU/GPU synchronization. They either wait for or query the status of a GPU operation. The `cudaStreamWaitEvent()` function is asynchronous with respect to the CPU and causes the specified *stream* to wait until an event has been recorded. The stream and event need not be associated with the same CUDA device. Section 9.3 describes how such inter-GPU synchronization may be performed and uses the feature to implement a peer-to-peer memcpy (see Listing 9.1).

6.8.1 STREAMS AND EVENTS ON MULTI-GPU: NOTES AND LIMITATIONS

- Streams and events exist in the scope of the context (or device). When `cuCtxDestroy()` or `cudaDeviceReset()` is called, the associated streams and events are destroyed.

- Kernel launches and `cu(da)EventRecord()` can only use CUDA streams in the same context/device.

- `cudaMemcpy()` can be called with any stream, but it is best to call it from the *source* context/device.

- `cudaStreamWaitEvent()` may be called on any event, using any stream.

6.9 Source Code Reference

The source code referenced in this chapter resides in the `concurrency` directory.

FILENAME	DESCRIPTION
`breakevenDtoHMemcpy.cu`	Measures the size of an asynchronous device→host memcpy before the amount of data copied "breaks even" with the driver overhead.

FILENAME	DESCRIPTION
breakevenHtoDMemcpy.cu	Measures the size of an asynchronous host→device memcpy before the amount of data copied "breaks even" with the driver overhead.
breakevenKernelAsync.cu	Measures the amount of work a kernel must do to "break even" with the driver overhead.
concurrencyKernelKernel.cu	Measures kernel-kernel concurrency within one GPU.
concurrencyKernelMapped.cu	Measures relative speed of concurrent memcpy/kernel processing using mapped pinned memory as compared to streams.
concurrencyMemcpyKernel.cu	Measures speedup due to concurrent memcpy and kernel processing for different amounts of work done by the kernel.
concurrencyMemcpyKernelMapped.cu	Measures speedup due to kernels running concurrently using mapped pinned memory.
memcpy16.cpp	SSE-optimized memcpy routine.
nullDtoHMemcpyAsync.cu	Measures throughput of one-byte asynchronous device→host memcpys.
nullDtoHMemcpySync.cu	Measures throughput of one-byte synchronous device→host memcpys.
nullHtoDMemcpyAsync.cu	Measures throughput of one-byte asynchronous host→device memcpys.
nullKernelAsync.cu	Measures throughput of asynchronous kernel launches.
nullKernelSync.cu	Measures throughput of synchronous kernel launches.
pageableMemcpyHtoD.cu	Illustrative example of pageable memcpy routine using standard CUDA programming constructions. Uses memcpy.
pageableMemcpyHtoD16.cu	Illustrative example of pageable memcpy routine using standard CUDA programming constructions.

continues

FILENAME	DESCRIPTION
pageableMemcpyHtoD16Blocking.cu	Identical to pageableMemcpyHtoD16.cu, but uses blocking events for synchronization.
pageableMemcpyHtoD16Broken.cu	Identical to pageableMemcpyHtoD16.cu, with the event synchronization removed.
pageableMemcpyHtoD16Synchronous.cu	Identical to pageableMemcpyHtoD16.cu, but with the event synchronization in a slightly different place that breaks CPU/GPU concurrency.
peer2peerMemcpy.cu	Peer-to-peer memcpy that stages through portable pinned buffers.

Chapter 7

Kernel Execution

This chapter gives a detailed description of how kernels are executed on the GPU: how they are launched, their execution characteristics, how they are organized into grids of blocks of threads, and resource management considerations. The chapter concludes with a description of dynamic parallelism—the new CUDA 5.0 feature that enables CUDA kernels to launch work for the GPU.

7.1 Overview

CUDA kernels execute on the GPU and, since the very first version of CUDA, always have executed concurrently with the CPU. In other words, kernel launches are *asynchronous*: Control is returned to the CPU before the GPU has completed the requested operation. When CUDA was first introduced, there was no need for developers to concern themselves with the asynchrony (or lack thereof) of kernel launches; data had to be copied to and from the GPU explicitly, and the memcpy commands would be enqueued after the commands needed to launch kernels. It was not possible to write CUDA code that exposed the asynchrony of kernel launches; the main side effect was to hide driver overhead when performing multiple kernel launches consecutively.

With the introduction of mapped pinned memory (host memory that can be directly accessed by the GPU), the asynchrony of kernel launches becomes more important, especially for kernels that write to host memory (as opposed to read from it). If a kernel is launched and writes host memory without explicit synchronization (such as with CUDA events), the code suffers from a race condition between the CPU and GPU and may not run correctly. Explicit synchronization often is not needed for kernels that *read* via mapped pinned memory, since any pending writes by the CPU will be posted before the kernel launches. But for kernels that are returning results to CPU by writing to mapped pinned memory, synchronizing to avoid write-after-read hazards is essential.

Once a kernel is launched, it runs as a *grid* of *blocks* of *threads*. Not all blocks run concurrently, necessarily; each block is assigned to a streaming multiprocessor (SM), and each SM can maintain the context for multiple blocks. To cover both memory and instruction latencies, the SM generally needs more warps than a single block can contain. The maximum number of blocks per SM cannot be queried, but it is documented by NVIDIA as having been 8 before SM 3.x and 16 on SM 3.x and later hardware.

The programming model makes no guarantees whatsoever as to the order of execution or whether certain blocks or threads can run concurrently. Developers can never assume that all the threads in a kernel launch are executing concurrently. It is easy to launch more threads than the machine can hold, and some will not start executing until others have finished. Given the lack of ordering guarantees, even initialization of global memory at the beginning of a kernel launch is a difficult proposition.

Dynamic parallelism, a new feature added with the Tesla K20 (GK110), the first SM 3.5–capable GPU, enables kernels to launch other kernels and perform synchronization between them. These capabilities address some of the limitations that were present in CUDA in previous hardware. For example, a dynamically parallel kernel can perform initialization by launching and waiting for a child grid.

7.2 Syntax

When using the CUDA runtime, a kernel launch is specified using the familiar triple-angle-bracket syntax.

```
Kernel<<<gridSize, blockSize, sharedMem, Stream>>>( Parameters… )
```

Kernel specifies the kernel to launch.

gridSize specifies the size of the grid in the form of a dim3 structure.

blockSize specifies the dimension of each threadblock as a dim3 .

sharedMem specifies additional shared memory[1] to reserve for each block.

Stream specifies the stream in which the kernel should be launched.

The dim3 structure used to specify the grid and block sizes has 3 members (x, y, and z) and, when compiling with C++, a constructor with default parameters such that the y and z members default to 1. See Listing 7.1, which is excerpted from the NVIDIA SDK file vector_types.h.

Listing 7.1 dim3 structure.

```
struct __device_builtin__ dim3
{
    unsigned int x, y, z;
#if defined(__cplusplus)
    __host__ __device__ dim3(
    unsigned int vx = 1,
    unsigned int vy = 1,
    unsigned int vz = 1) : x(vx), y(vy), z(vz) {}
    __host__ __device__ dim3(uint3 v) : x(v.x), y(v.y), z(v.z) {}
    __host__ __device__ operator uint3(void) {
        uint3 t;
        t.x = x;
        t.y = y;
        t.z = z;
        return t;
    }
#endif /* __cplusplus */
};
```

Kernels can be launched via the driver API using cuLaunchKernel(), though that function takes the grid and block dimensions as discrete parameters rather than dim3.

```
CUresult cuLaunchKernel (
    CUfunction kernel,
    unsigned int gridDimX,
    unsigned int gridDimY,
    unsigned int gridDimZ,
    unsigned int blockDimX,
    unsigned int blockDimY,
    unsigned int blockDimZ,
    unsigned int sharedMemBytes,
    CUstream hStream,
    void **kernelParams,
    void **extra
);
```

---

1. The amount of shared memory available to the kernel is the sum of this parameter and the amount of shared memory that was statically declared within the kernel.

As with the triple-angle-bracket syntax, the parameters to `cuLaunchKernel()` include the kernel to invoke, the grid and block sizes, the amount of shared memory, and the stream. The main difference is in how the parameters to the kernel itself are given: Since the kernel microcode emitted by `ptxas` contains metadata that describes each kernel's parameters,[2] `kernelParams` is an array of `void *`, where each element corresponds to a kernel parameter. Since the type is known by the driver, the correct amount of memory (4 bytes for an `int`, 8 bytes for a `double`, etc.) will be copied into the command buffer as part of the hardware-specific command used to invoke the kernel.

7.2.1 LIMITATIONS

All C++ classes participating in a kernel launch must be "plain old data" (POD) with the following characteristics.

- No user-declared constructors

- No user-defined copy assignment operator

- No user-defined destructor

- No nonstatic data members that are not themselves PODs

- No private or protected nonstatic data

- No base classes

- No virtual functions

Note that classes that violate these rules may be used in CUDA, or even in CUDA kernels; they simply cannot be used for a kernel launch. In that case, the classes used by a CUDA kernel can be constructed using the POD input data from the launch.

CUDA kernels also do not have return values. They must report their results back via device memory (which must be copied back to the CPU explicitly) or mapped host memory.

---

2. `cuLaunchKernel()` will fail on binary images that were not compiled with CUDA 3.2 or later, since that is the first version to include kernel parameter metadata.

7.2.2 CACHES AND COHERENCY

The GPU contains numerous caches to accelerate computation when reuse occurs. The constant cache is optimized for broadcast to the execution units within an SM; the texture cache reduces external bandwidth usage. Neither of these caches is kept coherent with respect to writes to memory by the GPU. For example, there is no protocol to enforce coherency between these caches and the L1 or L2 caches that serve to reduce latency and aggregate bandwidth to global memory. That means two things.

1. When a kernel is running, it must take care not to write memory that it (or a concurrently running kernel) also is accessing via constant or texture memory.

2. The CUDA driver must invalidate the constant cache and texture cache before each kernel launch.

For kernels that do not contain TEX instructions, there is no need for the CUDA driver to invalidate the texture cache; as a result, kernels that do not use texture incur less driver overhead.

7.2.3 ASYNCHRONY AND ERROR HANDLING

Kernel launches are *asynchronous*: As soon as a kernel is submitted to the hardware, it begins executing in parallel with the CPU.[3] This asynchrony complicates error handling. If a kernel encounters an error (for example, if it reads an invalid memory location), the error is reported to the driver (and the application) sometime after the kernel launch. The surest way to check for such errors is to synchronize with the GPU using cudaDeviceSynchronize() or cuCtxSynchronize(). If an error in kernel execution has occurred, the error code "unspecified launch failure" is returned.

Besides explicit CPU/GPU synchronization calls such as cudaDevice-Synchronize() or cuCtxSynchronize(), this error code may be returned by functions that implicitly synchronize with the CPU, such as synchronous memcpy calls.

---

3. On most platforms, the kernel will start executing on the GPU microseconds after the CPU has finished processing the launch command. But on the Windows Display Driver Model (WDDM), it may take longer because the driver must perform a kernel thunk in order to submit the launch to the hardware, and work for the GPU is enqueued in user mode to amortize the overhead of the user→kernel transition.

Invalid Kernel Launches

It is possible to request a kernel launch that the hardware cannot perform—for example, by specifying more threads per block than the hardware supports. When possible, the driver detects these cases and reports an error rather than trying to submit the launch to the hardware.

The CUDA runtime and the driver API handle this case differently. When an invalid parameter is specified, the driver API's explicit API calls such as cuLaunchGrid() and cuLaunchKernel() return error codes. But when using the CUDA runtime, since kernels are launched in-line with C/C++ code, there is no API call to return an error code. Instead, the error is "recorded" into a thread-local slot and applications can query the error value with cudaGetLastError(). This same error handling mechanism is used for kernel launches that are invalid for other reasons, such as a memory access violation.

7.2.4 TIMEOUTS

Because the GPU is not able to context-switch in the midst of kernel execution, a long-running CUDA kernel may negatively impact the interactivity of a system that uses the GPU to interact with the user. As a result, many CUDA systems implement a "timeout" that resets the GPU if it runs too long without context switching.

On WDDM (Windows Display Driver Model), the timeout is enforced by the operating system. Microsoft has documented how this "Timeout Detection and Recovery" (TDR) works. See http://bit.ly/WPPSdQ, which includes the Registry keys that control TDR behavior.[4] TDR can be safely disabled by using the Tesla Compute Cluster (TCC) driver, though the TCC driver is not available for all hardware.

On Linux, the NVIDIA driver enforces a default timeout of 2 seconds. No timeout is enforced on secondary GPUs that are not being used for display. Developers can query whether a runtime limit is being enforced on a given GPU by calling cuDeviceGetAttribute() with CU_DEVICE_ATTRIBUTE_KERNEL_EXEC_ TIMEOUT, or by examining cudaDeviceProp:: kernelExecTimeoutEnabled.

7.2.5 LOCAL MEMORY

Since local memory is per-thread, and a grid in CUDA can contain thousands of threads, the amount of local memory needed by a CUDA grid can be

---

4. Modifying the Registry should only be done for test purposes, of course.

considerable. The developers of CUDA took pains to preallocate resources to minimize the likelihood that operations such as kernel launches would fail due to a lack of resources, but in the case of local memory, a conservative allocation simply would have consumed too much memory. As a result, kernels that use a large amount of local memory take longer and may be synchronous because the CUDA driver must allocate memory before performing the kernel launch. Furthermore, if the memory allocation fails, the kernel launch will fail due to a lack of resources.

By default, when the CUDA driver must allocate local memory to run a kernel, it frees the memory after the kernel has finished. This behavior additionally makes the kernel launch synchronous. But this behavior can be inhibited by specifying `CU_CTX_LMEM_RESIZE_TO_MAX` to `cuCtxCreate()` or by calling `cudaSetDeviceFlags()` with `cudaDeviceLmemResizeToMax` before the primary context is created. In this case, the increased amount of local memory available will persist after launching a kernel that required more local memory than the default.

7.2.6 SHARED MEMORY

Shared memory is allocated when the kernel is launched, and it stays allocated for the duration of the kernel's execution. Besides static allocations that can be declared in the kernel, shared memory can be declared as an unsized `extern`; in that case, the amount of shared memory to allocate for the unsized array is specified as the third parameter of the kernel launch, or the `sharedMemBytes` parameter to `cuLaunchKernel()`.

7.3 Blocks, Threads, Warps, and Lanes

Kernels are launched as *grids* of *blocks* of threads. Threads can further be divided into 32-thread *warps*, and each thread in a warp is called a *lane*.

7.3.1 GRIDS OF BLOCKS

Thread blocks are separately scheduled onto SMs, and threads within a given block are executed by the same SM. Figure 7.1 shows a 2D grid (8W × 6H) of 2D blocks (8W × 8H). Figure 7.2 shows a 3D grid (8W × 6H × 6D) of 3D blocks (8W × 8H × 4D).

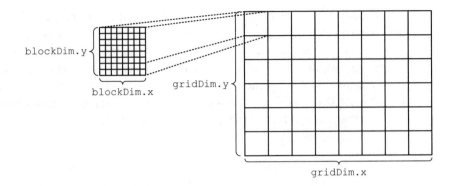

Figure 7.1 2D grid and thread block.

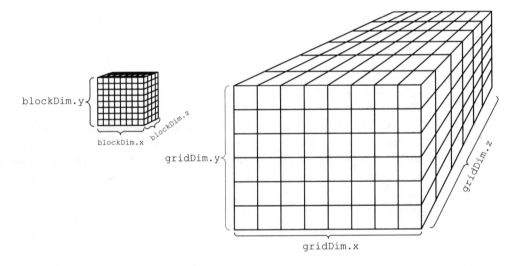

Figure 7.2 3D grid and thread block.

Grids can be up to 65535 x 65535 blocks (for SM 1.x hardware) or 65535 x 65535 x 65535 blocks (for SM 2.x hardware).[5] Blocks may be up to 512 or 1024 threads in size,[6] and threads within a block can communicate via the SM's shared memory. Blocks within a grid are likely to be assigned to different SMs; to maxi-

---

5. The maximum grid size is queryable via CU_DEVICE_ATTRIBUTE_MAX_GRID_DIM_X, CU_DEVICE_ATTRIBUTE_MAX_GRID_DIM_Y, or CU_DEVICE_ATTRIBUTE_MAX_GRID_DIM_Z; or by calling cudaGetDeviceGetProperties() and examining cudaDeviceProp::maxGridSize.
6. The maximum block size is queryable via CU_DEVICE_ATTRIBUTE_MAX_THREADS_PER_BLOCK, or deviceProp.maxThreadsPerBlock.

mize throughput of the hardware, a given SM can run threads and warps from different blocks at the same time. The warp schedulers dispatch instructions as needed resources become available.

Threads

Each threads gets a full complement of registers[7] and a thread ID that is unique within the threadblock. To obviate the need to pass the size of the grid and threadblock into every kernel, the grid and block size also are available for kernels to read at runtime. The built-in variables used to reference these registers are given in Table 7.1. They are all of type `dim3`.

Taken together, these variables can be used to compute which part of a problem the thread will operate on. A "global" index for a thread can be computed as follows.

```
int globalThreadId =
threadIdx.x+blockDim.x*(threadIdx.y+blockDim.y*threadIdx.z);
```

Warps, Lanes, and ILP

The threads themselves are executed together, in SIMD fashion, in units of 32 threads called a *warp*, after the collection of parallel threads in a loom.[8] (See Figure 7.3.) All 32 threads execute the same instruction, each using its private set of registers to perform the requested operation. In a triumph of mixed metaphor, the ID of a thread within a warp is called its *lane*.

Table 7.1 Built-In Variables

BUILT-IN VARIABLE	DESCRIPTION
`gridDim`	Dimension of grid (in thread blocks)
`blockDim`	Dimension of thread block (in threads)
`blockIdx`	Block index (within the grid)
`threadIdx`	Thread index (within the block)

---

7. The more registers needed per thread, the fewer threads can "fit" in a given SM. The percentage of warps executing in an SM as compared to the theoretical maximum is called *occupancy* (see Section 7.4).

8. The warp size can be queried, but it imposes such a huge compatibility burden on the hardware that developers can rely on it staying fixed at 32 for the foreseeable future.

Figure 7.3 Loom.

The warp ID and lane ID can be computed using a global thread ID as follows.

```
int warpID = globalThreadId >> 5;
int laneID = globalThreadId & 31;
```

Warps are an important unit of execution because they are the granularity with which GPUs can cover latency. It has been well documented how GPUs use parallelism to cover memory latency. It takes hundreds of clock cycles to satisfy a global memory request, so when a texture fetch or read is encountered, the GPU issues the memory request and then schedules other instructions until the data arrives. Once the data has arrived, the warp becomes eligible for execution again.

What has been less well documented is that GPUs also use parallelism to exploit ILP ("instruction level parallelism"). ILP refers to fine-grained parallelism that occurs during program execution; for example, when computing `(a+b) * (c+d)`, the addition operations `a+b` and `c+d` can be performed in parallel before the multiplication must be performed. Because the SMs already have a tremendous amount of logic to track dependencies and cover latency, they are very good at covering instruction latency through parallelism (which is effectively ILP) as well as memory latency. GPUs' support for ILP is part of the reason loop unrolling is such an effective optimization strategy. Besides slightly reducing the number of instructions per loop iteration, it exposes more parallelism for the warp schedulers to exploit.

Object Scopes

The scopes of objects that may be referenced by a kernel grid are summarized in Table 7.2, from the most local (registers in each thread) to the most global (global memory and texture references are per grid). Before the advent of dynamic parallelism, thread blocks served primarily as a mechanism for interthread synchronization within a thread block (via intrinsics such as __syncthreads()) and communication (via shared memory). Dynamic parallelism adds resource management to the mix, since streams and events created within a kernel are only valid for threads within the same thread block.

7.3.2 EXECUTION GUARANTEES

It is important that developers never make any assumptions about the order in which blocks or threads will execute. In particular, there is no way to know which block or thread will execute first, so initialization generally should be performed by code outside the kernel invocation.

Table 7.2 Object Scopes

OBJECT	SCOPE
Registers	Thread
Shared memory	Thread block
Local memory	Warp*
Constant memory	Grid
Global memory	Grid
Texture references	Grid
Stream**	Thread block
Event**	Thread block

* In order to execute, a kernel only needs enough local memory to service the maximum number of active warps.

** Streams and events can only be created by CUDA kernels using dynamic parallelism.

Execution Guarantees and Interblock Synchronization

Threads within a given thread block are guaranteed to be resident within the same SM, so they can communicate via shared memory and synchronize execution using intrinsics such as __syncthreads(). But thread blocks do not have any similar mechanisms for data interchange or synchronization.

More sophisticated CUDA developers may ask, *But what about atomic operations in global memory?* Global memory can be updated in a thread-safe manner using atomic operations, so it is tempting to build something like a __syncblocks() function that, like __syncthreads(), waits until all blocks in the kernel launch have arrived before proceeding. Perhaps it would do an atomicInc() on a global memory location and, if atomicInc() did not return the block count, poll that memory location until it did.

The problem is that the execution pattern of the kernel (for example, the mapping of thread blocks onto SMs) varies with the hardware configuration. For example, the number of SMs—and unless the GPU context is big enough to hold the entire grid—*some thread blocks may execute to completion before other thread blocks have started running.* The result is deadlock: Because not all blocks are necessarily resident in the GPU, the blocks that are polling the shared memory location prevent other blocks in the kernel launch from executing.

There are a few special cases when interblock synchronization can work. If simple mutual exclusion is all that's desired, atomicCAS() certainly can be used to provide that. Also, thread blocks can use atomics to signal when they've completed, so the last thread block in a grid can perform some operation before it exits, knowing that all the other thread blocks have completed execution. This strategy is employed by the threadFenceReduction SDK sample and the reduction4SinglePass.cu sample that accompanies this book (see Section 12.2).

7.3.3 BLOCK AND THREAD IDS

A set of special read-only registers give each thread context in the form of a *thread ID* and *block ID*. The thread and block IDs are assigned as a CUDA kernel begins execution; for 2D and 3D grids and blocks, they are assigned in row-major order.

Thread block sizes are best specified in multiples of 32, since warps are the finest possible granularity of execution on the GPU. Figure 7.4 shows how thread IDs are assigned in 32-thread blocks that are 32Wx1H, 16Wx2H, and 8Wx4H, respectively.

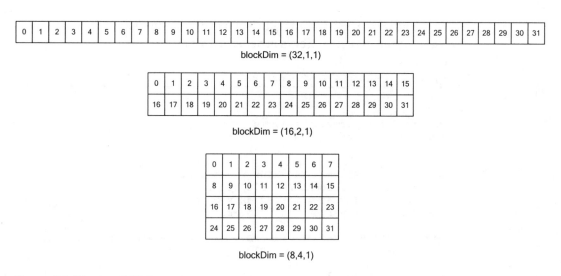

Figure 7.4 Blocks of 32 threads.

For blocks with a thread count that is not a multiple of 32, some warps are not fully populated with active threads. Figure 7.5 shows thread ID assignments for 28-thread blocks that are 28Wx1H, 14Wx2H, and 7Wx4H; in each case, 4 threads in the 32-thread warp are inactive for the duration of the kernel launch. For any thread block size not divisible by 32, some execution resources are wasted, as some warps will be launched with lanes that are disabled for the duration of the kernel execution. There is no performance benefit to 2D or 3D blocks or grids, but they sometimes make for a better match to the application.

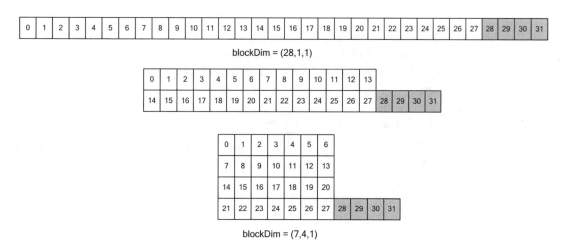

Figure 7.5 Blocks of 28 threads.

The `reportClocks.cu` program illustrates how thread IDs are assigned and how warp-based execution works in general (Listing 7.2).

Listing 7.2 `WriteClockValues` kernel.

```
__global__ void
WriteClockValues(
    unsigned int *completionTimes,
    unsigned int *threadIDs
)
{
    size_t globalBlock = blockIdx.x+blockDim.x*
        (blockIdx.y+blockDim.y*blockIdx.z);
    size_t globalThread = threadIdx.x+blockDim.x*
        (threadIdx.y+blockDim.y*threadIdx.z);

    size_t totalBlockSize = blockDim.x*blockDim.y*blockDim.z;
    size_t globalIndex = globalBlock*totalBlockSize + globalThread;

    completionTimes[globalIndex] = clock();
    threadIDs[globalIndex] = threadIdx.y<<4|threadIdx.x;
}
```

`WriteClockValues()` writes to the two output arrays using a global index computed using the block and thread IDs, and the grid and block sizes. One output array receives the return value from the `clock()` intrinsic, which returns a high-resolution timer value that increments for each warp. In the case of this program, we are using `clock()` to identify which warp processed a given value. `clock()` returns the value of a per-multiprocessor clock cycle counter, so we normalize the values by computing the minimum and subtracting it from all clock cycles values. We call the resulting values the thread's "completion time."

Let's take a look at completion times for threads in a pair of 16Wx8H blocks (Listing 7.3) and compare them to completion times for 14Wx8H blocks (Listing 7.4). As expected, they are grouped in 32s, corresponding to the warp size.

Listing 7.3 Completion times (16W×8H blocks).

```
0.01 ms for 256 threads = 0.03 us/thread
Completion times (clocks):
Grid (0, 0, 0) - slice 0:
    4   4   4   4   4   4   4   4   4   4   4   4   4   4   4   4
    4   4   4   4   4   4   4   4   4   4   4   4   4   4   4   4
    6   6   6   6   6   6   6   6   6   6   6   6   6   6   6   6
    6   6   6   6   6   6   6   6   6   6   6   6   6   6   6   6
```

```
   8   8   8   8   8   8   8   8   8   8   8   8   8   8   8   8
   8   8   8   8   8   8   8   8   8   8   8   8   8   8   8   8
   a   a   a   a   a   a   a   a   a   a   a   a   a   a   a   a
   a   a   a   a   a   a   a   a   a   a   a   a   a   a   a   a
Grid (1, 0, 0) - slice 0:
   0   0   0   0   0   0   0   0   0   0   0   0   0   0   0   0
   0   0   0   0   0   0   0   0   0   0   0   0   0   0   0   0
   2   2   2   2   2   2   2   2   2   2   2   2   2   2   2   2
   2   2   2   2   2   2   2   2   2   2   2   2   2   2   2   2
   4   4   4   4   4   4   4   4   4   4   4   4   4   4   4   4
   4   4   4   4   4   4   4   4   4   4   4   4   4   4   4   4
   6   6   6   6   6   6   6   6   6   6   6   6   6   6   6   6
   6   6   6   6   6   6   6   6   6   6   6   6   6   6   6   6
Thread IDs:
Grid (0, 0, 0) - slice 0:
   0   1   2   3   4   5   6   7   8   9   a   b   c   d   e   f
  10  11  12  13  14  15  16  17  18  19  1a  1b  1c  1d  1e  1f
  20  21  22  23  24  25  26  27  28  29  2a  2b  2c  2d  2e  2f
  30  31  32  33  34  35  36  37  38  39  3a  3b  3c  3d  3e  3f
  40  41  42  43  44  45  46  47  48  49  4a  4b  4c  4d  4e  4f
  50  51  52  53  54  55  56  57  58  59  5a  5b  5c  5d  5e  5f
  60  61  62  63  64  65  66  67  68  69  6a  6b  6c  6d  6e  6f
  70  71  72  73  74  75  76  77  78  79  7a  7b  7c  7d  7e  7f
Grid (1, 0, 0) - slice 0:
   0   1   2   3   4   5   6   7   8   9   a   b   c   d   e   f
  10  11  12  13  14  15  16  17  18  19  1a  1b  1c  1d  1e  1f
  20  21  22  23  24  25  26  27  28  29  2a  2b  2c  2d  2e  2f
  30  31  32  33  34  35  36  37  38  39  3a  3b  3c  3d  3e  3f
  40  41  42  43  44  45  46  47  48  49  4a  4b  4c  4d  4e  4f
  50  51  52  53  54  55  56  57  58  59  5a  5b  5c  5d  5e  5f
  60  61  62  63  64  65  66  67  68  69  6a  6b  6c  6d  6e  6f
  70  71  72  73  74  75  76  77  78  79  7a  7b  7c  7d  7e  7f
```

Listing 7.4 Completion times (14W×8H blocks).

```
Completion times (clocks):
Grid (0, 0, 0) - slice 0:
   6   6   6   6   6   6   6   6   6   6   6   6   6   6
   6   6   6   6   6   6   6   6   6   6   6   6   6   6
   6   6   6   6   8   8   8   8   8   8   8   8   8   8
   8   8   8   8   8   8   8   8   8   8   8   8   8   8
   8   8   8   8   8   8   8   8   a   a   a   a   a   a
   a   a   a   a   a   a   a   a   a   a   a   a   a   a
   a   a   a   a   a   a   a   a   a   a   a   a   c   c
   c   c   c   c   c   c   c   c   c   c   c   c   c   c
Grid (1, 0, 0) - slice 0:
   0   0   0   0   0   0   0   0   0   0   0   0   0   0
   0   0   0   0   0   0   0   0   0   0   0   0   0   0
   0   0   0   0   2   2   2   2   2   2   2   2   2   2
   2   2   2   2   2   2   2   2   2   2   2   2   2   2
   2   2   2   2   2   2   2   4   4   4   4   4   4   4
   4   4   4   4   4   4   4   4   4   4   4   4   4   4
```

```
 4   4   4   4   4   4   4   4   4   4   4   4   6   6
 6   6   6   6   6   6   6   6   6   6   6   6   6   6
Thread IDs:
Grid (0, 0, 0) - slice 0:
  0   1   2   3   4   5   6   7   8   9   a   b   c   d
 10  11  12  13  14  15  16  17  18  19  1a  1b  1c  1d
 20  21  22  23  24  25  26  27  28  29  2a  2b  2c  2d
 30  31  32  33  34  35  36  37  38  39  3a  3b  3c  3d
 40  41  42  43  44  45  46  47  48  49  4a  4b  4c  4d
 50  51  52  53  54  55  56  57  58  59  5a  5b  5c  5d
 60  61  62  63  64  65  66  67  68  69  6a  6b  6c  6d
 70  71  72  73  74  75  76  77  78  79  7a  7b  7c  7d
Grid (1, 0, 0) - slice 0:
  0   1   2   3   4   5   6   7   8   9   a   b   c   d
 10  11  12  13  14  15  16  17  18  19  1a  1b  1c  1d
 20  21  22  23  24  25  26  27  28  29  2a  2b  2c  2d
 30  31  32  33  34  35  36  37  38  39  3a  3b  3c  3d
 40  41  42  43  44  45  46  47  48  49  4a  4b  4c  4d
 50  51  52  53  54  55  56  57  58  59  5a  5b  5c  5d
 60  61  62  63  64  65  66  67  68  69  6a  6b  6c  6d
 70  71  72  73  74  75  76  77  78  79  7a  7b  7c  7d
```

The completion times for the 14Wx8H blocks given in Listing 7.4 underscore how the thread IDs map to warps. In the case of the 14Wx8H blocks, every warp holds only 28 threads; 12.5% of the number of possible thread lanes are idle throughout the kernel's execution. To avoid this waste, developers always should try to make sure blocks contain a multiple of 32 threads.

7.4 Occupancy

Occupancy is a ratio that measures the number of threads/SM that *will* run in a given kernel launch, as opposed to the maximum number of threads that *potentially could be running* on that SM.

$$\frac{Warps\ per\ SM}{Max.Warps\ per\ SM}$$

The denominator (maximum warps per SM) is a constant that depends only on the compute capability of the device. The numerator of this expression, which determines the occupancy, is a function of the following.

- Compute capability (1.0, 1.1, 1.2, 1.3, 2.0, 2.1, 3.0, 3.5)

- Threads per block

- Registers per thread

- Shared memory configuration[9]

- Shared memory per block

To help developers assess the tradeoffs between these parameters, the CUDA Toolkit includes an occupancy calculator in the form of an Excel spreadsheet.[10] Given the inputs above, the spreadsheet will calculate the following results.

- Active thread count

- Active warp count

- Active block count

- Occupancy (active warp count divided into the hardware's maximum number of active warps)

The spreadsheet also identifies whichever parameter is limiting the occupancy.

- Registers per multiprocessor

- Maximum number of warps or blocks per multiprocessor

- Shared memory per multiprocessor

Note that occupancy is not the be-all and end-all of CUDA performance;[11] often it is better to use more registers per thread and rely on instruction-level parallelism (ILP) to deliver performance. NVIDIA has a good presentation on warps and occupancy that discusses the tradeoffs.[12]

An example of a low-occupancy kernel that can achieve near-maximum global memory bandwidth is given in Section 5.2.10 (Listing 5.5). The inner loop of the GlobalReads kernel can be unrolled according to a template parameter; as the number of unrolled iterations increases, the number of needed registers increases and the occupancy goes down. For the Tesla M2050's in the cg1.4xlarge instance type, for example, the peak read bandwidth reported (with ECC disabled) is 124GiB/s, with occupancy of 66%. Volkov reports achieving

---

9. For SM 2.x and later only. Developers can split the 64K L1 cache in the SM as 16K shared/48K L1 or 48K shared/16K L1. (SM 3.x adds the ability to split the cache evenly as 32K shared/32K L1.)
10. Typically it is in the tools subdirectory—for example, %CUDA_PATH%/tools (Windows) or $CUDA_PATH/tools.
11. Vasily Volkov emphatically makes this point in his presentation "Better Performance at Lower Occupancy." It is available at http://bit.ly/YdScNG.
12. http://bit.ly/WHTb5m

near-peak memory bandwidth when running kernels whose occupancy is in the
single digits.

7.5 Dynamic Parallelism

Dynamic parallelism, a new capability that works only on SM 3.5–class hardware,
enables CUDA kernels to launch other CUDA kernels, and also to invoke various
functions in the CUDA runtime. When using dynamic parallelism, a subset of
the CUDA runtime (known as the *device runtime*) becomes available for use by
threads running on the device.

Dynamic parallelism introduces the idea of "parent" and "child" grids. Any
kernel invoked by another CUDA kernel (as opposed to host code, as done in all
previous CUDA versions) is a "child kernel," and the invoking grid is its "parent."
By default, CUDA supports two (2) nesting levels (one for the parent and one for
the child), a number that may be increased by calling `cudaSetDeviceLimit()`
with `cudaLimitDevRuntimeSyncDepth`.

Dynamic parallelism was designed to address applications that previously had
to deliver results to the CPU so the CPU could specify which work to perform
on the GPU. Such "handshaking" disrupts CPU/GPU concurrency in the execution pipeline described in Section 2.5.1, in which the CPU produces commands
for consumption by the GPU. The GPU's time is too valuable for it to wait for the
CPU to read and analyze results before issuing more work. Dynamic parallelism
avoids these pipeline bubbles by enabling the GPU to launch work for itself from
kernels.

Dynamic parallelism can improve performance in several cases.

- It enables initialization of data structures needed by a kernel before the kernel can begin execution. Previously, such initialization had to be taken care of
  in host code or by previously invoking a separate kernel.

- It enables simplified recursion for applications such as Barnes-Hut gravitational integration or hierarchical grid evaluation for aerodynamic simulations.

NOTE
Dynamic parallelism only works within a given GPU. Kernels can invoke
memory copies or other kernels, but they cannot submit work to other
GPUs.

7.5.1 SCOPING AND SYNCHRONIZATION

With the notable exception of block and grid size, child grids inherit most kernel configuration parameters, such as the shared memory configuration (set by `cudaDeviceSetCacheConfig()`), from their parents. Thread blocks are a unit of scope: Streams and events created by a thread block can only be used by that thread block (they are not even inherited for use by child grids), and they are automatically destroyed when the thread block exits.

NOTE

Resources created on the device via dynamic parallelism are strictly separated from resources created on the host. Streams and events created on the host may not be used on the device via dynamic parallelism, and vice versa.

CUDA guarantees that a parent grid is not considered complete until all of its children have finished. Although the parent may execute concurrently with the child, there is no guarantee that a child grid will begin execution until its parent calls `cudaDeviceSynchronize()`.

If all threads in a thread block exit, execution of the thread block is suspended until all child grids have finished. If that synchronization is not sufficient, developers can use CUDA streams and events for explicit synchronization. As on the host, operations within a given stream are performed in the order of submission. Operations can only execute concurrently if they are specified in different streams, and there is no guarantee that operations will, in fact, execute concurrently. If needed, synchronization primitives such as `__syncthreads()` can be used to coordinate the order of submission to a given stream.

NOTE

Streams and events created on the device may not be used outside the thread block that created them.

`cudaDeviceSynchronize()` synchronizes on all pending work launched by any thread in the thread block. It does not, however, perform any interthread synchronization, so if there is a desire to synchronize on work launched by other threads, developers must use `__syncthreads()` or other block-level synchronization primitives (see Section 8.6.2).

7.5.2 MEMORY MODEL

Parent and child grids share the same global and constant memory storage, but they have distinct local and shared memory.

Global Memory

There are two points in the execution of a child grid when its view of memory is fully consistent with the parent grid: when the child grid is invoked by the parent and when the child grid completes as signaled by a synchronization API invocation in the parent thread.

All global memory operations in the parent thread prior to the child thread's invocation are visible to the child grid. All memory operations of the child grid are visible to the parent after the parent has synchronized on the child grid's completion. Zero-copy memory has the same coherence and consistency guarantees as global memory.

Constant Memory

Constants are immutable and may not be modified from the device during kernel execution. Taking the address of a constant memory object from within a kernel thread has the same semantics as for all CUDA programs,[13] and passing that pointer between parents and their children is fully supported.

Shared and Local Memory

Shared and local memory is private to a thread block or thread, respectively, and is not visible or coherent between parent and child. When an object in one of these locations is referenced outside its scope, the behavior is undefined and would likely cause an error.

If nvcc detects an attempt to misuse a pointer to shared or local memory, it will issue a warning. Developers can use the __isGlobal() intrinsic to determine whether a given pointer references global memory. Pointers to shared or local memory are not valid parameters to cudaMemcpy*Async() or cudaMemset*Async().

Local Memory

Local memory is private storage for an executing thread and is not visible outside of that thread. It is illegal to pass a pointer to local memory as a launch

---

13. Note that in device code, the address must be taken with the "address-of" operator (unary operator&), since cudaGetSymbolAddress() is not supported by the device runtime.

argument when launching a child kernel. The result of dereferencing such a local memory pointer from a child will be undefined. To guarantee that this rule is not inadvertently violated by the compiler, all storage passed to a child kernel should be allocated explicitly from the global memory heap.

Texture Memory

Concurrent accesses by parent and child may result in inconsistent data and should be avoided. That said, a degree of coherency between parent and child is enforced by the runtime. A child kernel can use texturing to access memory written by its parent, but writes to memory by a child will not be reflected in the texture memory accesses by a parent until *after* the parent synchronizes on the child's completion. Texture objects are well supported in the device runtime. They cannot be created or destroyed, but they can be passed in and used by any grid in the hierarchy (parent or child).

7.5.3 STREAMS AND EVENTS

Streams and events created by the device runtime can be used only within the thread block that created the stream. The NULL stream has different semantics in the device runtime than in the host runtime. On the host, synchronizing with the NULL stream forces a "join" of all the other streamed operations on the GPU (as described in Section 6.2.3); on the device, the NULL stream is its own stream, and any interstream synchronization must be performed using events.

When using the device runtime, streams must be created with the cudaStream-NonBlocking flag (a parameter to cudaStreamCreateWithFlags()). The cudaStreamSynchronize() call is not supported; synchronization must be implemented in terms of events and cudaStreamWaitEvent().

Only the interstream synchronization capabilities of CUDA events are supported. As a consequence, cudaEventSynchronize(), cudaEventElapsedTime(), and cudaEventQuery() are not supported. Additionally, because timing is not supported, events must be created by passing the cudaEventDisableTiming flag to cudaEventCreateWithFlags().

7.5.4 ERROR HANDLING

Any function in the device runtime may return an error (cudaError_t). The error is recorded in a per-thread slot that can be queried by calling cudaGetLastError(). As with the host-based runtime, CUDA makes a distinction between errors that can be returned immediately (e.g., if an invalid parameter is passed to a memcpy function) and errors that must be reported asynchronously (e.g., if a launch performed an invalid memory access). If a child grid causes an error at runtime, CUDA will return an error to the host, not to the parent grid.

7.5.5 COMPILING AND LINKING

Unlike the host runtime, developers must explicitly link against the device runtime's static library when using the device runtime. On Windows, the device runtime is cudadevrt.lib; on Linux and MacOS, it is cudadevrt.a. When building with nvcc, this may be accomplished by appending -lcudadevrt to the command line.

7.5.6 RESOURCE MANAGEMENT

Whenever a kernel launches a child grid, the child is considered a new *nesting level*, and the total number of levels is the *nesting depth* of the program. In contrast, the deepest level at which the program will explicitly synchronize on a child launch is called the *synchronization depth*. Typically the synchronization depth is one less than the nesting depth of the program, but if the program does not always need to call cudaDeviceSynchronize(), then it may be substantially less than the nesting depth.

The theoretical maximum nesting depth is 24, but in practice it is governed by the device limit cudaLimitDevRuntimeSyncDepth. Any launch that would result in a kernel at a deeper level than the maximum will fail. The default maximum synchronization depth level is 2. The limits must be configured before the top-level kernel is launched from the host.

NOTE

Calling a device runtime function such as cudaMemcpyAsync() may invoke a kernel, increasing the nesting depth by 1.

For parent kernels that never call cudaDeviceSynchronize(), the system does not have to reserve space for the parent kernel. In this case, the memory footprint required for a program will be much less than the conservative maximum. Such a program could specify a shallower maximum synchronization depth to avoid overallocation of backing store.

Memory Footprint

The device runtime system software reserves device memory for the following purposes.

- To track pending grid launches

- To save saving parent-grid state during synchronization

- To serve as an allocation heap for `malloc()` and `cudaMalloc()` calls from kernels

This memory is not available for use by the application, so some applications may wish to reduce the default allocations, and some applications may have to increase the default values in order to operate correctly. To change the default values, developers call `cudaDeviceSetLimit()`, as summarized in Table 7.3. The limit `cudaLimitDevRuntimeSyncDepth` is especially important, since each nesting level costs up to 150MB of device memory.

Pending Kernel Launches

When a kernel is launched, all associated configuration and parameter data is tracked until the kernel completes. This data is stored within a

Table 7.3 `cudaDeviceSetLimit()` Values

LIMIT	BEHAVIOR
`cudaLimitDevRuntimeSyncDepth`	Sets the maximum depth at which `cudaDevice-Synchronize()` may be called. Launches may be performed deeper than this, but explicit synchronization deeper than this limit will return the error `cudaErrorLaunchMaxDepthExceeded`. The default maximum sync depth is 2.
`cudaLimitDevRuntimePendingLaunchCount`	Controls the amount of memory set aside for buffering kernel launches that have not yet begun to execute, due either to unresolved dependencies or lack of execution resources. When the buffer is full, launches will set the thread's last error to `cudaErrorLaunchPendingCountExceeded`. The default pending launch count is 2048 launches.
`cudaLimitMallocHeapSize`	Sets the size of the device runtime's heap that can be allocated by calling `malloc()` or `cudaMalloc()` from a kernel.

system-managed launch pool. The size of the launch pool is configurable by calling `cudaDeviceSetLimit()` from the host and specifying `cudaLimitDevRuntimePendingLaunchCount`.

Configuration Options

Resource allocation for the device runtime system software is controlled via the `cudaDeviceSetLimit()` API from the host program. Limits must be set before any kernel is launched and may not be changed while the GPU is actively running programs.

Memory allocated by the device runtime must be freed by the device runtime. Also, memory is allocated by the device runtime out of a preallocated heap whose size is specified by the device limit `cudaLimitMallocHeapSize`. The named limits in Table 7.3 may be set.

7.5.7 SUMMARY

Table 7.4 summarizes the key differences and limitations between the device runtime and the host runtime. Table 7.5 lists the subset of functions that may be called from the device runtime, along with any pertinent limitations.

Table 7.4 Device Runtime Limitations

CAPABILITY	LIMITATIONS AND DIFFERENCES
Events	Thread block scope only No query support No timing support; must be created with `cudaEventCreateWithFlags(cudaEventDisableTiming)` Limited synchronization support; use `cudaStreamWaitEvent()`
Local Memory	Local to grid only; cannot be passed to child grids
NULL Stream	Does not enforce join with other streams
Shared Memory	Local to grid only; cannot be passed to child grids
Streams	Thread block scope only No query support Limited synchronization support; use `cudaStreamWaitEvent()`

Table 7.4 Device Runtime Limitations *(Continued)*

CAPABILITY	LIMITATIONS AND DIFFERENCES
Textures	Texture references (pre–CUDA 5.0, module-scope textures) may be used only from top-level kernels launched from the host.
Texture and Surface Objects	SM 3.x–only texture and surface objects cannot be created or destroyed by the device runtime, but they can be used freely on the device.

Table 7.5 CUDA Device Runtime Functions

RUNTIME API FUNCTION	NOTES
cudaDeviceSynchronize	Synchronizes on work launched from thread's own thread block only
cudaDeviceGetCacheConfig	
cudaDeviceGetLimit	
cudaGetLastError	Last error is per-thread state, not per-block
cudaPeekAtLastError	
cudaGetErrorString	
cudaGetDeviceCount	
cudaGetDeviceProperty	Can return properties for any device
cudaGetDevice	Always returns current device ID as would be seen by the host
cudaStreamCreateWithFlags	Must pass cudaStreamNonBlocking flag
cudaStreamDestroy	
cudaStreamWaitEvent	
cudaEventCreateWithFlags	Must pass cudaEventDisableTiming flag

continues

Table 7.5 CUDA Device Runtime Functions *(Continued)*

RUNTIME API FUNCTION	NOTES
cudaEventRecord	
cudaEventDestroy	
cudaFuncGetAttributes	
cudaMemcpyAsync	
cudaMemcpy2DAsync	
cudaMemcpy3DAsync	
cudaMemsetAsync	
cudaMemset2DAsync	
cudaMemset3DAsync	
cudaRuntimeGetVersion	
cudaMalloc	Only may be freed by device
cudaFree	Can free memory allocated by device only

Chapter 8

Streaming Multiprocessors

The streaming multiprocessors (SMs) are the part of the GPU that runs our CUDA kernels. Each SM contains the following.

- Thousands of registers that can be partitioned among threads of execution

- Several caches:

  - *Shared memory* for fast data interchange between threads

  - *Constant cache* for fast broadcast of reads from constant memory

  - *Texture cache* to aggregate bandwidth from texture memory

  - *L1 cache* to reduce latency to local or global memory

- *Warp schedulers* that can quickly switch contexts between threads and issue instructions to warps that are ready to execute

- Execution cores for integer and floating-point operations:

  - Integer and single-precision floating point operations

  - Double-precision floating point

  - Special Function Units (SFUs) for single-precision floating-point transcendental functions

The reason there are many registers and the reason the hardware can context switch between threads so efficiently are to maximize the throughput of the hardware. The GPU is designed to have enough state to cover both execution latency and the memory latency of hundreds of clock cycles that it may take for data from device memory to arrive after a read instruction is executed.

The SMs are general-purpose processors, but they are designed very differently than the execution cores in CPUs: They target much lower clock rates; they support instruction-level parallelism, but not branch prediction or speculative execution; and they have less cache, if they have any cache at all. For suitable workloads, the sheer computing horsepower in a GPU more than makes up for these disadvantages.

The design of the SM has been evolving rapidly since the introduction of the first CUDA-capable hardware in 2006, with three major revisions, codenamed Tesla, Fermi, and Kepler. Developers can query the compute capability by calling `cudaGetDeviceProperties()` and examining `cudaDeviceProp.major` and `cudaDeviceProp.minor`, or by calling the driver API function `cuDevice-ComputeCapability()`. Compute capability 1.x, 2.x, and 3.x correspond to Tesla-class, Fermi-class, and Kepler-class hardware, respectively. Table 8.1 summarizes the capabilities added in each generation of the SM hardware.

Table 8.1 SM Capabilities

COMPUTE LEVEL	INTRODUCED ...
SM 1.1	Global memory atomics; mapped pinned memory; debuggable (e.g., breakpoint instruction)
SM 1.2	Relaxed coalescing constraints; warp voting (`any()` and `all()` intrinsics); atomic operations on shared memory
SM 1.3	Double precision support
SM 2.0	64-bit addressing; L1 and L2 cache; concurrent kernel execution; configurable 16K or 48K shared memory; bit manipulation instructions (`__clz()`, `__popc()`, `__ffs()`, `__brev()` intrinsics); directed rounding for single-precision floating-point values; fused multiply-add; 64-bit clock counter; surface load/store; 64-bit global atomic add, exchange, and compare-and-swap; global atomic add for single-precision floating-point values; warp voting (`ballot()` intrinsic); assertions and formatted output (`printf`).
SM 2.1	Function calls and indirect calls in kernels

Table 8.1 SM Capabilities *(Continued)*

COMPUTE LEVEL	INTRODUCED . . .
SM 3.0	Increase maximum grid size; warp shuffle; permute; 32K/32K shared memory configuration; configurable shared memory (32- or 64-bit mode) Bindless textures ("texture objects"); faster global atomics
SM 3.5	64-bit atomic min, max, AND, OR, and XOR; 64-bit funnel shift; read global memory via texture; dynamic parallelism

In Chapter 2, Figures 2.29 through 2.32 show block diagrams of different SMs. CUDA cores can execute integer and single-precision floating-point instructions; one double-precision unit implements double-precision support, if available; and Special Function Units implement reciprocal, reciprocal square root, sine/cosine, and logarithm/exponential functions. Warp schedulers dispatch instructions to these execution units as the resources needed to execute the instruction become available.

This chapter focuses on the instruction set capabilities of the SM. As such, it sometimes refers to the "SASS" instructions, the native instructions into which `ptxas` or the CUDA driver translate intermediate PTX code. Developers are not able to author SASS code directly; instead, NVIDIA has made these instructions visible to developers through the `cuobjdump` utility so they can direct optimizations of their source code by examining the compiled microcode.

8.1 Memory

8.1.1 REGISTERS

Each SM contains thousands of 32-bit registers that are allocated to threads as specified when the kernel is launched. Registers are both the fastest and most plentiful memory in the SM. As an example, the Kepler-class (SM 3.0) SMX contains 65,536 registers or 256K, while the texture cache is only 48K.

CUDA registers can contain integer or floating-point data; for hardware capable of performing double-precision arithmetic (SM 1.3 and higher), the operands are contained in even-valued register pairs. On SM 2.0 and higher hardware, register pairs also can hold 64-bit addresses.

CUDA hardware also supports wider memory transactions: The built-in int2/ float2 and int4/float4 data types, residing in aligned register pairs or quads, respectively, may be read or written using single 64- or 128-bit-wide loads or stores. Once in registers, the individual data elements can be referenced as .x/.y (for int2/float2) or .x/.y/.z/.w (for int4/float4).

Developers can cause nvcc to report the number of registers used by a kernel by specifying the command-line option --ptxas-options --verbose. The number of registers used by a kernel affects the number of threads that can fit in an SM and often must be tuned carefully for optimal performance. The maximum number of registers used for a compilation may be specified with --ptxas-options --maxregcount N.

Register Aliasing

Because registers can hold floating-point or integer data, some intrinsics serve only to coerce the compiler into changing its view of a variable. The __int_ as_float() and __float_as_int() intrinsics cause a variable to "change personalities" between 32-bit integer and single-precision floating point.

```
float   __int_as_float( int i );
int   __float_as_int( float f );
```

The __double2loint(), __double2hiint(), and __hiloint2double() intrinsics similarly cause registers to change personality (usually in-place). __double_as_longlong() and __longlong_as_double() coerce register pairs in-place; __double2loint() and __double2hiint() return the least and the most significant 32 bits of the input operand, respectively; and __hiloint2double() constructs a double out of the high and low halves.

```
int double2loint( double d );
int double2hiint( double d );
int hiloint2double( int hi, int lo );
double long_as_double(long long int i );
long long int __double_as_longlong( double d );
```

8.1.2 LOCAL MEMORY

Local memory is used to spill registers and also to hold local variables that are indexed and whose indices cannot be computed at compile time. Local memory is backed by the same pool of device memory as global memory, so it exhibits the same latency characteristics and benefits as the L1 and L2 cache hierarchy on Fermi and later hardware. Local memory is addressed in such a way that the memory transactions are automatically coalesced. The hardware includes special instructions to load and store local memory: The SASS variants are LLD/LST for Tesla and LDL/STL for Fermi and Kepler.

8.1.3 GLOBAL MEMORY

The SMs can read or write global memory using GLD/GST instructions (on Tesla) and LD/ST instructions (on Fermi and Kepler). Developers can use standard C operators to compute and dereference addresses, including pointer arithmetic and the dereferencing operators *, [], and ->. Operating on 64- or 128-bit built-in data types (int2/float2/int4/float4) automatically causes the compiler to issue 64- or 128-bit load and store instructions. Maximum memory performance is achieved through *coalescing* of memory transactions, described in Section 5.2.9.

Tesla-class hardware (SM 1.x) uses special address registers to hold pointers; later hardware implements a load/store architecture that uses the same register file for pointers; integer and floating-point values; and the same address space for constant memory, shared memory, and global memory.[1]

Fermi-class hardware includes several features not available on older hardware.

- 64-bit addressing is supported via "wide" load/store instructions in which addresses are held in even-numbered register pairs. 64-bit addressing is not supported on 32-bit host platforms; on 64-bit host platforms, 64-bit addressing is enabled automatically. As a result, code generated for the same kernels compiled for 32- and 64-bit host platforms may have different register counts and performance.

- The L1 cache may be configured to be 16K or 48K in size.[2] (Kepler added the ability to split the cache as 32K L1/32K shared.) Load instructions can include cacheability hints (to tell the hardware to pull the read into L1 or to bypass the L1 and keep the data only in L2). These may be accessed via inline PTX or through the command line option –X ptxas –dlcm=ca (cache in L1 and L2, the default setting) or –X ptxas –dlcm=cg (cache only in L2).

Atomic operations (or just "atomics") update a memory location in a way that works correctly even when multiple GPU threads are operating on the same

---

1. Both constant and shared memory exist in address windows that enable them to be referenced by 32-bit addresses even on 64-bit architectures.
2. The hardware can change this configuration per kernel launch, but changing this state is expensive and will break concurrency for concurrent kernel launches.

memory location. The hardware enforces mutual exclusion on the memory location for the duration of the operation. Since the order of operations is not guaranteed, the operators supported generally are associative.[3]

Atomics first became available for global memory for SM 1.1 and greater and for shared memory for SM 1.2 and greater. Until the Kepler generation of hardware, however, global memory atomics were too slow to be useful.

The global atomic intrinsics, summarized in Table 8.2, become automatically available when the appropriate architecture is specified to nvcc via --gpu-architecture. All of these intrinsics can operate on 32-bit integers. 64-bit support for atomicAdd(), atomicExch(), and atomicCAS() was added

Table 8.2 Atomic Operations

MNEMONIC	DESCRIPTION
atomicAdd	Addition
atomicSub	Subtraction
atomicExch	Exchange
atomicMin	Minimum
atomicMax	Maximum
atomicInc	Increment (add 1)
atomicDec	Decrement (subtract 1)
atomicCAS	Compare and swap
atomicAnd	AND
atomicOr	OR
atomicXor	XOR

---

3. The only exception is single-precision floating-point addition. Then again, floating-point code generally must be robust in the face of the lack of associativity of floating-point operations; porting to different hardware, or even just recompiling the same code with different compiler options, can change the order of floating-point operations and thus the result.

in SM 1.2. `atomicAdd()` of 32-bit floating-point values (`float`) was added in SM 2.0. 64-bit support for `atomicMin()`, `atomicMax()`, `atomicAnd()`, `atomicOr()`, and `atomicXor()` was added in SM 3.5.

NOTE

Because atomic operations are implemented using hardware in the GPU's integrated memory controller, they do not work across the PCI Express bus and thus do not work correctly on device memory pointers that correspond to host memory or peer memory.

At the hardware level, atomics come in two forms: atomic operations that return the value that was at the specified memory location before the operator was performed, and reduction operations that the developer can "fire and forget" at the memory location, ignoring the return value. Since the hardware can perform the operation more efficiently if there is no need to return the old value, the compiler detects whether the return value is used and, if it is not, emits different instructions. In SM 2.0, for example, the instructions are called ATOM and RED, respectively.

8.1.4 CONSTANT MEMORY

Constant memory resides in device memory, but it is backed by a different, read-only cache that is optimized to broadcast the results of read requests to threads that all reference the same memory location. Each SM contains a small, latency-optimized cache for purposes of servicing these read requests. Making the memory (and the cache) read-only simplifies cache management, since the hardware has no need to implement write-back policies to deal with memory that has been updated.

SM 2.x and subsequent hardware includes a special optimization for memory that is not denoted as constant but that the compiler has identified as (1) read-only and (2) whose address is not dependent on the block or thread ID. The "load uniform" (LDU) instruction reads memory using the constant cache hierarchy and broadcasts the data to the threads.

8.1.5 SHARED MEMORY

Shared memory is very fast, on-chip memory in the SM that threads can use for data interchange within a thread block. Since it is a per-SM resource, shared memory usage can affect occupancy, the number of warps that the SM can keep resident. SMs load and store shared memory with special instructions: G2R/R2G on SM 1.x, and LDS/STS on SM 2.x and later.

Shared memory is arranged as interleaved *banks* and generally is optimized for 32-bit access. If more than one thread in a warp references the same bank, a *bank conflict* occurs, and the hardware must handle memory requests consecutively until all requests have been serviced. Typically, to avoid bank conflicts, applications access shared memory with an interleaved pattern based on the thread ID, such as the following.

```
extern __shared__ float shared[];
float data = shared[BaseIndex + threadIdx.x];
```

Having all threads in a warp read from the same 32-bit shared memory location also is fast. The hardware includes a broadcast mechanism to optimize for this case. Writes to the same bank are serialized by the hardware, reducing performance. Writes to the same *address* cause race conditions and should be avoided.

For 2D access patterns (such as tiles of pixels in an image processing kernel), it's good practice to pad the shared memory allocation so the kernel can reference adjacent rows without causing bank conflicts. SM 2.x and subsequent hardware has 32 banks,[4] so for 2D tiles where threads in the same warp may access the data by row, it is a good strategy to pad the tile size to a multiple of 33 32-bit words.

On SM 1.x hardware, shared memory is about 16K in size;[5] on later hardware, there is a total of 64K of L1 cache that may be configured as 16K or 48K of shared memory, of which the remainder is used as L1 cache.[6]

Over the last few generations of hardware, NVIDIA has improved the hardware's handling of operand sizes other than 32 bits. On SM 1.x hardware, 8- and 16-bit reads from the same bank caused bank conflicts, while SM 2.x and later hardware can broadcast reads of any size out of the same bank. Similarly, 64-bit operands (such as double) in shared memory were so much slower than 32-bit operands on SM 1.x that developers sometimes had to resort to storing the data as separate high and low halves. SM 3.x hardware adds a new feature for

---

4. SM 1.x hardware had 16 banks (memory traffic from the first 16 threads and the second 16 threads of a warp was serviced separately), but strategies that work well on subsequent hardware also work well on SM 1.x.
5. 256 bytes of shared memory was reserved for parameter passing; in SM 2.x and later, parameters are passed via constant memory.
6. SM 3.x hardware adds the ability to split the cache evenly as 32K L1/32K shared.

kernels that predominantly use 64-bit operands in shared memory: a mode that increases the bank size to 64 bits.

Atomics in Shared Memory

SM 1.2 added the ability to perform atomic operations in shared memory. Unlike global memory, which implements atomics using single instructions (either GATOM or GRED, depending on whether the return value is used), shared memory atomics are implemented with explicit lock/unlock semantics, and the compiler emits code that causes each thread to loop over these lock operations until the thread has performed its atomic operation.

Listing 8.1 gives the source code to atomic32Shared.cu, a program specifically intended to be compiled to highlight the code generation for shared memory atomics. Listing 8.2 shows the resulting microcode generated for SM 2.0. Note how the LDSLK (load shared with lock) instruction returns a predicate that tells whether the lock was acquired, the code to perform the update is predicated, and the code loops until the lock is acquired and the update performed.

The lock is performed per 32-bit word, and the index of the lock is determined by bits 2–9 of the shared memory address. Take care to avoid contention, or the loop in Listing 8.2 may iterate up to 32 times.

Listing 8.1. atomic32Shared.cu.

```
__global__ void
Return32( int *sum, int *out, const int *pIn )
{
    extern __shared__ int s[];
    s[threadIdx.x] = pIn[threadIdx.x];
    __syncthreads();
    (void) atomicAdd( &s[threadIdx.x], *pIn );
    __syncthreads();
    out[threadIdx.x] = s[threadIdx.x];
}
```

Listing 8.2 atomic32Shared.cubin (microcode compiled for SM 2.0).

```
code for sm_20
      Function : _Z8Return32PiS_PKi
/*0000*/      MOV R1, c [0x1] [0x100];
/*0008*/      S2R R0, SR_Tid_X;
/*0010*/      SHL R3, R0, 0x2;
/*0018*/      MOV R0, c [0x0] [0x28];
/*0020*/      IADD R2, R3, c [0x0] [0x28];
```

```
/*0028*/        IMAD.U32.U32 RZ, R0, R1, RZ;
/*0030*/        LD R2, [R2];
/*0038*/        STS [R3], R2;
/*0040*/        SSY 0x80;
/*0048*/        BAR.RED.POPC RZ, RZ;
/*0050*/        LD R0, [R0];
/*0058*/        LDSLK P0, R2, [R3];
/*0060*/        @P0 IADD R2, R2, R0;
/*0068*/        @P0 STSUL [R3], R2;
/*0070*/        @!P0 BRA 0x58;
/*0078*/        NOP.S CC.T;
/*0080*/        BAR.RED.POPC RZ, RZ;
/*0088*/        LDS R0, [R3];
/*0090*/        IADD R2, R3, c [0x0] [0x24];
/*0098*/        ST [R2], R0;
/*00a0*/        EXIT;
```

. . . .

8.1.6 BARRIERS AND COHERENCY

The familiar __syncthreads() intrinsic waits until all the threads in the thread block have arrived before proceeding. It is needed to maintain coherency of shared memory within a thread block.[7] Other, similar memory barrier instructions can be used to enforce some ordering on broader scopes of memory, as described in Table 8.3.

Table 8.3 Memory Barrier Intrinsics

INTRINSIC	DESCRIPTION
__syncthreads()	Waits until all shared memory accesses made by the calling thread are visible to all threads in the threadblock
threadfence_block()	Waits until all global and shared memory accesses made by the calling thread are visible to all threads in the threadblock
threadfence()	Waits until all global and shared memory accesses made by the calling thread are visible to • All threads in the threadblock for shared memory accesses • All threads in the device for global memory accesses

---

7. Note that threads within a warp run in lockstep, sometimes enabling developers to write so-called "warp synchronous" code that does not call __syncthreads(). Section 7.3 describes thread and warp execution in detail, and Part III includes several examples of warp synchronous code.

Table 8.3 Memory Barrier Intrinsics *(Continued)*

INTRINSIC	DESCRIPTION
`threadfence_system()` (SM 2.x only)	Waits until all global and shared memory accesses made by the calling thread are visible to • All threads in the threadblock for shared memory accesses • All threads in the device for global memory accesses • Host threads for page-locked host memory accesses

8.2 Integer Support

The SMs have the full complement of 32-bit integer operations.

• Addition with optional negation of an operand for subtraction

• Multiplication and multiply-add

• Integer division

• Logical operations

• Condition code manipulation

• Conversion to/from floating point

• Miscellaneous operations (e.g., SIMD instructions for narrow integers, population count, find first zero)

CUDA exposes most of this functionality through standard C operators. Nonstandard operations, such as 24-bit multiplication, may be accessed using inline PTX assembly or intrinsic functions.

8.2.1 MULTIPLICATION

Multiplication is implemented differently on Tesla- and Fermi-class hardware. Tesla implements a 24-bit multiplier, while Fermi implements a 32-bit multiplier. As a consequence, full 32-bit multiplication on SM 1.x hardware requires four instructions. For performance-sensitive code targeting Tesla-class

Table 8.4 Multiplication Intrinsics

INTRINSIC	DESCRIPTION
__[u]mul24	Returns the least significant 32 bits of the product of the 24 least significant bits of the integer parameters. The 8 most significant bits of the inputs are ignored.
__[u]mulhi	Returns the most significant 32 bits of the product of the inputs.
__[u]mul64hi	Returns the most significant 64 bits of the products of the 64-bit inputs.

hardware, it is a performance win to use the intrinsics for 24-bit multiply.[8] Table 8.4 shows the intrinsics related to multiplication.

8.2.2 MISCELLANEOUS (BIT MANIPULATION)

The CUDA compiler implements a number of intrinsics for bit manipulation, as summarized in Table 8.5. On SM 2.x and later architectures, these intrinsics

Table 8.5 Bit Manipulation Intrinsics

INTRINSIC	SUMMARY	DESCRIPTION
__brev(x)	Bit reverse	Reverses the order of bits in a word
__byte_perm(x,y,s)	Permute bytes	Returns a 32-bit word whose bytes were selected from the two inputs according to the selector parameter s
__clz(x)	Count leading zeros	Returns number of zero bits (0–32) before most significant set bit
__ffs(x)	Find first sign bit	Returns the position of the least significant set bit. The least significant bit is position 1. For an input of 0, __ffs() returns 0.
__popc(x)	Population count	Returns the number of set bits
__[u]sad(x,y,z)	Sum of absolute differences	Adds |x-y| to z and returns the result

---

8. Using __mul24() or __umul24() on SM 2.x and later hardware, however, is a performance penalty.

map to single instructions. On pre-Fermi architectures, they are valid but may compile into many instructions. When in doubt, disassemble and look at the microcode! 64-bit variants have "ll" (two ells for "long long") appended to the intrinsic name `__clzll()`, `ffsll()`, `popcll()`, `brevll()`.

8.2.3 FUNNEL SHIFT (SM 3.5)

GK110 added a 64-bit "funnel shift" instruction that concatenates two 32-bit values together (the least significant and most significant halves are specified as separate 32-bit inputs, but the hardware operates on an aligned register pair), shifts the resulting 64-bit value left or right, and then returns the most significant (for left shift) or least significant (for right shift) 32 bits.

Funnel shift may be accessed with the intrinsics given in Table 8.6. These intrinsics are implemented as inline device functions (using inline PTX assembler) in `sm_35_intrinsics.h`. By default, the least significant 5 bits of the shift count are masked off; the `_lc` and `_rc` intrinsics clamp the shift value to the range 0..32.

Applications for funnel shift include the following.

- Multiword shift operations

- Memory copies between misaligned buffers using aligned loads and stores

- Rotate

Table 8.6 Funnel Shift Intrinsics

INTRINSIC	DESCRIPTION
`__funnelshift_l(hi, lo, sh)`	Concatenates [hi:lo] into a 64-bit quantity, shifts it left by (`sh&31`) bits, and returns the most significant 32 bits
`__funnelshift_lc(hi, lo, sh)`	Concatenates [hi:lo] into a 64-bit quantity, shifts it left by `min(sh,32)` bits, and returns the most significant 32 bits
`__funnelshift_r(hi, lo, sh)`	Concatenates [hi:lo] into a 64-bit quantity, shifts it right by (`sh&31`) bits, and returns the least significant 32 bits
`__funnelshift_rc(hi, lo, sh)`	Concatenates [hi:lo] into a 64-bit quantity, shifts it right by `min(sh,32)` bits, and returns the least significant 32 bits

To right-shift data sizes greater than 64 bits, use repeated `__funnelshift_r()` calls, operating from the least significant to the most significant word. The most significant word of the result is computed using `operator>>`, which shifts in zero or sign bits as appropriate for the integer type. To left-shift data sizes greater than 64 bits, use repeated `__funnelshift_l()` calls, operating from the most significant to the least significant word. The least significant word of the result is computed using `operator<<`. If the `hi` and `lo` parameters are the same, the funnel shift effects a rotate operation.

8.3 Floating-Point Support

Fast native floating-point hardware is the *raison d'être* for GPUs, and in many ways they are equal to or superior to CPUs in their floating-point implementation. Denormals are supported at full speed,[9] directed rounding may be specified on a per-instruction basis, and the Special Function Units deliver high-performance approximation functions to six popular single-precision transcendentals. In contrast, x86 CPUs implement denormals in microcode that runs perhaps 100x slower than operating on normalized floating-point operands. Rounding direction is specified by a control word that takes dozens of clock cycles to change, and the only transcendental approximation functions in the SSE instruction set are for reciprocal and reciprocal square root, which give 12-bit approximations that must be refined with a Newton-Raphson iteration before being used.

Since GPUs' greater core counts are offset somewhat by their lower clock frequencies, developers can expect at most a 10x (or thereabouts) speedup on a level playing field. If a paper reports a 100x or greater speedup from porting an optimized CPU implementation to CUDA, chances are one of the above-described "instruction set mismatches" played a role.

8.3.1 FORMATS

Figure 8.2 depicts the three (3) IEEE standard floating-point formats supported by CUDA: double precision (64-bit), single precision (32-bit), and half precision (16-bit). The values are divided into three fields: sign, exponent, and mantissa.

---

9. With the exception that single-precision denormals are not supported at all on SM 1.x hardware.

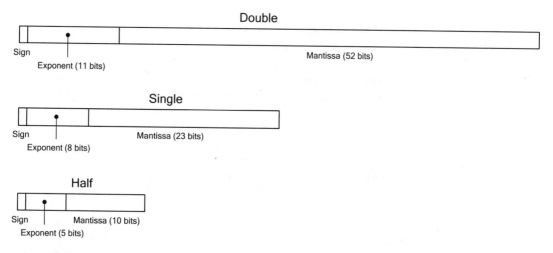

Figure 8.2 Floating-point formats.

For double, single, and half, the exponent fields are 11, 8, and 5 bits in size, respectively; the corresponding mantissa fields are 52, 23, and 10 bits.

The exponent field changes the interpretation of the floating-point value. The most common ("normal") representation encodes an implicit 1 bit into the mantissa and multiplies that value by 2^{e-bias}, where *bias* is the value added to the actual exponent before encoding into the floating-point representation. The bias for single precision, for example, is 127.

Table 8.7 summarizes how floating-point values are encoded. For most exponent values (so-called "normal" floating-point values), the mantissa is assumed to have an implicit 1, and it is multiplied by the biased value of the exponent. The maximum exponent value is reserved for infinity and Not-A-Number values. Dividing by zero (or overflowing a division) yields infinity; performing an invalid operation (such as taking the square root or logarithm of a negative number) yields a NaN. The minimum exponent value is reserved for values too small to represent with the implicit leading 1. As the so-called *denormals*[10] get closer to zero, they lose bits of effective precision, a phenomenon known as *gradual underflow*. Table 8.8 gives the encodings and values of certain extreme values for the three formats.

---

10. Sometimes called *subnormals*.

Table 8.7 Floating-Point Representations

DOUBLE PRECISION			
EXPONENT	MANTISSA	VALUE	CASE NAME
0	0	± 0	Zero
0	Nonzero	$\pm 2^{-1022}(0.mantissa)$	Denormal
1 to 2046	Any	$\pm 2^{e-1023}(1.mantissa)$	Normal
2047	0	$\pm\infty$	Infinity
2047	Nonzero		Not-A-Number

SINGLE PRECISION			
EXPONENT	MANTISSA	VALUE	CASE NAME
0	0	± 0	Zero
0	Nonzero	$\pm 2^{-126}(0.mantissa)$	Denormal
1 to 254	Any	$\pm 2^{e-127}(1.mantissa)$	Normal
255	0	$\pm\infty$	Infinity
255	Nonzero		Not-A-Number

HALF PRECISION			
EXPONENT	MANTISSA	VALUE	CASE NAME
0	0	± 0	Zero
0	Nonzero	$\pm 2^{-14}(0.mantissa)$	Denormal
1 to 30	Any	$\pm 2^{e-15}(1.mantissa)$	Normal
31	0	$\pm\infty$	Infinity
31	Nonzero		Not-A-Number

Table 8.8 Floating-Point Extreme Values

DOUBLE PRECISION		
	HEXADECIMAL	EXACT VALUE
Smallest denormal	`0...0001`	2^{-1074}
Largest denormal	`000F...F`	$2^{-1022}(1-2^{-52})$
Smallest normal	`0010...0`	2^{-1022}
1.0	`3FF0...0`	1
Maximum integer	`4340...0`	2^{53}
Largest normal	`7F7FFFFF`	$2^{1024}(1-2^{-53})$
Infinity	`7FF00000`	Infinity
SINGLE PRECISION		
	HEXADECIMAL	EXACT VALUE
Smallest denormal	`00000001`	2^{-149}
Largest denormal	`007FFFFF`	$2^{-126}(1-2^{-23})$
Smallest normal	`00800000`	2^{-126}
1.0	`3F800000`	1
Maximum integer	`4B800000`	2^{24}
Largest normal	`7F7FFFFF`	$2^{128}(1-2^{-24})$
Infinity	`7F800000`	Infinity

continues

Table 8.8 Floating-Point Extreme Values *(Continued)*

	HALF PRECISION	
	HEXADECIMAL	EXACT VALUE
Smallest denormal	0001	2^{-24}
Largest denormal	07FF	$2^{-14}(1-2^{-10})$
Smallest normal	0800	2^{-14}
1.0	3c00	1
Maximum integer	6800	2^{11}
Largest normal	7BFF	$2^{16}(1-2^{-11})$
Infinity	7C00	Infinity

Rounding

The IEEE standard provides for four (4) round modes.

- Round-to-nearest-even (also called "round-to-nearest")

- Round toward zero (also called "truncate" or "chop")

- Round down (or "round toward negative infinity")

- Round up (or "round toward positive infinity")

Round-to-nearest, where intermediate values are rounded to the nearest representable floating-point value after each operation, is by far the most commonly used round mode. Round up and round down (the "directed rounding modes") are used for *interval arithmetic*, where a pair of floating-point values are used to bracket the intermediate result of a computation. To correctly bracket a result, the lower and upper values of the interval must be rounded toward negative infinity ("down") and toward positive infinity ("up"), respectively.

The C language does not provide any way to specify round modes on a per-instruction basis, and CUDA hardware does not provide a control word to implicitly specify rounding modes. Consequently, CUDA provides a set of intrinsics to specify the round mode of an operation, as summarized in Table 8.9.

Table 8.9 Intrinsics for Rounding

INTRINSIC	OPERATION
__fadd_[rn|rz|ru|rd]	Addition
__fmul_[rn|rz|ru|rd]	Multiplication
__fmaf_[rn|rz|ru|rd]	Fused multiply-add
__frcp_[rn|rz|ru|rd]	Recriprocal
__fdiv_[rn|rz|ru|rd]	Division
__fsqrt_[rn|rz|ru|rd]	Square root
__dadd_[rn|rz|ru|rd]	Addition
__dmul_[rn|rz|ru|rd]	Multiplication
__fma_[rn|rz|ru|rd]	Fused multiply-add
__drcp_[rn|rz|ru|rd]	Reciprocal
__ddiv_[rn|rz|ru|rd]	Division
__dsqrt_[rn|rz|ru|rd]	Square root

Conversion

In general, developers can convert between different floating-point representations and/or integers using standard C constructs: implicit conversion or explicit typecasts. If necessary, however, developers can use the intrinsics listed in Table 8.10 to perform conversions that are not in the C language specification, such as those with directed rounding.

Because half is not standardized in the C programming language, CUDA uses unsigned short in the interfaces for __half2float() and __float2half(). __float2half() only supports the round-to-nearest rounding mode.

```
float __half2float( unsigned short );
unsigned short __float2half( float );
```

Table 8.10 Intrinsics for Conversion

INTRINSIC	OPERATION
`__float2int_[rn|rz|ru|rd]`	float to int
`__float2uint_[rn|rz|ru|rd]`	float to unsigned int
`__int2float_[rn|rz|ru|rd]`	int to float
`__uint2float_[rn|rz|ru|rd]`	unsigned int to float
`__float2ll_[rn|rz|ru|rd]`	float to 64-bit int
`__ll2float_[rn|rz|ru|rd]`	64-bit int to float
`__ull2float_[rn|rz|ru|rd]`	unsigned 64-bit int to float
`__double2float_[rn|rz|ru|rd]`	double to float
`__double2int_[rn|rz|ru|rd]`	double to int
`__double2uint_[rn|rz|ru|rd]`	double to unsigned int
`__double2ll_[rn|rz|ru|rd]`	double to 64-bit int
`__double2ull_[rn|rz|ru|rd]`	double to 64-bit unsigned int
`__int2double_rn`	int to double
`__uint2double_rn`	unsigned int to double
`__ll2double_[rn|rz|ru|rd]`	64-bit int to double
`__ull2double_[rn|rz|ru|rd]`	unsigned 64-bit int to double

8.3.2 SINGLE PRECISION (32-BIT)

Single-precision floating-point support is the workhorse of GPU computation. GPUs have been optimized to natively deliver high performance on this data type,[11] not only for core standard IEEE operations such as addition and multiplication, but also for nonstandard operations such as approximations to transcendentals such as `sin()` and `log()`. The 32-bit values are held in the same register file as integers, so coercion between single-precision floating-point values and 32-bit integers (with `__float_as_int()` and `__int_as_float()`) is free.

Addition, Multiplication, and Multiply-Add

The compiler automatically translates +, –, and * operators on floating-point values into addition, multiplication, and multiply-add instructions. The `__fadd_rn()` and `__fmul_rn()` intrinsics may be used to suppress fusion of addition and multiplication operations into multiply-add instructions.

Reciprocal and Division

For devices of compute capability 2.x and higher, the division operator is IEEE-compliant when the code is compiled with `--prec-div=true`. For devices of compute capability 1.x or for devices of compute capability 2.x when the code is compiled with `--prec-div=false`, the division operator and `__fdividef(x,y)` have the same accuracy, but for $2^{126}<y<2^{128}$, `__fdividef(x,y)` delivers a result of zero, whereas the division operator delivers the correct result. Also, for $2^{126}<y<2^{128}$, if x is infinity, `__fdividef(x,y)` returns NaN, while the division operator returns infinity.

Transcendentals (SFU)

The Special Function Units (SFUs) in the SMs implement very fast versions of six common transcendental functions.

- Sine and cosine

- Logarithm and exponential

- Reciprocal and reciprocal square root

Table 8.11, excerpted from the paper on the Tesla architecture[12] summarizes the supported operations and corresponding precision. The SFUs do not implement full precision, but they are reasonably good approximations of these functions and they are *fast*. For CUDA ports that are significantly faster than an optimized CPU equivalent (say, 25x or more), the code most likely relies on the SFUs.

---

11. In fact, GPUs had full 32-bit floating-point support before they had full 32-bit integer support. As a result, some early GPU computing literature explained how to implement integer math with floating-point hardware!

12. Lindholm, Erik, John Nickolls, Stuart Oberman, and John Montrym. NVIDIA Tesla: A unified graphics and computing architecture. *IEEE Micro*, March–April 2008, p. 47.

Table 8.11 SFU Accuracy

FUNCTION	ACCURACY (GOOD BITS)	ULP ERROR
1/x	24.02	0.98
1/sqrt(x)	23.40	1.52
2^x	22.51	1.41
$\log2_x$	22.57	n/a
sin/cos	22.47	n/a

The SFUs are accessed with the intrinsics given in Table 8.12. Specifying the `--fast-math` compiler option will cause the compiler to substitute conventional C runtime calls with the corresponding SFU intrinsics listed above.

Table 8.12 SFU Intrinsics

INTRINSIC	OPERATION
__cosf(x)	cos x
__exp10f(x)	10^x
__expf(x)	e^x
__fdividef(x,y)	x/y
__logf(x)	ln x
__log2f(x)	$\log_2 x$
__log10f(x)	$\log_{10} x$
__powf(x,y)	x^y
__sinf(x)	sin x
__sincosf(x,sptr,cptr)	*s=sin(x); *c=cos(x);
__tanf(x)	tan x

Miscellaneous

__saturate(x) returns 0 if x<0, 1 if x>1, and x otherwise.

8.3.3 DOUBLE PRECISION (64-BIT)

Double-precision floating-point support was added to CUDA with SM 1.3 (first implemented in the GeForce GTX 280), and much improved double-precision support (both functionality and performance) became available with SM 2.0. CUDA's hardware support for double precision features full-speed denormals and, starting in SM 2.x, a native fused multiply-add instruction (FMAD), compliant with IEEE 754 c. 2008, that performs only one rounding step. Besides being an intrinsically useful operation, FMAD enables full accuracy on certain functions that are converged with the Newton-Raphson iteration.

As with single-precision operations, the compiler automatically translates standard C operators into multiplication, addition, and multiply-add instructions. The __dadd_rn() and __dmul_rn() intrinsics may be used to suppress fusion of addition and multiplication operations into multiply-add instructions.

8.3.4 HALF PRECISION (16-BIT)

With 5 bits of exponent and 10 bits of significand, half values have enough precision for HDR (high dynamic range) images and can be used to hold other types of values that do not require float precision, such as angles. Half precision values are intended for storage, not computation, so the hardware only provides instructions to convert to/from 32-bit.[13] These instructions are exposed as the __halftofloat() and __floattohalf() intrinsics.

```
float __halftofloat( unsigned short );
unsigned short __floattohalf( float );
```

These intrinsics use unsigned short because the C language has not standardized the half floating-point type.

8.3.5 CASE STUDY: float→half CONVERSION

Studying the float→half conversion operation is a useful way to learn the details of floating-point encodings and rounding. Because it's a simple unary

---

13. half floating-point values are supported as a texture format, in which case the TEX intrinsics return float and the conversion is automatically performed by the texture hardware.

operation, we can focus on the encoding and rounding without getting distracted by the details of floating-point arithmetic and the precision of intermediate representations.

When converting from float to half, the correct output for any float too large to represent is half infinity. Any float too small to represent as a half (even a denormal half) must be clamped to 0.0. The maximum float that rounds to half 0.0 is 0x32FFFFFF, or 2.98^{-8}, while the smallest float that rounds to half infinity is 65520.0. float values inside this range can be converted to half by propagating the sign bit, rebiasing the exponent (since float has an 8-bit exponent biased by 127 and half has a 5-bit exponent biased by 15), and rounding the float mantissa to the nearest half mantissa value. Rounding is straightforward in all cases except when the input value falls exactly between the two possible output values. When this is the case, the IEEE standard specifies rounding to the "nearest even" value. In decimal arithmetic, this would mean rounding 1.5 to 2.0, but also rounding 2.5 to 2.0 and (for example) rounding 0.5 to 0.0.

Listing 8.3 shows a C routine that exactly replicates the float-to-half conversion operation, as implemented by CUDA hardware. The variables exp and mag contain the input exponent and "magnitude," the mantissa and exponent together with the sign bit masked off. Many operations, such as comparisons and rounding operations, can be performed on the magnitude without separating the exponent and mantissa.

The macro LG_MAKE_MASK, used in Listing 8.3, creates a mask with a given bit count: #define LG_MAKE_MASK(bits) ((1<<bits)-1). A volatile union is used to treat the same 32-bit value as float and unsigned int; idioms such as *((float *) (&u)) are not portable. The routine first propagates the input sign bit and masks it off the input.

After extracting the magnitude and exponent, the function deals with the special case when the input float is INF or NaN, and does an early exit. Note that INF is signed, but NaN has a canonical unsigned value. Lines 50–80 clamp the input float value to the minimum or maximum values that correspond to representable half values and recompute the magnitude for clamped values. Don't be fooled by the elaborate code constructing f32MinRInfin and f32MaxRf16_zero; those are constants with the values 0x477ff000 and 0x32ffffff, respectively.

The remainder of the routine deals with the cases of output normal and denormal (input denormals are clamped in the preceding code, so mag corresponds to a normal float). As with the clamping code, f32Minf16Normal is a constant, and its value is 0x38ffffff.

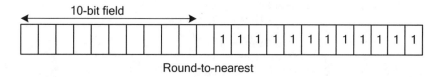

Figure 8.3 Rounding mask (half).

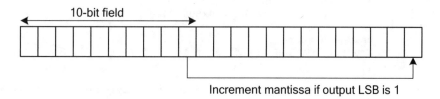

Figure 8.4 Round-to-nearest-even (half).

To construct a normal, the new exponent must be computed (lines 92 and 93) and the correctly rounded 10 bits of mantissa shifted into the output. To construct a denormal, the implicit 1 must be OR'd into the output mantissa and the resulting mantissa shifted by the amount corresponding to the input exponent. For both normals and denormals, the rounding of the output mantissa is accomplished in two steps. The rounding is accomplished by adding a mask of 1's that ends just short of the output's LSB, as seen in Figure 8.3.

This operation increments the output mantissa if bit 12 of the input is set; if the input mantissa is all 1's, the overflow causes the output exponent to correctly increment. If we added one more 1 to the MSB of this adjustment, we'd have elementary school–style rounding where the tiebreak goes to the larger number. Instead, to implement round-to-nearest even, we conditionally increment the output mantissa if the LSB of the 10-bit output is set (Figure 8.4). Note that these steps can be performed in either order or can be reformulated in many different ways.

Listing 8.3 ConvertToHalf().

```
/*
 * exponent shift and mantissa bit count are the same.
 *     When we are shifting, we use [f16|f32]ExpShift
 *     When referencing the number of bits in the mantissa,
 *          we use [f16|f32]MantissaBits
 */
```

```c
const int f16ExpShift = 10;
const int f16MantissaBits = 10;

const int f16ExpBias = 15;
const int f16MinExp = -14;
const int f16MaxExp = 15;
const int f16SignMask = 0x8000;

const int f32ExpShift = 23;
const int f32MantissaBits = 23;
const int f32ExpBias = 127;
const int f32SignMask = 0x80000000;

unsigned short
ConvertFloatToHalf( float f )
{
    /*
     * Use a volatile union to portably coerce
     * 32-bit float into 32-bit integer
     */
    volatile union {
        float f;
        unsigned int u;
    } uf;
    uf.f = f;

    // return value: start by propagating the sign bit.
    unsigned short w = (uf.u >> 16) & f16SignMask;

    // Extract input magnitude and exponent
    unsigned int mag = uf.u & ~f32SignMask;
    int exp = (int) (mag >> f32ExpShift) - f32ExpBias;

    // Handle float32 Inf or NaN
    if ( exp == f32ExpBias+1 ) {      // INF or NaN

        if ( mag & LG_MAKE_MASK(f32MantissaBits) )
            return 0x7fff; // NaN

        // INF - propagate sign
        return w|0x7c00;
    }

    /*
     * clamp float32 values that are not representable by float16
     */
    {
        // min float32 magnitude that rounds to float16 infinity

        unsigned int f32MinRInfin = (f16MaxExp+f32ExpBias) <<
            f32ExpShift;
        f32MinRInfin |= LG_MAKE_MASK( f16MantissaBits+1 ) <<
            (f32MantissaBits-f16MantissaBits-1);

        if (mag > f32MinRInfin)
            mag = f32MinRInfin;
    }
```

```
{
    // max float32 magnitude that rounds to float16 0.0

    unsigned int f32MaxRf16_zero = f16MinExp+f32ExpBias-
        (f32MantissaBits-f16MantissaBits-1);
    f32MaxRf16_zero <<= f32ExpShift;
    f32MaxRf16_zero |= LG_MAKE_MASK( f32MantissaBits );

    if (mag < f32MaxRf16_zero)
        mag = f32MaxRf16_zero;
}

/*
 * compute exp again, in case mag was clamped above
 */
exp = (mag >> f32ExpShift) - f32ExpBias;

// min float32 magnitude that converts to float16 normal
unsigned int f32Minf16Normal = ((f16MinExp+f32ExpBias)<<
    f32ExpShift);
f32Minf16Normal |= LG_MAKE_MASK( f32MantissaBits );
if ( mag >= f32Minf16Normal ) {
    //
    // Case 1: float16 normal
    //

    // Modify exponent to be biased for float16, not float32
    mag += (unsigned int) ((f16ExpBias-f32ExpBias)<<
        f32ExpShift);

    int RelativeShift = f32ExpShift-f16ExpShift;

    // add rounding bias
    mag += LG_MAKE_MASK(RelativeShift-1);

    // round-to-nearest even
    mag += (mag >> RelativeShift) & 1;

    w |= mag >> RelativeShift;
}
else {
    /*
     * Case 2: float16 denormal
     */

    // mask off exponent bits - now fraction only
    mag &= LG_MAKE_MASK(f32MantissaBits);

    // make implicit 1 explicit
    mag |= (1<<f32ExpShift);

    int RelativeShift = f32ExpShift-f16ExpShift+f16MinExp-exp;

    // add rounding bias
    mag += LG_MAKE_MASK(RelativeShift-1);
```

```
        // round-to-nearest even
        mag += (mag >> RelativeShift) & 1;

        w |= mag >> RelativeShift;
    }
    return w;
}
```

In practice, developers should convert `float` to `half` by using the `__floattohalf()` intrinsic, which the compiler translates to a single F2F machine instruction. This sample routine is provided purely to aid in understanding floating-point layout and rounding; also, examining all the special-case code for INF/NAN and denormal values helps to illustrate why these features of the IEEE spec have been controversial since its inception: They make hardware slower, more costly, or both due to increased silicon area and engineering effort for validation.

In the code accompanying this book, the `ConvertFloatToHalf()` routine in Listing 8.3 is incorporated into a program called `float_to_float16.cu` that tests its output for every 32-bit floating-point value.

8.3.6 MATH LIBRARY

CUDA includes a built-in math library modeled on the C runtime library, with a few small differences: CUDA hardware does not include a rounding mode register (instead, the round mode is encoded on a per-instruction basis),[14] so functions such as `rint()` that reference the current rounding mode always round-to-nearest. Additionally, the hardware does not raise floating-point exceptions; results of aberrant operations, such as taking the square root of a negative number, are encoded as NaNs.

Table 8.13 lists the math library functions and the maximum error in ulps for each function. Most functions that operate on `float` have an "f" appended to the function name—for example, the functions that compute the sine function are as follows.

```
double sin( double angle );
float sinf( float angle );
```

These are denoted in Table 8.13 as, for example, `sin[f]`.

---

14. Encoding a round mode per instruction and keeping it in a control register are not irreconcilable. The Alpha processor had a 2-bit encoding to specify the round mode per instruction, one setting of which was to use the rounding mode specified in a control register! CUDA hardware just uses a 2-bit encoding for the four round modes specified in the IEEE specification.

Table 8.13 Math Library

FUNCTION	OPERATION	EXPRESSION	ULP ERROR 32	ULP ERROR 64
x+y	Addition	x+y	0^1	0
x*y	Multiplication	x*y	0^1	0
x/y	Division	x/y	2^2	0
1/x	Reciprocal	1/x	1^2	0
acos[f](x)	Inverse cosine	$\cos^{-1} x$	3	2
acosh[f](x)	Inverse hyperbolic cosine	$\ln\left(x + \sqrt{x^2 + 1}\right)$	4	2
asin[f](x)	Inverse sine	$\sin^{-1} x$	4	2
asinh[f](x)	Inverse hyperbolic sine	$\text{sign}(x)\ln\left(\lvert x \rvert + \sqrt{1 + x^2}\right)$	3	2
atan[f](x)	Inverse tangent	$\tan^{-1} x$	2	2
atan2[f](y,x)	Inverse tangent of y/x	$\tan^{-1} x\left(\dfrac{y}{x}\right)$	3	2
atanh[f](x)	Inverse hyperbolic tangent	$\tanh^{-1}$	3	2
cbrt[f](x)	Cube root	$\sqrt[3]{x}$	1	1
ceil[f](x)	"Ceiling," nearest integer greater than or equal to *x*	$\lceil x \rceil$	0	
copysign[f](x,y)	Sign of y, magnitude of x		n/a	
cos[f](x)	Cosine	$\cos x$	2	1
cosh[f](x)	Hyperbolic cosine	$\dfrac{e^x + e^{-x}}{2}$	2	
cospi[f](x)	Cosine, scaled by π	$\cos \pi x$	2	

continues

Table 8.13 Math Library *(Continued)*

FUNCTION	OPERATION	EXPRESSION	ULP ERROR 32	ULP ERROR 64
erf[f](x)	Error function	$\dfrac{2}{\pi}\int_0^x e^{-t^2}$	3	2
erfc[f](x) •	Complementary error function	$1-\dfrac{2}{\pi}\int_0^x e^{-t^2}$	6	4
erfcinv[f](y)	Inverse complementary error function	Return x for which y=1-erff(x)	7	8
erfcx[f](x)	Scaled error function	e^{x^2} (erff(x))	6	3
erfinv[f](y)	Inverse error function	Return x for which y=erff(x)	3	5
exp[f](x)	Natural exponent	e^x	2	1
exp10[f](x)	Exponent (base 10)	10^x	2	1
exp2[f](x)	Exponent (base 2)	2^x	2	1
expm1[f](x)	Natural exponent, minus one	$e^x - 1$	1	1
fabs[f](x)	Absolute value	$\|x\|$	0	0
fdim[f](x,y)	Positive difference	$\begin{cases} x-y, x>y \\ +0, x\le y \\ \text{NAN, x or y NaN} \end{cases}$	0	0
floor[f](x)	"Floor," nearest integer less than or equal to x	$\lfloor x \rfloor$	0	0
fma[f](x,y,z)	Multiply-add	$xy + z$	0	0
fmax[f](x,y)	Maximum	$\begin{cases} x, x>y \text{ or isNaN(y)} \\ y, \text{otherwise} \end{cases}$	0	0

Table 8.13 Math Library *(Continued)*

FUNCTION	OPERATION	EXPRESSION	ULP ERROR 32	ULP ERROR 64
fmin[f](x,y)	Minimum	$\begin{cases} x, x < y \text{ or isNaN(y)} \\ y, \text{ otherwise} \end{cases}$	0	0
fmod[f](x,y)	Floating-point remainder		0	0
frexp[f](x,exp)	Fractional component		0	0
hypot[f](x,y)	Length of hypotenuse	$\sqrt{x^2 + y^2}$	3	2
ilogb[f](x)	Get exponent		0	0
isfinite(x)	Nonzero if x is not ±INF		n/a	
isinf(x)	Nonzero if x is ±INF		n/a	
isnan(x)	Nonzero if x is a NaN		n/a	
j0[f](x)	Bessel function of the first kind (n=0)	$J_0(x)$	9^3	7^3
j1[f](x)	Bessel function of the first kind (n=1)	$J_1(x)$	9^3	7^3
jn[f](n,x)	Bessel function of the first kind	$J_n(x)$	*	
ldexp[f](x,exp)	Scale by power of 2	$x2^{exp}$	0	0
lgamma[f](x)	Logarithm of gamma function	$\ln\left(\Gamma(x)\right)$	6^4	4^4
llrint[f](x)	Round to long long		0	0
llround[f](x)	Round to long long		0	0
lrint[f](x)	Round to long		0	0
lround[f](x)	Round to long		0	0
log[f](x)	Natural logarithm	$\ln(x)$	1	1
log10[f](x)	Logarithm (base 10)	$\log_{10} x$	3	1
log1p[f](x)	Natural logarithm of x+1	$\ln(x + 1)$	2	1

continues

Table 8.13 Math Library (Continued)

FUNCTION	OPERATION	EXPRESSION	ULP ERROR 32	ULP ERROR 64
log2[f](x)	Logarithm (base 2)	$\log_2 x$	3	1
logb[f](x)	Get exponent		0	0
modff(x,iptr)	Split fractional and integer parts		0	0
nan[f](cptr)	Returns NaN	NaN	n/a	
nearbyint[f](x)	Round to integer		0	0
nextafter[f](x,y)	Returns the FP value closest to x in the direction of y		n/a	
normcdf[f](x)	Normal cumulative distribution		6	5
normcdinv[f](x)	Inverse normal cumulative distribution		5	8
pow[f](x,y)	Power function	x^y	8	2
rcbrt[f](x)	Inverse cube root	$\dfrac{1}{\sqrt[3]{x}}$	2	1
remainder[f](x,y)	Remainder		0	0
remquo[f] (x,y,iptr)	Remainder (also returns quotient)		0	0
rsqrt[f](x)	Reciprocal	$\dfrac{1}{\sqrt{x}}$	2	1
rint[f](x)	Round to nearest int		0	0
round[f](x)	Round to nearest int		0	0
scalbln[f](x,n)	Scale x by 2^n (n is long int)	$x2^n$	0	0
scalbn[f](x,n)	Scale x by 2^n (n is int)	$x2^n$	0	0
signbit(x)	Nonzero if x is negative		n/a	0
sin[f](x)	Sine	sin x	2	1

Table 8.13 Math Library *(Continued)*

FUNCTION	OPERATION	EXPRESSION	ULP ERROR 32	ULP ERROR 64
sincos[f](x,s,c)	Sine and cosine	*s=sin(x); *c=cos(x);	2	1
sincospi[f](x,s,c)	Sine and cosine	*s=sin(πx); *c=cos(πx);	2	1
sinh[f](x)	Hyperbolic sine	$$\frac{e^x - e^{-x}}{2}$$	3	1
sinpi[f](x)	Sine, scaled by π	$\sin \pi x$	2	1
sqrt[f](x)	Square root	$\sqrt{x}$	3[5]	0
tan[f](x)	Tangent	$\tan x$	4	2
tanh[f](x)	Hyperbolic tangent	$$\frac{\sinh x}{\cosh x}$$	2	1
tgamma[f](x)	True gamma function	$\Gamma(x)$	11	8
trunc[f](x)	Truncate (round to integer toward zero)		0	0
y0[f](x)	Bessel function of the second kind (n=0)	$Y_0(x)$	9[3]	7[3]
y1[f](x)	Bessel function of the second kind (n=1)	$Y_1(x)$	9[3]	7[3]
yn[f](n,x)	Bessel function of the second kind	$Y_n(x)$	**	**

* For the Bessel functions jnf(n,x) and jn(n,x), for n=128 the maximum absolute error is 2.2×10^{-6} and 5×10^{-12}, respectively.

** For the Bessel function ynf(n,x), the error is $\lceil 2 + 2.5n \rceil$ for |x|; otherwise, the maximum absolute error is 2.2×10^{-6} for n=128. For yn(n,x), the maximum absolute error is 5×10^{-12}.

1. On SM 1.x class hardware, the precision of addition and multiplication operation that are merged into FMAD instructions will suffer due to truncation of the intermediate mantissa.

2. On SM 2.x and later hardware, developers can reduce this error rate to 0 ulps by specifying --prec-div=true.

3. For float, the error is 9 ulps for |x|<8; otherwise, the maximum absolute error is 2.2×10^{-6}. For double, the error is 7 ulps for |x|<8; otherwise, the maximum absolute error is 5×10^{-12}.

4. The error for lgammaf() is greater than 6 inside the interval –10.001, –2.264. The error for lgamma() is greater than 4 inside the interval –11.001, –2.2637.

5. On SM 2.x and later hardware, developers can reduce this error rate to 0 ulps by specifying --prec-sqrt=true.

Conversion to Integer

According to the C runtime library definition, the nearbyint() and rint() functions round a floating-point value to the nearest integer using the "current rounding direction," which in CUDA is always round-to-nearest-even. In the C runtime, nearbyint() and rint() differ only in their handling of the INEXACT exception. But since CUDA does not raise floating-point exceptions, the functions behave identically.

round() implements elementary school–style rounding: For floating-point values halfway between integers, the input is always rounded away from zero. NVIDIA recommends against using this function because it expands to eight (8) instructions as opposed to one for rint() and its variants. trunc() truncates or "chops" the floating-point value, rounding toward zero. It compiles to a single instruction.

Fractions and Exponents

```
float frexpf(float x, int *eptr);
```

frexpf() breaks the input into a floating-point significand in the range [0.5, 1.0) and an integral exponent for 2, such that

$$x = Significand \cdot 2^{Exponent}$$

```
float logbf( float x );
```

logbf() extracts the exponent from x and returns it as a floating-point value. It is equivalent to floorf(log2f(x)), except it is faster. If x is a denormal, logbf() returns the exponent that x would have if it were normalized.

```
float ldexpf( float x, int exp );
float scalbnf( float x, int n );
float scanblnf( float x, long n );
```

ldexpf(), scalbnf(), and scalblnf() all compute x2^n by direct manipulation of floating-point exponents.

Floating-Point Remainder

modff() breaks the input into fractional and integer parts.

```
float modff( float x, float *intpart );
```

The return value is the fractional part of x, with the same sign.

`remainderf(x,y)` computes the floating-point remainder of dividing x by y. The return value is `x-n*y`, where n is x/y, rounded to the nearest integer. If |x − ny| = 0.5, n is chosen to be even.

```
float remquof(float x, float y, int *quo);
```

computes the remainder and passes back the lower bits of the integral quotient x/y, with the same sign as x/y.

Bessel Functions

The Bessel functions of order n relate to the differential equation

$$x^2 \frac{d^2y}{dx^2} + x\frac{dy}{dx} + (x^2 - n^2)y = 0$$

n can be a real number, but for purposes of the C runtime, it is a nonnegative integer.

The solution to this second-order ordinary differential equation combines Bessel functions of the first kind and of the second kind.

$$y(x) = c_1 J_n(x) + c_2 Y_n(x)$$

The math runtime functions `jn[f]()` and `yn[f]()` compute $J_n(x)$ and $Y_n(x)$, respectively. `j0f()`, `j1f()`, `y0f()`, and `y1f()` compute these functions for the special cases of n=0 and n=1.

Gamma Function

The gamma function Γ is an extension of the factorial function, with its argument shifted down by 1, to real numbers. It has a variety of definitions, one of which is as follows.

$$\Gamma(x) = \int_0^\infty e^{-t} t^{x-1} dt$$

The function grows so quickly that the return value loses precision for relatively small input values, so the library provides the `lgamma()` function, which returns the natural logarithm of the gamma function, in addition to the `tgamma()` ("true gamma") function.

8.3.7 ADDITIONAL READING

Goldberg's survey (with the captivating title "What Every Computer Scientist Should Know About Floating Point Arithmetic") is a good introduction to the topic.

http://download.oracle.com/docs/cd/E19957-01/806-3568/ncg_goldberg.html

Nathan Whitehead and Alex Fit-Florea of NVIDIA have coauthored a white paper entitled "Precision & Performance: Floating Point and IEEE 754 Compliance for NVIDIA GPUs."

http://developer.download.nvidia.com/assets/cuda/files/NVIDIA-CUDA-Floating-Point.pdf

Increasing Effective Precision

Dekker and Kahan developed methods to almost double the effective precision of floating-point hardware using pairs of numbers in exchange for a slight reduction in exponent range (due to intermediate underflow and overflow at the far ends of the range). Some papers on this topic include the following.

Dekker, T.J. Point technique for extending the available precision. *Numer. Math.* 18, 1971, pp. 224–242.

Linnainmaa, S. Software for doubled-precision floating point computations. *ACM TOMS* 7, pp. 172–283 (1981).

Shewchuk, J.R. Adaptive precision floating-point arithmetic and fast robust geometric predicates. *Discrete & Computational Geometry* 18, 1997, pp. 305–363.

Some GPU-specific work on this topic has been done by Andrew Thall, Da Graça, and Defour.

Guillaume, Da Graça, and David Defour. Implementation of float-float operators on graphics hardware, *7th Conference on Real Numbers and Computers*, RNC7 (2006).

http://hal.archives-ouvertes.fr/docs/00/06/33/56/PDF/float-float.pdf

Thall, Andrew. Extended-precision floating-point numbers for GPU computation. 2007.

http://andrewthall.org/papers/df64_qf128.pdf

8.4 Conditional Code

The hardware implements "condition code" or CC registers that contain the usual 4-bit state vector (sign, carry, zero, overflow) used for integer comparison. These CC registers can be set using comparison instructions such as `ISET`, and they can direct the flow of execution via *predication* or *divergence*. Predication allows (or suppresses) the execution of instructions on a per-thread basis within a warp, while divergence is the conditional execution of longer instruction sequences. Because the processors within an SM execute instructions in SIMD fashion at warp granularity (32 threads at a time), divergence can result in fewer instructions executed, provided all threads within a warp take the same code path.

8.4.1 PREDICATION

Due to the additional overhead of managing divergence and convergence, the compiler uses predication for short instruction sequences. The effect of most instructions can be predicated on a condition; if the condition is not TRUE, the instruction is suppressed. This suppression occurs early enough that predicated execution of instructions such as load/store and `TEX` inhibits the memory traffic that the instruction would otherwise generate. Note that predication has no effect on the eligibility of memory traffic for global load/store coalescing. The addresses specified to all load/store instructions in a warp must reference consecutive memory locations, even if they are predicated.

Predication is used when the number of instructions that vary depending on a condition is small; the compiler uses heuristics that favor predication up to about 7 instructions. Besides avoiding the overhead of managing the branch synchronization stack described below, predication also gives the compiler more optimization opportunities (such as instruction scheduling) when emitting microcode. The ternary operator in C (? :) is considered a compiler hint to favor predication.

Listing 8.2 gives an excellent example of predication, as expressed in microcode. When performing an atomic operation on a shared memory location, the compiler emits code that loops over the shared memory location until it has successfully performed the atomic operation. The `LDSLK` (load shared and lock) instruction returns a condition code that tells whether the lock was acquired. The instructions to perform the operation then are predicated on that condition code.

```
/*0058*/ LDSLK P0, R2, [R3];
/*0060*/ @P0 IADD R2, R2, R0;
/*0068*/ @P0 STSUL [R3], R2;
/*0070*/ @!P0 BRA 0x58;
```

This code fragment also highlights how predication and branching sometimes work together. The last instruction, a conditional branch to attempt to reacquire the lock if necessary, also is predicated.

8.4.2 DIVERGENCE AND CONVERGENCE

Predication works well for small fragments of conditional code, especially if statements with no corresponding else. For larger amounts of conditional code, predication becomes inefficient because every instruction is executed, regardless of whether it will affect the computation. When the larger number of instructions causes the costs of predication to exceed the benefits, the compiler will use conditional branches. When the flow of execution within a warp takes different paths depending on a condition, the code is called *divergent*.

NVIDIA is close-mouthed about the details of how their hardware supports divergent code paths, and it reserves the right to change the hardware implementation between generations. The hardware maintains a bit vector of active threads within each warp. For threads that are marked inactive, execution is suppressed in a way similar to predication. Before taking a branch, the compiler executes a special instruction to push this active-thread bit vector onto a stack. The code is then executed *twice*, once for threads for which the condition was TRUE, then for threads for which the predicate was FALSE. This two-phased execution is managed with a *branch synchronization stack*, as described by Lindholm et al.[15]

> If threads of a warp diverge via a data-dependent conditional branch, the warp serially executes each branch path taken, disabling threads that are not on that path, and when all paths complete, the threads reconverge to the original execution path. The SM uses a branch synchronization stack to manage independent threads that diverge and converge. Branch divergence only occurs within a warp; different warps execute independently regardless of whether they are executing common or disjoint code paths.

The PTX specification makes no mention of a branch synchronization stack, so the only publicly available evidence of its existence is in the disassembly output of cuobjdump. The SSY instruction pushes a state such as the program counter and active thread mask onto the stack; the .S instruction prefix pops this state

---

15. Lindholm, Erik, John Nickolls, Stuart Oberman, and John Montrym. NVIDIA Tesla: A unified graphics and computing architecture. *IEEE Micro*, March–April 2008, pp. 39–55.

and, if any active threads did not take the branch, causes those threads to execute the code path whose state was snapshotted by SSY.

SSY/.S is only necessary when threads of execution may diverge, so if the compiler can guarantee that threads will stay uniform in a code path, you may see branches that are not bracketed by SSY/.S. The important thing to realize about branching in CUDA is that in all cases, it is most efficient for all threads within a warp to follow the same execution path.

The loop in Listing 8.2 also includes a good self-contained example of divergence and convergence. The SSY instruction (offset 0x40) and NOP.S instruction (offset 0x78) bracket the points of divergence and convergence, respectively. The code loops over the LDSLK and subsequent predicated instructions, retiring active threads until the compiler knows that all threads will have converged and the branch synchronization stack can be popped with the NOP.S instruction.

```
/*0040*/  SSY 0x80;
/*0048*/  BAR.RED.POPC RZ, RZ;
/*0050*/  LD R0, [R0];
/*0058*/  LDSLK P0, R2, [R3];
/*0060*/  @P0 IADD R2, R2, R0;
/*0068*/  @P0 STSUL [R3], R2;
/*0070*/  @!P0 BRA 0x58;
/*0078*/  NOP.S CC.T;
```

8.4.3 SPECIAL CASES: MIN, MAX, AND ABSOLUTE VALUE

Some conditional operations are so common that they are supported natively by the hardware. Minimum and maximum operations are supported for both integer and floating-point operands and are translated to a single instruction. Additionally, floating-point instructions include modifiers that can negate or take the absolute value of a source operand.

The compiler does a good job of detecting when min/max operations are being expressed, but if you want to take no chances, call the min()/max() intrinsics for integers or fmin()/fmax() for floating-point values.

8.5 Textures and Surfaces

The instructions that read and write textures and surfaces refer to much more implicit state than do other instructions; parameters such as the base address, dimensions, format, and interpretation of the texture contents are contained in a *header*, an intermediate data structure whose software abstraction is called a *texture reference* or *surface reference*. As developers manipulate the texture or surface references, the CUDA runtime and driver must translate those changes into the headers, which the texture or surface instruction references as an index.[16]

Before launching a kernel that operates on textures or surfaces, the driver must ensure that all this state is set correctly on the hardware. As a result, launching such kernels may take longer. Texture reads are serviced through a specialized cache subsystem that is separate from the L1/L2 caches in Fermi, and also separate from the constant cache. Each SM has an L1 texture cache, and the TPCs (texture processor clusters) or GPCs (graphics processor clusters) each additionally have L2 texture cache. Surface reads and writes are serviced through the same L1/L2 caches that service global memory traffic.

Kepler added two technologies of note with respect to textures: the ability to read from global memory via the texture cache hierarchy without binding a texture reference, and the ability to specify a texture header by address rather than by index. The latter technology is known as "bindless textures."

On SM 3.5 and later hardware, reading global memory via the texture cache can be requested by using `const __restrict` pointers or by explicitly invoking the `ldg()` intrinsics in `sm_35_intrinsics.h`.

8.6 Miscellaneous Instructions

8.6.1 WARP-LEVEL PRIMITIVES

It did not take long for the importance of warps as a primitive unit of execution (naturally residing between threads and blocks) to become evident to CUDA programmers. Starting with SM 1.x, NVIDIA began adding instructions that specifically operate on warps.

Vote

That CUDA architectures are 32-bit and that warps are comprised of 32 threads made an irresistible match to instructions that can evaluate a condition and

---

16. SM 3.x added *texture objects*, which enable texture and surface headers to be referenced by address rather than an index. Previous hardware generations could reference at most 128 textures or surfaces in a kernel, but with SM 3.x the number is limited only by memory.

broadcast a 1-bit result to every thread in the warp. The VOTE instruction (first available in SM 1.2) evaluates a condition and broadcasts the result to all threads in the warp. The __any() intrinsic returns 1 if the predicate is true for *any* of the 32 threads in the warp. The __all() intrinsic returns 1 if the predicate is true for *all* of the 32 threads in the warp.

The Fermi architecture added a new variant of VOTE that passes back the predicate result for every thread in the warp. The __ballot() intrinsic evaluates a condition for all threads in the warp and returns a 32-bit value where each bit gives the condition for the corresponding thread in the warp.

Shuffle

Kepler added *shuffle* instructions that enable data interchange between threads within a warp without staging the data through shared memory. Although these instructions execute with the same latency as shared memory, they have the benefit of doing the exchange without performing both a read and a write, and they can reduce shared memory usage.

The following instruction is wrapped in a number of device functions that use inline PTX assembly defined in sm_30_intrinsics.h.

```
int __shfl(int var, int srcLane, int width=32);
int __shfl_up(int var, unsigned int delta, int width=32);
int __shfl_down(int var, unsigned int delta, int width=32);
int __shfl_xor(int var, int laneMask, int width=32);
```

The width parameter, which defaults to the warp width of 32, must be a power of 2 in the range 2..32. It enables subdivision of the warp into segments; if width<32, each subsection of the warp behaves as a separate entity with a starting logical lane ID of 0. A thread may only exchange data with other threads in its subsection.

__shfl() returns the value of var held by the thread whose ID is given by srcLane. If srcLane is outside the range 0..width-1, the thread's own value of var is returned. This variant of the instruction can be used to broadcast values within a warp. __shfl_up() calculates a source lane ID by subtracting delta from the caller's lane ID and clamping to the range 0..width-1. __shfl_down() calculates a source lane ID by adding delta to the caller's lane ID.

__shfl_up() and __shfl_down() enable warp-level scan and reverse scan operations, respectively. __shfl_xor() calculates a source lane ID by performing a bitwise XOR of the caller's lane ID with laneMask; the value of var held by the resulting lane ID is returned. This variant can be used to do a reduction across the warps (or subwarps); each thread computes the reduction using a differently ordered series of the associative operator.

8.6.2 BLOCK-LEVEL PRIMITIVES

The `__syncthreads()` intrinsic serves as a barrier. It causes all threads to wait until every thread in the threadblock has arrived at the `__syncthreads()`. The Fermi instruction set (SM 2.x) added several new block-level barriers that aggregate information about the threads in the threadblock.

- `__syncthreads_count()`: evaluates a predicate and returns the sum of threads for which the predicate was true

- `__syncthreads_or()`: returns the OR of all the inputs across the threadblock

- `__syncthreads_and()`: returns the AND of all the inputs across the threadblock

8.6.3 PERFORMANCE COUNTER

Developers can define their own set of performance counters and increment them in live code with the `__prof_trigger()` intrinsic.

```
void __prof_trigger(int counter);
```

Calling this function increments the corresponding counter by 1 per warp. `counter` must be in the range 0..7; counters 8..15 are reserved. The value of the counters may be obtained by listing `prof_trigger_00..prof_trigger_07` in the profiler configuration file.

8.6.4 VIDEO INSTRUCTIONS

The video instructions described in this section are accessible only via the inline PTX assembler. Their basic functionality is described here to help developers to decide whether they might be beneficial for their application. Anyone intending to use these instructions, however, should consult the PTX ISA specification.

Scalar Video Instructions

The scalar video instructions, added with SM 2.0 hardware, enable efficient operations on the short (8- and 16-bit) integer types needed for video processing. As described in the PTX 3.1 ISA Specification, the format of these instructions is as follows.

```
vop.dtype.atype.btype{.sat} d, a{.asel}, b{.bsel};
vop.dtype.atype.btype{.sat}.secop d, a{.asel}, b{.bsel}, c;
```

The source and destination operands are all 32-bit registers. `dtype`, `atype`, and `btype` may be `.u32` or `.s32` for unsigned and signed 32-bit integers, respectively. The `asel`/`bsel` specifiers select which 8- or 16-bit value to extract from the source operands: `b0`, `b1`, `b2`, and `b3` select bytes (numbering from the least significant), and `h0`/`h1` select the least significant and most significant 16 bits, respectively.

Once the input values are extracted, they are sign- or zero-extended internally to signed 33-bit integers, and the primary operation is performed, producing a 34-bit intermediate result whose sign depends on `dtype`. Finally, the result is clamped to the output range, and one of the following operations is performed.

1. Apply a second operation (add, min or max) to the intermediate result and a third operand.

2. Truncate the intermediate result to an 8- or 16-bit value and merge into a specified position in the third operand to produce the final result.

The lower 32 bits are then written to the destination operand.

The `vset` instruction performs a comparison between the 8-, 16-, or 32-bit input operands and generates the corresponding predicate (1 or 0) as output. The PTX scalar video instructions and the corresponding operations are given in Table 8.14.

Table 8.14 Scalar Video Instructions.

MNEMONIC	OPERATION
vabsdiff	abs(a-b)
vadd	a+b
vavrg	(a+b)/2
vmad	a*b+c
vmax	max(a,b)

continues

273

Table 8.14 Scalar Video Instructions. *(Continued)*

MNEMONIC	OPERATION
vmin	min(a,b)
vset	Compare a and b
vshl	a<<b
vshr	a>>b
vsub	a-b

Vector Video Instructions (SM 3.0 only)

These instructions, added with SM 3.0, are similar to the scalar video instructions in that they promote the inputs to a canonical integer format, perform the core operation, and then clamp and optionally merge the output. But they deliver higher performance by operating on pairs of 16-bit values or quads of 8-bit values.

Table 8.15 summarizes the PTX instructions and corresponding operations implemented by these instructions. They are most useful for video processing and certain image processing operations (such as the median filter).

Table 8.15 Vector Video Instructions

MNEMONIC	OPERATION
vabsdiff[2|4]	abs(a-b)
vadd[2|4]	a+b
vavrg[2|4]	(a+b)/2
vmax[2|4]	max(a,b)
vmin[2|4]	min(a,b)
vset[2|4]	Compare a and b
vsub[2|4]	a-b

8.6.5 SPECIAL REGISTERS

Many special registers are accessed by referencing the built-in variables `threadIdx`, `blockIdx`, `blockDim`, and `gridDim`. These pseudo-variables, described in detail in Section 7.3, are 3-dimensional structures that specify the thread ID, block ID, thread count, and block count, respectively.

Besides those, another special register is the SM's clock register, which increments with each clock cycle. This counter can be read with the `__clock()` or `__clock64()` intrinsic. The counters are separately tracked for each SM and, like the time stamp counters on CPUs, are most useful for measuring relative performance of different code sequences and best avoided when trying to calculate wall clock times.

8.7 Instruction Sets

NVIDIA has developed three major architectures: Tesla (SM 1.x), Fermi (SM 2.x), and Kepler (SM 3.x). Within those families, new instructions have been added as NVIDIA updated their products. For example, global atomic operations were not present in the very first Tesla-class processor (the G80, which shipped in 2006 as the GeForce GTX 8800), but all subsequent Tesla-class GPUs included them. So when querying the SM version via `cuDeviceComputeCapability()`, the major and minor versions will be 1.0 for G80 and 1.1 (or greater) for all other Tesla-class GPUs. Conversely, if the SM version is 1.1 or greater, the application can use global atomics.

Table 8.16 gives the SASS instructions that may be printed by `cuobjdump` when disassembling microcode for Tesla-class (SM 1.x) hardware. The Fermi and Kepler instruction sets closely resemble each other, with the exception of the instructions that support surface load/store, so their instruction sets are given together in Table 8.17. In both tables, the middle column specifies the first SM version to support a given instruction.

Table 8.16 SM 1.x Instruction Set

OPCODE	SM	DESCRIPTION
FLOATING POINT		
COS	1.0	Cosine
DADD	1.3	Double-precision floating-point add
DFMA	1.3	Double-precision floating-point fused multiply-add
DMAX	1.3	Double-precision floating-point maximum
DMIN	1.3	Double-precision floating-point minimum
DMUL	1.3	Double-precision floating-point multiply
DSET	1.3	Double-precision floating-point condition set
EX2	1.0	Exponential (base 2)
FADD/FADD32/FADD32I	1.0	Single-precision floating-point add
FCMP	1.0	Single-precision floating-point compare
FMAD/FMAD32/FMAD32I	1.0	Single-precision floating-point multiply-add
FMAX	1.0	Single-precision floating-point maximum
FMIN	1.0	Single-precision floating-point minimum
FMUL/FMUL32/FMUL32I	1.0	Single-precision floating-point multiply
FSET	1.0	Single-precision floating-point conditional set
LG2	1.0	Single-precision floating-point logarithm (base 2)
RCP	1.0	Single-precision floating-point reciprocal
RRO	1.0	Range reduction operator (used before SIN/COS)
RSQ	1.0	Reciprocal square root
SIN	1.0	Sine

Table 8.16 SM 1.x Instruction Set *(Continued)*

OPCODE	SM	DESCRIPTION
FLOW CONTROL		
BAR	1.0	Barrier synchronization/__syncthreads()
BRA	1.0	Conditional branch
BRK	1.0	Conditional break from loop
BRX	1.0	Fetch an address from constant memory and branch to it
C2R	1.0	Condition code to data register
CAL	1.0	Unconditional subroutine call
RET	1.0	Conditional return from subroutine
SSY	1.0	Set synchronization point; used before potentially divergent instructions
DATA CONVERSION		
F2F	1.0	Copy floating-point value with conversion to floating point
F2I	1.0	Copy floating-point value with conversion to integer
I2F	1.0	Copy integer value to floating-point with conversion
I2I	1.0	Copy integer value to integer with conversion
INTEGER		
IADD/ IADD32/ IADD32I	1.0	Integer addition
IMAD/ IMAD32/ IMAD32I	1.0	Integer multiply-add
IMAX	1.0	Integer maximum
IMIN	1.0	Integer minimum
IMUL/ IMUL32/ IMUL32I	1.0	Integer multiply
ISAD/ ISAD32	1.0	Integer sum of absolute difference

continues

Table 8.16 SM 1.x Instruction Set *(Continued)*

OPCODE	SM	DESCRIPTION
ISET	1.0	Integer conditional set
SHL	1.0	Shift left
SHR	1.0	Shift right
MEMORY OPERATIONS		
A2R	1.0	Move address register to data register
ADA	1.0	Add immediate to address register
G2R	1.0	Move from shared memory to register. The .LCK suffix, used to implement shared memory atomics, causes the bank to be locked until an R2G.UNL has been performed.
GATOM.IADD/ EXCH/ CAS/ IMIN/ IMAX/ INC/ DEC/ IAND/ IOR/ IXOR	1.2	Global memory atomic operations; performs an atomic operation and returns the original value.
GLD	1.0	Load from global memory
GRED.IADD/ IMIN/ IMAX/ INC/ DEC/ IAND/ IOR/ IXOR	1.2	Global memory reduction operations; performs an atomic operation with no return value.
GST	1.0	Store to global memory
LLD	1.0	Load from local memory
LST	1.0	Store to local memory
LOP	1.0	Logical operation (AND/OR/XOR)
MOV/ MOV32	1.0	Move source to destination
MVC	1.0	Move from constant memory
MVI	1.0	Move immediate
R2A	1.0	Move register to address register
R2C	1.0	Move data register to condition code
R2G	1.0	Store to shared memory. When used with the .UNL suffix, releases a previously held lock on that shared memory bank.

Table 8.16 SM 1.x Instruction Set *(Continued)*

OPCODE	SM	DESCRIPTION
MISCELLANEOUS		
NOP	1.0	No operation
TEX/ TEX32	1.0	Texture fetch
VOTE	1.2	Warp-vote primitive.
S2R	1.0	Move special register (e.g., thread ID) to register

Table 8.17 SM 2.x and SM 3.x Instruction Sets

OPCODE	SM	DESCRIPTION
FLOATING POINT		
DADD	2.0	Double-precision add
DMUL	2.0	Double-precision multiply
DMNMX	2.0	Double-precision minimum/maximum
DSET	2.0	Double-precision set
DSETP	2.0	Double-precision predicate
DFMA	2.0	Double-precision fused multiply-add
FFMA	2.0	Single-precision fused multiply-add
FADD	2.0	Single-precision floating-point add
FCMP	2.0	Single-precision floating-point compare
FMUL	2.0	Single-precision floating-point multiply
FMNMX	2.0	Single-precision floating-point minimum/maximum
FSWZ	2.0	Single-precision floating-point swizzle

continues

Table 8.17 SM 2.x and SM 3.x Instruction Sets *(Continued)*

OPCODE	SM	DESCRIPTION
FSET	2.0	Single-precision floating-point set
FSETP	2.0	Single-precision floating-point set predicate
MUFU	2.0	MultiFunk (SFU) operator
RRO	2.0	Range reduction operator (used before MUFU sin/cos)
INTEGER		
BFE	2.0	Bit field extract
BFI	2.0	Bit field insert
FLO	2.0	Find leading one
IADD	2.0	Integer add
ICMP	2.0	Integer compare and select
IMAD	2.0	Integer multiply-add
IMNMX	2.0	Integer minimum/maximum
IMUL	2.0	Integer multiply
ISAD	2.0	Integer sum of absolute differences
ISCADD	2.0	Integer add with scale
ISET	2.0	Integer set
ISETP	2.0	Integer set predicate
LOP	2.0	Logical operation (AND/OR/XOR)
SHF	3.5	Funnel shift
SHL	2.0	Shift left
SHR	2.0	Shift right
POPC	2.0	Population count

Table 8.17 SM 2.x and SM 3.x Instruction Sets *(Continued)*

OPCODE	SM	DESCRIPTION
DATA CONVERSION		
F2F	2.0	Floating point to floating point
F2I	2.0	Floating point to integer
I2F	2.0	Integer to floating point
I2I	2.0	Integer to integer
SCALAR VIDEO		
VABSDIFF	2.0	Scalar video absolute difference
VADD	2.0	Scalar video add
VMAD	2.0	Scalar video multiply-add
VMAX	2.0	Scalar video maximum
VMIN	2.0	Scalar video minimum
VSET	2.0	Scalar video set
VSHL	2.0	Scalar video shift left
VSHR	2.0	Scalar video shift right
VSUB	2.0	Scalar video subtract
VECTOR (SIMD) VIDEO		
VABSDIFF2(4)	3.0	Vector video 2x16-bit (4x8-bit) absolute difference
VADD2(4)	3.0	Vector video 2x16-bit (4x8-bit) addition
VAVRG2(4)	3.0	Vector video 2x16-bit (4x8-bit) average
VMAX2(4)	3.0	Vector video 2x16-bit (4x8-bit) maximum
VMIN2(4)	3.0	Vector video 2x16-bit (4x8-bit) minimum
VSET2(4)	3.0	Vector video 2x16-bit (4x8-bit) set
VSUB2(4)	3.0	Vector video 2x16-bit (4x8-bit) subtraction

continues

Table 8.17 SM 2.x and SM 3.x Instruction Sets *(Continued)*

OPCODE	SM	DESCRIPTION
DATA MOVEMENT		
MOV	2.0	Move
PRMT	2.0	Permute
SEL	2.0	Select (conditional move)
SHFL	3.0	Warp shuffle
PREDICATE/CONDITION CODES		
CSET	2.0	Condition code set
CSETP	2.0	Condition code set predicate
P2R	2.0	Predicate to register
R2P	2.0	Register to predicate
PSET	2.0	Predicate set
PSETP	2.0	Predicate set predicate
TEXTURE		
TEX	2.0	Texture fetch
TLD	2.0	Texture load
TLD4	2.0	Texture load 4 texels
TXQ	2.0	Texture query
MEMORY OPERATIONS		
ATOM	2.0	Atomic memory operation
CCTL	2.0	Cache control
CCTLL	2.0	Cache control (local)
LD	2.0	Load from memory

Table 8.17 SM 2.x and SM 3.x Instruction Sets *(Continued)*

OPCODE	SM	DESCRIPTION
LDC	2.0	Load constant
LDG	3.5	Noncoherence global load (reads via texture cache)
LDL	2.0	Load from local memory
LDLK	2.0	Load and lock
LDS	2.0	Load from shared memory
LDSLK	2.0	Load from shared memory and lock
LDU	2.0	Load uniform
LD_LDU	2.0	Combines generic load LD with a load uniform LDU
LDS_LDU	2.0	Combines shared memory load LDS with a load uniform LDU
MEMBAR	2.0	Memory barrier
RED	2.0	Atomic memory reduction operation
ST	2.0	Store to memory
STL	2.0	Store to local memory
STUL	2.0	Store and unlock
STS	2.0	Store to shared memory
STSUL	2.0	Store to shared memory and unlock
SURFACE MEMORY (FERMI)		
SULD	2.0	Surface load
SULEA	2.0	Surface load effective address
SUQ	2.0	Surface query
SURED	2.0	Surface reduction
SUST	2.0	Surface store

continues

Table 8.17 SM 2.x and SM 3.x Instruction Sets (Continued)

OPCODE	SM	DESCRIPTION
SURFACE MEMORY (KEPLER)		
SUBFM	3.0	Surface bit field merge
SUCLAMP	3.0	Surface clamp
SUEAU	3.0	Surface effective address
SULDGA	3.0	Surface load generic address
SUSTGA	3.0	Surface store generic address
FLOW CONTROL		
BRA	2.0	Branch to relative address
BPT	2.0	Breakpoint/trap
BRK	2.0	Break from loop
BRX	2.0	Branch to relative indexed address
CAL	2.0	Call to relative address
CONT	2.0	Continue in loop
EXIT	2.0	Exit program
JCAL	2.0	Call to absolute address
JMP	2.0	Jump to absolute address
JMX	2.0	Jump to absolute indexed address
LONGJMP	2.0	Long jump
PBK	2.0	Pre-break relative address
PCNT	2.0	Pre-continue relative address
PLONGJMP	2.0	Pre-long jump relative address
PRET	2.0	Pre-return relative address

Table 8.17 SM 2.x and SM 3.x Instruction Sets *(Continued)*

OPCODE	SM	DESCRIPTION
RET	2.0	Return from call
SSY	2.0	Set synchronization point; used before potentially divergent instructions
MISCELLANEOUS		
B2R	2.0	Barrier to register
BAR	2.0	Barrier synchronization
LEPC	2.0	Load effective program counter
NOP	2.0	No operation
S2R	2.0	Special register to register (used to read, for example, the thread or block ID)
VOTE	2.0	Query condition across warp

Chapter 9

Multiple GPUs

This chapter describes CUDA's facilities for multi-GPU programming, including threading models, peer-to-peer, and inter-GPU synchronization. As an example, we'll first explore inter-GPU synchronization using CUDA streams and events by implementing a peer-to-peer memcpy that stages through portable pinned memory. We then discuss how to implement the N-body problem (fully described in Chapter 14) with single- and multithreaded implementations that use multiple GPUs.

9.1 Overview

Systems with multiple GPUs generally contain multi-GPU boards with a PCI Express bridge chip (such as the GeForce GTX 690) or multiple PCI Express slots, or both, as described in Section 2.3. Each GPU in such a system is separated by PCI Express bandwidth, so there is always a huge disparity in bandwidth between memory connected directly to a GPU (its device memory) and its connections to other GPUs as well as the CPU.

Many CUDA features designed to run on multiple GPUs, such as peer-to-peer addressing, require the GPUs to be identical. For applications that can make assumptions about the target hardware (such as vertical applications built for specific hardware configurations), this requirement is innocuous enough. But applications targeting systems with a variety of GPUs (say, a low-power one for everyday use and a powerful one for gaming) may have to use heuristics to decide which GPU(s) to use or load-balance the workload across GPUs so the faster ones contribute more computation to the final output, commensurate with their higher performance.

A key ingredient to all CUDA applications that use multiple GPUs is *portable pinned memory*. As described in Section 5.1.2, portable pinned memory is pinned memory that is mapped for all CUDA contexts such that any GPU can read or write the memory directly.

CPU Threading Models

Until CUDA 4.0, the only way to drive multiple GPUs was to create a CPU thread for each one. The `cudaSetDevice()` function had to be called once per CPU thread, before any CUDA code had executed, in order to tell CUDA which device to initialize when the CPU thread started to operate on CUDA. Whichever CPU thread made that call would then get exclusive access to the GPU, because the CUDA driver had not yet been made thread-safe in a way that would enable multiple threads to access the same GPU at the same time.

In CUDA 4.0, `cudaSetDevice()` was modified to implement the semantics that everyone had previously expected: It tells CUDA which GPU should perform subsequent CUDA operations. Having multiple threads operating on the same GPU at the same time may incur a slight performance hit, but it should be expected to work. Our example N-body application, however, only has one CPU thread operating on any given device at a time. The multithreaded formulation has each of *N* threads operate on a specific device, and the single-threaded formulation has one thread operate on each of the *N* devices in turn.

9.2 Peer-to-Peer

When multiple GPUs are used by a CUDA program, they are known as "peers" because the application generally treats them equally, as if they were coworkers collaborating on a project. CUDA enables two flavors of peer-to-peer: explicit memcpy and peer-to-peer addressing.[1]

9.2.1 PEER-TO-PEER MEMCPY

Memory copies can be performed between the memories of any two different devices. When UVA (Unified Virtual Addressing) is in effect, the ordinary family of memcpy function can be used for peer-to-peer memcpy, since CUDA can infer which device "owns" which memory. If UVA is not in effect, the peer-to-peer

---

1. For peer-to-peer addressing, the term *peer* also harkens to the requirement that the GPUs be identical.

memcpy must be done explicitly using `cudaMemcpyPeer()`, `cudaMemcpy-PeerAsync()`, `cudaMemcpy3DPeer()`, or `cudaMemcpy3DPeerAsync()`.

NOTE

CUDA can copy memory between any two devices, not just devices that can directly address one another's memory. If necessary, CUDA will stage the memory copy through host memory, which can be accessed by any device in the system.

Peer-to-peer memcpy operations do not run concurrently with any other operation. Any pending operations on either GPU must complete before the peer-to-peer memcpy can begin, and no subsequent operations can start to execute until after the peer-to-peer memcpy is done. When possible, CUDA will use direct peer-to-peer mappings between the two pointers. The resulting copies are faster and do not have to be staged through host memory.

9.2.2 PEER-TO-PEER ADDRESSING

Peer-to-peer mappings of device memory, shown in Figure 2.20, enable a kernel running on one GPU to read or write memory that resides in another GPU. Since the GPUs can only use peer-to-peer to read or write data at PCI Express rates, developers have to partition the workload in such a way that

1. Each GPU has about an equal amount of work to do.

2. The GPUs only need to interchange modest amounts of data.

Examples of such systems might be a pipelined computer vision system where each stage in the pipeline of GPUs computes an intermediate data structure (e.g., locations of identified features) that needs to be further analyzed by the next GPU in the pipeline or a large so-called "stencil" computation in which separate GPUs can perform most of the computation independently but must exchange edge data between computation steps.

In order for peer-to-peer addressing to work, the following conditions apply.

- Unified virtual addressing (UVA) must be in effect.

- Both GPUs must be SM 2.x or higher and must be based on the same chip.

- The GPUs must be on the same I/O hub.

cu(da)DeviceCanAccessPeer () may be called to query whether the current device can map another device's memory.

```
cudaError_t cudaDeviceCanAccessPeer(int *canAccessPeer, int device,
int peerDevice);
CUresult cuDeviceCanAccessPeer(int *canAccessPeer, CUdevice device,
CUdevice peerDevice);
```

Peer-to-peer mappings are not enabled automatically; they must be specifically requested by calling cudaDeviceEnablePeerAccess () or cuCtxEnablePeerAccess ().

```
cudaError_t cudaDeviceEnablePeerAccess(int peerDevice, unsigned int
flags);
CUresult cuCtxEnablePeerAccess(CUcontext peerContext, unsigned int
Flags);
```

Once peer-to-peer access has been enabled, all memory in the peer device—including new allocations—is accessible to the current device until cudaDeviceDisablePeerAccess () or cuCtxDisablePeerAccess () is called.

Peer-to-peer access uses a small amount of extra memory (to hold more page tables) and makes memory allocation more expensive, since the memory must be mapped for all participating devices. Peer-to-peer functionality enables contexts to read and write memory belonging to other contexts, both via memcpy (which may be implemented by staging through system memory) and directly by having kernels read or write global memory pointers.

The cudaDeviceEnablePeerAccess () function maps the memory belonging to another device. Peer-to-peer memory addressing is asymmetric; it is possible for GPU A to map GPU B's allocations without its allocations being available to GPU B. In order for two GPUs to see each other's memory, each GPU must explicitly map the other's memory.

```
// tell device 1 to map device 0 memory
cudaSetDevice( 1 );
cudaDeviceEnablePeerAccess( 0, cudaPeerAccessDefault );
// tell device 0 to map device 1 memory
cudaSetDevice( 0 );
cudaDeviceEnablePeerAccess( 1, cudaPeerAccessDefault );
```

NOTE

On GPU boards with PCI Express 3.0–capable bridge chips (such as the Tesla K10), the GPUs can communicate at PCI Express 3.0 speeds even if the board is plugged into a PCI Express 2.0 slot.

9.3 UVA: Inferring Device from Address

Since UVA is always enabled on peer-to-peer-capable systems, the address ranges for different devices do not overlap, and the driver can infer the owning device from a pointer value. The cuPointerGetAttribute() function may be used to query information about UVA pointers, including the owning context.

```
CUresult CUDAAPI cuPointerGetAttribute(void *data, CUpointer_
attribute attribute, CUdeviceptr ptr);
```

cuPointerGetAttribute() or cudaPointerGetAttributes() may be used to query the attributes of a pointer. Table 9.1 gives the values that can be passed into cuPointerGetAttribute(); the structure passed back by cudaPointerGetAttributes() is as follows.

```
struct cudaPointerAttributes {
    enum cudaMemoryType memoryType;
    int device;
    void *devicePointer;
    void *hostPointer;
}
```

Table 9.1 cuPointerGetAttribute() Attributes

ATTRIBUTE	PASSBACK TYPE	DESCRIPTION
CU_POINTER_ATTRIBUTE_CONTEXT	CUcontext	Context in which a pointer was allocated or registered
CU_POINTER_ATTRIBUTE_MEMORY_TYPE	CUmemorytype	Physical location of a pointer
CU_POINTER_ATTRIBUTE_DEVICE_POINTER	CUdeviceptr	Pointer at which the memory may be accessed by the GPU
CU_POINTER_ATTRIBUTE_HOST_POINTER	void *	Pointer at which the memory may be accessed by the host

memoryType may be cudaMemoryTypeHost or cudaMemoryTypeDevice.

device is the device for which the pointer was allocated. For device memory, device identifies the device where the memory corresponding to ptr was allocated. For host memory, device identifies the device that was current when the allocation was performed.

devicePointer gives the device pointer value that may be used to reference ptr from the current device. If ptr cannot be accessed by the current device, devicePointer is NULL.

hostPointer gives the host pointer value that may be used to reference ptr from the CPU. If ptr cannot be accessed by the current host, hostPointer is NULL.

9.4 Inter-GPU Synchronization

CUDA events may be used for inter-GPU synchronization using cu(da) StreamWaitEvent(). If there is a producer/consumer relationship between two GPUs, the application can have the producer GPU record an event and then have the consumer GPU insert a stream-wait on that event into its command stream. When the consumer GPU encounters the stream-wait, it will stop processing commands until the producer GPU has passed the point of execution where cu(da)EventRecord() was called.

NOTE

In CUDA 5.0, the device runtime, described in Section 7.5, does not enable any inter-GPU synchronization whatsoever. That limitation may be relaxed in a future release.

Listing 9.1 gives chMemcpyPeerToPeer(),[2] an implementation of peer-to-peer memcpy that uses portable memory and inter-GPU synchronization to implement the same type of memcpy that CUDA uses under the covers, if no direct mapping between the GPUs exists. The function works similarly to the chMemcpyHtoD() function in Listing 6.2 that performs host→device memcpy:

---

2. The CUDART_CHECK error handling has been removed for clarity.

A staging buffer is allocated in host memory, and the memcpy begins by having the source GPU copy source data into the staging buffer and recording an event. But unlike the host→device memcpy, there is never any need for the CPU to synchronize because all synchronization is done by the GPUs. Because both the memcpy and the event-record are asynchronous, immediately after kicking off the initial memcpy and event-record, the CPU can request that the destination GPU wait on that event and kick off a memcpy of the same buffer. Two staging buffers and two CUDA events are needed, so the two GPUs can copy to and from staging buffers concurrently, much as the CPU and GPU concurrently operate on staging buffers during the host→device memcpy. The CPU loops over the input buffer and output buffers, issuing memcpy and event-record commands and ping-ponging between staging buffers, until it has requested copies for all bytes and all that's left to do is wait for both GPUs to finish processing.

NOTE

As with the implementations in the CUDA support provided by NVIDIA, our peer-to-peer memcpy is synchronous.

Listing 9.1 `chMemcpyPeerToPeer()`.

```
cudaError_t
chMemcpyPeerToPeer(
    void *_dst, int dstDevice,
    const void *_src, int srcDevice,
    size_t N )
{
    cudaError_t status;
    char *dst = (char *) _dst;
    const char *src = (const char *) _src;
    int stagingIndex = 0;
    while ( N ) {
        size_t thisCopySize = min( N, STAGING_BUFFER_SIZE );

        cudaSetDevice( srcDevice );
        cudaStreamWaitEvent( 0, g_events[dstDevice][stagingIndex],0);
        cudaMemcpyAsync( g_hostBuffers[stagingIndex], src,
            thisCopySize, cudaMemcpyDeviceToHost, NULL );
        cudaEventRecord( g_events[srcDevice][stagingIndex] );

        cudaSetDevice( dstDevice );
        cudaStreamWaitEvent( 0, g_events[srcDevice][stagingIndex],0);
        cudaMemcpyAsync( dst, g_hostBuffers[stagingIndex],
            thisCopySize, cudaMemcpyHostToDevice, NULL );
        cudaEventRecord( g_events[dstDevice][stagingIndex] );
```

```
        dst += thisCopySize;
        src += thisCopySize;
        N -= thisCopySize;
        stagingIndex = 1 - stagingIndex;
    }
    // Wait until both devices are done
    cudaSetDevice( srcDevice );
    cudaDeviceSynchronize();

    cudaSetDevice( dstDevice );
    cudaDeviceSynchronize();

Error:
    return status;
}
```

9.5 Single-Threaded Multi-GPU

When using the CUDA runtime, a single-threaded application can drive multiple GPUs by calling cudaSetDevice() to specify which GPU will be operated by the calling CPU thread. This idiom is used in Listing 9.1 to switch between the source and destination GPUs during the peer-to-peer memcpy, as well as the single-threaded, multi-GPU implementation of N-body described in Section 9.5.2. In the driver API, CUDA maintains a stack of current contexts so that subroutines can easily change and restore the caller's current context.

9.5.1 CURRENT CONTEXT STACK

Driver API applications can manage the current context with the current-context stack: cuCtxPushCurrent() makes a new context current, pushing it onto the top of the stack, and cuCtxPopCurrent() pops the current context and restores the previous current context. Listing 9.2 gives a driver API version of chMemcpyPeerToPeer(), which uses cuCtxPopCurrent() and cuCtx-PushCurrent() to perform a peer-to-peer memcpy between two contexts.

The current context stack was introduced to CUDA in v2.2, and at the time, the CUDA runtime and driver API could not be used in the same application. That restriction has been relaxed in subsequent versions.

Listing 9.2 `chMemcpyPeerToPeer` (driver API version).

```
CUresult
chMemcpyPeerToPeer(
    void *_dst, CUcontext dstContext, int dstDevice,
    const void *_src, CUcontext srcContext, int srcDevice,
    size_t N )
{
    CUresult status;
    CUdeviceptr dst = (CUdeviceptr) (intptr_t) _dst;
    CUdeviceptr src = (CUdeviceptr) (intptr_t) _src;
    int stagingIndex = 0;

    while ( N ) {
        size_t thisCopySize = min( N, STAGING_BUFFER_SIZE );

        CUDA_CHECK( cuCtxPushCurrent( srcContext ) );
        CUDA_CHECK( cuStreamWaitEvent(
            NULL, g_events[dstDevice][stagingIndex], 0 ) );
        CUDA_CHECK( cuMemcpyDtoHAsync(
            g_hostBuffers[stagingIndex],
            src,
            thisCopySize,
            NULL ) );
        CUDA_CHECK( cuEventRecord(
            g_events[srcDevice][stagingIndex],
            0 ) );

        CUDA_CHECK( cuCtxPopCurrent( &srcContext ) );
        CUDA_CHECK( cuCtxPushCurrent( dstContext ) );
        CUDA_CHECK( cuStreamWaitEvent(
            NULL,
            g_events[srcDevice][stagingIndex],
            0 ) );
        CUDA_CHECK( cuMemcpyHtoDAsync(
            dst,
            g_hostBuffers[stagingIndex],
            thisCopySize,
            NULL ) );
        CUDA_CHECK( cuEventRecord(
            g_events[dstDevice][stagingIndex],
            0 ) );

        CUDA_CHECK( cuCtxPopCurrent( &dstContext ) );

        dst += thisCopySize;
        src += thisCopySize;
        N -= thisCopySize;
        stagingIndex = 1 - stagingIndex;
    }

    // Wait until both devices are done
    CUDA_CHECK( cuCtxPushCurrent( srcContext ) );
```

```
        CUDA_CHECK( cuCtxSynchronize() );
        CUDA_CHECK( cuCtxPopCurrent( &srcContext ) );

        CUDA_CHECK( cuCtxPushCurrent( dstContext ) );
        CUDA_CHECK( cuCtxSynchronize() );
        CUDA_CHECK( cuCtxPopCurrent( &dstContext ) );

Error:
        return status;
}
```

9.5.2 N-BODY

The N-body computation (described in detail in Chapter 14) computes N forces in $O(N^2)$ time, and the outputs may be computed independently. On a system with k GPUs, our multi-GPU implementation splits the computation into k parts.

Our implementation makes the common assumption that the GPUs are identical, so it divides the computation evenly. Applications targeting GPUs of unequal performance, or whose workloads have less predictable runtimes, can divide the computation more finely and have the host code submit work items to the GPUs from a queue.

Listing 9.3 gives a modified version of Listing 14.3 that takes two additional parameters (a base index base and size n of the subarray of forces) to compute a subset of the output array for an N-body computation. This __device__ function is invoked by wrapper kernels that are declared as __global__. It is structured this way to reuse the code without incurring link errors. If the function were declared as __global__, the linker would generate an error about duplicate symbols.[3]

Listing 9.3 N-body kernel (multi-GPU).

```
inline __device__ void
ComputeNBodyGravitation_Shared_multiGPU(
    float *force,
    float *posMass,
    float softeningSquared,
    size_t base,
    size_t n,
    size_t N )
```

---

3. This is a bit of an old-school workaround. CUDA 5.0 added a linker that enables the __global__ function to be compiled into a static library and linked into the application.

```
{
    float4 *posMass4 = (float4 *) posMass;
    extern __shared__ float4 shPosMass[];
    for ( int m = blockIdx.x*blockDim.x + threadIdx.x;
              m < n;
              m += blockDim.x*gridDim.x )
    {
        size_t i = base+m;
        float acc[3] = {0};
        float4 myPosMass = posMass4[i];
#pragma unroll 32
        for ( int j = 0; j < N; j += blockDim.x ) {
            shPosMass[threadIdx.x] = posMass4[j+threadIdx.x];
            __syncthreads();
            for ( size_t k = 0; k < blockDim.x; k++ ) {
                float fx, fy, fz;
                float4 bodyPosMass = shPosMass[k];

                bodyBodyInteraction(
                    &fx, &fy, &fz,
                    myPosMass.x, myPosMass.y, myPosMass.z,
                    bodyPosMass.x,
                    bodyPosMass.y,
                    bodyPosMass.z,
                    bodyPosMass.w,
                    softeningSquared );
                acc[0] += fx;
                acc[1] += fy;
                acc[2] += fz;
            }
            __syncthreads();
        }
        force[3*m+0] = acc[0];
        force[3*m+1] = acc[1];
        force[3*m+2] = acc[2];
    }
}
```

The host code for a single-threaded, multi-GPU version of N-body is shown in Listing 9.4.[4] The arrays `dptrPosMass` and `dptrForce` track the device pointers for the input and output arrays for each GPU (the maximum number of GPUs is declared as a constant in `nbody.h`; default is 32). Similar to dispatching work into CUDA streams, the function uses separate loops for different stages of the computation: The first loop allocates and populates the input array for each GPU; the second loop launches the kernel and an asynchronous copy of the output data; and the third loop calls `cudaDeviceSynchronize()` on each GPU in turn. Structuring the function this way maximizes CPU/GPU overlap. During

---

4. To avoid awkward formatting, error checking has been removed.

the first loop, asynchronous host→device memcpys to GPUs 0..*i*-1 can proceed while the CPU is busy allocating memory for GPU *i*. If the kernel launch and asynchronous device→host memcpy were in the first loop, the synchronous cudaMalloc() calls would decrease performance because they are synchronous with respect to the current GPU.

Listing 9.4 N-body host code (single-threaded multi-GPU).

```
float
ComputeGravitation_multiGPU_singlethread(
    float *force,
    float *posMass,
    float softeningSquared,
    size_t N
)
{
    cudaError_t status;

    float ret = 0.0f;

    float *dptrPosMass[g_maxGPUs];
    float *dptrForce[g_maxGPUs];

    chTimerTimestamp start, end;
    chTimerGetTime( &start );

    memset( dptrPosMass, 0, sizeof(dptrPosMass) );
    memset( dptrForce, 0, sizeof(dptrForce) );
    size_t bodiesPerGPU = N / g_numGPUs;
    if ( (0 != N % g_numGPUs) || (g_numGPUs > g_maxGPUs) ) {
        return 0.0f;
    }

    // kick off the asynchronous memcpy's - overlap GPUs pulling
    // host memory with the CPU time needed to do the memory
    // allocations.
    for ( int i = 0; i < g_numGPUs; i++ ) {
        cudaSetDevice( i );
        cudaMalloc( &dptrPosMass[i], 4*N*sizeof(float) );
        cudaMalloc( &dptrForce[i], 3*bodiesPerGPU*sizeof(float) );
        cudaMemcpyAsync(
            dptrPosMass[i],
            g_hostAOS_PosMass,
            4*N*sizeof(float),
            cudaMemcpyHostToDevice );
    }
    for ( int i = 0; i < g_numGPUs; i++ ) {
        cudaSetDevice( i );
        ComputeNBodyGravitation_Shared_device<<<
            300,256,256*sizeof(float4)>>>(
            dptrForce[i],
            dptrPosMass[i],
```

```
                softeningSquared,
                i*bodiesPerGPU,
                bodiesPerGPU,
                N );
            cudaMemcpyAsync(
                g_hostAOS_Force+3*bodiesPerGPU*i,
                dptrForce[i],
                3*bodiesPerGPU*sizeof(float),
                cudaMemcpyDeviceToHost );
        }
        // Synchronize with each GPU in turn.
        for ( int i = 0; i < g_numGPUs; i++ ) {
            cudaSetDevice( i );
            cudaDeviceSynchronize();
        }
        chTimerGetTime( &end );
        ret = chTimerElapsedTime( &start, &end ) * 1000.0f;
Error:
        for ( int i = 0; i < g_numGPUs; i++ ) {
            cudaFree( dptrPosMass[i] );
            cudaFree( dptrForce[i] );
        }
        return ret;
}
```

9.6 Multithreaded Multi-GPU

CUDA has supported multiple GPUs since the beginning, but until CUDA 4.0, each GPU had to be controlled by a separate CPU thread. For workloads that required a lot of CPU power, that requirement was never very onerous because the full power of modern multicore processors can be unlocked only through multithreading.

The multithreaded implementation of multi-GPU N-Body creates one CPU thread per GPU, and it delegates the dispatch and synchronization of the work for a given N-body pass to each thread. The main thread splits the work evenly between GPUs, delegates work to each worker thread by signaling an event (or a semaphore, on POSIX platforms such as Linux), and then waits for all of the worker threads to signal completion before proceeding. As the number of GPUs grows, synchronization overhead starts to chip away at the benefits from parallelism.

This implementation of N-body uses the same multithreading library as the multithreaded implementation of N-body, described in Section 14.9. The workerThread class, described in Appendix A.2, enables the application thread to "delegate" work to CPU threads, then synchronize on the worker threads' completion of the delegated task.

Listing 9.5 gives the host code that creates and initializes the CPU threads. Two globals, g_numGPUs and g_GPUThreadPool, contain the GPU count and a worker thread for each. After each CPU thread is created, it is initialized by synchronously calling the initializeGPU() function, which affiliates the CPU thread with a given GPU—an affiliation that never changes during the course of the application's execution.

Listing 9.5 Multithreaded multi-GPU initialization code.

```
workerThread *g_CPUThreadPool;
int g_numCPUCores;

workerThread *g_GPUThreadPool;
int g_numGPUs;

struct gpuInit_struct
{
    int iGPU;

    cudaError_t status;
};

void
initializeGPU( void *_p )
{
    cudaError_t status;

    gpuInit_struct *p = (gpuInit_struct *) _p;
    CUDART_CHECK( cudaSetDevice( p->iGPU ) );
    CUDART_CHECK( cudaSetDeviceFlags( cudaDeviceMapHost ) );
    CUDART_CHECK( cudaFree(0) );
Error:
    p->status = status;
}

// ... below is from main()

    if ( g_numGPUs ) {
        chCommandLineGet( &g_numGPUs, "numgpus", argc, argv );
        g_GPUThreadPool = new workerThread[g_numGPUs];
        for ( size_t i = 0; i < g_numGPUs; i++ ) {
            if ( ! g_GPUThreadPool[i].initialize( ) ) {
                fprintf( stderr, "Error initializing thread pool\n" );
                return 1;
            }
        }
        for ( int i = 0; i < g_numGPUs; i++ ) {
            gpuInit_struct initGPU = {i};
```

```
        g_GPUThreadPool[i].delegateSynchronous(
            initializeGPU,
            &initGPU );
        if ( cudaSuccess != initGPU.status ) {
            fprintf( stderr, "Initializing GPU %d failed "
                "with %d (%s)\n",
                i,
                initGPU.status,
                cudaGetErrorString( initGPU.status ) );
            return 1;
        }
    }
}
```

Once the worker threads are initialized, they suspend waiting on a thread synchronization primitive until the application thread dispatches work to them. Listing 9.6 shows the host code that dispatches work to the GPUs: The gpuDelegation structure encapsulates the work that a given GPU must do, and the gpuWorkerThread function is invoked for each of the worker threads created by the code in Listing 9.5. The application thread code, shown in Listing 9.7, creates a gpuDelegation structure for each worker thread and calls the delegateAsynchronous() method to invoke the code in Listing 9.6. The waitAll() method then waits until all of the worker threads have finished. The performance and scaling results of the single-threaded and multithreaded version of multi-GPU N-body are summarized in Section 14.7.

Listing 9.6 Host code (worker thread).

```
struct gpuDelegation {
    size_t i;    // base offset for this thread to process
    size_t n;    // size of this thread's problem
    size_t N;    // total number of bodies

    float *hostPosMass;
    float *hostForce;
    float softeningSquared;

    cudaError_t status;
};

void
gpuWorkerThread( void *_p )
{
    cudaError_t status;
    gpuDelegation *p = (gpuDelegation *) _p;
    float *dptrPosMass = 0;
    float *dptrForce = 0;

    //
    // Each GPU has its own device pointer to the host pointer.
    //
```

```
    CUDART_CHECK( cudaMalloc( &dptrPosMass, 4*p->N*sizeof(float) ) );
    CUDART_CHECK( cudaMalloc( &dptrForce, 3*p->n*sizeof(float) ) );
    CUDART_CHECK( cudaMemcpyAsync(
        dptrPosMass,
        p->hostPosMass,
        4*p->N*sizeof(float),
        cudaMemcpyHostToDevice ) );
    ComputeNBodyGravitation_multiGPU<<<300,256,256*sizeof(float4)>>>(
        dptrForce,
        dptrPosMass,
        p->softeningSquared,
        p->i,
        p->n,
        p->N );
    // NOTE: synchronous memcpy, so no need for further
    // synchronization with device
    CUDART_CHECK( cudaMemcpy(
        p->hostForce+3*p->i,
        dptrForce,
        3*p->n*sizeof(float),
        cudaMemcpyDeviceToHost ) );
Error:
    cudaFree( dptrPosMass );
    cudaFree( dptrForce );
    p->status = status;
}
```

Listing 9.7 ?Host code (application thread)

```
float
ComputeGravitation_multiGPU_threaded(
    float *force,
    float *posMass,
    float softeningSquared,
    size_t N
)
{
    chTimerTimestamp start, end;
    chTimerGetTime( &start );
    {
        gpuDelegation *pgpu = new gpuDelegation[g_numGPUs];
        size_t bodiesPerGPU = N / g_numGPUs;
        if ( N % g_numGPUs ) {
            return 0.0f;
        }

        size_t i;
        for ( i = 0; i < g_numGPUs; i++ ) {
            pgpu[i].hostPosMass = g_hostAOS_PosMass;
            pgpu[i].hostForce = g_hostAOS_Force;

            pgpu[i].softeningSquared = softeningSquared;
```

```
            pgpu[i].i = bodiesPerGPU*i;
            pgpu[i].n = bodiesPerGPU;
            pgpu[i].N = N;

            g_GPUThreadPool[i].delegateAsynchronous(
                gpuWorkerThread,
                &pgpu[i] );
        }
        workerThread::waitAll( g_GPUThreadPool, g_numGPUs );
        delete[] pgpu;
    }

    chTimerGetTime( &end );
    return chTimerElapsedTime( &start, &end ) * 1000.0f;
}
```

Chapter 10

Texturing

10.1 Overview

In CUDA, a software technology for general-purpose parallel computing, texture support could not have been justified if the hardware hadn't already been there, due to its graphics-accelerating heritage. Nevertheless, the texturing hardware accelerates enough useful operations that NVIDIA saw fit to include support. Although many CUDA applications may be built without ever using texture, some rely on it to be competitive with CPU-based code.

Texture mapping was invented to enable richer, more realistic-looking objects by enabling images to be "painted" onto geometry. Historically, the hardware interpolated texture coordinates along with the X, Y, and Z coordinates needed to render a triangle, and for each output pixel, the texture value was fetched (optionally with bilinear interpolation), processed by blending with interpolated shading factors, and blended into the output buffer. With the introduction of programmable graphics and texture-like data that might not include color data (for example, bump maps), graphics hardware became more sophisticated. The shader programs included TEX instructions that specified the coordinates to fetch, and the results were incorporated into the computations used to generate the output pixel. The hardware improves performance using texture caches, memory layouts optimized for dimensional locality, and a dedicated hardware pipeline to transform texture coordinates into hardware addresses.

Because the functionality grew organically and was informed by a combination of application requirements and hardware costs, the texturing features are not very orthogonal. For example, the "wrap" and "mirror" texture addressing modes do not work unless the texture coordinates are normalized. This chapter explains every detail of the texture hardware as supported by CUDA. We will cover everything from normalized versus unnormalized coordinates to addressing modes to the limits of linear interpolation; 1D, 2D, 3D, and layered textures; and how to use these features from both the CUDA runtime and the driver API.

10.1.1 TWO USE CASES

In CUDA, there are two significantly different uses for texture. One is to simply use texture as a read path: to work around coalescing constraints or to use the texture cache to reduce external bandwidth requirements, or both. The other use case takes advantage of the fixed-function hardware that the GPU has in place for graphics applications. The texture hardware consists of a configurable pipeline of computation stages that can do all of the following.

- Scale normalized texture coordinates

- Perform boundary condition computations on the texture coordinates

- Convert texture coordinates to addresses with 2D or 3D locality

- Fetch 2, 4, or 8 texture elements for 1D, 2D, or 3D textures and linearly interpolate between them

- Convert the texture values from integers to unitized floating-point values

Textures are read through *texture references* that are bound to underlying memory (either CUDA arrays or device memory). The memory is just an unshaped bucket of bits; it is the texture reference that tells the hardware how to interpret the data and deliver it into registers when a TEX instruction is executed.

10.2 Texture Memory

Before describing the features of the fixed-function texturing hardware, let's spend some time examining the underlying memory to which texture references may be bound. CUDA can texture from either device memory or CUDA arrays.

10.2.1 DEVICE MEMORY

In device memory, the textures are addressed in row-major order. A 1024x768 texture might look like Figure 10.1, where *Offset* is the offset (in elements) from the base pointer of the image.

$$Offset = Y * Width + X \quad \text{(Equation 10.1)}$$

For a byte offset, multiply by the size of the elements.

$$ByteOffset = sizeof(T) * (Y * Width + X) \quad \text{(Equation 10.2)}$$

In practice, this addressing calculation only works for the most convenient of texture widths: 1024 happens to be convenient because it is a power of 2 and conforms to all manner of alignment restrictions. To accommodate less convenient texture sizes, CUDA implements *pitch-linear addressing*, where the width of the texture memory is different from the width of the texture. For less convenient widths, the hardware enforces an alignment restriction and the width in elements is treated differently from the width of the texture memory. For a texture width of 950, say, and an alignment restriction of 64 bytes, the width-in-bytes is padded to 964 (the next multiple of 64), and the texture looks like Figure 10.2.

In CUDA, the padded width in bytes is called the *pitch*. The total amount of device memory used by this image is 964x768 elements. The offset into the image now is computed in bytes, as follows.

$$ByteOffset = Y * Pitch + XInBytes$$

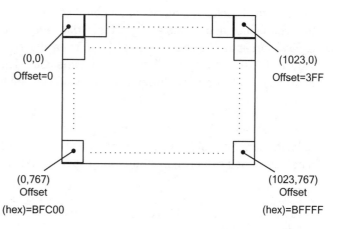

(0,0)
Offset=0

(1023,0)
Offset=3FF

(0,767)
Offset
(hex)=BFC00

(1023,767)
Offset
(hex)=BFFFF

Figure 10.1 1024x768 image.

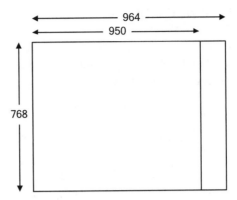

Figure 10.2 950x768 image, with pitch.

Applications can call `cudaMallocPitch()`/`cuMemAllocPitch()` to delegate selection of the pitch to the CUDA driver.[1] In 3D, pitch-linear images of a given *Depth* are exactly like 2D images, with *Depth* 2D slices laid out contiguously in device memory.

10.2.2 CUDA ARRAYS AND BLOCK LINEAR ADDRESSING

CUDA arrays are designed specifically to support texturing. They are allocated from the same pool of physical memory as device memory, but they have an opaque layout and cannot be addressed with pointers. Instead, memory locations in a CUDA array must be identified by the array handle and a set of 1D, 2D, or 3D coordinates.

CUDA arrays perform a more complicated addressing calculation, designed so that contiguous addresses exhibit 2D or 3D locality. The addressing calculation is hardware-specific and changes from one hardware generation to the next. Figure 10.1 illustrates one of the mechanisms used: The two least significant address bits of row and column have been interleaved before undertaking the addressing calculation.

As you can see in Figure 10.3, bit interleaving enables contiguous addresses to have "dimensional locality": A cache line fill pulls in a block of pixels in a neighborhood rather than a horizontal span of pixels.[2] When taken to the

---

1. Code that delegates to the driver is more future-proof than code that tries to perform allocations that comply with the documented alignment restrictions, since those restrictions are subject to change.
2. 3D textures similarly interleave the X, Y, and Z coordinate bits.

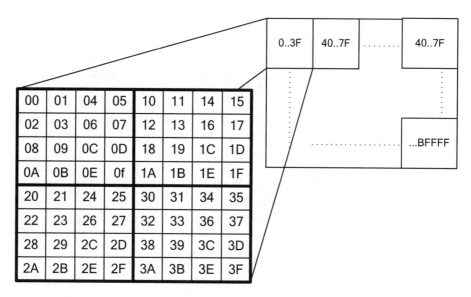

Figure 10.3 1024x768 image, interleaved bits.

limit, bit interleaving imposes some inconvenient requirements on the texture dimensions, so it is just one of several strategies used for the so-called "block linear" addressing calculation.

In device memory, the location of an image element can be specified by any of the following.

- The base pointer, pitch, and a *(XInBytes, Y)* or *(XInBytes, Y, Z)* tuple

- The base pointer and an offset as computed by Equation 10.1

- The device pointer with the offset already applied

In contrast, when CUDA arrays do not have device memory addresses, so memory locations must be specified in terms of the CUDA array and a tuple *(XInBytes, Y)* or *(XInBytes, Y, Z)*.

Creating and Destroying CUDA Arrays

Using the CUDA runtime, CUDA arrays may be created by calling `cudaMallocArray()`.

```
cudaError_t cudaMallocArray(struct cudaArray **array, const struct
cudaChannelFormatDesc *desc, size_t width, size_t height __dv(0),
unsigned int flags __dv(0));
```

array passes back the array handle, and desc specifies the number and type of components (e.g., 2 floats) in each array element. width specifies the width of the array *in bytes*. height is an optional parameter that specifies the height of the array; if the height is not specified, cudaMallocArray() creates a 1D CUDA array.

The flags parameter is used to hint at the CUDA array's usage. As of this writing, the only flag is cudaArraySurfaceLoadStore, which must be specified if the CUDA array will be used for surface read/write operations as described later in this chapter.

The __dv macro used for the height and flags parameters causes the declaration to behave differently, depending on the language. When compiled for C, it becomes a simple parameter, but when compiled for C++, it becomes a parameter with the specified default value.

The structure cudaChannelFormatDesc describes the contents of a texture.

```
struct cudaChannelFormatDesc {
    int x, y, z, w;
    enum cudaChannelFormatKind f;
};
```

The x, y, z, and w members of the structure specify the number of bits in each member of the texture element. For example, a 1-element float texture will contain x==32 and the other elements will be 0. The cudaChannelFormat-Kind structure specifies whether the data is signed integer, unsigned integer, or floating point.

```
enum cudaChannelFormatKind
{
    cudaChannelFormatKindSigned = 0,
    cudaChannelFormatKindUnsigned = 1,
    cudaChannelFormatKindFloat = 2,
    cudaChannelFormatKindNone = 3
};
```

Developers can create cudaChannelFormatDesc structures using the cuda-CreateChannelDesc function.

```
cudaChannelFormatDesc cudaCreateChannelDesc(int x, int y, int z, int w,
cudaChannelFormatKind kind);
```

Alternatively, a templated family of functions can be invoked as follows.

```
template<class T> cudaCreateChannelDesc<T>();
```

where T may be any of the native formats supported by CUDA. Here are two examples of the specializations of this template.

```
template<> __inline__ __host__ cudaChannelFormatDesc
cudaCreateChannelDesc<float>(void)
{
    int e = (int)sizeof(float) * 8;

    return cudaCreateChannelDesc(e, 0, 0, 0, cudaChannelFormatKindFloat);
}


template<> __inline__ __host__ cudaChannelFormatDesc
cudaCreateChannelDesc<uint2>(void)
{
 int e = (int)sizeof(unsigned int) * 8;

 return cudaCreateChannelDesc(e, e, 0, 0,
cudaChannelFormatKindUnsigned);
}
```

CAUTION

When using the `char` data type, be aware that some compilers assume `char` is signed, while others assume it is unsigned. You can always make this distinction unambiguous with the `signed` keyword.

3D CUDA arrays may be allocated with `cudaMalloc3DArray()`.

```
cudaError_t cudaMalloc3DArray(struct cudaArray** array, const struct
cudaChannelFormatDesc* desc, struct cudaExtent extent, unsigned int
flags __dv(0));
```

Rather than taking width, height, and depth parameters, `cudaMalloc3DArray()` takes a `cudaExtent` structure.

```
struct cudaExtent {
    size_t width;
    size_t height;
    size_t depth;
};
```

The `flags` parameter, like that of `cudaMallocArray()`, must be `cudaArraySurfaceLoadStore` if the CUDA array will be used for surface read/write operations.

NOTE

For array handles, the CUDA runtime and driver API are compatible with one another. The pointer passed back by `cudaMallocArray()` can be cast to `CUarray` and passed to driver API functions such as `cuArrayGetDescriptor()`.

Driver API

The driver API equivalents of cudaMallocArray() and cudaMalloc3DArray() are cuArrayCreate() and cuArray3DCreate(), respectively.

```
CUresult cuArrayCreate(CUarray *pHandle, const CUDA_ARRAY_DESCRIPTOR
*pAllocateArray);
CUresult cuArray3DCreate(CUarray *pHandle, const CUDA_ARRAY3D_
DESCRIPTOR *pAllocateArray);
```

cuArray3DCreate() can be used to allocate 1D or 2D CUDA arrays by specifying 0 as the height or depth, respectively. The CUDA_ARRAY3D_DESCRIPTOR structure is as follows.

```
typedef struct CUDA_ARRAY3D_DESCRIPTOR_st
{
    size_t Width;
    size_t Height;
    size_t Depth;
    CUarray_format Format;
    unsigned int NumChannels;
    unsigned int Flags;
} CUDA_ARRAY3D_DESCRIPTOR;
```

Together, the Format and NumChannels members describe the size of each element of the CUDA array: NumChannels may be 1, 2, or 4, and Format specifies the channels' type, as follows.

```
typedef enum CUarray_format_enum {
    CU_AD_FORMAT_UNSIGNED_INT8  = 0x01,
    CU_AD_FORMAT_UNSIGNED_INT16 = 0x02,
    CU_AD_FORMAT_UNSIGNED_INT32 = 0x03,
    CU_AD_FORMAT_SIGNED_INT8    = 0x08,
    CU_AD_FORMAT_SIGNED_INT16   = 0x09,
    CU_AD_FORMAT_SIGNED_INT32   = 0x0a,
    CU_AD_FORMAT_HALF           = 0x10,
    CU_AD_FORMAT_FLOAT          = 0x20
} CUarray_format;
```

NOTE

The format specified in CUDA_ARRAY3D_DESCRIPTOR is just a convenient way to specify the amount of data in the CUDA array. Textures bound to the CUDA array can specify a different format, as long as the bytes per element is the same. For example, it is perfectly valid to bind a texture<int> reference to a CUDA array containing 4-component bytes (32 bits per element).

Sometimes CUDA array handles are passed to subroutines that need to query the dimensions and/or format of the input array. The following `cuArray3DGet-Descriptor()` function is provided for that purpose.

```
CUresult cuArray3DGetDescriptor(CUDA_ARRAY3D_DESCRIPTOR
*pArrayDescriptor, CUarray hArray);
```

Note that this function may be called on 1D and 2D CUDA arrays, even those that were created with `cuArrayCreate()`.

10.2.3 DEVICE MEMORY VERSUS CUDA ARRAYS

For applications that exhibit sparse access patterns, especially patterns with dimensional locality (for example, computer vision applications), CUDA arrays are a clear win. For applications with regular access patterns, especially those with little to no reuse or whose reuse can be explicitly managed by the application in shared memory, device pointers are the obvious choice.

Some applications, such as image processing applications, fall into a gray area where the choice between device pointers and CUDA arrays is not obvious. All other things being equal, device memory is probably preferable to CUDA arrays, but the following considerations may be used to help in the decision-making process.

- Until CUDA 3.2, CUDA kernels could not write to CUDA arrays. They were only able to read from them via texture intrinsics. CUDA 3.2 added the ability for Fermi-class hardware to access 2D CUDA arrays via "surface read/write" intrinsics.

- CUDA arrays do not consume any CUDA address space.

- On WDDM drivers (Windows Vista and later), the system can automatically manage the residence of CUDA arrays. They can be swapped into and out of device memory transparently, depending on whether they are needed by the CUDA kernels that are executing. In contrast, WDDM requires all device memory to be resident in order for any kernel to execute.

- CUDA arrays can reside only in device memory, and if the GPU contains copy engines, it can convert between the two representations while transferring the data across the bus. For some applications, keeping a pitch representation in host memory and a CUDA array representation in device memory is the best fit.

10.3 1D Texturing

For illustrative purposes, we will deal with 1D textures in detail and then expand the discussion to include 2D and 3D textures.

10.3.1 TEXTURE SETUP

The data in textures can consist of 1, 2, or 4 elements of any of the following types.

- Signed or unsigned 8-, 16-, or 32-bit integers

- 16-bit floating-point values

- 32-bit floating-point values

In the `.cu` file (whether using the CUDA runtime or the driver API), the texture reference is declared as follows.

```
texture<ReturnType, Dimension, ReadMode> Name;
```

where `ReturnType` is the value returned by the texture intrinsic; `Dimension` is 1, 2, or 3 for 1D, 2D, or 3D, respectively; and `ReadMode` is an optional parameter type that defaults to `cudaReadModeElementType`. The read mode only affects integer-valued texture data. By default, the texture passes back integers when the texture data is integer-valued, promoting them to 32-bit if necessary. But when `cudaReadModeNormalizedFloat` is specified as the read mode, 8- or 16-bit integers can be promoted to floating-point values in the range [0.0, 1.0] according to the formulas in Table 10.1.

Table 10.1 Floating-Point Promotion (Texture)

FORMAT	CONVERSION FORMULA TO FLOAT
`char c`	$\begin{cases} -1.0, c == 0x80 \\ c/127.0, \textit{otherwise} \end{cases}$
`short s`	$\begin{cases} -1.0, s == 0x8000 \\ \dfrac{s}{32767.0}, \textit{otherwise} \end{cases}$
`unsigned char uc`	$uc/255.0$
`unsigned short us`	$us/65535.0$

The C versions of this conversion operation are given in Listing 10.1.

Listing 10.1 Texture unit floating-point conversion.

```
float
TexPromoteToFloat( signed char c )
{
    if ( c == (signed char) 0x80 ) {
        return -1.0f;
    }
    return (float) c / 127.0f;
}

float
TexPromoteToFloat( short s )
{
    if ( s == (short) 0x8000 ) {
        return -1.0f;
    }
    return (float) s / 32767.0f;
}

float
TexPromoteToFloat( unsigned char uc )
{
    return (float) uc / 255.0f;
}

float
TexPromoteToFloat( unsigned short us )
{
    return (float) us / 65535.0f;
}
```

Once the texture reference is declared, it can be used in kernels by invoking texture intrinsics. Different intrinsics are used for different types of texture, as shown in Table 10.2.

Texture references have file scope and behave similarly to global variables. They cannot be created, destroyed, or passed as parameters, so wrapping them in higher-level abstractions must be undertaken with care.

CUDA Runtime

Before invoking a kernel that uses a texture, the texture must be *bound* to a CUDA array or device memory by calling cudaBindTexture(), cudaBindTexture2D(), or cudaBindTextureToArray(). Due to the

Table 10.2 Texture Intrinsics

TEXTURE TYPE	INTRINSIC
Linear device memory	`tex1Dfetch( int index );`
1D CUDA array	`tex1D(float x);`
2D CUDA array 2D device memory	`tex2D(float x, float y);`
3D CUDA array	`tex3D(float x, float y, float z);`
1D layered texture	`tex1DLayered(float x, int layer);`
2D layered texture	`tex2DLayered(float x, float y, int layer);`

language integration of the CUDA runtime, the texture can be referenced by name, such as the following.

```
texture<float, 2, cudaReadModeElementType> tex;
...
  CUDART_CHECK(cudaBindTextureToArray(tex, texArray));
```

Once the texture is bound, kernels that use that texture reference will read from the bound memory until the texture binding is changed.

Driver API

When a texture is declared in a `.cu` file, driver applications must query it using `cuModuleGetTexRef()`. In the driver API, the immutable attributes of the texture must be set explicitly, and they must agree with the assumptions used by the compiler to generate the code. For most textures, this just means the format must agree with the format declared in the `.cu` file; the exception is when textures are set up to promote integers or 16-bit floating-point values to normalized 32-bit floating-point values.

The `cuTexRefSetFormat()` function is used to specify the format of the data in the texture.

```
CUresult CUDAAPI cuTexRefSetFormat(CUtexref hTexRef, CUarray_format
fmt, int NumPackedComponents);
```

The array formats are as follows.

ENUMERATION VALUE	TYPE
CU_AD_FORMAT_UNSIGNED_INT8	unsigned char
CU_AD_FORMAT_UNSIGNED_INT16	unsigned short
CU_AD_FORMAT_UNSIGNED_INT32	unsigned int
CU_AD_FORMAT_SIGNED_INT8	signed char
CU_AD_FORMAT_SIGNED_INT16	short
CU_AD_FORMAT_SIGNED_INT32	int
CU_AD_FORMAT_SIGNED_HALF	half (IEEE 754 "binary16" format)
CU_AD_FORMAT_SIGNED_FLOAT	float

NumPackedComponents specifies the number of components in each texture element. It may be 1, 2, or 4. 16-bit floats (half) are a special data type that are well suited to representing image data with high integrity.[3] With 10 bits of floating-point mantissa (effectively 11 bits of precision for normalized numbers), there is enough precision to represent data generated by most sensors, and 5 bits of exponent gives enough dynamic range to represent starlight and sunlight in the same image. Most floating-point architectures do not include native instructions to process 16-bit floats, and CUDA is no exception. The texture hardware promotes 16-bit floats to 32-bit floats automatically, and CUDA kernels can convert between 16- and 32-bit floats with the __float2half_rn() and __half2float_rn() intrinsics.

10.4 Texture as a Read Path

When using texture as a read path—that is, using the texturing hardware to get around awkward coalescing constraints or to take advantage of the texture cache as opposed to accessing hardware features such as linear

---

3. Section 8.3.4 describes 16-bit floats in detail.

interpolation—many texturing features are unavailable. The highlights of this usage for texture are as follows.

- The texture reference must be bound to device memory with `cudaBind-Texture()` or `cuTexRefSetAddress()`.

- The `tex1Dfetch()` intrinsic must be used. It takes a 27-bit integer index.[4]

- `tex1Dfetch()` optionally can convert the texture contents to floating-point values. Integers are converted to floating-point values in the range [0.0, 1.0], and 16-bit floating-point values are promoted to `float`.

The benefits of reading device memory via `tex1Dfetch()` are twofold. First, memory reads via texture do not have to conform to the coalescing constraints that apply when reading global memory. Second, the texture cache can be a useful complement to the other hardware resources, even the L2 cache on Fermi-class hardware. When an out-of-range index is passed to `tex1Dfetch()`, it returns 0.

10.4.1 INCREASING EFFECTIVE ADDRESS COVERAGE

Since the 27-bit index specifies which texture element to fetch, and the texture elements may be up to 16 bytes in size, a texture being read via `tex1Dfetch()` can cover up to 31 bits $(2^{27}+2^4)$ worth of memory. One way to increase the amount of data being effectively covered by a texture is to use wider texture elements than the actual data size. For example, the application can texture from `float4` instead of `float`, then select the appropriate element of the `float4`, depending on the least significant bits of the desired index. Similar techniques can be applied to integer data, especially 8- or 16-bit data where global memory transactions are always uncoalesced. Alternatively, applications can alias multiple textures over different segments of the device memory and perform predicated texture fetches from each texture in such a way that only one of them is "live."

Microdemo: **tex1dfetch_big.cu**

This program illustrates using `tex1Dfetch()` to read from large arrays using both multiple components per texture and multiple textures. It is invoked as follows.

```
tex1dfetch_big <NumMegabytes>
```

---

4. All CUDA-capable hardware has the same 27-bit limit, so there is not yet any way to query a device for the limit.

The application allocates the specified number of megabytes of device memory (or mapped pinned host memory, if the device memory allocation fails), fills the memory with random numbers, and uses 1-, 2-, and 4-component textures to compute checksums on the data. Up to four textures of `int4` can be used, enabling the application to texture from up to 8192M of memory.

For clarity, `tex1dfetch_big.cu` does not perform any fancy parallel reduction techniques. Each thread writes back an intermediate sum, and the final checksums are accumulated on the CPU. The application defines the 27-bit hardware limits.

```
#define CUDA_LG_MAX_TEX1DFETCH_INDEX 27
#define CUDA_MAX_TEX1DFETCH_INDEX
(((size_t)1<<CUDA_LG_MAX_TEX1DFETCH_INDEX)-1)
```

And it defines four textures of `int4`.

```
texture<int4, 1, cudaReadModeElementType> tex4_0;
texture<int4, 1, cudaReadModeElementType> tex4_1;
texture<int4, 1, cudaReadModeElementType> tex4_2;
texture<int4, 1, cudaReadModeElementType> tex4_3;
```

A device function `tex4Fetch()` takes an index and teases it apart into a texture ordinal and a 27-bit index to pass to `tex1Dfetch()`.

```
__device__ int4
tex4Fetch( size_t index )
{
    int texID = (int) (index>>CUDA_LG_MAX_TEX1DFETCH_INDEX);
    int i = (int) (index & (CUDA_MAX_TEX1DFETCH_INDEX_SIZE_T-1));
    int4 i4;

    if ( texID == 0 ) {
        i4 = tex1Dfetch( tex4_0, i );
    }
    else if ( texID == 1 ) {
        i4 = tex1Dfetch( tex4_1, i );
    }
    else if ( texID == 2 ) {
        i4 = tex1Dfetch( tex4_2, i );
    }
    else if ( texID == 3 ) {
        i4 = tex1Dfetch( tex4_3, i );
    }
    return i4;
}
```

This device function compiles to a small amount of code that uses four predicated TEX instructions, only one of which is "live." If random access is desired, the application also can use predication to select from the `.x`, `.y`, `.z`, or `.w` component of the `int4` return value.

Binding the textures, shown in Listing 10.2, is a slightly tricky business. This code creates two small arrays `texSizes[]` and `texBases[]` and sets them up to cover the device memory range. The `for` loop ensures that all four textures have a valid binding, even if fewer than four are needed to map the device memory.

Listing 10.2 `tex1dfetch_big.cu` (excerpt).

```
int iTexture;
cudaChannelFormatDesc int4Desc = cudaCreateChannelDesc<int4>();
size_t numInt4s = numBytes / sizeof(int4);
int numTextures = (numInt4s+CUDA_MAX_TEX1DFETCH_INDEX)>>

    CUDA_LG_MAX_TEX1DFETCH_INDEX;
size_t Remainder = numBytes & (CUDA_MAX_BYTES_INT4-1);
if ( ! Remainder ) {
    Remainder - CUDA_MAX_BYTES_INT4;
}

size_t texSizes[4];
char *texBases[4];
for ( iTexture = 0; iTexture < numTextures; iTexture++ ) {
    texBases[iTexture] = deviceTex+iTexture*CUDA_MAX_BYTES_INT4;
    texSizes[iTexture] = CUDA_MAX_BYTES_INT4;
}
texSizes[iTexture-1] = Remainder;
while ( iTexture < 4 ) {
    texBases[iTexture] = texBases[iTexture-1];
    texSizes[iTexture] = texSizes[iTexture-1];
    iTexture++;
}
cudaBindTexture( NULL, tex4_0, texBases[0], int4Desc, texSizes[0] );
cudaBindTexture( NULL, tex4_1, texBases[1], int4Desc, texSizes[1] );
cudaBindTexture( NULL, tex4_2, texBases[2], int4Desc, texSizes[2] );
cudaBindTexture( NULL, tex4_3, texBases[3], int4Desc, texSizes[3] );
```

Once compiled and run, the application can be invoked with different sizes to see the effects. On a CG1 instance running in Amazon's EC2 cloud compute offering, invocations with 512M, 768M, 1280M, and 8192M worked as follows.

```
$ ./tex1dfetch_big 512
Expected checksum: 0x7b7c8cd3
 tex1 checksum: 0x7b7c8cd3
 tex2 checksum: 0x7b7c8cd3
 tex4 checksum: 0x7b7c8cd3
$ ./tex1dfetch_big 768
Expected checksum: 0x559a1431
 tex1 checksum: (not performed)
 tex2 checksum: 0x559a1431
 tex4 checksum: 0x559a1431
```

```
$ ./tex1dfetch_big 1280
Expected checksum: 0x66a4f9d9
 tex1 checksum: (not performed)
 tex2 checksum: (not performed)
 tex4 checksum: 0x66a4f9d9
$ ./tex1dfetch_big 8192
Device alloc of 8192 Mb failed, trying mapped host memory
Expected checksum: 0xf049c607
 tex1 checksum: (not performed)
 tex2 checksum: (not performed)
 tex4 checksum: 0xf049c607
```

Each int4 texture can "only" read 2G, so invoking the program with numbers greater than 8192 causes it to fail. This application highlights the demand for indexed textures, where the texture being fetched can be specified as a parameter at runtime, but CUDA does not expose support for this feature.

10.4.2 TEXTURING FROM HOST MEMORY

Using texture as a read path, applications can read from host memory by allocating mapped pinned memory, fetching the device pointer, and then specifying that device pointer to cudaBindAddress() or cuTexRefSetAddress(). The capability is there, but reading host memory via texture is *slow*. Tesla-class hardware can texture over PCI Express at about 2G/s, and Fermi hardware is much slower. You need some other reason to do it, such as code simplicity.

Microdemo: tex1dfetch_int2float.cu

This code fragment uses texture-as-a-read path and texturing from host memory to confirm that the TexPromoteToFloat() functions work properly. The CUDA kernel that we will use for this purpose is a straightforward, blocking-agnostic implementation of a memcpy function that reads from the texture and writes to device memory.

```
texture<signed char, 1, cudaReadModeNormalizedFloat> tex;

extern "C" __global__ void
TexReadout( float *out, size_t N )
{
    for ( size_t i = blockIdx.x*blockDim.x + threadIdx.x;
                 i < N;
                 i += gridDim.x*blockDim.x )
    {
        out[i] = tex1Dfetch( tex, i );
    }
}
```

Since promoting integers to floating point only works on 8- and 16-bit values, we can test every possible conversion by allocating a small buffer, texturing from it, and confirming that the output meets our expectations. Listing 10.3 gives an excerpt from `tex1dfetch_int2float.cu`. Two host buffers are allocated: `inHost` holds the input buffer of 256 or 65536 input values, and `fOutHost` holds the corresponding float-valued outputs. The device pointers corresponding to these mapped host pointers are fetched into `inDevice` and `foutDevice`.

The input values are initialized to every possible value of the type to be tested, and then the input device pointer is bound to the texture reference using `cudaBindTexture()`. The `TexReadout()` kernel is then invoked to read each value from the input texture and write as output the values returned by `tex1Dfetch()`. In this case, both the input and output buffers reside in mapped host memory. Because the kernel is writing directly to host memory, we must call `cudaDeviceSynchronize()` to make sure there are no race conditions between the CPU and GPU. At the end of the function, we call the `TexPromote-ToFloat()` specialization corresponding to the type being tested and confirm that it is equal to the value returned by the kernel. If all tests pass, the function returns `true`; if any API functions or comparisons fail, it returns `false`.

Listing 10.3 `tex1d_int2float.cu` (excerpt).

```
template<class T>
void
CheckTexPromoteToFloat( size_t N )
{
    T *inHost, *inDevice;
    float *foutHost, *foutDevice;
    cudaError_t status;

    CUDART_CHECK(cudaHostAlloc( (void **) &inHost,
                                N*sizeof(T),
                                cudaHostAllocMapped));
    CUDART_CHECK(cudaHostGetDevicePointer( (void **) &inDevice,
                                           inHost,
                                           0 ));
    CUDART_CHECK(cudaHostAlloc( (void **) &foutHost,
                                N*sizeof(float),
                                cudaHostAllocMapped));
    CUDART_CHECK(cudaHostGetDevicePointer( (void **) &foutDevice,
                                           foutHost,
                                           0 ));

    for ( int i = 0; i < N; i++ ) {
        inHost[i] = (T) i;
    }
    memset( foutHost, 0, N*sizeof(float) );
```

```
CUDART_CHECK( cudaBindTexture( NULL,
                               tex,
                               inDevice,
                               cudaCreateChannelDesc<T>(),
                               N*sizeof(T)));
TexReadout<<<2,384>>>( foutDevice, N );
CUDART_CHECK(cudaDeviceSynchronize());

for ( int i = 0; i < N; i++ ) {
    printf( "%.2f ", foutHost[i] );
    assert( foutHost[i] == TexPromoteToFloat( (T) i ) );
}
printf( "\n" );
Error:
    cudaFreeHost( inHost );
    cudaFreeHost( foutHost );
}
```

10.5 Texturing with Unnormalized Coordinates

All texture intrinsics except `tex1Dfetch()` use floating-point values to specify coordinates into the texture. When using *unnormalized coordinates*, they fall in the range [0, *MaxDim*), where *MaxDim* is the width, height, or depth of the texture. Unnormalized coordinates are an intuitive way to index into a texture, but some texturing features are not available when using them.

An easy way to study texturing behavior is to populate a texture with elements that contain the index into the texture. Figure 10.4 shows a float-valued 1D texture with 16 elements, populated by the identity elements and annotated with some of the values returned by `tex1D()`.

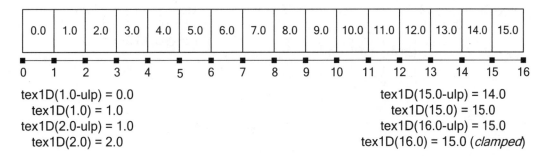

Figure 10.4 Texturing with unnormalized coordinates (without linear filtering).

Not all texturing features are available with unnormalized coordinates, but they can be used in conjunction with *linear filtering* and a limited form of *texture addressing.* The texture addressing mode specifies how the hardware should deal with out-of-range texture coordinates. For unnormalized coordinates, the Figure 10.4 illustrates the default texture addressing mode of clamping to the range [0, *MaxDim*) before fetching data from the texture: The value 16.0 is out of range and clamped to fetch the value 15.0. Another texture addressing option available when using unnormalized coordinates is the "border" addressing mode where out-of-range coordinates return zero.

The default filtering mode, so-called "point filtering," returns one texture element depending on the value of the floating-point coordinate. In contrast, linear filtering causes the texture hardware to fetch the two neighboring texture elements and linearly interpolate between them, weighted by the texture coordinate. Figure 10.5 shows the 1D texture with 16 elements, with some sample values returned by tex1D(). Note that you must add 0.5f to the texture coordinate to get the identity element.

Many texturing features can be used in conjunction with one another; for example, linear filtering can be combined with the previously discussed promotion from integer to floating point. In that case, the floating-point outputs produced by tex1D() intrinsics are accurate interpolations between the promoted floating-point values of the two participating texture elements.

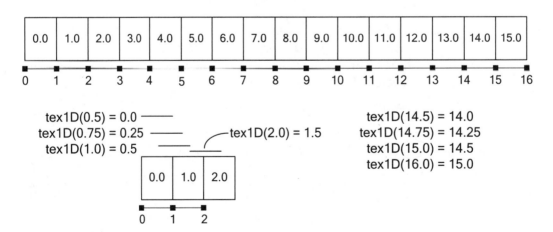

Figure 10.5 Texturing with unnormalized coordinates (with linear filtering).

Microdemo: `tex1d_unnormalized.cu`

The microdemo `tex1d_unnormalized.cu` is like a microscope to closely examine texturing behavior by printing the coordinate and the value returned by the `tex1D()` intrinsic together. Unlike the `tex1dfetch_int2float.cu` microdemo, this program uses a 1D CUDA array to hold the texture data. A certain number of texture fetches is performed, along a range of floating-point values specified by a base and increment; the interpolated values and the value returned by `tex1D()` are written together into an output array of `float2`. The CUDA kernel is as follows.

```
texture<float, 1> tex;

extern "C" __global__ void
TexReadout( float2 *out, size_t N, float base, float increment )
{
    for ( size_t i = blockIdx.x*blockDim.x + threadIdx.x;
                 i < N;
                 i += gridDim.x*blockDim.x )
    {
        float x = base + (float) i * increment;
        out[i].x = x;
        out[i].y = tex1D( tex, x );
    }
}
```

A host function `CreateAndPrintTex()`, given in Listing 10.4, takes the size of the texture to create, the number of texture fetches to perform, the base and increment of the floating-point range to pass to `tex1D()`, and optionally the filter and addressing modes to use on the texture. This function creates the CUDA array to hold the texture data, optionally initializes it with the caller-provided data (or identity elements if the caller passes NULL), binds the texture to the CUDA array, and prints the `float2` output.

Listing 10.4 `CreateAndPrintTex()`.

```
template<class T>
void
CreateAndPrintTex( T *initTex, size_t texN, size_t outN,
    float base, float increment,
    cudaTextureFilterMode filterMode = cudaFilterModePoint,
    cudaTextureAddressMode addressMode = cudaAddressModeClamp )
{
    T *texContents = 0;
    cudaArray *texArray = 0;

    float2 *outHost = 0, *outDevice = 0;
    cudaError_t status;
    cudaChannelFormatDesc channelDesc = cudaCreateChannelDesc<T>();
```

```
        // use caller-provided array, if any, to initialize texture
        if ( initTex ) {
            texContents = initTex;
        }
        else {
            // default is to initialize with identity elements
            texContents = (T *) malloc( texN*sizeof(T) );
            if ( ! texContents )
                goto Error;
            for ( int i = 0; i < texN; i++ ) {
                texContents[i] = (T) i;
            }
        }

        CUDART_CHECK(cudaMallocArray(&texArray, &channelDesc, texN));

        CUDART_CHECK(cudaHostAlloc( (void **) &outHost,
                                    outN*sizeof(float2),
                                    cudaHostAllocMapped));
        CUDART_CHECK(cudaHostGetDevicePointer( (void **)
                                               &outDevice,
                                               outHost, 0 ));

        CUDART_CHECK(cudaMemcpyToArray( texArray,
                                        0, 0,
                                        texContents,
                                        texN*sizeof(T),
                                        cudaMemcpyHostToDevice));
        CUDART_CHECK(cudaBindTextureToArray(tex, texArray));

        tex.filterMode = filterMode;
        tex.addressMode[0] = addressMode;
        CUDART_CHECK(cudaHostGetDevicePointer(&outDevice, outHost, 0));
        TexReadout<<<2,384>>>( outDevice, outN, base, increment );
        CUDART_CHECK(cudaThreadSynchronize());

        for ( int i = 0; i < outN; i++ ) {
            printf( "(%.2f, %.2f)\n", outHost[i].x, outHost[i].y );
        }
        printf( "\n" );

Error:
        if ( ! initTex ) free( texContents );
        if ( texArray ) cudaFreeArray( texArray );
        if ( outHost ) cudaFreeHost( outHost );
}
```

The main() function for this program is intended to be modified to study texturing behavior. This version creates an 8-element texture and writes the output of tex1D() from 0.0 .. 7.0.

```
int
main( int argc, char *argv[] )
{
 cudaError_t status;
 CUDA_CHECK(cudaSetDeviceFlags(cudaDeviceMapHost));

 CreateAndPrintTex<float>( NULL, 8, 8, 0.0f, 1.0f );
 CreateAndPrintTex<float>( NULL, 8, 8, 0.0f, 1.0f,
cudaFilterModeLinear );

 return 0;
}
```

The output from this program is as follows.

```
(0.00, 0.00)      <- output from the first CreateAndPrintTex()
(1.00, 1.00)
(2.00, 2.00)
(3.00, 3.00)
(4.00, 4.00)
(5.00, 5.00)
(6.00, 6.00)
(7.00, 7.00)

(0.00, 0.00)      <- output from the second CreateAndPrintTex()
(1.00, 0.50)
(2.00, 1.50)
(3.00, 2.50)
(4.00, 3.50)
(5.00, 4.50)
(6.00, 5.50)
(7.00, 6.50)
```

If we change `main()` to invoke `CreateAndPrintTex()` as follows.

```
CreateAndPrintTex<float>( NULL, 8, 20, 0.9f, 0.01f,
cudaFilterModePoint );
```

The resulting output highlights that when point filtering, 1.0 is the dividing line between texture elements 0 and 1.

```
(0.90, 0.00)
(0.91, 0.00)
(0.92, 0.00)
(0.93, 0.00)
(0.94, 0.00)
(0.95, 0.00)
(0.96, 0.00)
(0.97, 0.00)
(0.98, 0.00)
(0.99, 0.00)
(1.00, 1.00)      <- transition point
(1.01, 1.00)
(1.02, 1.00)
(1.03, 1.00)
```

```
(1.04,  1.00)
(1.05,  1.00)
(1.06,  1.00)
(1.07,  1.00)
(1.08,  1.00)
(1.09,  1.00)
```

One limitation of linear filtering is that it is performed with 9-bit weighting factors. It is important to realize that the precision of the interpolation depends not on that of the texture elements but on the weights. As an example, let's take a look at a 10-element texture initialized with normalized identity elements—that is, (0.0, 0.1, 0.2, 0.3, ... 0.9) instead of (0, 1, 2, ... 9). CreateAndPrintTex() lets us specify the texture contents, so we can do so as follows.

```
{
    float texData[10];
    for ( int i = 0; i < 10; i++ ) {
        texData[i] = (float) i / 10.0f;
    }
     CreateAndPrintTex<float>( texData, 10, 10, 0.0f, 1.0f );
}
```

The output from an unmodified CreateAndPrintTex() looks innocuous enough.

```
(0.00,  0.00)
(1.00,  0.10)
(2.00,  0.20)
(3.00,  0.30)
(4.00,  0.40)
(5.00,  0.50)
(6.00,  0.60)
(7.00,  0.70)
(8.00,  0.80)
(9.00,  0.90)
```

Or if we invoke CreateAndPrintTex() with linear interpolation between the first two texture elements (values 0.1 and 0.2), we get the following.

```
CreateAndPrintTex<float>(tex,10,10,1.5f,0.1f,cudaFilterModeLinear);
```

The resulting output is as follows.

```
(1.50,  0.10)
(1.60,  0.11)
(1.70,  0.12)
(1.80,  0.13)
(1.90,  0.14)
(2.00,  0.15)
(2.10,  0.16)
(2.20,  0.17)
(2.30,  0.18)
(2.40,  0.19)
```

Rounded to 2 decimal places, this data looks very well behaved. But if we modify `CreateAndPrintTex()` to output hexadecimal instead, the output becomes

```
(1.50, 0x3dcccccd)
(1.60, 0x3de1999a)
(1.70, 0x3df5999a)
(1.80, 0x3e053333)
(1.90, 0x3e0f3333)
(2.00, 0x3e19999a)
(2.10, 0x3e240000)
(2.20, 0x3e2e0000)
(2.30, 0x3e386667)
(2.40, 0x3e426667)
```

It is clear that most fractions of 10 are not exactly representable in floating point. Nevertheless, when performing interpolation that does not require high precision, these values are interpolated at full precision.

Microdemo: `tex1d_9bit.cu`

To explore this question of precision, we developed another microdemo, `tex1d_9bit.cu`. Here, we've populated a texture with 32-bit floating-point values that require full precision to represent. In addition to passing the base/increment pair for the texture coordinates, another base/increment pair specifies the "expected" interpolation value, assuming full-precision interpolation.

In `tex1d_9bit`, the `CreateAndPrintTex()` function is modified to write its output as shown in Listing 10.5.

Listing 10.5 `Tex1d_9bit.cu` (excerpt).

```
printf( "X\tY\tActual Value\tExpected Value\tDiff\n" );
for ( int i = 0; i < outN; i++ ) {
    T expected;
    if ( bEmulateGPU ) {
        float x = base+(float)i*increment - 0.5f;
        float frac = x - (float) (int) x;
        {
            int frac256 = (int) (frac*256.0f+0.5f);
            frac = frac256/256.0f;
        }
        int index = (int) x;
        expected = (1.0f-frac)*initTex[index] +
                        frac*initTex[index+1];
    }
    else {
        expected = expectedBase + (float) i*expectedIncrement;
    }
    float diff = fabsf( outHost[i].y - expected );
    printf( "%.2f\t%.2f\t", outHost[i].x, outHost[i].y );
    printf( "%08x\t", *(int *) (&outHost[i].y) );
```

```
        printf( "%08x\t", *(int *) (&expected) );
        printf( "%E\n", diff );
    }
    printf( "\n" );
```

For the just-described texture with 10 values (incrementing by 0.1), we can use this function to generate a comparison of the actual texture results with the expected full-precision result. Calling the function

```
CreateAndPrintTex<float>( tex, 10, 4, 1.5f, 0.25f, 0.1f, 0.025f );
CreateAndPrintTex<float>( tex, 10, 4, 1.5f, 0.1f, 0.1f, 0.01f );
```

yields this output.

```
X      Y      Actual Value  Expected Value  Diff
1.50   0.10   3dcccccd      3dcccccd        0.000000E+00
1.75   0.12   3e000000      3e000000        0.000000E+00
2.00   0.15   3e19999a      3e19999a        0.000000E+00
2.25   0.17   3e333333      3e333333        0.000000E+00

X      Y      Actual Value  Expected Value  Diff
1.50   0.10   3dcccccd      3dcccccd        0.000000E+00
1.60   0.11   3de1999a      3de147ae        1.562536E-04
1.70   0.12   3df5999a      3df5c290        7.812679E-05
1.80   0.13   3e053333      3e051eb8        7.812679E-05
```

As you can see from the "Diff" column on the right, the first set of outputs were interpolated at full precision, while the second were not. The explanation for this difference lies in Appendix F of the *CUDA Programming Guide*, which describes how linear interpolation is performed for 1D textures.

$$tex(x) = (1 - \alpha)T(i) + \alpha T(i + 1)$$

where

$$i = floor(X_B), \alpha + frac(X_B), X_B = x - 0.5$$

and α is stored in a 9-bit fixed-point format with 8 bits of fractional value.

In Listing 10.5, this computation in C++ is emulated in the bEmulateGPU case. The code snippet to emulate 9-bit weights can be enabled in tex1d_9bit.cu by passing true as the bEmulateGPU parameter of CreateAndPrintTex(). The output then becomes

```
X      Y      Actual Value  Expected Value  Diff
1.50   0.10   3dcccccd      3dcccccd        0.000000E+00
1.75   0.12   3e000000      3e000000        0.000000E+00
2.00   0.15   3e19999a      3e19999a        0.000000E+00
2.25   0.17   3e333333      3e333333        0.000000E+00
```

```
X      Y      Actual Value   Expected Value   Diff
1.50   0.10   3dcccccd       3dcccccd         0.000000E+00
1.60   0.11   3de1999a       3de1999a         0.000000E+00
1.70   0.12   3df5999a       3df5999a         0.000000E+00
1.80   0.13   3e053333       3e053333         0.000000E+00
```

As you can see from the rightmost column of 0's, when computing the interpolated value with 9-bit precision, the differences between "expected" and "actual" output disappear.

10.6 Texturing with Normalized Coordinates

When texturing with normalized coordinates, the texture is addressed by coordinates in the range [0.0, 1.0) instead of the range [0, MaxDim). For a 1D texture with 16 elements, the normalized coordinates are as in Figure 10.6.

Other than having texture coordinates that are independent of the texture dimension, the texture is dealt with in largely the same way, except that the full range of CUDA's texturing capabilities become available. With normalized coordinates, more texture addressing mode besides clamp and border addressing becomes available: the *wrap* and *mirror* addressing modes, whose formulas are as follows.

Wrap	$x' = x - \lfloor x \rfloor$
Mirror	$x' = \begin{cases} x - \lfloor x \rfloor, & \lfloor x \rfloor \text{ is even} \\ 1 - x - \lfloor x \rfloor, & \lfloor x \rfloor \text{ is odd} \end{cases}$

The four texture addressing modes supported in CUDA in Figure 10.7 show which in-range texture element is fetched by the first two out-of-range

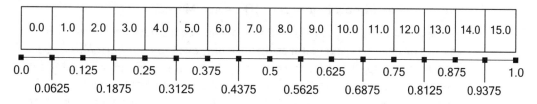

Figure 10.6 Texturing with normalized coordinates.

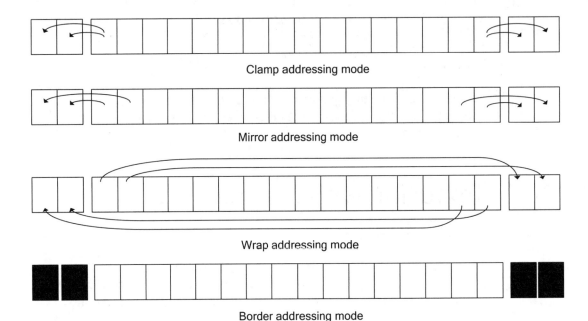

Clamp addressing mode

Mirror addressing mode

Wrap addressing mode

Border addressing mode

Figure 10.7 Texture addressing modes.

coordinates on each end. If you are having trouble visualizing the behavior of these addressing modes, check out the `tex2d_opengl.cu` microdemo in the next section.

IMPORTANT NOTE

In the driver API, changes to the texture reference are codified by the `cuTexRefSetArray()` or `cuTexRefSetAddress()` function. In other words, calls to functions that make state changes, such as `cuTexRefSet-FilterMode()` or `cuTexRefSetAddressMode()`, have no effect until the texture reference is bound to memory.

Floating-Point Coordinates with 1D Device Memory

For applications that wish to use floating-point coordinates to address the texture or use texturing features that are only available for normalized coordinates, use `cudaBindTexture2D()` / `cuTexRefSetAddress2D()` to specify the base address. Specify a height of 1 and pitch of `N*sizeof(T)`. The kernel can then call `tex2D(x,0.0f)` to read the 1D texture with floating-point coordinates.

10.7 1D Surface Read/Write

Until SM 2.0 hardware became available, CUDA kernels could access the contents of CUDA arrays only via texturing. Other access to CUDA arrays, including all write access, could be performed only via memcpy functions such as `cudaMemcpyToArray()`. The only way for CUDA kernels to both texture from and write to a given region of memory was to bind the texture reference to linear device memory.

But with the surface read/write functions newly available in SM 2.x, developers can bind CUDA arrays to *surface references* and use the `surf1Dread()` and `surf1Dwrite()` intrinsics to read and write the CUDA arrays from a kernel. Unlike texture reads, which have dedicated cache hardware, these reads and writes go through the same L2 cache as global loads and stores.

NOTE

In order for a surface reference to be bound to a CUDA array, the CUDA array must have been created with the `cudaArraySurfaceLoadStore` flag.

The 1D surface read/write intrinsics are declared as follows.

```
template<class Type> Type surf1Dread(surface<void, 1> surfRef, int x,
boundaryMode = cudaBoundaryModeTrap);
template<class Type> void surf1Dwrite(Type data, surface<void, 1>
surfRef, int x, boundaryMode = cudaBoundaryModeTrap);
```

These intrinsics are not type-strong—as you can see, surface references are declared as `void`—and the size of the memory transaction depends on `sizeof(Type)` for a given invocation of `surf1Dread()` or `surf1Dwrite()`. The x offset is in bytes and must be naturally aligned with respect to `sizeof(Type)`. For 4-byte operands such as `int` or `float`, `offset` must be evenly divisible by 4, for `short` it must be divisible by 2, and so on.

Support for surface read/write is far less rich than texturing functionality.[5] Only unformatted reads and writes are supported, with no conversion or interpolation functions, and the border handling is restricted to only two modes.

---

5. In fact, CUDA could have bypassed implementation of surface references entirely, with the intrinsics operating directly on CUDA arrays. Surface references were included for orthogonality with texture references to provide for behavior defined on a per-surfref basis as opposed to per-instruction.

Boundary conditions are handled differently for surface read/write than for texture reads. For textures, this behavior is controlled by the addressing mode in the texture reference. For surface read/write, the method of handling out-of-range offset values is specified as a parameter of surf1Dread() or surf1Dwrite(). Out-of-range indices can either cause a hardware exception (cudaBoundaryModeTrap) or read as 0 for surf1Dread() and are ignored for surf1Dwrite() (cudaBoundaryModeZero).

Because of the untyped character of surface references, it is easy to write a templated 1D memset routine that works for all types.

```
surface<void, 1> surf1D;

template <typename T>
__global__ void
surf1Dmemset( int index, T value, size_t N )
{
    for ( size_t i = blockIdx.x*blockDim.x + threadIdx.x;
                 i < N;
                 i += blockDim.x*gridDim.x )
    {
        surf1Dwrite( value, surf1D, (index+i)*sizeof(T) );
    }
}
```

This kernel is in the microdemo surf1Dmemset.cu, which creates a 64-byte CUDA array for illustrative purposes, initializes it with the above kernel, and prints the array in float and integer forms.

A generic template host function wraps this kernel with a call to cudaBindSurfaceToArray().

```
template<typename T>
cudaError_t
surf1Dmemset( cudaArray *array, int offset, T value, size_t N )
{
    cudaError_t status;
    CUDART_CHECK(cudaBindSurfaceToArray(surf1D, array));
    surf1Dmemset_kernel<<<2,384>>>( 0, value, 4*NUM_VALUES );
Error:
    return status;
}
```

The untyped character of surface references makes this template structure much easier to pull off than for textures. Because texture references are both type-strong and global, they cannot be templatized in the parameter list of a would-be generic function. A one-line change from

```
CUDART_CHECK(surf1Dmemset(array, 0, 3.141592654f, NUM_VALUES));
```

to

```
CUDART_CHECK(surf1Dmemset(array, 0, (short) 0xbeef, 2*NUM_VALUES));
```

will change the output of this program from

```
0x40490fdb 0x40490fdb ... (16 times)
3.141593E+00 3.141593E+00 ... (16 times)
```

to

```
0xbeefbeef 0xbeefbeef ... (16 times)
-4.68253E-01 -4.68253E-01 ... (16 times)
```

10.8 2D Texturing

In most ways, 2D texturing is similar to 1D texturing as described above. Applications optionally may promote integer texture elements to floating point, and they can use unnormalized or normalized coordinates. When linear filtering is supported, bilinear filtering is performed between four texture values, weighted by the fractional bits of the texture coordinates. The hardware can perform a different addressing mode for each dimension. For example, the X coordinate can be clamped while the Y coordinate is wrapped.

10.8.1 MICRODEMO: TEX2D_OPENGL.CU

This microdemo graphically illustrates the effects of the different texturing modes. It uses OpenGL for portability and the GL Utility Library (GLUT) to minimize the amount of setup code. To keep distractions to a minimum, this application does not use CUDA's OpenGL interoperability functions. Instead, we allocate mapped host memory and render it to the frame buffer using glDrawPixels(). To OpenGL, the data might as well be coming from the CPU.

The application supports normalized and unnormalized coordinates and clamp, wrap, mirror, and border addressing in both the X and Y directions. For unnormalized coordinates, the following kernel is used to write the texture contents into the output buffer.

```
__global__ void
RenderTextureUnnormalized( uchar4 *out, int width, int height )
{
    for ( int row = blockIdx.x; row < height; row += gridDim.x ) {
        out = (uchar4 *) (((char *) out)+row*4*width);
```

```
        for ( int col = threadIdx.x; col < width; col += blockDim.x ) {
            out[col] = tex2D( tex2d, (float) col, (float) row );
        }
    }
}
```

This kernel fills the rectangle of width × height pixels with values read from the texture using texture coordinates corresponding to the pixel locations. For out-of-range pixels, you can see the effects of the clamp and border addressing modes.

For normalized coordinates, the following kernel is used to write the texture contents into the output buffer.

```
__global__ void
RenderTextureNormalized(
    uchar4 *out,
    int width,
    int height,
    int scale )
{
    for ( int j = blockIdx.x; j < height; j += gridDim.x ) {
        int row = height-j-1;
        out = (uchar4 *) (((char *) out)+row*4*width);
        float texRow = scale * (float) row / (float) height;
        float invWidth = scale / (float) width;
        for ( int col = threadIdx.x; col < width; col += blockDim.x ) {
            float texCol = col * invWidth;
            out[col] = tex2D( tex2d, texCol, texRow );
        }
    }
}
```

The scale parameter specifies the number of times to tile the texture into the output buffer. By default, scale=1.0, and the texture is seen only once. When running the application, you can hit the 1–9 keys to replicate the texture that many times. The C, W, M, and B keys set the addressing mode for the current direction; the X and Y keys specify the current direction.

KEY	ACTION
1–9	Set number of times to replicate the texture.
W	Set wrap addressing mode.
C	Set clamp addressing mode.
M	Set mirror addressing mode.

KEY	ACTION
B	Set border addressing mode.
N	Toggle normalized and unnormalized texturing.
X	The C, W, M, or B keys will set the addressing mode in the X direction.
Y	The C, W, M, or B keys will set the addressing mode in the Y direction.
T	Toggle display of the overlaid text.

Readers are encouraged to run the program, or especially to modify and run the program, to see the effects of different texturing settings. Figure 10.8 shows the output of the program for the four permutations of X Wrap/Mirror and Y Wrap/Mirror when replicating the texture five times.

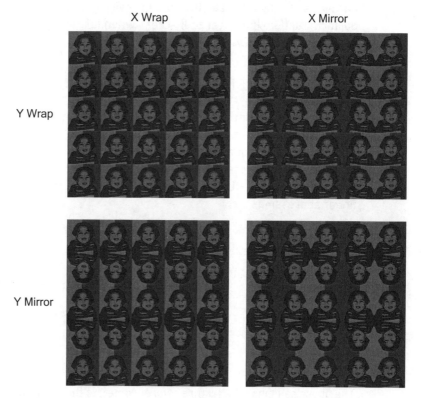

Figure 10.8 Wrap and mirror addressing modes.

10.9 2D Texturing: Copy Avoidance

When CUDA was first introduced, CUDA kernels could read from CUDA arrays only via texture. Applications could write to CUDA arrays only with memory copies; in order for CUDA kernels to write data that would then be read through texture, they had to write to device memory and then perform a device→array memcpy. Since then, two mechanisms have been added that remove this step for 2D textures.

- A 2D texture can be bound to a pitch-allocated range of linear device memory.

- Surface load/store intrinsics enable CUDA kernels to write to CUDA arrays directly.

3D texturing from device memory and 3D surface load/store are not supported.

For applications that read most or all the texture contents with a regular access pattern (such as a video codec) or applications that must work on Tesla-class hardware, it is best to keep the data in device memory. For applications that perform random (but localized) access when texturing, it is probably best to keep the data in CUDA arrays and use surface read/write intrinsics.

10.9.1 2D TEXTURING FROM DEVICE MEMORY

Texturing from 2D device memory does not have any of the benefits of "block linear" addressing—a cache line fill into the texture cache pulls in a horizontal span of texels, not a 2D or 3D block of them—but unless the application performs random access into the texture, the benefits of avoiding a copy from device memory to a CUDA array likely outweigh the penalties of losing block linear addressing.

To bind a 2D texture reference to a device memory range, call cudaBindTexture2D().

```
cudaBindTexture2D(
    NULL,
    &tex,
    texDevice,
    &channelDesc,
    inWidth,
    inHeight,
    texPitch );
```

The above call binds the texture reference tex to the 2D device memory range given by texDevice / texPitch. The base address and pitch must conform to hardware-specific alignment constraints.[6] The base address must be aligned with respect to `cudaDeviceProp.textureAlignment`, and the pitch must be aligned with respect to `cudaDeviceProp.texturePitchAlignment`.[7] The microdemo `tex2d_addressing_device.cu` is identical to `tex2d_addressing.cu`, but it uses device memory to hold the texture data. The two programs are designed to be so similar that you can look at the differences. A device pointer/pitch tuple is declared instead of a CUDA array.

```
< cudaArray *texArray = 0;
> T *texDevice = 0;
> size_t texPitch;
```

`cudaMallocPitch()` is called instead of calling `cudaMallocArray()`. `cudaMallocPitch()` delegates selection of the base address and pitch to the driver, so the code will continue working on future generations of hardware (which have a tendency to increase alignment requirements).

```
< CUDART_CHECK(cudaMallocArray( &texArray,
< &channelDesc,
< inWidth,
> CUDART_CHECK(cudaMallocPitch( &texDevice,
> &texPitch,
> inWidth*sizeof(T),
  inHeight));
```

Next, `cudaTextureBind2D()` is called instead of `cudaBindTextureToArray()`.

```
< CUDART_CHECK(cudaBindTextureToArray(tex, texArray));
> CUDART_CHECK(cudaBindTexture2D( NULL,
> &tex,
> texDevice,
> &channelDesc,
> inWidth,
> inHeight,
> texPitch ));
```

The final difference is that instead of freeing the CUDA array, `cudaFree()` is called on the pointer returned by `cudaMallocPitch()`.

```
< cudaFreeArray( texArray );
> cudaFree( texDevice );
```

---

6. CUDA arrays must conform to the same constraints, but in that case, the base address and pitch are managed by CUDA and hidden along with the memory layout.
7. In the driver API, the corresponding device attribute queries are CU_DEVICE_ATTRIBUTE_TEX-TURE_ALIGNMENT and CU_DEVICE_ATTRIBUTE_TEXTURE_PITCH_ALIGNMENT.

10.9.2 2D SURFACE READ/WRITE

As with 1D surface read/write, Fermi-class hardware enables kernels to write directly into CUDA arrays with intrinsic surface read/write functions.

```
template<class Type> Type surf2Dread(surface<void, 1> surfRef, int x,
int y, boundaryMode = cudaBoundaryModeTrap);
template<class Type> Type surf2Dwrite(surface<void, 1> surfRef, Type
data, int x, int y, boundaryMode = cudaBoundaryModeTrap);
```

The surface reference declaration and corresponding CUDA kernel for 2D surface memset, given in surf2Dmemset.cu, is as follows.

```
surface<void, 2> surf2D;

template<typename T>
__global__ void
surf2Dmemset_kernel( T value,
                     int xOffset, int yOffset,
                     int Width, int Height )
{
    for ( int row = blockIdx.y*blockDim.y + threadIdx.y;
                row < Height;
                row += blockDim.y*gridDim.y )
    {
        for ( int col = blockIdx.x*blockDim.x + threadIdx.x;
                    col < Width;
                    col += blockDim.x*gridDim.x )
        {
            surf2Dwrite( value,
                         surf2D,
                         (xOffset+col)*sizeof(T),
                         yOffset+row );
        }
    }
}
```

Remember that the X offset parameter to surf2Dwrite() is given in *bytes*.

10.10 3D Texturing

Reading from 3D textures is similar to reading from 2D textures, but there are more limitations.

- 3D textures have smaller limits (2048x2048x2048 instead of 65536x32768).

- There are no copy avoidance strategies: CUDA does not support 3D texturing from device memory or surface load/store on 3D CUDA arrays.

Other than that, the differences are straightforward: Kernels can read from 3D textures using a `tex3D()` intrinsic that takes 3 floating-point parameters, and the underlying 3D CUDA arrays must be populated by 3D memcpys. Trilinear filtering is supported; 8 texture elements are read and interpolated according to the texture coordinates, with the same 9-bit precision limit as 1D and 2D texturing.

The 3D texture size limits may be queried by calling `cuDeviceGetAttribute()` with `CU_DEVICE_ATTRIBUTE_MAXIMUM_TEXTURE3D_WIDTH`, `CU_DEVICE_ATTRIBUTE_MAXIMUM_TEXTURE3D_HEIGHT`, and `CU_DEVICE_ATTRIBUTE_MAXIMUM_TEXTURE3D_DEPTH`, or by calling `cudaGetDeviceProperties()` and examining `cudaDeviceProp.maxTexture3D`. Due to the much larger number of parameters needed, 3D CUDA arrays must be created and manipulated using a different set of APIs than 1D or 2D CUDA arrays.

To create a 3D CUDA array, the `cudaMalloc3DArray()` function takes a `cudaExtent` structure instead of width and height parameters.

```
cudaError_t cudaMalloc3DArray(struct cudaArray** array, const struct
cudaChannelFormatDesc* desc, struct cudaExtent extent, unsigned int
flags __dv(0));
```

`cudaExtent` is defined as follows.

```
struct cudaExtent {
    size_t width;
    size_t height;
    size_t depth;
};
```

Describing 3D memcpy operations is sufficiently complicated that both the CUDA runtime and the driver API use structures to specify the parameters. The runtime API uses the `cudaMemcpy3DParams` structure, which is declared as follows.

```
struct cudaMemcpy3DParms {
    struct cudaArray *srcArray;
    struct cudaPos srcPos;
    struct cudaPitchedPtr srcPtr;
    struct cudaArray *dstArray;
    struct cudaPos dstPos;
    struct cudaPitchedPtr dstPtr;
    struct cudaExtent extent;
    enum cudaMemcpyKind kind;
};
```

Most of these structure members are themselves structures: extent gives the width, height, and depth of the copy. The `srcPos` and `dstPos` members are cudaPos structures that specify the start points for the source and destination of the copy.

```
struct cudaPos {
    size_t x;
    size_t y;
    size_t z;
};
```

The cudaPitchedPtr is a structure that was added with 3D memcpy to contain a pointer/pitch tuple.

```
struct cudaPitchedPtr
{
    void *ptr; /**< Pointer to allocated memory */
    size_t pitch; /**< Pitch of allocated memory in bytes */
    size_t xsize; /**< Logical width of allocation in elements */
    size_t ysize; /**< Logical height of allocation in elements */
};
```

A cudaPitchedPtr structure may be created with the function make_cudaPitchedPtr, which takes the base pointer, pitch, and logical width and height of the allocation. make_cudaPitchedPtr just copies its parameters into the output struct; however,

```
struct cudaPitchedPtr
make_cudaPitchedPtr(void *d, size_t p, size_t xsz, size_t ysz)
{
    struct cudaPitchedPtr s;

    s.ptr = d;
    s.pitch = p;
    s.xsize = xsz;
    s.ysize = ysz;

    return s;
}
```

The simpleTexture3D sample in the SDK illustrates how to do 3D texturing with CUDA.

10.11 Layered Textures

Layered textures are known in the graphics world as *texture arrays* because they enable 1D or 2D textures to be arranged as arrays accessed by an integer index. The main advantage of layered textures over vanilla 2D or 3D textures is that they support larger extents within the slices. There is no performance advantage to using layered textures.

Layered textures are laid out in memory differently than 2D or 3D textures, in such a way that 2D or 3D textures will not perform as well if they use the layout optimized for layered textures. As a result, when creating the CUDA array, you must specify `cudaArrayLayered` to `cudaMalloc3DArray()` or specify `CUDA_ARRAY3D_LAYERED` to `cuArray3DCreate()`. The `simpleLayered-Texture` sample in the SDK illustrates how to use layered textures.

10.11.1 1D LAYERED TEXTURES

The 1D layered texture size limits may be queried by calling `cuDeviceGet-Attribute()` with `CU_DEVICE_ATTRIBUTE_MAXIMUM_TEXTURE1D_LAYERED_WIDTH` and `CU_DEVICE_ATTRIBUTE_MAXIMUM_TEXTURE1D_LAYERED_LAYERS` or by calling `cudaGetDeviceProperties()` and examining `cudaDeviceProp.maxTexture1DLayered`.

10.11.2 2D LAYERED TEXTURES

The 2D layered texture size limits may be queried by calling `cuDeviceGet-Attribute()` with `CU_DEVICE_ATTRIBUTE_MAXIMUM_TEXTURE2D_LAYERED_WIDTH` and `CU_DEVICE_ATTRIBUTE_MAXIMUM_TEXTURE2D_LAYERED_HEIGHT` or `CU_DEVICE_ATTRIBUTE_MAXIMUM_TEXTURE2D_LAYERED_LAYERS` or by calling `cudaGetDeviceProperties()` and examining `cudaDeviceProp.maxTexture2DLayered`. The layered texture size limits may be queried `cudaGetDeviceProperties()` and examining `cudaDeviceProp.maxTexture2DLayered`.

10.12 Optimal Block Sizing and Performance

When the texture coordinates are generated in the "obvious" way, such as in `tex2d_addressing.cu`

```
row = blockIdx.y*blockDim.y + threadIdx.y;
col = blockIdx.x*blockDim.x + threadIdx.x;
... tex2D( tex, (float) col, (float) row);
```

then texturing performance is dependent on the block size.

To find the optimal size of a thread block, the `tex2D_shmoo.cu` and `surf2Dmemset_shmoo.cu` programs time the performance of thread blocks whose width and height vary from 4..64, inclusive. Some combinations of these thread block sizes are not valid because they have too many threads.

For this exercise, the texturing kernel is designed to do as little work as possible (maximizing exposure to the performance of the texture hardware), while still "fooling" the compiler into issuing the code. Each thread computes the floating-point sum of the values it reads and writes the sum if the output parameter is non-NULL. The trick is that we never pass a non-NULL pointer to this kernel! The reason the kernel is structured this way is because if it never wrote any output, the compiler would see that the kernel was not doing any work and would emit code that did not perform the texturing operations at all.

```
extern "C" __global__ void
TexSums( float *out, size_t Width, size_t Height )
{
    float sum = 0.0f;
    for ( int row = blockIdx.y*blockDim.y + threadIdx.y;
                row < Height;
                row += blockDim.y*gridDim.y )
    {
        for ( int col = blockIdx.x*blockDim.x + threadIdx.x;
                    col < Width;
                    col += blockDim.x*gridDim.x )
        {
            sum += tex2D( tex, (float) col, (float) row );
        }
    }
    if ( out ) {
        out[blockIdx.x*blockDim.x+threadIdx.x] = sum;
    }
}
```

Even with our "trick," there is a risk that the compiler will emit code that checks the `out` parameter and exits the kernel early if it's equal to NULL. We'd have to synthesize some output that wouldn't affect performance too much (for example, have each thread block compute the reduction of the sums in shared memory and write them to `out`). But by compiling the program with the `--keep` option and using `cuobjdump ---dump-sass` to examine the microcode, we can see that the compiler doesn't check `out` until after the doubly-nested `for` loop as executed.

10.12.1 RESULTS

On a GeForce GTX 280 (GT200), the optimal block size was found to be 128 threads, which delivered 35.7G/s of bandwidth. Thread blocks of size 32W × 4H were about the same speed as 16W × 8H or 8W × 16H, all traversing a 4K × 4K texture of `float` in 1.88 ms. On a Tesla M2050, the optimal block size was found to be 192 threads, which delivered 35.4G/s of bandwidth. As with the GT200, different-sized thread blocks were the same speed, with 6W × 32H, 16W × 12H, and 8W × 24H blocks delivering about the same performance.

The shmoo over 2D surface memset was less conclusive: Block sizes of at least 128 threads generally had good performance, provided the thread count was evenly divisible by the warp size of 32. The fastest 2D surface memset performance reported on a `cg1.4xlarge` without ECC enabled was 48Gb/s.

For `float`-valued data for both boards we tested, the peak bandwidth numbers reported by texturing and surface write are about ¼ and ½ of the achievable peaks for global load/store, respectively.

10.13 Texturing Quick References

10.13.1 HARDWARE CAPABILITIES

Hardware Limits

CAPABILITY	SM 1.X	SM 2.X
Maximum width—1D CUDA array	8192	32768
Maximum width—1D device memory	2^{27}	
Maximum width and number of layers—1D layered texture	8192x512	16384x2048
Maximum extents for 2D texture	65536x32768	
Maximum extents and number of layers—2D layered texture	8192x 8192x 512	16384x 16384x 2048
Maximum extents—3D CUDA array	2048x2048x2048	
Maximum number of textures that may be bound to a kernel	128	
Maximum extents for a 2D surface reference bound to a CUDA kernel	n/a	8192x8192
Maximum number of surfaces that may be bound to a kernel		8

Queries—Driver API

Most of the hardware limits listed above can be queried with `cuDevice-Attribute()`, which may be called with the following values to query.

ATTRIBUTE	CUDEVICE_ATTRIBUTE VALUE
Maximum width—1D CUDA array	`CU_DEVICE_ATTRIBUTE_MAXIMUM_TEXTURE1D_WIDTH`
Maximum width of 1D layered texture	`CU_DEVICE_ATTRIBUTE_MAXIMUM_TEXTURE1D_LAYERED_WIDTH`
Maximum number of layers of 1D layered texture	`CU_DEVICE_ATTRIBUTE_MAXIMUM_TEXTURE1D_LAYERED_LAYERS`
Maximum width of 2D texture	`CU_DEVICE_ATTRIBUTE_MAXIMUM_TEXTURE2D_WIDTH`
Maximum height of 2D texture	`CU_DEVICE_ATTRIBUTE_MAXIMUM_TEXTURE2D_HEIGHT`
Maximum width of 2D layered texture	`CU_DEVICE_ATTRIBUTE_MAXIMUM_TEXTURE2D_LAYERED_WIDTH`
Maximum height of 2D layered texture	`CU_DEVICE_ATTRIBUTE_MAXIMUM_TEXTURE2D_LAYERED_HEIGHT`
Maximum number of layers of 2D layered texture	`CU_DEVICE_ATTRIBUTE_MAXIMUM_TEXTURE2D_LAYERED_LAYERS`
Maximum width—3D CUDA array	`CU_DEVICE_ATTRIBUTE_MAXIMUM_TEXTURE3D_WIDTH`
Maximum height—3D CUDA array	`CU_DEVICE_ATTRIBUTE_MAXIMUM_TEXTURE3D_HEIGHT`
Maximum depth—3D CUDA array	`CU_DEVICE_ATTRIBUTE_MAXIMUM_TEXTURE3D_DEPTH`

Queries—CUDA Runtime

The following members of `cudaDeviceProp` contain hardware limits as listed above.

CAPABILITY	CUDADEVICEPROP MEMBER
Maximum width—1D CUDA array	`int maxTexture1D;`
Maximum width and number of layers—1D layered texture	`int maxTextureLayered[2];`
Maximum extents for 2D texture	`int maxTexture2D[2];`
Maximum extents and number of layers—2D layered texture	`int maxTextureLayered[2];`
Maximum extents—3D CUDA array	`int maxTexture3D[3];`

10.13.2 CUDA RUNTIME

1D Textures

OPERATION	DEVICE MEMORY	CUDA ARRAYS
Allocate with . . .	`cudaMalloc()`	`cudaMallocArray()`
Free with . . .	`cudaFree()`	`cudaFreeArray()`
Bind with . . .	`cudaBindTexture()`	`cudaBindTextureToArray()`
Texture with . . .	`tex1Dfetch()`	`tex1D()`

2D Textures

OPERATION	DEVICE MEMORY	CUDA ARRAYS
Allocate with . . .	`cudaMallocPitch()`	`cudaMalloc2DArray()` *
Free with . . .	`cudaFree()`	`cudaFreeArray()`
Bind with . . .	`cudaBindTexture2D()`	`cudaBindTextureToArray()`
Texture with . . .	`tex2D()`	

* If surface load/store is desired, specify the `cudaArraySurfaceLoadStore` flag.

3D Textures

OPERATION	DEVICE MEMORY	CUDA ARRAYS
Allocate with . . .	*(not supported)*	`cudaMalloc3DArray()`
Free with . . .		`cudaFreeArray()`
Bind with . . .		`cudaBindTextureToArray()`
Texture with . . .		`tex3D()`

1D Layered Textures

OPERATION	DEVICE MEMORY	CUDA ARRAYS
Allocate with . . .	*(not supported)*	`cudaMalloc2DArray()` - specify `cudaArrayLayered`.
Free with . . .		`cudaFreeArray()`
Bind with . . .		`cudaBindTextureToArray()`
Texture with . . .		`tex1DLayered()`

2D Layered Textures

OPERATION	DEVICE MEMORY	CUDA ARRAYS
Allocate with . . .	*(not supported)*	`cudaMalloc3DArray()` - specify `cudaArrayLayered`.
Free with . . .		`cudaFreeArray()`
Bind with . . .		`cudaBindTextureToArray()`
Texture with . . .		`tex1DLayered()`

10.13.3 DRIVER API

1D Textures

OPERATION	DEVICE MEMORY	CUDA ARRAYS
Allocate with . . .	cuMemAlloc()	cuArrayCreate()
Free with . . .	cuMemFree()	cuArrayDestroy()
Bind with . . .	cuTexRefSetAddress()	cuTexRefSetArray()
Texture with . . .	tex1Dfetch()	tex1D()
Size Limit	2^{27} elements (128M)	65536

The texture size limit for device memory is not queryable; it is 2^{27} elements on all CUDA-capable GPUs. The texture size limit for 1D CUDA arrays may be queried by calling cuDeviceGetAttribute() with CU_DEVICE_ATTRIBUTE_MAXIMUM_TEXTURE1D_WIDTH.

2D Textures

OPERATION	DEVICE MEMORY	CUDA ARRAYS
Allocate with . . .	cuMemAllocPitch()	cuArrayCreate()
Free with . . .	cuMemFree()	cudaFreeArray()
Bind with . . .	cuTexRefSetAddress2D()	cuTexRefSetArray()
Texture with . . .	tex2D()	

3D Textures

OPERATION	DEVICE MEMORY	CUDA ARRAYS
Allocate with . . .	*(not supported)*	`cudaMalloc3DArray()`
Free with . . .		`cudaFreeArray()`
Bind with . . .		`cudaBindTextureToArray()`
Texture with . . .		`tex3D()`

1D Layered Textures

OPERATION	DEVICE MEMORY	CUDA ARRAYS
Allocate with . . .	*(not supported)*	`cuArray3DCreate()` - specify `CUDA_ARRAY3D_LAYERED`
Free with . . .		`cudaFreeArray()`
Bind with . . .		`cuTexRefSetArray()`
Texture with . . .		`tex1DLayered()`

2D Layered Textures

OPERATION	DEVICE MEMORY	CUDA ARRAYS
Allocate with . . .	*(not supported)*	`cuArray3DCreate()` - specify `CUDA_ARRAY3D_LAYERED`
Free with . . .		`cuArrayDestroy()`
Bind with . . .		`cuTexRefSetArray()`
Texture with . . .		`tex2DLayered()`

PART III

Chapter 11

Streaming Workloads

Streaming workloads are among the simplest that can be ported to CUDA: computations where each data element can be computed independently of the others, often with such low computational density that the workload is bandwidth-bound. Streaming workloads do not use many of the hardware resources of the GPU, such as caches and shared memory, that are designed to optimize reuse of data.

Since GPUs give the biggest benefits on workloads with *high* computational density, it might be useful to review some cases when it still makes sense for streaming workloads to port to GPUs.

- If the input and output are in device memory, it doesn't make sense to transfer the data back to the CPU just to perform one operation.

- If the GPU has much better instruction-level support than the CPU for the operation (e.g., Black-Scholes options computation, which uses Special Function Unit instructions intensively), the GPU can outperform the CPU despite memory transfer overhead.

- The GPU operating concurrently with the CPU can approximately double performance, even if they are the same speed.

- The CUDA code for a given workload may be more readable or maintainable than highly optimized CPU code for the same computation.

- On integrated systems (i.e., systems-on-a-chip with CPU and CUDA-capable GPU operating on the same memory), there is no transfer overhead. CUDA can use "zero-copy" methods and avoid the copy entirely.

This chapter covers every aspect of streaming workloads, giving different formulations of the same workload to highlight the different issues that arise. The workload in question—the SAXPY operation from the BLAS library— performs a scalar multiplication and vector addition together in a single operation.

Listing 11.1 gives a trivial C implementation of SAXPY. For corresponding elements in the two input arrays, one element is scaled by a constant, added to the other, and written to the output array. Both input arrays and the output arrays consist of N elements. Since GPUs have a native multiply-add instruction, the innermost loop of SAXPY has an extremely modest number of instructions per memory access.

Listing 11.1 saxpyCPU.

```
void
saxpyCPU(
    float *out,
    const float *x,
    const float *y,
    size_t N,
    float alpha )
{
    for ( size_t i = 0; i < N; i++ ) {
        out[i] += alpha*x[i]+y[i];
    }
}
```

Listing 11.2 gives a trivial CUDA implementation of SAXPY. This version works for any grid or block size, and it performs adequately for most applications. This kernel is so bandwidth-bound that most applications would benefit more from restructuring the application to increase the computational density than from optimizing this tiny kernel.

Listing 11.2 saxpyGPU.

```
__global__ void
saxpyGPU(
    float *out,
    const float *x,
    const float *y,
    size_t N,
    float alpha )
{
```

```
for ( size_t i = blockIdx.x*blockDim.x + threadIdx.x;
            i < N;
            i += blockDim.x*gridDim.x ) {
    out[i] = alpha*x[i]+y[i];
    }
}
```

The bulk of this chapter discusses how to move data to and from host memory efficiently, but first we'll spend a moment examining how to improve this kernel's performance when operating on device memory.

11.1 Device Memory

If the input and output data are in device memory, optimizing a low-density computation such as SAXPY is a matter of optimizing the global memory access. Besides alignment and coalescing constraints that inform performance, CUDA kernels are sensitive to the number of blocks and threads per block. The globalRead, globalWrite, globalCopy, and globalCopy2 applications (in the memory/ subdirectory of the source code) generate reports for the bandwidths achieved for a variety of operand sizes, block sizes, and loop unroll factors. A sample report generated by globalCopy2 (which follows a memory access pattern similar to SAXPY: two reads and one write per loop iteration) is given in Listing 11.3.

If we reference the globalCopy2.cu application from Chapter 5 (see Listing 5.8), running it on a GK104 gets us the output in Listing 11.3 for 4-byte operands. The top row (unroll factor of 1) corresponds to the naïve implementation (similar to Listing 11.2); a slight performance benefit is observed when the loop is unrolled. An unroll factor of 4 gives a speedup of about 10%, delivering 128 GiB/s of bandwidth as opposed to the naïve implementation's 116 GiB/s.

Interestingly, using the #pragma unroll compiler directive only increases performance to about 118 GiB/s, while modifying the templated kernel from globalCopy2.cu to perform SAXPY increases performance to 135 GiB/s. Listing 11.4 gives the resulting kernel, which is implemented in the stream1Device.cu application (cudahandbook/streaming/).

For most applications, these small performance differences don't justify rewriting kernels in this way. But if kernels are written to be "blocking-agnostic" (i.e., to work correctly for any grid or block size), then the optimal settings can be determined empirically without too much effort.

Listing 11.3 `globalCopy2` output (GK104).

```
Operand size: 4 bytes
Input size: 16M operands
                        Block Size
Unroll  32      64      128     256     512     maxBW   maxThreads
1       63.21   90.89   104.64  113.45  116.06  116.06  512
2       66.43   92.89   105.09  116.35  120.66  120.66  512
3       87.23   100.70  112.07  110.85  121.36  121.36  512
4       99.54   103.53  113.58  119.52  128.64  128.64  512
5       94.27   103.56  108.02  122.82  124.88  124.88  512
6       100.67  104.18  115.10  122.05  122.46  122.46  512
7       94.56   106.09  116.30  117.63  114.50  117.63  256
8       58.27   45.10   47.07   46.29   45.18   58.27   32
9       41.20   34.74   35.87   35.49   34.58   41.20   32
10      33.59   31.97   32.42   31.43   30.61   33.59   32
11      27.76   28.17   28.46   27.83   26.79   28.46   128
12      25.59   26.42   26.54   25.72   24.51   26.54   128
13      22.69   23.07   23.54   22.50   20.71   23.54   128
14      22.19   22.40   22.23   21.10   19.00   22.40   64
15      20.94   21.14   20.98   19.62   17.31   21.14   64
16      18.86   19.01   18.97   17.66   15.40   19.01   64
```

Listing 11.4 saxpyGPU (templated unroll).

```
template<const int n>
__device__ void
saxpy_unrolled(
    float *out,
    const float *px,
    const float *py,
    size_t N,
    float alpha )
{
    float x[n], y[n];
    size_t i;
    for ( i = n*blockIdx.x*blockDim.x+threadIdx.x;
          i < N-n*blockDim.x*gridDim.x;
          i += n*blockDim.x*gridDim.x ) {
        for ( int j = 0; j < n; j++ ) {
            size_t index = i+j*blockDim.x;
            x[j] = px[index];
            y[j] = py[index];
        }
```

```
        for ( int j = 0; j < n; j++ ) {
            size_t index = i+j*blockDim.x;
            out[index] = alpha*x[j]+y[j];
        }
    }
    // to avoid the (index<N) conditional in the inner loop,
    // we left off some work at the end
    for ( int j = 0; j < n; j++ ) {
        for ( int j = 0; j < n; j++ ) {
            size_t index = i+j*blockDim.x;
            if ( index<N ) {
                x[j] = px[index];
                y[j] = py[index];
            }
        }
        for ( int j = 0; j < n; j++ ) {
            size_t index = i+j*blockDim.x;
            if ( index<N ) out[index] = alpha*x[j]+y[j];
        }
    }
}

__global__ void
saxpyGPU( float *out, const float *px, const float *py, size_t N,
float alpha )
{
    saxpy_unrolled<4>( out, px, py, N, alpha );
}
```

The `stream1Device.cu` application reports the total wall clock time needed to transfer data from pageable system memory to device memory, operate on the data with the kernel in Listing 11.4, and transfer the data back. On a test system with an Intel i7 running Windows 7 on a GeForce GTX 680, the output of this application is as follows.

```
Measuring times with 128M floats (use --N to specify number of Mfloats)
Memcpy( host->device ): 365.95 ms (2934.15 MB/s)
Kernel processing : 11.94 ms (134920.75 MB/s)
Memcpy (device->host ): 188.72 ms (2844.73 MB/s)

Total time (wall clock): 570.22 ms (2815.30 MB/s)
```

The kernel takes a tiny amount of the overall execution time—about 2% of the wall clock time. The other 98% of time is spent transferring data to and from the GPU! For transfer-bound workloads like this one, if some or all of the data being operated on is in host memory, the best way to optimize the application is to improve CPU/GPU overlap and transfer performance.

11.2 Asynchronous Memcpy

Unless the input and output data can stay resident on the GPU, the logistics of streaming the data through the GPU—copying the input and output data to and from device memory—become the primary consideration. The two tools best suited to improve transfer performance are pinned memory and asynchronous memcpy (which can only operate on pinned memory).

The `stream2Async.cu` application illustrates the effect of moving the page-able memory of `stream1Device.cu` to pinned memory and invoking the memcpys asynchronously.

```
Measuring times with 128M floats (use --N to specify number of Mfloats)
Memcpy( host->device ): 181.03 ms (5931.33 MB/s)
Kernel processing : 13.87 ms (116152.99 MB/s)
Memcpy (device->host ): 90.07 ms (5960.35 MB/s)

Total time (wall clock): 288.68 ms (5579.29 MB/s)
```

Listing 11.5 contrasts the difference between the timed portions of `stream1-Device.cu` (which performs synchronous transfers) and `stream2Async.cu` (which performs asynchronous transfers).[1] In both cases, four CUDA events are used to record the times at the start, after the host→device transfers, after the kernel launch, and at the end. For `stream2Async.cu`, all of these operations are requested of the GPU in quick succession, and the GPU records the event times as it performs them. For `stream1Device.cu`, the GPU event-based times are a bit suspect, since for any `cudaMemcpy()`, calls must wait for the GPU to complete before proceeding, causing a pipeline bubble before the `cudaEventRecord()` calls for `evHtoD` and `evDtoH` are processed.

Note that despite using the slower, naïve implementation of `saxpyGPU` (from Listing 11.2), the wall clock time from this application shows that it completes the computation almost twice as fast: 289 ms versus 570.22 ms. The combination of faster transfers and asynchronous execution delivers much better performance.

Despite the improved performance, the application output highlights another performance opportunity: Some of the kernel processing can be performed concurrently with transfers. The next two sections describe two different methods to overlap kernel execution with transfers.

---

1. Error checking has been removed for clarity.

Listing 11.5 Synchronous (`stream1Device.cu`) versus asynchronous (`stream2Async.cu`).

```
//
// from stream1Device.cu
//
cudaEventRecord( evStart, 0 );
cudaMemcpy( dptrX, hptrX, ..., cudaMemcpyHostToDevice );
cudaMemcpy( dptrY, hptrY, ..., cudaMemcpyHostToDevice );
cudaEventRecord( evHtoD, 0 );
    saxpyGPU<<<nBlocks, nThreads>>>( dptrOut, dptrX, dptrY, N, alpha;
cudaEventRecord( evKernel, 0 );
cudaMemcpy( hptrOut, dptrOut, N*sizeof(float), cudaMemcpyDeviceToHost );
cudaEventRecord( evDtoH, 0 );
cudaDeviceSynchronize();

//
// from stream2Async.cu
//
cudaEventRecord( evStart, 0 );
cudaMemcpyAsync( dptrX, hptrX, ..., cudaMemcpyHostToDevice, NULL );
cudaMemcpyAsync( dptrY, hptrY, ..., cudaMemcpyHostToDevice, NULL );
cudaEventRecord( evHtoD, 0 );
    saxpyGPU<<<nBlocks, nThreads>>>( dptrOut, dptrX, dptrY, N, alpha;
cudaEventRecord( evKernel, 0 );
cudaMemcpyAsync( hptrOut, dptrOut, N*sizeof(float), ... , NULL );
cudaEventRecord( evDtoH, 0 );
cudaDeviceSynchronize();
```

11.3 Streams

For workloads that benefit from concurrent memcpy and kernel execution (GPU/GPU overlap), CUDA streams can be used to coordinate execution. The `stream3Streams.cu` application splits the input and output arrays into k streams and then invokes k host→device memcpys, kernels, and device→host memcpys, each in their own stream. Associating the transfers and computations with different streams lets CUDA know that the computations are completely independent, and CUDA will exploit whatever parallelism opportunities the hardware can support. On GPUs with multiple copy engines, the GPU may be transferring data both to and from device memory while processing other data with the SMs.

Listing 11.6 shows an excerpt from `stream3Streams.cu`, the same portion of the application as shown in Listing 11.5. On the test system, the output from this application reads as follows.

```
Measuring times with 128M floats
Testing with default max of 8 streams (set with --maxStreams <count>)

Streams  Time (ms)  MB/s
1        290.77 ms  5471.45
2        273.46 ms  5820.34
3        277.14 ms  5744.49
4        278.06 ms  5725.76
5        277.44 ms  5736.52
6        276.56 ms  5751.87
7        274.75 ms  5793.43
8        275.41 ms  5779.51
```

The GPU in question has only one copy engine, so it is not surprising that the case with 2 streams delivers the highest performance. If the kernel execution time were more in line with the transfer time, it would likely be beneficial to split the arrays into more than 2 subarrays. As things stand, the first kernel launch cannot begin processing until the first host→device memcpy is done, and the final device→host memcpy cannot begin until the last kernel launch is done. If the kernel processing took more time, this "overhang" would be more pronounced. For our application, the wall clock time of 273 ms shows that most of the kernel processing (13.87 ms) has been hidden.

Note that in this formulation, partly due to hardware limitations, we are not trying to insert any `cudaEventRecord()` calls between operations, as we did in Listing 11.5. On most CUDA hardware, trying to record events between the streamed operations in Listing 11.6 would break concurrency and reduce performance. Instead, we bracket the operations with one `cudaEventRecord()` before and one `cudaEventRecord()` after.

Listing 11.6 `stream3Streams.cu` excerpt.

```
for ( int iStream = 0; iStream < nStreams; iStream++ ) {
    CUDART_CHECK( cudaMemcpyAsync(
                    dptrX+iStream*streamStep,
                    hptrX+iStream*streamStep,
                    streamStep*sizeof(float),
                    cudaMemcpyHostToDevice,
                    streams[iStream] ) );
    CUDART_CHECK( cudaMemcpyAsync(
                    dptrY+iStream*streamStep,
                    hptrY+iStream*streamStep,
                    streamStep*sizeof(float),
```

```
                       cudaMemcpyHostToDevice,
                       streams[iStream] ) );
    }

    for ( int iStream = 0; iStream < nStreams; iStream++ ) {
        saxpyGPU<<<nBlocks, nThreads, 0, streams[iStream]>>>(
            dptrOut+iStream*streamStep,
            dptrX+iStream*streamStep,
            dptrY+iStream*streamStep,
            streamStep,
            alpha );
    }

    for ( int iStream = 0; iStream < nStreams; iStream++ ) {
        CUDART_CHECK( cudaMemcpyAsync(
                        hptrOut+iStream*streamStep,
                        dptrOut+iStream*streamStep,
                        streamStep*sizeof(float),
                        cudaMemcpyDeviceToHost,
                        streams[iStream] ) );
    }
```

11.4 Mapped Pinned Memory

For transfer-bound, streaming workloads such as SAXPY, reformulating the application to use mapped pinned memory for both the input and output confers a number of benefits.

- As shown by the excerpt from `stream4Mapped.cu` (Listing 11.7), it eliminates the need to call `cudaMemcpy()`.

- It eliminates the need to allocate device memory.

- For discrete GPUs, mapped pinned memory performs bus transfers but minimizes the amount of "overhang" alluded to in the previous section. Instead of waiting for a host→device memcpy to finish, input data can be processed by the SMs as soon as it arrives. Instead of waiting for a kernel to complete before initiating a device →host transfer, the data is posted to the bus as soon as the SMs are done processing.

- For integrated GPUs, host and device memory exist in the same memory pool, so mapped pinned memory enables "zero copy" and eliminates any need to transfer data over the bus at all.

Listing 11.7 `stream4Mapped` excerpt.

```
chTimerGetTime( &chStart );
cudaEventRecord( evStart, 0 );
    saxpyGPU<<<nBlocks, nThreads>>>( dptrOut, dptrX, dptrY, N, alpha );
cudaEventRecord( evStop, 0 );
cudaDeviceSynchronize();
```

Mapped pinned memory works especially well when writing to host memory (for example, to deliver the result of a reduction to the host) because unlike reads, there is no need to wait until writes arrive before continuing execution.[2] Workloads that read mapped pinned memory are more problematic. If the GPU cannot sustain full bus performance while reading from mapped pinned memory, the smaller transfer performance may overwhelm the benefits of a smaller overhang. Also, for some workloads, the SMs have better things to do than drive (and wait for) PCI Express bus traffic.

In the case of our application, on our test system, mapped pinned memory is a definite win.

```
Measuring times with 128M floats (use --N to specify number of Mfloats)
Total time: 204.54 ms (7874.45 MB/s)
```

It completes the computation in 204.54 ms, significantly faster than the 273 ms of the second-fastest implementation. The effective bandwidth of 7.9 GiB/s shows that the GPU is pushing both directions of PCI Express.

Not all combinations of systems and GPUs can sustain such high levels of performance with mapped pinned memory. If there's any doubt, keep the data in device memory and use the asynchronous memcpy formulations, similar to `stream2Async.cu`.

11.5 Performance and Summary

This chapter covers four different implementations of SAXPY, emphasizing different strategies of data movement.

- Synchronous memcpy to and from device memory

- Asynchronous memcpy to and from device memory

---

2. Hardware designers call this "covering the latency."

- Asynchronous memcpy using streams

- Mapped pinned memory

Table 11.1 and Figure 11.1 summarize the relative performance of these implementations for 128M floats on GK104s plugged into two different test systems: the Intel i7 system (PCI Express 2.0) and an Intel Xeon E5-2670 (PCI Express 3.0). The benefits of PCI Express 3.0 are evident, as they are about twice as fast. Additionally, the overhead of CPU/GPU synchronization is higher on the E5-2670, since the pageable memcpy operations are slower.

Table 11.1 Streaming Performance

	BANDWIDTH (MB/S)	
VERSION	INTEL I7	INTEL SANDY BRIDGE
stream1Device.cu	2815	2001
stream2Async.cu	5579	10502
stream3Streams.cu	5820	14051
stream4Mapped.cu	7874	17413

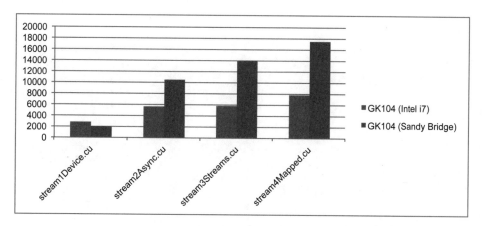

Figure 11.1 Bandwidth (GeForce GTX 680 on Intel i7 versus Sandy Bridge)

Chapter 12

Reduction

Reduction is a class of parallel algorithms that pass over $O(N)$ input data and generate a $O(1)$ result computed with a binary associative operator $\oplus$. Examples of such operations include minimum, maximum, sum, sum of squares, AND, OR, and the dot product of two vectors. Reduction is also an important primitive used as a subroutine in other operations, such as Scan (covered in the next chapter).

Unless the operator $\oplus$ is extremely expensive to evaluate, reduction tends to be bandwidth-bound. Our treatment of reduction begins with several two-pass implementations based on the `reduction` SDK sample. Next, the `threadFenceReduction` SDK sample shows how to perform reduction in a single pass so only one kernel must be invoked to perform the operation. Finally, the chapter concludes with a discussion of fast binary reduction with the `__syncthreads_count()` intrinsic (added with SM 2.0) and how to perform reduction using the warp shuffle instruction (added with SM 3.0).

12.1 Overview

Since the binary operator is associative, the $O(N)$ operations to compute a reduction may be performed in any order.

$$\sum_i a_i = a_0 \oplus a_1 \oplus a_2 \oplus a_3 \oplus a_4 \oplus a_5 \oplus a_6 \oplus a_7$$

Figure 12.1 shows some different options to process an 8-element array. The serial implementation is shown for contrast. Only one execution unit that can

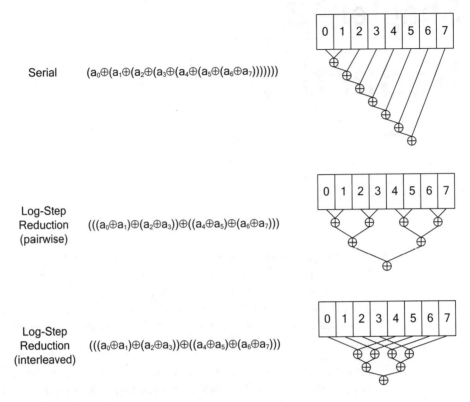

Serial $\qquad (a_0 \oplus (a_1 \oplus (a_2 \oplus (a_3 \oplus (a_4 \oplus (a_5 \oplus (a_6 \oplus a_7)))))))$

Log-Step
Reduction $\qquad (((a_0 \oplus a_1) \oplus (a_2 \oplus a_3)) \oplus ((a_4 \oplus a_5) \oplus (a_6 \oplus a_7)))$
(pairwise)

Log-Step
Reduction $\qquad (((a_0 \oplus a_1) \oplus (a_2 \oplus a_3)) \oplus ((a_4 \oplus a_5) \oplus (a_6 \oplus a_7)))$
(interleaved)

Figure 12.1. Reduction of 8 elements.

perform the $\oplus$ operator is needed, but performance is poor because it takes 7 steps to complete the computation.

The pairwise formulation is intuitive and only requires $O(\lg N)$ steps (3 in this case) to compute the result, but it exhibits poor performance in CUDA. When reading global memory, having a single thread access adjacent memory locations causes uncoalesced memory transactions. When reading shared memory, the pattern shown will cause bank conflicts.

For both global memory and shared memory, an interleaving-based strategy works better. In Figure 12.1, the interleaving factor is 4; for global memory, interleaving by a multiple of `blockDim.x *gridDim.x` has good performance because all memory transactions are coalesced. For shared memory, best performance is achieved by accumulating the partial sums with an interleaving factor chosen to avoid bank conflicts and to keep adjacent threads in the thread block active.

Once a thread block has finished processing its interleaved subarray, it writes the result to global memory for further processing by a subsequent kernel launch. It may seem expensive to launch multiple kernels, but kernel launches are asynchronous, so the CPU can request the next kernel launch while the GPU is executing the first; every kernel launch represents an opportunity to specify different launch configurations.

Since the performance of a kernel can vary with different thread and block sizes, it's a good idea to write the kernel so it will work correctly for any valid combination of thread and block sizes. The optimal thread/block configuration then can be determined empirically.

The initial reduction kernels in this chapter illustrate some important CUDA programming concepts that may be familiar.

- *Coalesced memory operations* to maximize bandwidth

- *Variable-sized shared memory* to facilitate collaboration between threads

- Avoiding shared memory *bank conflicts*

The optimized reduction kernels illustrate more advanced CUDA programming idioms.

- *Warp synchronous* coding avoids unneeded thread synchronization.

- *Atomic operations* and *memory fences* eliminate the need to invoke multiple kernels.

- The *shuffle* instruction enables warp-level reductions without the use of shared memory.

12.2 Two-Pass Reduction

This algorithm operates in two stages. A kernel performs *NumBlocks* reductions in parallel, where *NumBlocks* is the number of blocks used to invoke the kernel; the results are written to an intermediate array. The final result is generated by invoking the same kernel to perform a second pass on the intermediate array with a single block. Listing 12.1 gives a two-pass reduction kernel that computes the sum of an array of integers.

Listing 12.1 Two-pass reduction kernel.

```
__global__ void
Reduction1_kernel( int *out, const int *in, size_t N )
{
    extern __shared__ int sPartials[];
    int sum = 0;
    const int tid = threadIdx.x;
    for ( size_t i = blockIdx.x*blockDim.x + tid;
            i < N;
            i += blockDim.x*gridDim.x ) {
        sum += in[i];
    }
    sPartials[tid] = sum;
    __syncthreads();

    for ( int activeThreads = blockDim.x>>1;
              activeThreads;
              activeThreads >>= 1 ) {
        if ( tid < activeThreads ) {
            sPartials[tid] += sPartials[tid+activeThreads];
        }
        __syncthreads();
    }

    if ( tid == 0 ) {
        out[blockIdx.x] = sPartials[0];
    }
}

void
Reduction1( int *answer, int *partial,
            const int *in, size_t N,
            int numBlocks, int numThreads )
{
    unsigned int sharedSize = numThreads*sizeof(int);
    Reduction1_kernel<<<
        numBlocks, numThreads, sharedSize>>>(
            partial, in, N );
    Reduction1_kernel<<<
        1, numThreads, sharedSize>>>(
            answer, partial, numBlocks );
}
```

The shared memory array is used to accumulate the reduction within each thread block. Its size depends on the number of threads in the block, so it must be specified when the kernel is launched. *Note:* The number of threads in the block must be a power of 2!

The first `for` loop computes the thread's sum over the input array. If the input pointer is properly aligned, all of the memory transactions by this code are coalesced, and it will maximize the memory bandwidth. Each thread then writes its accumulated sum to shared memory and synchronizes before starting the log-step reduction.

The second `for` loop performs a log-step reduction over the values in shared memory. The values in the upper half of shared memory are added to the values in the lower half, and the number of participating threads is successively halved until one value in `shared_sum[0]` contains the output for that block. This part of the kernel is the one that requires that the thread block size be a power of 2.

Finally, the output value of the thread block is written to global memory. This kernel is intended to be invoked twice, as shown in the host function: once with *N* blocks, where *N* is chosen for maximum performance in performing the reduction over the input array, and then with 1 block to accumulate the final output. Listing 12.2 shows the host function that invokes `Reduction1_kernel()`. Note that an array for the partial sums is allocated and passed in separately. Also note that since the kernel uses an unsized shared memory array, the amount of shared memory needed by the kernel must be specified as the third parameter in the `<<< >>>` syntax.

The CUDA SDK discusses several optimizations of this kernel that focus on reducing the amount of conditional code in the log-step reduction. Part of the `for` loop that performs the log-step reduction—the later part, when the thread count is 32 or fewer—can be implemented with *warp-synchronous* code. Since the warps in each thread block execute each instruction in lockstep, the `__syncthreads()` intrinsics are no longer needed when the number of active threads in a block drops below the hardware's warp size of 32. The resulting kernel, located in the `reduction2.cu` source code file, is shown in Listing 12.2.

IMPORTANT NOTE

When writing warp synchronous code, the `volatile` keyword must be used for the pointers into shared memory. Otherwise, the compiler may introduce optimizations that change the order of memory operations and the code will not work correctly.

Listing 12.2 Reduction with unrolled, warp-synchronous finish.

```
__global__ void
Reduction2_kernel( int *out, const int *in, size_t N )
{
    extern __shared__ int sPartials[];
    int sum = 0;
    const int tid = threadIdx.x;
    for ( size_t i = blockIdx.x*blockDim.x + tid;
          i < N;
          i += blockDim.x*gridDim.x ) {
        sum += in[i];
    }
    sPartials[tid] = sum;
    __syncthreads();

    for ( int activeThreads = blockDim.x>>1;
              activeThreads > 32;
              activeThreads >>= 1 ) {
        if ( tid < activeThreads ) {
            sPartials[tid] += sPartials[tid+activeThreads];
        }
        __syncthreads();
    }
    if ( threadIdx.x < 32 ) {
        volatile int *wsSum = sPartials;
        if ( blockDim.x > 32 ) wsSum[tid] += wsSum[tid + 32];
        wsSum[tid] += wsSum[tid + 16];
        wsSum[tid] += wsSum[tid + 8];
        wsSum[tid] += wsSum[tid + 4];
        wsSum[tid] += wsSum[tid + 2];
        wsSum[tid] += wsSum[tid + 1];
        if ( tid == 0 ) {
            volatile int *wsSum = sPartials;
            out[blockIdx.x] = wsSum[0];
        }
    }
}
```

The warp synchronous optimization can be taken a step further by lofting the thread count into a template parameter, enabling the log-step reduction to be unrolled completely. Listing 12.3 gives the complete optimized kernel. Following Mark Harris's reduction presentation,[1] the code evaluated at compile time is italicized.

---

1. http://bit.ly/WNmH9Z

Listing 12.3 Templatized, fully unrolled log-step reduction.

```
template<unsigned int numThreads>
__global__ void
Reduction3_kernel( int *out, const int *in, size_t N )
{
    extern __shared__ int sPartials[];
    const unsigned int tid = threadIdx.x;
    int sum = 0;
    for ( size_t i = blockIdx.x*numThreads + tid;
          i < N;
          i += numThreads*gridDim.x )
    {
        sum += in[i];
    }
    sPartials[tid] = sum;
    __syncthreads();

    if (numThreads >= 1024) {
        if (tid < 512) {
            sPartials[tid] += sPartials[tid + 512];
        }
        __syncthreads();
    }
    if (numThreads >= 512) {
        if (tid < 256) {
            sPartials[tid] += sPartials[tid + 256];
        }
        __syncthreads();
    }
    if (numThreads >= 256) {
        if (tid < 128) {
            sPartials[tid] += sPartials[tid + 128];
        }
        __syncthreads();
    }
    if (numThreads >= 128) {
        if (tid <  64) {
            sPartials[tid] += sPartials[tid +  64];
        }
        __syncthreads();
    }

    // warp synchronous at the end
    if ( tid < 32 ) {
        volatile int *wsSum = sPartials;
        if (numThreads >=  64) { wsSum[tid] += wsSum[tid + 32]; }
        if (numThreads >=  32) { wsSum[tid] += wsSum[tid + 16]; }
        if (numThreads >=  16) { wsSum[tid] += wsSum[tid +  8]; }
        if (numThreads >=   8) { wsSum[tid] += wsSum[tid +  4]; }
        if (numThreads >=   4) { wsSum[tid] += wsSum[tid +  2]; }
        if (numThreads >=   2) { wsSum[tid] += wsSum[tid +  1]; }
```

```
        if ( tid == 0 ) {
            out[blockIdx.x] = wsSum[0];
        }
    }
}
```

To instantiate the function template in Listing 12.3, it must be invoked explicitly in a separate host function. Listing 12.4 shows how `Reduction3_kernel`
is invoked by another function template, and the host function uses a `switch`
statement to invoke that template for each possible block size.

Listing 12.4 Template instantiations for unrolled reduction.

```
template<unsigned int numThreads>
void
Reduction3_template( int *answer, int *partial,
                     const int *in, size_t N,
                     int numBlocks )
{
    Reduction3_kernel<numThreads><<<
        numBlocks, numThreads, numThreads*sizeof(int)>>>(
            partial, in, N );
    Reduction3_kernel<numThreads><<<
        1, numThreads, numThreads*sizeof(int)>>>(
            answer, partial, numBlocks );
}

void
Reduction3( int *out, int *partial,
            const int *in, size_t N,
            int numBlocks, int numThreads )
{
    switch ( numThreads ) {
        case    1: return Reduction3_template<    1>( ... );
        case    2: return Reduction3_template<    2>( ... );
        case    4: return Reduction3_template<    4>( ... );
        case    8: return Reduction3_template<    8>( ... );
        case   16: return Reduction3_template<   16>( ... );
        case   32: return Reduction3_template<   32>( ... );
        case   64: return Reduction3_template<   64>( ... );
        case  128: return Reduction3_template<  128>( ... );
        case  256: return Reduction3_template<  256>( ... );
        case  512: return Reduction3_template<  512>( ... );
        case 1024: return Reduction3_template<1024>( ... );
    }
}
```

12.3 Single-Pass Reduction

The two-pass reduction approach is in part a workaround for the inability of CUDA blocks to synchronize with one another. In the absence of interblock synchronization to determine when processing of the final output can begin, a second kernel invocation is needed.

The second kernel invocation can be avoided by using a combination of atomic operations and shared memory, as described in the `threadfenceReduction` sample in the CUDA SDK. A single device memory location tracks which thread blocks have finished writing their partial sums. Once all blocks have finished, one block performs the final log-step reduction to write the output.

Since this kernel performs several log-step reductions from shared memory, the code in Listing 12.3 that conditionally adds based on the templated thread count is pulled into a separate device function for reuse.

Listing 12.5 `Reduction4_LogStepShared`.

```
template<unsigned int numThreads>
__device__ void
Reduction4_LogStepShared( int *out, volatile int *partials )
{
    const int tid = threadIdx.x;
    if (numThreads >= 1024) {
        if (tid < 512) {
            partials[tid] += partials[tid + 512];
        }
        __syncthreads();
    }
    if (numThreads >= 512) {
        if (tid < 256) {
            partials[tid] += partials[tid + 256];
        }
        __syncthreads();
    }
    if (numThreads >= 256) {
        if (tid < 128) {
            partials[tid] += partials[tid + 128];
        }
        __syncthreads();
    }
    if (numThreads >= 128) {
        if (tid <  64) {
            partials[tid] += partials[tid +  64];
        }
        __syncthreads();
    }
```

```
    // warp synchronous at the end
    if ( tid < 32 ) {
        if (numThreads >= 64) { partials[tid] += partials[tid + 32]; }
        if (numThreads >= 32) { partials[tid] += partials[tid + 16]; }
        if (numThreads >= 16) { partials[tid] += partials[tid +  8]; }
        if (numThreads >=  8) { partials[tid] += partials[tid +  4]; }
        if (numThreads >=  4) { partials[tid] += partials[tid +  2]; }
        if (numThreads >=  2) { partials[tid] += partials[tid +  1]; }
        if ( tid == 0 ) {
            *out = partials[0];
        }
    }
}
```

The Reduction4_LogStepShared() function, shown in Listing 12.5, writes the reduction for the thread block, whose partial sums are given by par-tials to the pointer to the memory location specified by out. Listing 12.6 gives the single-pass reduction using Reduction4_LogStepShared() as a subroutine.

Listing 12.6 Single-pass reduction kernel (reduction4SinglePass.cuh).

```
// Global variable used by reduceSinglePass to count blocks
__device__ unsigned int retirementCount = 0;

template <unsigned int numThreads>
__global__ void
reduceSinglePass( int *out, int *partial,
                  const int *in, unsigned int N )
{
    extern __shared__ int sPartials[];
    unsigned int tid = threadIdx.x;
    int sum = 0;
    for ( size_t i = blockIdx.x*numThreads + tid;
                 i < N;
                 i += numThreads*gridDim.x ) {
        sum += in[i];
    }
    sPartials[tid] = sum;
    __syncthreads();

    if (gridDim.x == 1) {
        Reduction4_LogStepShared<numThreads>( &out[blockIdx.x],
                                              sPartials );

        return;
    }
    Reduction4_LogStepShared<numThreads>( &partial[blockIdx.x],
                                          sPartials );
```

```
    __shared__ bool lastBlock;

    // wait for outstanding memory instructions in this thread
    __threadfence();

    // Thread 0 takes a ticket
    if( tid==0 ) {
        unsigned int ticket = atomicAdd(&retirementCount, 1);

        //
        // If the ticket ID is equal to the number of blocks,
        // we are the last block!
        //
        lastBlock = (ticket == gridDim.x-1);
    }
    __syncthreads();

    // One block performs the final log-step reduction
    if( lastBlock ) {
        int sum = 0;
        for ( size_t i = tid;
                    i < gridDim.x;
                    i += numThreads ) {
            sum += partial[i];
        }
        sPartials[threadIdx.x] = sum;
        __syncthreads();
        Reduction4_LogStepShared<numThreads>( out, sPartials );
        retirementCount = 0;
    }
}
```

The kernel starts out with familiar code that has each thread compute a partial reduction across the input array and write the results to shared memory. Once this is done, the single-block case is treated specially, since the output of the log-step reduction from shared memory can be written directly and not to the array of partial sums. The remainder of the kernel is executed only on kernels with multiple thread blocks.

The shared Boolean lastBlock is used to evaluate a predicate that must be communicated to all threads in the final block. The __threadfence() causes all threads in the block to wait until any pending memory transactions have been posted to device memory. When __threadfence() is executed, writes to global memory are visible to all threads, not just the calling thread or threads in the block.

As each block exits, it performs an `atomicAdd()` to check whether it is the one block that needs to perform the final log-step reduction. Since `atomicAdd()` returns the *previous* value of the memory location, the block that increments `retirementCount` and gets a value equal to `gridDim.x-1` can be deemed the "last thread" and can perform the final reduction. The `lastBlock` shared memory location communicates that result to all threads in the block, and `__syncthreads()` then must be called so the write to `lastBlock` will be visible to all threads in the block. The final block performs the final log-step reduction of the partial sums and writes the result. Finally, `retirementCount` is set back to 0 for subsequent invocations of `reduceSinglePass()`.

12.4 Reduction with Atomics

For reductions whose ⊕ operator is supported natively by an atomic operator implemented in hardware, a simpler approach to reduction is possible: Just loop over the input data and "fire and forget" the inputs into the output memory location to receive the output value. The `Reduction5` kernel given in Listing 12.7 is much simpler than previous formulations. Each thread computes a partial sum over the inputs and performs an `atomicAdd` on the output at the end.

Note that `Reduction5_kernel` does not work properly unless the memory location pointed to by `out` is initialized to 0.[2] Like the `threadFenceReduction` sample, this kernel has the advantage that only one kernel invocation is needed to perform the operation.

Listing 12.7 Reduction with global atomics (`reduction5Atomics.cuh`).

```
__global__ void
Reduction5_kernel( int *out, const int *in, size_t N )
{
    const int tid = threadIdx.x;
    int partialSum = 0;
    for ( size_t i = blockIdx.x*blockDim.x + tid;
          i < N;
          i += blockDim.x*gridDim.x ) {
        partialSum += in[i];
    }
    atomicAdd( out, partialSum );
}
```

---

2. The kernel itself cannot perform this initialization because CUDA's execution model does not enable the race condition to be resolved between thread blocks. See Section 7.3.1.

```
void
Reduction5 ( int *answer, int *partial,
             const int *in, size_t N,
             int numBlocks, int numThreads )
{
    cudaMemset ( answer, 0, sizeof(int) );
    Reduction5_kernel<<< numBlocks, numThreads>>>( answer, in, N );
}
```

12.5 Arbitrary Block Sizes

So far, all of the reduction implementations that use shared memory require the block size to be a power of 2. With a small amount of additional code, the reduction can be made to work on arbitrary block sizes. Listing 12.8 gives a kernel derived from the very first two-pass kernel given in Listing 12.1, modified to operate on any block size. The floorPow2 variable computes the power of 2 that is less than or equal to the block size, and the contribution from any threads above that power of 2 is added before continuing on to the loop that implements the log-step reduction.

Listing 12.8 Reduction (arbitrary block size) (reduction6AnyBlockSize.cuh).

```
__global__ void
Reduction6_kernel ( int *out, const int *in, size_t N )
{
    extern __shared__ int sPartials[];
    int sum = 0;
    const int tid = threadIdx.x;
    for ( size_t i = blockIdx.x*blockDim.x + tid;
          i < N;
          i += blockDim.x*gridDim.x ) {
        sum += in[i];
    }
    sPartials[tid] = sum;
    __syncthreads();

    // start the shared memory loop on the next power of 2 less
    // than the block size.  If block size is not a power of 2,
    // accumulate the intermediate sums in the remainder range.
    int floorPow2 = blockDim.x;

    if ( floorPow2 & (floorPow2-1) ) {
        while ( floorPow2 & (floorPow2-1) ) {
            floorPow2 &= floorPow2-1;
        }
```

```
        if ( tid >= floorPow2 ) {
            sPartials[tid - floorPow2] += sPartials[tid];
        }
        __syncthreads();
    }

    for ( int activeThreads = floorPow2>>1;
            activeThreads;
            activeThreads >>= 1 ) {
        if ( tid < activeThreads ) {
            sPartials[tid] += sPartials[tid+activeThreads];
        }
        __syncthreads();
    }

    if ( tid == 0 ) {
        out[blockIdx.x] = sPartials[0];
    }
}
```

12.6 Reduction Using Arbitrary Data Types

So far, we have only developed reduction kernels that can compute the sum of
an array of integers. To generalize these kernels to perform a broader set of
operations, we turn to C++ templates. With the exception of the algorithms that
use atomics, all of the kernels that have appeared so far can be adapted to use
templates. In the source code accompanying the book, they are in the CUDA
headers reduction1Templated.cuh, reduction2Templated.cuh, and
so on. Listing 12.9 gives the templated version of the reduction kernel from
Listing 12.1.

Listing 12.9 Templated reduction kernel.

```
template<typename ReductionType, typename T>
__global__ void
Reduction_templated( ReductionType *out, const T *in, size_t N )
{
    SharedMemory<ReductionType> sPartials;
    ReductionType sum;
    const int tid = threadIdx.x;
    for ( size_t i = blockIdx.x*blockDim.x + tid;
            i < N;
            i += blockDim.x*gridDim.x ) {
        sum += in[i];
    }
```

```
    sPartials[tid] = sum;
    __syncthreads();

    for ( int activeThreads = blockDim.x>>1;
            activeThreads;
            activeThreads >>= 1 ) {
        if ( tid < activeThreads ) {
            sPartials[tid] += sPartials[tid+activeThreads];
        }
        __syncthreads();
    }
    if ( tid == 0 ) {
        out[blockIdx.x] = sPartials[0];
    }
}
```

Note that since we want to be able to compute a variety of output types for a given type of input (for example, we would like to build kernels that compute any combination of the minimum, maximum, sum, or the sum of squares of an array of integers), we've used two different template parameters: T is the type being reduced, and ReductionType is the type used for partial sums and for the final result.

The first few lines of code use the += operator to "rake" through the input, accumulating a partial sum for each thread in the block.[3] Execution then proceeds exactly as in Listing 12.1, except that the code is operating on ReductionType instead of int. To avoid alignment-related compilation errors, this kernel uses an idiom from the CUDA SDK to declare the variable-sized shared memory.

```
template<class T>
struct SharedMemory
{
    __device__ inline operator         T*()
    {
        extern __shared__ int __smem[];
        return (T*) (void *) __smem;
    }

    __device__ inline operator const T*() const
    {
        extern __shared__ int __smem[];
        return (T*) (void *) __smem;
    }
};
```

---

3. We just as easily could have defined a function to wrap the binary operator being evaluated by the reduction. The Thrust library defines a functor plus.

Listing 12.10 shows an example of a class intended to be used with templated reduction functions such as `Reduction_templated`. This class computes both the sum and the sum of squares of an array of integers.[4] Besides defining `operator+=`, a specialization of the `SharedMemory` template must be declared; otherwise, the compiler will generate the following error.

```
Error: Unaligned memory accesses not supported
```

The `reductionTemplated.cu` program in the accompanying source code shows how the function templates from the CUDA headers can be invoked.

```
Reduction1<CReduction_Sumi_isq, int>( ... );
```

Listing 12.10 `CReduction_Sumi_isq` class.

```
struct CReduction_Sumi_isq {
public:
    CReduction_Sumi_isq();
    int sum;
    long long sumsq;

    CReduction_Sumi_isq& operator +=( int a );
    volatile CReduction_Sumi_isq& operator +=( int a ) volatile;

    CReduction_Sumi_isq& operator +=( const CReduction_Sumi_isq& a );
    volatile CReduction_Sumi_isq& operator +=(
        volatile CReduction_Sumi_isq& a ) volatile;

};

inline __device__ __host__
CReduction_Sumi_isq::CReduction_Sumi_isq()
{
    sum = 0;
    sumsq = 0;
}

inline __device__ __host__
CReduction_Sumi_isq&
CReduction_Sumi_isq::operator +=( int a )
{
    sum += a;
    sumsq += (long long) a*a;
    return *this;
}

inline __device__ __host__
volatile CReduction_Sumi_isq&
CReduction_Sumi_isq::operator +=( int a ) volatile
```

---

4. You could compute a whole suite of statistics on the input array in a single pass, but we are keeping things simple here for illustrative purposes.

```
{
    sum += a;
    sumsq += (long long) a*a;
    return *this;
}

inline __device__ __host__
CReduction_Sumi_isq&
CReduction_Sumi_isq::operator +=( const CReduction_Sumi_isq& a )
{
    sum += a.sum;
    sumsq += a.sumsq;
    return *this;
}

inline __device__ __host__
volatile CReduction_Sumi_isq&
CReduction_Sumi_isq::operator +=(
    volatile CReduction_Sumi_isq& a ) volatile
{
    sum += a.sum;
    sumsq += a.sumsq;
    return *this;
}

inline int
operator!=( const CReduction_Sumi_isq& a,
            const CReduction_Sumi_isq& b )
{
    return a.sum != b.sum && a.sumsq != b.sumsq;
}


//
// from Reduction SDK sample:
// specialize to avoid unaligned memory
// access compile errors
//
template<>
struct SharedMemory<CReduction_Sumi_isq>
{
    __device__ inline operator        CReduction_Sumi_isq*()
    {
        extern __shared__ CReduction_Sumi_isq
            __smem_CReduction_Sumi_isq[];
        return (CReduction_Sumi_isq*)__smem_CReduction_Sumi_isq;
    }

    __device__ inline operator const CReduction_Sumi_isq*() const
    {
        extern __shared__ CReduction_Sumi_isq
            __smem_CReduction_Sumi_isq[];
        return (CReduction_Sumi_isq*)__smem_CReduction_Sumi_isq;
    }
};
```

12.7 Predicate Reduction

Predicates or truth values (true/false) can be represented compactly, since each predicate only occupies 1 bit. In SM 2.0, NVIDIA added a number of instructions to make predicate manipulation more efficient. The `__ballot()` and `__popc()` intrinsics can be used for warp-level reduction, and the `__syncthreads_count()` intrinsic can be used for block-level reduction.

```
int __ballot( int p );
```

`__ballot()` evaluates a condition for all threads in the warp and returns a 32-bit word, where each bit gives the condition for the corresponding thread in the warp. Since `__ballot()` broadcasts its result to every thread in the warp, it is effectively a reduction across the warp. Any thread that wants to count the number of threads in the warp for which the condition was true can call the `__popc()` intrinsic

```
int __popc( int i );
```

which returns the number of set bits in the input word.

SM 2.0 also introduced `__syncthreads_count()`.

```
int __syncthreads_count( int p );
```

This intrinsic waits until all warps in the threadblock have arrived, then broadcasts to all threads in the block the number of threads for which the input condition was true.

Since the 1-bit predicates immediately turn into 5- and 9- or 10-bit values after a warp- or block-level reduction, these intrinsics only serve to reduce the amount of shared memory needed for the lowest-level evaluation and reduction. Still, they greatly amplify the number of elements that can be considered by a single thread block.

12.8 Warp Reduction with Shuffle

SM 3.0 introduced the "shuffle" instruction, described in Section 8.6.1, that can be used to perform a reduction across the 32 threads in a warp. By using the "butterfly" variant of the shuffle instruction, the final 5 steps of the log-step reduction

```
wsSum[tid] += wsSum[tid+16];
wsSum[tid] += wsSum[tid+8];
wsSum[tid] += wsSum[tid+4];
wsSum[tid] += wsSum[tid+2];
wsSum[tid] += wsSum[tid+1];
```

can be rewritten as

```
int mySum = wsSum[tid];
mySum += __shuf_xor( mySum, 16 );
mySum += __shuf_xor( mySum, 8 );
mySum += __shuf_xor( mySum, 4 );
mySum += __shuf_xor( mySum, 2 );
mySum += __shuf_xor( mySum, 1 );
```

All threads in the warp then contain the reduction in mySum. Figure 12.2 illustrates the operation of this warp scan primitive. Each thread's sum is shown as a 4W × 8H rectangle, with a dark square showing which threads have contributed to each thread's partial sum. (Besides the inset, the top row shows which squares correspond to each thread's contribution.) With each step in the log-step reduction, the number of contributions doubles until every thread has a full reduction.[5]

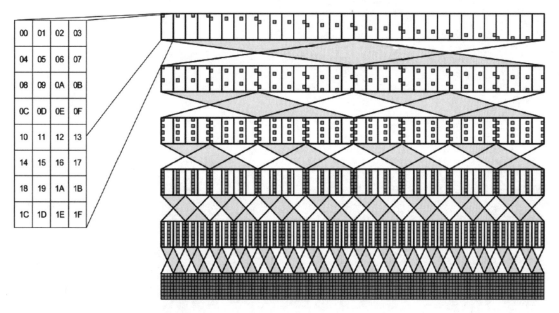

Figure 12.2 Reduction using shuffle instruction.

---

5. The shuffle-up or shuffle-down variants can be used to implement reduction, but they take just as long as the butterfly (XOR) variant and only make the reduction value available to a single thread.

Chapter 13

Scan

Scan, also known as *prefix scan*, *prefix sum*, or *parallel prefix sum*, is an important primitive in parallel programming and is used as a building block for many different algorithms, including but not limited to the following.

- Radix sort

- Quicksort

- Stream compaction and stream splitting

- Sparse matrix-vector multiplication

- Minimum spanning tree construction

- Computation of summed area tables

This chapter starts with a description of the algorithm and a few variations, discusses an early implementation strategy and how Scan algorithms can be described in terms of circuit diagrams, and then provides detailed descriptions of Scan implementations for CUDA. The References section covers both the Scan algorithm and the parallel prefix sum circuit problem in hardware design.

13.1 Definition and Variations

Inclusive scan takes a binary associative operator $\oplus$ and an array of length N

$$[a_0, a_1, \ldots a_{N-1}]$$

and returns the array

$$[a_0, (a_0 \oplus a_1), \ldots (a_0 \oplus a_1 \oplus \ldots \oplus a_{N-1})].$$

Each element of the output depends on the preceding elements in the input.

Exclusive scan is defined similarly but shifts the output and uses an *identity element $id_\oplus$* that has no effect on a value when $\oplus$ is performed with it (for example, 0 for integer addition, 1 for multiplication, etc.).

$$[id_\oplus, a_0, a_0 \oplus a_1, \ldots a_0 \oplus a_1 \oplus \ldots \oplus a_{N-2}].$$

Inclusive and exclusive scans can be transformed between each other by adding or subtracting the input array element by element, as shown in Figure 13.1.

Stream compaction is an operation that separates elements in an array according to a criterion. If a predicate (0 or 1) is computed for each element of the input array to determine whether it should be included in the output stream, then an exclusive scan on the predicates computes the indices of the output elements. A variation of stream compaction, known as *stream splitting*, writes the compact output separately for each value of the predicate. *Segmented scan* is a variation that takes a set of input flags (one per array element) in addition to the array and performs scans on the subarrays delineated by the flags.

Due to the importance of the Scan primitive, an enormous amount of effort has been put into developing optimized scan implementations for CUDA. A list of references is given at the end of this chapter. Both the CUDPP and Thrust libraries include families of optimized Scan primitives that use templates for the best tradeoff between generality and performance. All that said, however, applications that use Scan as a primitive usually can benefit from custom implementations that take advantage of specific knowledge about the problem.

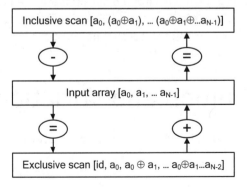

Figure 13.1 Inclusive and exclusive scan.

13.2 Overview

A simple implementation in C++ looks like Listing 13.1.

Listing 13.1 Inclusive scan (in C++).

```
template<class T>
T
InclusiveScan( T *out, const T *in, size_t N )
{
    T sum(0);
    for ( size_t i = 0; i < N; i++ ) {
        sum += in[i];
        out[i] = sum;
    }
    return sum;
}
```

For these serial implementations in Listings 13.1 and 13.2, the only difference between inclusive and exclusive scan is that the lines

```
out[i] = sum;
```

and

```
sum += in[i];
```

are swapped.[1]

Listing 13.2 Exclusive scan (in C++).

```
template<class T>
T
ExclusiveScan( T *out, const T *in, size_t N )
{
    T sum(0);
    for ( size_t i = 0; i < N; i++ ) {
        out[i] = sum;
        sum += in[i];
    }
    return sum;
}
```

---

1. As written, the implementation of exclusive scan does not support an in-place computation. To enable the input and output arrays to be the same, `in[i]` must be saved in a temporary variable.

The serial implementations of Scan are so obvious and trivial that you are for-given if you're wondering what a parallel implementation would look like! The so-called *prefix dependency,* where each output depends on all of the preceding inputs, may have some wondering if it's even possible. But, upon reflection, you can see that the operations for neighboring pairs ($a_i \oplus a_{i+1}$ for $0 \leq i < N - 1$) could be computed in parallel; for $i = 0$, $a_i \oplus a_{i+1}$ computes a final output of the Scan, and otherwise these pairwise operations compute partial sums that can be used to contribute to the final output, much as we used partial sums in Chapter 12.

Blelloch[2] describes a two-pass algorithm with an *upsweep* phase that com-putes the reduction of the array, storing intermediate results along the way, and followed by a *downsweep* that computes the final output of the scan. Pseudocode for the upsweep as is follows.

```
upsweep(a, N)
for d from 0 to (lg N) - 1
in parallel for i from 0 to N - 1 by 2^(d+1)
            a[i + 2^(d+1) - 1] += a[i + 2^(d - 1)]
```

The operation resembles the log-step reduction we have discussed before, except intermediate sums are stored for later use in generating the final output of the scan.

After Blelloch, Figure 13.2 shows an example run of this upsweep algorithm on an 8-element array using addition on integers. The "upsweep" terminology stems from thinking of the array as a balanced tree (Figure 13.3).

Once the upsweep has been completed, a *downsweep* propagates intermediate sums into the leaves of the tree. Pseudocode for the downsweep is as follows.

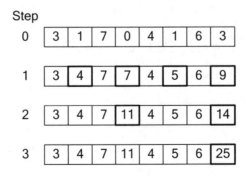

Figure 13.2 Upsweep pass (array view).

---

2. http://bit.ly/YmTmGP

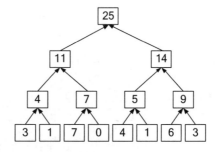

Figure 13.3 Upsweep pass (tree view).

```
downsweep(a, N)
    a[N-1] = 0
    for d from (lg N)-1 downto 0
        in parallel for i from 0 to N-1 by 2^(d+1)
            t  := a[i+2^d-1]
            a[i+2^d-1] = a[i + 2^(d+1)-1]
            a[i+2^(d+1)-1] += t
```

Figure 13.4 shows how the example array is transformed during the downsweep, and Figure 13.5 shows the downsweep in tree form. Early implementations of Scan for CUDA followed this algorithm closely, and it does make a good introduction to thinking about possible parallel implementations. Unfortunately, it is not a great match to CUDA's architecture; a naïve implementation suffers from shared memory bank conflicts, and addressing schemes to compensate for the bank conflicts incurs enough overhead that the costs outweigh the benefits.

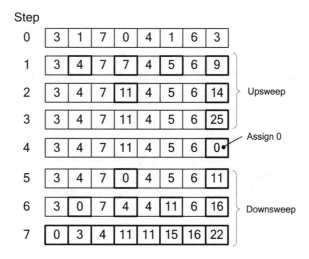

Figure 13.4 Downsweep (array view).

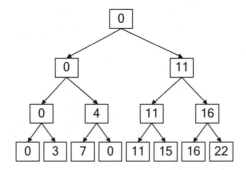

Figure 13.5 Downsweep (tree view).

13.3 Scan and Circuit Design

Having explored one possible parallel algorithm for Scan, it may now be clear that there are many different ways to implement parallel Scan algorithms. In reasoning about other possible implementations, we can take advantage of design methodologies for integer addition hardware that performs a similar function: Instead of propagating an arbitrary binary associative operator ⊕ across an array, culminating in the output from a reduction, hardware adders propagate partial addition results, culminating in the carry bit to be propagated for multiprecision arithmetic.

Hardware designers use directed acyclic, oriented graphs to represent different implementations of Scan "circuits." These diagrams compactly express both the data flow and the parallelism. A diagram of the serial implementation of Listing 13.1 is given in Figure 13.6. The steps proceed downward as time advances; the vertical lines denote wires where the signal is propagated. Nodes of in-degree 2 ("operation nodes") apply the operator ⊕ to their inputs.

Note that the circuit diagrams show inclusive scans, not exclusive ones. For circuit diagrams, the difference is minor; to turn the inclusive scan in Figure 13.6 into an exclusive scan, a 0 is wired into the first output and the sum is wired into the output, as shown in Figure 13.7. Note that both inclusive and exclusive scans generate the reduction of the input array as output, a characteristic that we will exploit in building efficient scan algorithms. (For purposes of clarity, all circuit diagrams other than Figure 13.7 will depict inclusive scans.)

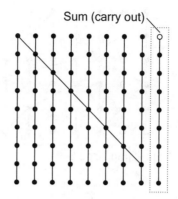

Figure 13.6 Serial scan.

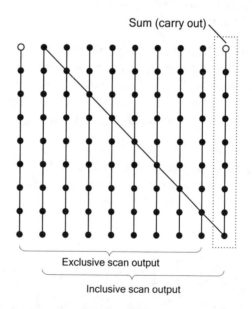

Figure 13.7 Serial scan (inclusive and exclusive).

The Scan algorithm described by Blelloch corresponds to a circuit design known as Brent-Kung, a recursive decomposition in which every second output is fed into a Brent-Kung circuit of half the width. Figure 13.8 illustrates a Brent-Kung circuit operating on our example length of 8, along with Blelloch's upsweep and downsweep phases. Nodes that broadcast their output to multiple nodes in the next stage are known as *fans*. Brent-Kung circuits are notable for having a constant fan-out of 2.

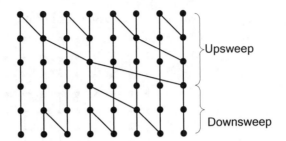

Figure 13.8 Brent-Kung circuit.

The structure of a Brent-Kung circuit becomes clearer on larger circuits; see, for example, the circuit that processes 16 inputs in Figure 13.9. Figure 13.9 also highlights the *spine* of the circuit, the longest subgraph that generates the last element of the scan output.

The depth of the Brent-Kung circuit grows logarithmically in the number of inputs, illustrating its greater efficiency than (for example) the serial algorithm. But because each stage in the recursive decomposition increases the depth by 2, the Brent-Kung circuit is not of minimum depth. Sklansky described a method to build circuits of minimum depth by recursively decomposing them as shown in Figure 13.10.

Two (*N*/2)-input circuits are run in parallel, and the output of the spine of the left circuit is added to each element of the right circuit. For our 16-element example, the left-hand subgraph of the recursion is highlighted in Figure 13.10.

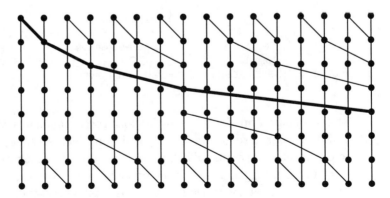

Figure 13.9 Brent-Kung circuit (16 inputs).

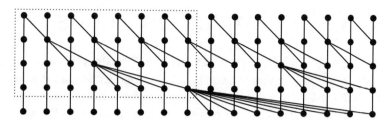

Figure 13.10 Sklansky (minimum-depth) circuit.

Another minimum-depth scan circuit, known as Kogge-Stone, has a constant fan-out of 2, which is a desirable characteristic for hardware implementation, but, as you can see in Figure 13.11, it has many operation nodes; software implementations analogous to Kogge-Stone are work-inefficient.

Any scan circuit can be constructed from a combination of *scans* (which perform the parallel prefix computation and generate the sum of the input array as output) and *fans* (which add an input to each of their remaining outputs). The minimum-depth circuit in Figure 13.10 makes heavy use of fans in its recursive definition.

For an optimized CUDA implementation, a key insight is that a fan doesn't need to take its input from a Scan *per se*; any reduction will do. And from Chapter 12, we have a highly optimized reduction algorithm.

If, for example, we split the input array into subarrays of length *b* and compute the sum of each subarray using our optimized reduction routine, we end up with an array of $\left\lceil \frac{N}{b} \right\rceil$ reduction values. *If we then perform an exclusive scan on that array, it becomes an array of fan inputs (seeds) for scans of each subarray.* The number of values that can be efficiently scanned in one pass over global memory is limited by CUDA's thread block and shared memory size, so for larger inputs, the approach must be applied recursively.

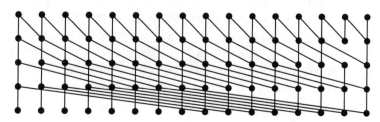

Figure 13.11 Kogge-Stone circuit.

13.4 CUDA Implementations

Designing Scan algorithms and studying circuit diagrams is instructive, but in order to implement Scan for CUDA, we need to map the algorithms onto registers, memory and addressing schemes, and correct synchronization. The optimal CUDA implementation of Scan depends on the size of the scan being performed. Different schemes are best for warp-sized scans, scans that can fit in shared memory, and scans that must spill to global memory. Because blocks cannot reliably exchange data through global memory, scans too large to fit in shared memory *must* perform multiple kernel invocations.[3]

Before examining special cases (such as scanning of predicates), we will examine three (3) approaches to doing Scan on CUDA.

- Scan-then-fan (recursive)

- Reduce-then-scan (recursive)

- Two-level reduce-then-scan

13.4.1 SCAN-THEN-FAN

The scan-then-fan approach uses a similar decomposition for global and shared memory. Figure 13.12 shows the approach used to scan a threadblock: A scan is performed on each 32-thread warp, and the reduction of that 32-element sub-array is written to shared memory. A single warp then scans the array of partial sums. A single warp is sufficient because CUDA does not support threadblocks with more than 1024 threads. Finally, the base sums are fanned out to each warp's output elements. Note that Figure 13.12 shows an inclusive scan being performed in step 2, so the first element of its output must be fanned out to the second warp, and so on.

The code to implement this algorithm is given in Listing 13.3. The input array is assumed to have been loaded into shared memory already, and the parameters `sharedPartials` and `idx` specify the base address and index of the warp to scan, respectively. (In our first implementation, `threadIdx.x` is passed as the parameter `idx`.) Lines 9–13 implement step 1 in Figure 13.12; lines 16–21 implement step 2; and lines 31–45 implement step 3. The output value written by this thread is returned to the caller but is used only if it happens to be the thread block's reduction.

---

3. With CUDA 5.0 and SM 3.5 hardware, dynamic parallelism can move most of the kernel launches to be "child grids" as opposed to kernel launches initiated by the host.

1. Scan warps and write each sum (reduction) into shared array of partial sums.

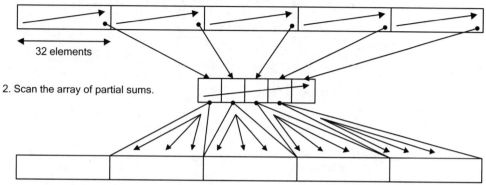

2. Scan the array of partial sums.

3. Fan each base sum into its corresponding subarray.

Figure 13.12 Scan-then-fan (shared memory).

Listing 13.3 scanBlock: Block portion of scan-then-fan for thread blocks.

```
template<class T>
inline __device__ T
scanBlock( volatile T *sPartials )
{
    extern __shared__ T warpPartials[];
    const int tid = threadIdx.x;
    const int lane = tid & 31;
    const int warpid = tid >> 5;

    //
    // Compute this thread's partial sum
    //
    T sum = scanWarp<T>( sPartials );
    __syncthreads();

    //
    // Write each warp's reduction to shared memory
    //
    if ( lane == 31 ) {
        warpPartials[16+warpid] = sum;
    }
    __syncthreads();

    //
    // Have one warp scan reductions
    //
    if ( warpid==0 ) {
        scanWarp<T>( 16+warpPartials+tid );
    }
    __syncthreads();
```

```
    //
    // Fan out the exclusive scan element (obtained
    // by the conditional and the decrement by 1)
    // to this warp's pending output
    //
    if ( warpid > 0 ) {
        sum += warpPartials[16+warpid-1];
    }
    __syncthreads();

    //
    // Write this thread's scan output
    //
    *sPartials = sum;
    __syncthreads();

    //
    // The return value will only be used by caller if it
    // contains the spine value (i.e., the reduction
    // of the array we just scanned).
    //
    return sum;
}
```

Figure 13.13 shows how this approach is adapted to global memory. A kernel scans *b*-element subarrays, where *b* is the block size. The partial sums are written to global memory, and another 1-block kernel invocation scans these partial sums, which are then fanned into the final output in global memory.

1. Scan subarrays and write each sum (reduction) into global array of partial sums.

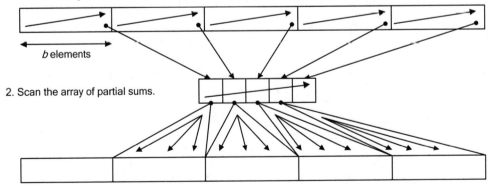

b elements

2. Scan the array of partial sums.

3. Fan each base sum into the final output array.

Figure 13.13 Scan-then-fan (global memory).

Listing 13.4 gives the CUDA code for the Scan kernel in step 1 in Figure 13.13. It loops over the threadblocks to process, staging the input array into and out of shared memory. The kernel then optionally writes the spine value to global memory at the end. At the bottom level of the recursion, there is no need to record spine values, so the bWriteSpine template parameter enables the kernel to avoid dynamically checking the value of partialsOut.

Listing 13.4 scanAndWritePartials.

```
template<class T, bool bWriteSpine>
__global__ void
scanAndWritePartials(
    T *out,
    T *gPartials,
    const T *in,
    size_t N,
    size_t numBlocks )
{
    extern volatile __shared__ T sPartials[];
    const int tid = threadIdx.x;
    volatile T *myShared = sPartials+tid;

    for ( size_t iBlock = blockIdx.x;
                 iBlock < numBlocks;
                 iBlock += gridDim.x ) {
        size_t index = iBlock*blockDim.x+tid;

        *myShared = (index < N) ? in[index] : 0;
        __syncthreads();

        T sum = scanBlock( myShared );
        __syncthreads();
        if ( index < N ) {
            out[index] = *myShared;
        }
        //
        // write the spine value to global memory
        //
        if ( bWriteSpine && (threadIdx.x==(blockDim.x-1)) )
        {
            gPartials[iBlock] = sum;
        }
    }
}
```

Listing 13.5 gives the host function that uses Listings 13.3 to 13.4 to implement an inclusive scan on an array in global memory. Note that the function recurses for scans too large to perform in shared memory. The first conditional in the function serves both as the base case for the recursion and to short-circuit scans small enough to perform in shared memory alone, avoiding any need to allocate global memory. Note how the amount of shared memory needed by the kernel (b*sizeof(T)) is specified at kernel invocation time.

For larger scans, the function computes the number of partial sums needed $\left\lceil \dfrac{N}{b} \right\rceil$, allocates global memory to hold them, and follows the pattern in Figure 3.13, writing partial sums to the global array for later use by the scanAndWritePartials kernel in Listing 13.4.

Each level of recursion reduces the number of elements being processed by a factor of b, so for $b = 128$ and $N = 1048576$, for example, two levels of recursion are required: one of size 8192 and one of size 64.

Listing 13.5 scanFan host function.

```
template<class T>
void
scanFan( T *out, const T *in, size_t N, int b )
{
    cudaError_t status;

    if ( N <= b ) {
        scanAndWritePartials<T, false><<<1,b,b*sizeof(T)>>>(
            out, 0, in, N, 1 );
        return;
    }

    //
    // device pointer to array of partial sums in global memory
    //
    T *gPartials = 0;

    //
    // ceil(N/b)
    //
    size_t numPartials = (N1)/b;

    //
    // number of CUDA threadblocks to use.  The kernels are
    // blocking agnostic, so we can clamp to any number
    // within CUDA's limits and the code will work.
    //
    const unsigned int maxBlocks = 150;    // maximum blocks to launch
    unsigned int numBlocks = min( numPartials, maxBlocks );

    CUDART_CHECK( cudaMalloc( &gPartials,
                              numPartials*sizeof(T) ) );
```

```
scanAndWritePartials<T, true><<<numBlocks,b,b*sizeof(T)>>>(
    out, gPartials, in, N, numPartials );
scanFan<T>( gPartials, gPartials, numPartials, b );
scanAddBaseSums<T><<<numBlocks, b>>>( out, gPartials, N,
    numPartials );

Error:
    cudaFree( gPartials );
}
```

Listing 13.6 completes the picture with a very simple kernel to fan-out results from global memory to global memory.

Listing 13.6 scanAddBaseSums kernel.

```
template<class T>
__global__ void
scanAddBaseSums(
    T *out,
    T *gBaseSums,
    size_t N,
    size_t numBlocks )
{
    const int tid = threadIdx.x;

    T fan_value = 0;
    for ( size_t iBlock = blockIdx.x;
                 iBlock < numBlocks;
                 iBlock += gridDim.x ) {
        size_t index = iBlock*blockDim.x+tid;
        if ( iBlock > 0 ) {
            fan_value = gBaseSums[iBlock-1];
        }
        out[index] += fan_value;
    }
}
```

At the highest level of recursion, the scan-then-fan strategy performs $4N$ global memory operations. The initial scan performs one read and one write, and then the fan in Listing 13.4 performs another read and write. We can decrease the number of global memory writes by first computing only reductions on the input array.

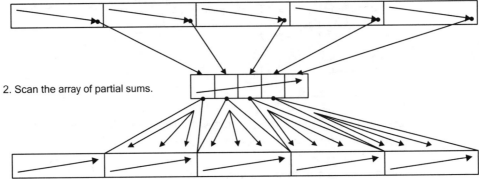

1. Compute reduction of each subarray and write into global array of partial sums.

2. Scan the array of partial sums.

3. Scan output array in subarrays, adding the corresponding partial sum into the output.

Figure 13.14 Reduce-then-scan.

13.4.2 REDUCE-THEN-SCAN (RECURSIVE)

Figure 13.14 shows how this strategy works. As before, an array of $\left\lceil \dfrac{N}{b} \right\rceil$ partial sums of the input is computed and scanned to compute an array of base sums. But instead of doing the scan in the first pass, we compute only the partial sums in the first pass. The scan of the final output is then performed, adding the base sum along the way.

Listing 13.7 gives the code used to compute the array of partial sums, which uses the reduction code from Listing 12.3 as a subroutine. As with the reduction code, the kernel is templatized according to block size, and a wrapper template uses a switch statement to invoke specializations of the template.

Listing 13.7 scanReduceBlocks.

```
template<class T, int numThreads>
__global__ void
scanReduceBlocks( T *gPartials, const T *in, size_t N )
{
    extern volatile __shared__ T sPartials[];

    const int tid = threadIdx.x;
    gPartials += blockIdx.x;
```

```
    for ( size_t i = blockIdx.x*blockDim.x;
                   i < N;
                   i += blockDim.x*gridDim.x ) {
        size_t index = i+tid;
        sPartials[tid] = (index < N) ? in[index] : 0;
        __syncthreads();

        reduceBlock<T,numThreads>( gPartials, sPartials );
        __syncthreads();
        gPartials += gridDim.x;
    }
}

template<class T>
void
scanReduceBlocks(
    T *gPartials,
    const T *in,
    size_t N,
    int numThreads,
    int numBlocks )
{
    switch ( numThreads ) {
        case  128: return scanReduceBlocks<T,  128> ... ( ... );
        case  256: return scanReduceBlocks<T,  256> ... ( ... );
        case  512: return scanReduceBlocks<T,  512> ... ( ... );
        case 1024: return scanReduceBlocks<T,1024> ... ( ... );
    }
}
```

Listing 13.8 gives the kernel used to perform the scans. The main difference from Listing 13.4 is that instead of writing the sum of the input subarrays to global memory, the kernel adds the base sum corresponding to each subarray to the output elements before writing them.

Listing 13.8 scanWithBaseSums.

```
template<class T>
__global__ void
scanWithBaseSums(
    T *out,
    const T *gBaseSums,
    const T *in,
    size_t N,
    size_t numBlocks )
{
    extern volatile __shared__ T sPartials[];
    const int tid = threadIdx.x;
```

```
for ( size_t iBlock = blockIdx.x;
                iBlock < numBlocks;
                iBlock += gridDim.x ) {
    T base_sum = 0;
    size_t index = iBlock*blockDim.x+tid;

    if ( iBlock > 0 && gBaseSums ) {
        base_sum = gBaseSums[iBlock-1];
    }
    sPartials[tid] = (index < N) ? in[index] : 0;
    __syncthreads();

    scanBlock( sPartials+tid );
    __syncthreads();
    if ( index < N ) {
        out[index] = sPartials[tid]+base_sum;
    }
}
}
}
```

The host code for the reduce-then-scan strategy is given in Listing 13.9. At the highest level of recursion, the reduce-then-scan strategy performs 3*N* global memory operations. The initial reduction pass performs one read per element, and then the scan in Listing 13.9 performs another read and a write. As with fan-then-scan, each level of recursion reduces the number of elements being processed by a factor of *b*.

Listing 13.9 scanReduceThenScan.

```
template<class T>
void
scanReduceThenScan( T *out, const T *in, size_t N, int b )
{
    cudaError_t status;

    if ( N <= b ) {
        return scanWithBaseSums<T><<<1,b,b*sizeof(T)>>>(
            out, 0, in, N, 1 );
    }

    //
    // device pointer to array of partial sums in global memory
    //
    T *gPartials = 0;

    //
    // ceil(N/b) = number of partial sums to compute
    //
    size_t numPartials = (N1)/b;
```

```
    //
    // number of CUDA threadblocks to use.  The kernels are blocking
    // agnostic, so we can clamp to any number within CUDA's limits
    // and the code will work.
    //
    const unsigned int maxBlocks = 150;
    unsigned int numBlocks = min( numPartials, maxBlocks );

    CUDART_CHECK( cudaMalloc( &gPartials, numPartials*sizeof(T) ) );

    scanReduceBlocks<T>( gPartials, in, N, b, numBlocks );
    scanReduceThenScan<T>( gPartials, gPartials, numPartials, b );
    scanWithBaseSums<T><<<numBlocks,b,b*sizeof(T)>>>(
        out,
        gPartials,
        in,
        N,
        numPartials );
Error:
    cudaFree( gPartials );

}
```

13.4.3 REDUCE-THEN-SCAN (TWO PASS)

Merrill[4] describes another formulation of Scan that uses a small, fixed-size number of base sums. The algorithm is the same as Figure 13.14, except that the array in step 2 is a relatively small, fixed size of perhaps a few hundred instead of $\left\lceil \dfrac{N}{b} \right\rceil$ partial sums. The number of partial sums is the same as the number of threadblocks to use, both for the reduction pass and for the Scan pass. Listing 13.10 shows the code to compute these partial sums, which is updated to compute reductions for subarrays of size elementsPerPartial as opposed to the thread block size.

Listing 13.10 scanReduceSubarrays.

```
template<class T, int numThreads>
__device__ void
scanReduceSubarray(
    T *gPartials,
    const T *in,
    size_t iBlock,
```

---

4. http://bit.ly/ZKtlh1

```
        size_t N,
        int elementsPerPartial )
    {
        extern volatile __shared__ T sPartials[];
        const int tid = threadIdx.x;

        size_t baseIndex = iBlock*elementsPerPartial;

        T sum = 0;
        for ( int i = tid; i < elementsPerPartial; i += blockDim.x ) {
            size_t index = baseIndex+i;
            if ( index < N )
                sum += in[index];
        }
        sPartials[tid] = sum;
        __syncthreads();

        reduceBlock<T,numThreads>( &gPartials[iBlock], sPartials );
    }

/*
 * Compute the reductions of each subarray of size
 * elementsPerPartial, and write them to gPartials.
 */
template<class T, int numThreads>
__global__ void
scanReduceSubarrays(
        T *gPartials,
        const T *in,
        size_t N,
        int elementsPerPartial )
    {
        extern volatile __shared__ T sPartials[];

        for ( int iBlock = blockIdx.x;
                iBlock*elementsPerPartial < N;
                iBlock += gridDim.x )
        {
            scanReduceSubarray<T,numThreads>(
                gPartials,
                in,
                iBlock,
                N,
                elementsPerPartial );
        }
    }
```

Listing 13.11 gives the Scan code, which has been modified to carry over each block's sum as the Scan of that block is completed. The bZeroPad template parameter in Listing 13.11 and the utility function scanSharedIndex that uses it are described in more detail in Section 13.5.1.

Listing 13.11 scan2Level_kernel.

```
template<class T, bool bZeroPad>
__global__ void
scan2Level_kernel(
    T *out,
    const T *gBaseSums,
    const T *in,
    size_t N,
    size_t elementsPerPartial )
{
    extern volatile __shared__ T sPartials[];
    const int tid = threadIdx.x;
    int sIndex = scanSharedIndex<bZeroPad>( threadIdx.x );

    if ( bZeroPad ) {
        sPartials[sIndex-16] = 0;
    }
    T base_sum = 0;
    if ( blockIdx.x && gBaseSums ) {
        base_sum = gBaseSums[blockIdx.x-1];
    }
    for ( size_t i = 0;
                 i < elementsPerPartial;
                 i += blockDim.x ) {
        size_t index = blockIdx.x*elementsPerPartial + i + tid;
        sPartials[sIndex] = (index < N) ? in[index] : 0;
        __syncthreads();

        scanBlock<T,bZeroPad>( sPartials+sIndex );
        __syncthreads();
        if ( index < N ) {
            out[index] = sPartials[sIndex]+base_sum;
        }
        __syncthreads();

        // carry forward from this block to the next.
        base_sum += sPartials[
            scanSharedIndex<bZeroPad>( blockDim.x-1 ) ];
        __syncthreads();
    }
}
```

Listing 13.12 gives the host code for Merrill's two-pass reduce-then-scan algorithm. Since the number of partials computed is small and never varies, the host code never has to allocate global memory in order to perform the scan; instead, we declare a __device__ array that is allocated at module load time

```
__device__ int g_globalPartials[MAX_PARTIALS];
```

and obtain its address by calling cudaGetSymbolAddress().

```
status = cudaGetSymbolAddress(
        (void **) &globalPartials,
        g_globalPartials );
```

The routine then computes the number of elements per partial and number of
threadblocks to use and invokes the three (3) kernels needed to perform the
computation.

Listing 13.12 scan2Level.

```
template<class T, bool bZeroPad>
void
scan2Level( T *out, const T *in, size_t N, int b )
{
    int sBytes = scanSharedMemory<T,bZeroPad>( b );

    if ( N <= b ) {
        return scan2Level_kernel<T, bZeroPad><<<1,b,sBytes>>>(
            out, 0, in, N, N );
    }

    cudaError_t status;
    T *gPartials = 0;
    status = cudaGetSymbolAddress(
                (void **) &gPartials,
                g_globalPartials );

    if ( cudaSuccess ==  status )
    {
        //
        // ceil(N/b) = number of partial sums to compute
        //
        size_t numPartials = (N+b-1)/b;

        if ( numPartials > MAX_PARTIALS ) {
            numPartials = MAX_PARTIALS;
        }

        //
        // elementsPerPartial has to be a multiple of b
        //
        unsigned int elementsPerPartial =
            (N+numPartials-1)/numPartials;
        elementsPerPartial = b * ((elementsPerPartial+b-1)/b);
        numPartials = (N+elementsPerPartial-1)/elementsPerPartial;

        //
        // number of CUDA threadblocks to use.  The kernels are
        // blocking agnostic, so we can clamp to any number within
        // CUDA's limits and the code will work.
        //
        const unsigned int maxBlocks = MAX_PARTIALS;
        unsigned int numBlocks = min( numPartials, maxBlocks );
```

```
        scanReduceSubarrays<T>(
            gPartials,
            in,
            N,
            elementsPerPartial,
            numBlocks,
            b );
        scan2Level_kernel<T, bZeroPad><<<1,b,sBytes>>>(
            gPartials,
            0,
            gPartials,
            numPartials,
            numPartials );
        scan2Level_kernel<T, bZeroPad><<<numBlocks,b,sBytes>>>(
            out,
            gPartials,
            in,
            N,
            elementsPerPartial );
    }
}
```

13.5 Warp Scans

So far, we've focused on constructing our Scan implementations from the top down. At the bottom of all three of our Scan implementations, however, lurks an entirely different software approach to Scan. For subarrays of size 32 or less, we use a special *warp scan* modeled on the Kogge-Stone circuit (Figure 13.11). Kogge-Stone circuits are *work-inefficient*, meaning they perform many operations despite their small depth, but at the warp level, where execution resources of CUDA hardware are available whether or not the developer uses them, Kogge-Stone works well on CUDA hardware.

Listing 13.13 gives a __device__ routine that is designed to operate on shared memory, the fastest way for threads to exchange data with one another. Because there are no shared memory conflicts and the routine executes at warp granularity, no thread synchronization is needed during updates to the shared memory.

Listing 13.13 scanWarp.

```
template<class T>
inline __device__ T
scanWarp( volatile T *sPartials )
{
```

```
    const int tid = threadIdx.x;
    const int lane = tid & 31;

    if ( lane >=  1 ) sPartials[0] += sPartials[- 1];
    if ( lane >=  2 ) sPartials[0] += sPartials[- 2];
    if ( lane >=  4 ) sPartials[0] += sPartials[- 4];
    if ( lane >=  8 ) sPartials[0] += sPartials[- 8];
    if ( lane >= 16 ) sPartials[0] += sPartials[-16];
    return sPartials[0];
}
```

13.5.1 ZERO PADDING

We can reduce the number of machine instructions needed to implement the warp scan by interleaving the warps' data with 16-element arrays of 0's, enabling the conditionals to be removed. Listing 13.14 gives a version of scanWarp that assumes 16 zero elements preceding the base address in shared memory.

Listing 13.14 scanWarp0.

```
template<class T>
__device__ T scanWarp0( volatile T *sharedPartials, int idx )
{
    const int tid = threadIdx.x;
    const int lane = tid & 31;

    sharedPartials[idx] += sharedPartials[idx -  1];
    sharedPartials[idx] += sharedPartials[idx -  2];
    sharedPartials[idx] += sharedPartials[idx -  4];
    sharedPartials[idx] += sharedPartials[idx -  8];
    sharedPartials[idx] += sharedPartials[idx - 16];
    return sharedPartials[idx];
}
```

Figure 13.15 shows how the interleaving works for a 256-thread block, which contains 8 warps. The shared memory index is computed as follows.

```
const int tid = threadIdx.x;
const int warp = tid >> 5;
const int lane = tid & 31;
const int sharedIndex = 49 * warp + 32 + lane;
```

The initialization to 0 is then done as follows.

```
partials[sharedIndex-16] = 0;
```

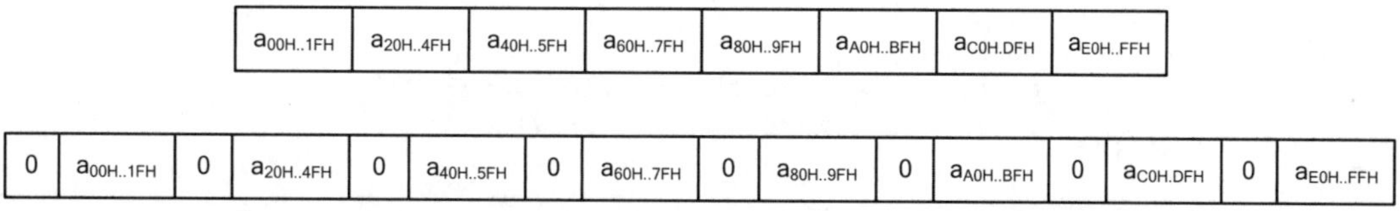

$a_{00H..1FH}$	$a_{20H..4FH}$	$a_{40H..5FH}$	$a_{60H..7FH}$	$a_{80H..9FH}$	$a_{A0H..BFH}$	$a_{C0H.DFH}$	$a_{E0H..FFH}$

0	$a_{00H..1FH}$	0	$a_{20H..4FH}$	0	$a_{40H..5FH}$	0	$a_{60H..7FH}$	0	$a_{80H..9FH}$	0	$a_{A0H..BFH}$	0	$a_{C0H.DFH}$	0	$a_{E0H..FFH}$

Figure 13.15 Interleaved zeros for warp scan.

The other area where this change affects the shared memory addressing is in the block scan subroutine. The index for each partial sum for each warp must be offset by 16 to enable the single warp scan that computes the base sums to work. Finally, the kernel invocation must reserve enough shared memory to hold both the partial sums and the zeros.

13.5.2 TEMPLATED FORMULATIONS

The faster, zero-padded implementation of Scan requires more shared memory, a resource requirement that not all applications can accommodate. To enable our code to support both versions, Listing 13.15 shows utility functions that take a bool template parameter bZeroPad. The scanSharedMemory function returns the amount of shared memory needed for a given block size. scanSharedIndex returns the shared memory index corresponding to a given thread. In turn, Listing 13.16 gives the templated version of scanWarp that works for both the zero-padded and non-zero-padded cases.

Listing 13.15 Shared memory utilities for zero padding.

```
template<bool bZeroPad>
inline __device__ int
scanSharedIndex( int tid )
{
    if ( bZeroPad ) {
        const int warp = tid >> 5;
        const int lane = tid & 31;
        return 49 * warp + 16 + lane;
    }
    else {
        return tid;
    }
}

template<typename T, bool bZeroPad>
inline __device__ __host__ int
scanSharedMemory( int numThreads )
```

```
{
    if ( bZeroPad ) {
        const int warpcount = numThreads>>5;
        return (49 * warpcount + 16)*sizeof(T);
    }
    else {
        return numThreads*sizeof(T);
    }
}
```

Listing 13.16 scanWarp (templated).

```
template<class T, bool bZeroPadded>
inline __device__ T
scanWarp( volatile T *sPartials )
{
    T t = sPartials[0];
    if ( bZeroPadded ) {
        t += sPartials[- 1]; sPartials[0] = t;
        t += sPartials[- 2]; sPartials[0] = t;
        t += sPartials[- 4]; sPartials[0] = t;
        t += sPartials[- 8]; sPartials[0] = t;
        t += sPartials[-16]; sPartials[0] = t;
    }
    else {
        const int tid = threadIdx.x;
        const int lane = tid & 31;
        if ( lane >=  1 ) { t += sPartials[- 1]; sPartials[0] = t; }
        if ( lane >=  2 ) { t += sPartials[- 2]; sPartials[0] = t; }
        if ( lane >=  4 ) { t += sPartials[- 4]; sPartials[0] = t; }
        if ( lane >=  8 ) { t += sPartials[- 8]; sPartials[0] = t; }
        if ( lane >= 16 ) { t += sPartials[-16]; sPartials[0] = t; }
    }
    return t;
}
```

13.5.3 WARP SHUFFLE

The SM 3.0 instruction set added the warp shuffle instruction, which enables registers to be exchanged within the 32 threads of a warp. The "up" and "down" variants of the warp shuffle can be used to implement scan and reverse scan, respectively. The shuffle instruction takes a register to exchange and an offset to apply to the lane ID. It returns a predicate that is false for inactive threads or threads whose offset is outside the warp.

Listing 13.17 gives `scanWarpShuffle`, a device function that implements an inclusive warp scan with the shuffle instruction. The template parameter is an integer, and typically the value 5 is passed because 5 is the base 2 logarithm of the warp size of 32. `scanWarpShuffle` uses a utility function `scanWarpShuffle_step`, implemented in inline PTX, because the compiler does not emit efficient code to deal with the predicate returned by the shuffle instruction.

Listing 13.17 scanWarpShuffle device function.

```
__device__ __forceinline__
int
scanWarpShuffle_step(int partial, int offset)
{
    int result;
    asm(
        "{.reg .u32 r0;"
        ".reg .pred p;"
        "shfl.up.b32 r0|p, %1, %2, 0;"
        "@p add.u32 r0, r0, %3;"
        "mov.u32 %0, r0;}"
        : "=r"(result) : "r"(partial), "r"(offset), "r"(partial));
    return result;
}

template <int levels>
__device__ __forceinline__
int
scanWarpShuffle(int mysum)
{
    for(int i = 0; i < levels; ++i)
        mysum = scanWarpShuffle_step(mysum, 1 << i);
    return mysum;
}
```

Listing 13.18 illustrates how to extend `scanWarpShuffle` to scan the values across a thread block using shared memory. Following the same pattern as the block scan in Listing 13.3, `scanBlockShuffle` uses the warp shuffle to scan each warp. Each warp writes its partial sum to shared memory, and then the warp shuffle is used again, this time by a single warp, to scan these base sums. Finally, each warp adds its corresponding base sum to compute the final output value.

Listing 13.18 scanBlockShuffle device function.

```
template <int logBlockSize>
__device__
int
scanBlockShuffle(int val, const unsigned int idx)
```

```
{
    const unsigned int lane   = idx & 31;
    const unsigned int warpid = idx >> 5;
    __shared__ int sPartials[32];

    // Intra-warp scan in each warp
    val = scanWarpShuffle<5>(val);

    // Collect per-warp results
    if (lane == 31) sPartials[warpid] = val;
    __syncthreads();

    // Use first warp to scan per-warp results
    if (warpid == 0) {
        int t = sPartials[lane];
        t = scanWarpShuffle<logBlockSize-5>( t );
        sPartials[lane] = t;
    }

    __syncthreads();

    // Add scanned base sum for final result
    if (warpid > 0) {
        val += sPartials[warpid - 1];
    }
    return val;
}
```

13.5.4 INSTRUCTION COUNTS

To examine the tradeoffs between the different variations of warp scan discussed in this section, we compiled for SM 3.0 and used cuobjdump to disassemble the three implementations.

- The non-zero-padded implementation given in Listing 13.19 is 30 instructions and includes a great deal of branching (the SSY/.S instruction pairs push and pop the divergence stack, as described in Section 8.4.2).

- The zero-padded implementation given in Listing 13.20 is 17 instructions because it does not check the lane ID before performing its shared memory reads. Note that because the shared memory operations are guaranteed to be contained within a warp, there is no need for barrier synchronization via the __syncthreads() intrinsic, which compiles to BAR.SYNC instructions in SASS.

- The shuffle-based implementation given in Listing 13.21 is only 11 instructions.

We confirmed that the shuffle-based implementation is, in fact, significantly faster (about 2x) than the general case given in Listing 13.19, running on a synthetic workload that isolates the warp scan.

Listing 13.19 SASS for warp scan (no zero padding).

```
/*0070*/        SSY 0xa0;
/*0078*/        @P0 NOP.S CC.T;
/*0088*/        LDS R5, [R3+-0x4];
/*0090*/        IADD R0, R5, R0;
/*0098*/        STS.S [R3], R0;
/*00a0*/        ISETP.LT.U32.AND P0, pt, R4, 0x2, pt;
/*00a8*/        SSY 0xd8;
/*00b0*/        @P0 NOP.S CC.T;
/*00b8*/        LDS R5, [R3+-0x8];
/*00c8*/        IADD R0, R5, R0;
/*00d0*/        STS.S [R3], R0;
/*00d8*/        ISETP.LT.U32.AND P0, pt, R4, 0x4, pt;
/*00e0*/        SSY 0x110;
/*00e8*/        @P0 NOP.S CC.T;
/*00f0*/        LDS R5, [R3+-0x10];
/*00f8*/        IADD R0, R5, R0;
/*0108*/        STS.S [R3], R0;
/*0110*/        ISETP.LT.U32.AND P0, pt, R4, 0x8, pt;
/*0118*/        SSY 0x140;
/*0120*/        @P0 NOP.S CC.T;
/*0128*/        LDS R5, [R3+-0x20];
/*0130*/        IADD R0, R5, R0;
/*0138*/        STS.S [R3], R0;
/*0148*/        ISETP.LT.U32.AND P0, pt, R4, 0x10, pt;
/*0150*/        SSY 0x178;
/*0158*/        @P0 NOP.S CC.T;
/*0160*/        LDS R4, [R3+-0x40];
/*0168*/        IADD R0, R4, R0;
/*0170*/        STS.S [R3], R0;
/*0178*/        BAR.SYNC 0x0;
```

Listing 13.20 SASS for warp scan (with zero padding).

```
/*0058*/        LDS R4, [R3+-0x4];
/*0060*/        LDS R0, [R3];
/*0068*/        IADD R4, R4, R0;
/*0070*/        STS [R3], R4;
/*0078*/        LDS R0, [R3+-0x8];
/*0088*/        IADD R4, R4, R0;
/*0090*/        STS [R3], R4;
/*0098*/        LDS R0, [R3+-0x10];
/*00a0*/        IADD R4, R4, R0;
/*00a8*/        STS [R3], R4;
/*00b0*/        LDS R0, [R3+-0x20];
```

```
/*00b8*/        IADD R4, R4, R0;
/*00c8*/        STS [R3], R4;
/*00d0*/        LDS R0, [R3+-0x40];
/*00d8*/        IADD R0, R4, R0;
/*00e0*/        STS [R3], R0;
/*00e8*/        BAR.SYNC 0x0;
```

Listing 13.21 SASS for warp scan (using shuffle).

```
/*0050*/        SHFL.UP P0, R4, R0, 0x1, 0x0;
/*0058*/        IADD.X R3, R3, c [0x0] [0x144];
/*0060*/        @P0 IADD R4, R4, R0;
/*0068*/        SHFL.UP P0, R0, R4, 0x2, 0x0;
/*0070*/        @P0 IADD R0, R0, R4;
/*0078*/        SHFL.UP P0, R4, R0, 0x4, 0x0;
/*0088*/        @P0 IADD R4, R4, R0;
/*0090*/        SHFL.UP P0, R0, R4, 0x8, 0x0;
/*0098*/        @P0 IADD R0, R0, R4;
/*00a0*/        SHFL.UP P0, R4, R0, 0x10, 0x0;
/*00a8*/        @P0 IADD R4, R4, R0;
```

13.6 Stream Compaction

Scan implementations often operate on *predicates*—truth values (0 or 1) computed by evaluating a condition. As mentioned at the beginning of the chapter, an exclusive scan of predicates can be used to implement *stream compaction*, a class of parallel problems where only the "interesting" elements of an input array are written to the output. For predicate values where the predicate is equal to 1 for "interesting" elements, the exclusive scan computes the output index of the element.

As an example, let's write a Scan implementation that operates on an array of int and emits all ints that are odd.[5] Our implementation is based on Merrill's reduce-then-scan with a fixed number of blocks *b*.

1. A first reduction pass over the input data gives the number of elements in each $\left\lceil \dfrac{N}{b} \right\rceil$ subarray that meets the criteria.

---

5. The code is easily modified to evaluate more complicated predicates.

2. A scan is performed on the array of *b* counts, giving the base index for the output of each subarray.

3. A scan is performed on the input array, evaluating the criteria and using the "seed" value as the base index for each subarray's output.

Listing 13.22 shows the code for step 1: `predicateReduceSubarrays_odd()` function invokes subroutines `predicateReduceSubarray_odd()` and `isOdd()` to evaluate the predicate for each array element, compute the reduction, and write it to the array of base sums.

Listing 13.22 `predicateReduceSubarrays_odd`.

```
template<class T>
__host__ __device__ bool
isOdd( T x )
{
    return x & 1;
}

template<class T, int numThreads>
__device__ void
predicateReduceSubarray_odd(
    int *gPartials,
    const T *in,
    size_t iBlock,
    size_t N,
    int elementsPerPartial )
{
    extern volatile __shared__ int sPartials[];
    const int tid = threadIdx.x;

    size_t baseIndex = iBlock*elementsPerPartial;

    int sum = 0;
    for ( int i = tid; i < elementsPerPartial; i += blockDim.x ) {
        size_t index = baseIndex+i;
        if ( index < N )
            sum += isOdd( in[index] );
    }
    sPartials[tid] = sum;
    __syncthreads();

    reduceBlock<int,numThreads>( &gPartials[iBlock], sPartials );
}

/*
 * Compute the reductions of each subarray of size
 * elementsPerPartial, and write them to gPartials.
 */
```

415

```
template<class T, int numThreads>
__global__ void
predicateReduceSubarrays_odd(
    int *gPartials,
    const T *in,
    size_t N,
    int elementsPerPartial )
{
    extern volatile __shared__ int sPartials[];

    for ( int iBlock = blockIdx.x;
            iBlock*elementsPerPartial < N;
            iBlock += gridDim.x )
    {
        predicateReduceSubarray_odd<T,numThreads>(
            gPartials,
            in,
            iBlock,
            N,
            elementsPerPartial );
    }
}
```

Computing the scan of the array of base sums is done by invoking the kernel in Listing 13.23. Once this is done, each base sum element contains the number of preceding array elements for which the predicate is true, which also is the start index of the corresponding block's output array.

Listing 13.23 streamCompact_odd kernel.

```
template<class T, bool bZeroPad>
__global__ void
streamCompact_odd(
    T *out,
    int *outCount,
    const int *gBaseSums,
    const T *in,
    size_t N,
    size_t elementsPerPartial )
{
    extern volatile __shared__ int sPartials[];
    const int tid = threadIdx.x;
    int sIndex = scanSharedIndex<bZeroPad>( threadIdx.x );

    if ( bZeroPad ) {
        sPartials[sIndex-16] = 0;
    }
    // exclusive scan element gBaseSums[blockIdx.x]
    int base_sum = 0;
```

```
    if ( blockIdx.x && gBaseSums ) {
        base_sum = gBaseSums[blockIdx.x-1];
    }
    for ( size_t i = 0;
                    i < elementsPerPartial;
                    i += blockDim.x ) {
        size_t index = blockIdx.x*elementsPerPartial + i + tid;
        int value = (index < N) ? in[index] : 0;
        sPartials[sIndex] = (index < N) ? isOdd( value ) : 0;
        __syncthreads();

        scanBlock<int,bZeroPad>( sPartials+sIndex );
        __syncthreads();
        if ( index < N && isOdd( value ) ) {
            int outIndex = base_sum;
            if ( tid ) {
                outIndex += sPartials[
                    scanSharedIndex<bZeroPad>(tid-1)];
            }
            out[outIndex] = value;
        }
        __syncthreads();

        // carry forward from this block to the next.
        {
            int inx = scanSharedIndex<bZeroPad>( blockDim.x-1 );
            base_sum += sPartials[ inx ];
        }
        __syncthreads();
    }
    if ( threadIdx.x == 0 && blockIdx.x == 0 ) {
        if ( gBaseSums ) {
            *outCount = gBaseSums[gridDim.x-1];
        }
        else {
            int inx = scanSharedIndex<bZeroPad>( blockDim.x-1 );
            *outCount = sPartials[ inx ];
        }
    }
}
```

Listing 13.23 shows the code for step 3, which takes the input array and the array of base sums, evaluates the predicate again for each input array element, and writes the element to the correctly indexed output element if the predicate is true. The host code is analogous to Listing 13.12, with minor changes, and is not shown here.

13.7 References (Parallel Scan Algorithms)

The recursive scan-then-fan is described in the NVIDIA Technical Report NVR-2008-003 by Sengupta et al. The recursive reduce-then-scan algorithm is described by Dotsenko et al. The two-level reduce-then-scan algorithm is due to Merrill. Merrill's paper is extremely valuable reading, both for background and for an overview of negative results—for example, an attempted formulation of Scan modeled on Sklansky's minimum-depth circuit whose performance was disappointing.

Blelloch, Guy E. Prefix sums and their applications. Technical Report CMU-CS-90-190.

Dotsenko, Yuri, Naga K. Govindaraju, Peter-Pike Sloan, Charles Boyd, and John Manferdelli. Fast scan algorithms in graphics processors. In *Proceedings of the 22nd Annual International Conference on Supercomputing*, ACM, 2008, pp. 205–213.

Fellner, D., and S. Spender, eds. SIGGRAPH/Eurographics Conference on Graphics Hardware. Eurographics Association, Aire-la-Ville, Switzerland, pp. 97–106.

Harris, Mark, and Michael Garland. Optimizing parallel prefix operations for the Fermi architecture. In *GPU Computing Gems, Jade Edition*, Wen-Mei Hwu, ed. Morgan Kaufmann, Waltham, MA, 2012, pp. 29–38.

Harris, Mark, Shubhabrata Sengupta, and John Owens. Parallel prefix sum (scan) with CUDA. In *GPU Gems 3*, H. Nguyen, ed. Addison-Wesley, Boston, MA, Aug. 2007.

Merrill, Duane, and Andrew Grimshaw. Parallel scan for stream architectures. Technical Report CS2009-14. Department of Computer Science, University of Virginia.

Sengupta, Shubhabrata, Mark Harris, and Michael Garland. Efficient parallel scan algorithms for GPUs. NVIDIA Technical Report NVR-2008-003. December 2008.

http://research.nvidia.com/publication/efficient-parallel-scan-algorithms-gpus

Sengupta, Shubhabrata, Mark Harris, ZhangYao Zhang, and John D. Owens. Scan primitives for GPU computing. In *Proceedings of the 22nd ACM SIGGRAPH/ Eurographics Symposium on Graphics Hardware.* San Diego, CA, August 4–5, 2007.

13.8 Further Reading (Parallel Prefix Sum Circuits)

There is a rich literature on circuits to compute parallel prefix sums. Besides the Brent-Kung, Sklansky, and Kogge-Stone formulations, other examples of scan circuits include Ladner-Fischer and more recent work by Lin and Hsiao. Hinze describes an algebra of scans that can be used to reason about Scan implementations. The details of his work are outside the scope of this book, but his paper is highly recommended reading.

Sean Baxter's Web site, http://www.moderngpu.com, is an excellent resource for optimized Scan and its applications.

Brent, Richard P., and H.T. Kung. A regular layout for parallel adders. *IEEE Transactions on Computers* C-31, 1982, pp. 260–264.

Hinze, Ralf. An algebra of scans. In *Mathematics of Program Construction*, Springer, 2004, Stirling, Scotland, pp. 186–210.

Kogge, Peter M., and Harold S. Stone. A parallel algorithm for the efficient solution of a general class of recurrence equations. *IEEE Transactions on Computers* C-22, 1973, pp. 783–791.

Sklansky, J. Conditional sum addition logic. *IRE Trans. Electron. Comput.* 9 (2), June 1960, pp. 226–231.

Chapter 14

N-Body

N-Body computations are a family of computation that models a set of particles (known as *bodies*), each of which must consider all the other bodies during the computation. Example applications of N-Body include (but are not limited to) the following.

- Gravitational simulation in which stars exert gravitational forces

- Molecular modeling in which ions exert electrostatic forces

- Particle systems in computer graphics to simulate water and fire

- "Boids," a technique for computer animation designed to simulate flocking behavior

Typically the paths of the bodies are being simulated per timestep, and computing each timestep costs $O(N^2)$ operations for N bodies. In most formulations, the forces quickly decrease with distance, leading to hierarchical algorithms in which (for example) the mass and location of the center-of-mass for a collection of bodies are used to avoid performing the full $O(N^2)$ computations needed otherwise. Barnes-Hut algorithms reduce the runtime to $O(N\lg N)$ by introducing a spatial hierarchy that approximates the forces between clusters of objects; for applications where the "leaf nodes" of the computation contain k bodies, $O(k^2)$ computations must be performed in a given leaf. It is this $O(k^2)$ portion of the computation at which GPUs excel.

N-Body workloads have proven the most effective way for GPUs to approach their theoretical limit in processing power. In their GPU Gems 3 paper "Fast N-Body Simulation with CUDA,"[1] Harris et al. frequently cite this theoretical limit

---

1. http.developer.nvidia.com/GPUGems3/gpugems3_ch31.html

in explaining why further performance improvements are not possible. The GPU in question, NVIDIA GeForce 8800 GTX, was so effective at N-Body computations that it outperformed custom GRAPE-6 hardware that had been specifically designed to perform astrophysics computation.

In the hopes that readers will be able to "plug in" their computation and find the fastest method, this chapter illustrates several different ways to implement N-Body and related computations using CUDA.

- A naïve implementation illustrates the technique and underscores the effectiveness of caches and the importance of loop unrolling.

- A shared memory implementation (for our gravitational computation, the fastest) duplicates Harris et al.'s result, tiling the computation over thread-block-sized collections of bodies to minimize memory latencies in the inner-most loop.

- A constant memory implementation, inspired by Stone et al.'s implementation of Direct Coulomb Summation (DCS),[2] uses constant memory to hold body descriptions, freeing shared memory for other uses.

Because readers' applications may not happen to be gravitational N-Body, these different implementations are not presented with the singular goal of optimizing that particular computation. It may make sense to adapt a different implementation, depending on the target SM architecture, problem size, and details of the central calculation.

Since gravitational N-Body has been presented as a poster child for theoretical performance of GPUs, with speedups of up to 400x reported, the chapter concludes by presenting an implementation optimized for CPUs. By rewriting the calculation to use SSE (Streaming SIMD Extensions) and multithreading, a speedup of more than 300x is obtained. Nevertheless, as reported in Section 14.9, a GK104-based GPU is significantly faster than a high-end server with a pair of Intel Xeon E2670 CPUs. The CUDA implementation is faster, more readable, and more maintainable than the optimized CPU implementation.

Throughout the chapter, performance results are reported using a server-class machine with two Xeon E2670 "Sandy Bridge" CPUs and up to four GK104 GPUs that are underclocked to conserve power and minimize heat dissipation. Rather than reporting results in GFLOPS, we report performance results in terms of body-body interactions per second.

---

2. www.ncbi.nlm.nih.gov/pubmed/17894371

14.1 Introduction

Given N bodies with positions $\mathbf{x}_i$ and velocities $\mathbf{v}_i$ for $1 \le i \le N$, the force vector $\mathbf{f}_{ij}$ on body i caused by body j is given by

$$f_{ij} = G \frac{m_i m_j}{\left\| d_{ij} \right\|^2} \cdot \frac{d_{ij}}{\left\| d_{ij} \right\|}$$

where m_i and m_j are the masses of bodies i and j, respectively; $\mathbf{d}_{ij}$ is the difference vector from body i to body j; and G is the gravitational constant. Due to divide overflow, this express diverges for $\mathbf{d}_{ij}$ with small magnitude; to compensate, it is common practice to apply a *softening factor* that models the interaction between two Plummer masses—masses that behave as if they were spherical galaxies. For a softening factor ε, the resulting expression is

$$f_{ij} = G \frac{m_i m_j d_{ij}}{\left(\left\| d_{ij} \right\|^2 + \varepsilon^2 \right)^{3/2}}$$

The total force $\mathbf{F}_i$ on body i, due to its interactions with the other $N - 1$ bodies, is obtained by summing all interactions.

$$F_i = \sum_{j=1}^{N} \mathbf{f}_{ij} = G m_i \sum_{j=1}^{N} \frac{m_i m_j d_{ij}}{\left(\left\| d_{ij} \right\|^2 + \varepsilon^2 \right)^{3/2}}$$

To update the position and velocity of each body, the force (acceleration) applied for body i is $\mathbf{a}_i = \mathbf{F}_i / m_i$, so the $\mathbf{m}_i$ term can be removed from the numerator, as follows.

$$F_i = \sum_{\substack{1 \le j \le N \\ j \ne i}}^{N} \mathbf{f}_{ij} = G m_i \sum_{j=1}^{N} \frac{m_j d_{ij}}{\left(\left\| d_{ij} \right\|^2 + \varepsilon^2 \right)^{3/2}}$$

Like Nyland et al., we use a leapfrog Verlet algorithm to apply a timestep to the simulation. The values of the positions and velocities are offset by half a timestep from one another, a characteristic that is not obvious from the code because in our sample, the positions and velocities are initially assigned random values. Our leapfrog Verlet integration updates the velocity, then the position.

$$\mathbf{V}_i\left(t+\frac{1}{2}\partial t\right)=\mathbf{V}_i\left(t-\frac{1}{2}\partial t\right)+\partial t\mathbf{F}_i$$

$$\mathbf{P}_i\left(t+\partial t\right)=\mathbf{P}_i\left(t\right)+\partial t\mathbf{V}_i\left(t+\frac{1}{2}\partial t\right)$$

This method is just one of many different integration algorithms that can be used to update the simulation, but an extensive discussion is outside the scope of this book.

Since the integration has a runtime of $O(N)$ and computing the forces has a runtime of $O(N^2)$, the biggest performance benefits from porting to CUDA stem from optimizing the force computation. Optimizing this portion of the calculation is the primary focus of this chapter.

14.1.1 A MATRIX OF FORCES

A naïve implementation of the N-Body algorithm consists of a doubly nested loop that, for each body, computes the sum of the forces exerted on that body by every other body. The $O(N^2)$ body-body forces can be thought of as an $N{\times}N$ matrix, where the sum of each row i is the total gravitational force exerted on body i.

$$F_i=\sum_{j=1}^{N}f_{ij}$$

The diagonals of this "matrix" are zeroes corresponding to each body's influence on itself, which can be ignored.

Because each element in the matrix may be computed independently, there is a tremendous amount of potential parallelism. The sum of each row is a reduction that may be computed by a single thread or by combining results from multiple threads as described in Chapter 12.

Figure 14.1 shows an 8-body "matrix" being processed. The rows correspond to the sums that are the output of the computation. When using CUDA, N-Body implementations typically have one thread compute the sum for each row.

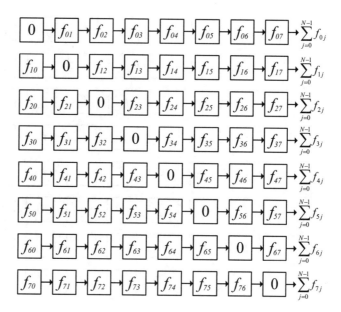

Figure 14.1 "Matrix" of forces (8 bodies).

Since every element in the "matrix" is independent, they also may be computed in parallel *within* a given row: Compute the sum of every fourth element, for example, and then add the four partial sums to compute the final output. Harris et al. describe using this method for small N where there are not enough threads to cover the latencies in the GPU: Launch more threads, compute partial sums in each thread, and accumulate the final sums with reductions in shared memory. Harris et al. reported a benefit for $N \leq 4096$.

For physical forces that are symmetric (i.e., the force exerted on body i by body j is equal in magnitude but has the opposite sign of the force exerted by body j on i), such as gravitation, the transpose "elements" of the matrix have the opposite sign.

$$\mathbf{f}_{ij} = -\mathbf{f}_{ji}$$

In this case, the "matrix" takes the form shown in Figure 14.2. When exploiting the symmetry, an implementation need only compute the upper right triangle of the "matrix," performing about half as many body-body computations.[3]

---

3. $\dfrac{N(N-1)}{2}$, to be exact.

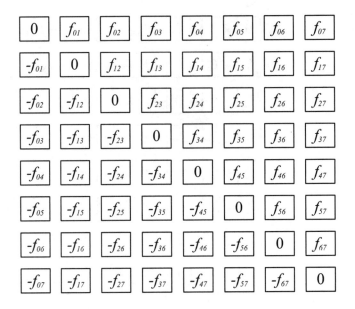

Figure 14.2 Matrix with symmetric forces.

The problem is that unlike the brute force method outlined in Figure 14.1, when exploiting symmetric forces, different threads may have contributions to add to a given output sum. Partial sums must be accumulated and either written to temporary locations for eventual reduction or the system must protect the final sums with mutual exclusion (by using atomics or thread synchronization). Since the body-body computation is about 20 FLOPS (for single precision) or 30 FLOPS (for double precision), subtracting from a sum would seem like a decisive performance win.

Unfortunately, the overhead often overwhelms the benefit of performing half as many body-body computations. For example, a completely naïve implementation that does two (2) floating-point atomic adds per body-body computation is prohibitively slower than the brute force method.

Figure 14.3 shows a compromise between the two extremes: By tiling the computation, only the upper right diagonal of *tiles* needs to be computed. For a tile size of k, this method performs k^2 body-body computations each on $$\frac{N/k\left(N/k - 1\right)}{2}$$ nondiagonal tiles, plus $k(k-1)$ body-body computations each on

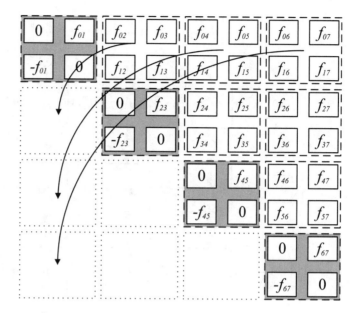

Figure 14.3 Tiled N-Body ($k = 2$).

N/k diagonal tiles. For large N, the savings in body-body computations are about the same,[4] but because the tiles can locally accumulate partial sums to contribute to the final answer, the synchronization overhead is reduced. Figure 14.3 shows a tile size with $k = 2$, but a tile size corresponding to the warp size ($k = 32$) is more practical.

Figure 14.4 shows how the partial sums for a given tile are computed. The partial sums for the rows and columns are computed—adding and subtracting, respectively—in order to arrive at partial sums that must be added to the corresponding output sums.

The popular AMBER application for molecular modeling exploits symmetry of forces, performing the work on tiles tuned to the warp size of 32,[5] but in extensive testing, the approach has not proven fruitful for the more lightweight computation described here.

---

4. For example, with $N = 65536$ and $k = 32$, the tiled approach performs 51.5% of the body-body computations performed by the brute force algorithm, or 3% more than the ideal symmetric algorithm.
5. Götz, Andreas, Mark J. Williamson, Dong Xu, Duncan Poole, Scott Le Grand, and Ross C. Walker. Routine microsecond molecular dynamics simulations with AMBER on GPUs—Part I: Generalized Born, *J. Chem. Theory Comput.* 8, no. 5 (2012), pp. 1542–1555.

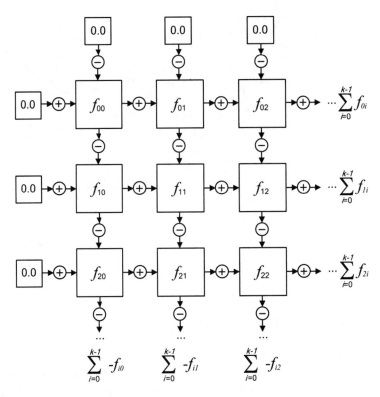

Figure 14.4 N-Body tile.

14.2 Naïve Implementation

Listing 14.1 gives a function that implements the body-body interaction described in the previous section; by annotating it with both the __host__ and __device__ keywords, the CUDA compiler knows it is valid for both the CPU and GPU. The function is templated so it may be invoked for both float and double values (though for this book, only float is fully implemented). It passes back the 3D force vector in the (fx, fy, fz) tuple.

Listing 14.1 bodyBodyInteraction.

```
template <typename T>
__host__ __device__ void bodyBodyInteraction(
    T& ax, T& ay, T& az,
```

```
    T x0, T y0, T z0,
    T x1, T y1, T z1, T mass1,
    T softeningSquared)
{
    T dx = x1 - x0;
    T dy = y1 - y0;
    T dz = z1 - z0;

    T distSqr = dx*dx + dy*dy + dz*dz;
    distSqr += softeningSquared;

    T invDist = (T)1.0 / (T)sqrt(distSqr);

    T invDistCube =  invDist * invDist * invDist;
    T s = mass1 * invDistCube;

    ax = dx * s;
    ay = dy * s;
    az = dz * s;
}
```

Listing 14.2 gives the function that computes the total gravitational force exerted on each body. For each body, it loads that body's position into (myX, myY, myZ) and then, for every other body, calls bodyBodyInteraction<float> to compute the force exerted between the two. The "AOS" in the function name denotes that the input data comes in the form of an "array of structures": four packed float values that give the (x, y, z, mass) tuple that specifies a body's position and mass. The float4 representation is a convenient size for GPU implementation, with native hardware support for loads and stores. Our optimized CPU implementations, described in Section 14.9, use so-called "structure of arrays" (SOA) representation where four arrays of float contain packed x, y, z, and *mass* elements for easier processing by SIMD instruction sets. SOA is not a good fit for GPU implementation because the 4 base pointers needed by an SOA representation cost too many registers.

Listing 14.2 ComputeGravitation_AOS (CPU implementation).

```
float
ComputeGravitation_AOS(
    float *force,
    float *posMass,
    float softeningSquared,
    size_t N
)
{
    chTimerTimestamp start, end;
    chTimerGetTime( &start );
```

```
for ( size_t i = 0; i < N; i++ )
{
    float ax = 0.0f;
    float ay = 0.0f;
    float az = 0.0f;
    float myX = posMass[i*4+0];
    float myY = posMass[i*4+1];
    float myZ = posMass[i*4+2];

    for ( size_t j = 0; j < N; j++ ) {
        float acc[3];
        float bodyX = posMass[j*4+0];
        float bodyY = posMass[j*4+1];
        float bodyZ = posMass[j*4+2];
        float bodyMass = posMass[j*4+3];

        bodyBodyInteraction<float>(
            ax, ay, az,
            myX, myY, myZ,
            bodyX, bodyY, bodyZ, bodyMass,
            softeningSquared );
        ax += acc[0];
        ay += acc[1];
        az += acc[2];
    }

    force[3*i+0] = ax;
    force[3*i+1] = ay;
    force[3*i+2] = az;
}
chTimerGetTime( &end );
return (float) chTimerElapsedTime( &start, &end ) * 1000.0f;
}
```

Listing 14.3 gives the GPU equivalent to Listing 14.2. For each body, it sums the accelerations due to every other body, then writes that value out to the force array. The L1 and L2 caches in SM 2.x and later GPUs accelerate this workload well, since there is a great deal of reuse in the innermost loop.

Both the outer loop and the inner loop cast the input array posMass to float4 to ensure that the compiler correctly emits a single 16-byte load instruction. Loop unrolling is an oft-cited optimization for N-Body calculations on GPUs, and it's not hard to imagine why: Branch overhead is much higher on GPUs than CPUs, so the reduced instruction count per loop iteration has a bigger benefit, and the unrolled loop exposes more opportunities for ILP (instruction level parallelism), in which the GPU covers latency of instruction execution as well as memory latency.

Table 14.1 Loop Unrolling in the Naïve Kernel

UNROLL FACTOR	BODY-BODY INTERACTIONS PER SECOND (BILLIONS)
1	25
2	30
16	34.3

To get the benefits of loop unrolling in our N-Body application, we need only insert the line

```
#pragma unroll <factor>
```

in front of the `for` loop over `j`. Unfortunately, the optimal loop unrolling factor must be determined empirically. Table 14.1 summarizes the effects of unrolling the loop in this kernel.

In the case of this kernel, in the absence of unrolling, it only delivers 25 billion body-body interactions per second. Even an unroll factor of 2 increases this performance to 30 billion; increasing the unroll factor to 16 delivers the highest performance observed with this kernel: 34.3 billion body-body interactions per second, a 37% performance improvement.

Listing 14.3 `ComputeNBodyGravitation_GPU_AOS`.

```
template<typename T>
__global__ void
ComputeNBodyGravitation_GPU_AOS(
    T *force,
    T *posMass,
    size_t N,
    T softeningSquared )
{
    for ( int i = blockIdx.x*blockDim.x + threadIdx.x;
              i < N;
              i += blockDim.x*gridDim.x )
    {
        T acc[3] = {0};
        float4 me = ((float4 *) posMass)[i];
        T myX = me.x;
        T myY = me.y;
```

```
        T myZ = me.z;
        for ( int j = 0; j < N; j++ ) {
            float4 body = ((float4 *) posMass)[j];
            float fx, fy, fz;
            bodyBodyInteraction(
                &fx, &fy, &fz,
                myX, myY, myZ,
                body.x, body.y, body.z, body.w,
                softeningSquared);
            acc[0] += fx;
            acc[1] += fy;
            acc[2] += fz;
        }
        force[3*i+0] = acc[0];
        force[3*i+1] = acc[1];
        force[3*i+2] = acc[2];
    }
}
```

14.3 Shared Memory

There is enough locality and reuse in the innermost loop of the N-Body calculation that caches work well without any involvement from the programmer; but on CUDA architectures, there is a benefit to using shared memory to explicitly cache the data[6], as shown in Listing 14-4. The inner loop is *tiled* using two loops: an outer one that strides through the N bodies, a thread block at a time, loading shared memory, and an inner one that iterates through the body descriptions in shared memory. Shared memory always has been optimized to broadcast to threads within a warp if they are reading the same shared memory location, so this usage pattern is a good fit with the hardware architecture.

This approach is the same one reported by Harris et al. that achieved the highest performance for large N and that approached the theoretical limits of the GPU's performance.

Listing 14.4 ComputeNBodyGravitation_Shared.

```
__global__ void
ComputeNBodyGravitation_Shared(
    float *force,
```

---

6. Shared memory is a must on SM 1.x architectures, which did not include caches. But it turns out to be a win on all CUDA architectures, albeit a slight one on SM 2.x and SM 3.x.

```
        float *posMass,
        float softeningSquared,
        size_t N )
{
    float4 *posMass4 = posMass;
    extern __shared__ float4 shPosMass[];
    for ( int i = blockIdx.x*blockDim.x + threadIdx.x;
              i < N;
              i += blockDim.x*gridDim.x )
    {
        float acc[3] = {0};
        float4 myPosMass = posMass4[i];
#pragma unroll 32
        for ( int j = 0; j < N; j += blockDim.x ) {
            shPosMass[threadIdx.x] = posMass4[j+threadIdx.x];
            __syncthreads();
            for ( size_t k = 0; k < blockDim.x; k++ ) {
                float fx, fy, fz;
                float4 bodyPosMass = shPosMass[k];

                bodyBodyInteraction(
                    &fx, &fy, &fz,
                    myPosMass.x, myPosMass.y, myPosMass.z,
                    bodyPosMass.x,
                    bodyPosMass.y,
                    bodyPosMass.z,
                    bodyPosMass.w,
                    softeningSquared );
                acc[0] += fx;
                acc[1] += fy;
                acc[2] += fz;
            }
            __syncthreads();
        }
        force[3*i+0] = acc[0];
        force[3*i+1] = acc[1];
        force[3*i+2] = acc[2];
    }
}
```

As with the previous kernel, loop unrolling delivers higher performance. Table 14.2 summarizes the effects of loop unrolling in the shared memory implementation. The optimal unroll factor of 4 delivers 18% higher performance.

Table 14.2 Loop Unrolling in the Shared Memory Kernel

UNROLL FACTOR	BODY-BODY INTERACTIONS PER SECOND (BILLIONS)
1	38.2
2	44.5
3	42.6
4	45.2

14.4 Constant Memory

Stone et al. describe a method of Direct Coulomb Summation (DCS) that uses shared memory to hold potential map lattice points for a molecular modeling application[7] so it must use constant memory to hold body descriptions. Listing 14.5 shows a CUDA kernel that uses the same method for our gravitational simulation. Since only 64K of constant memory is available to developers for a given kernel, each kernel invocation can only process about 4000 16-byte body descriptions. The constant g_bodiesPerPass specifies the number of bodies that can be considered by the innermost loop.

Since every thread in the innermost loop is reading the same body description, constant memory works well because it is optimized to broadcast reads to all threads in a warp.

Listing 14.5 N-Body (constant memory).

```
const int g_bodiesPerPass = 4000;
__constant__ __device__ float4 g_constantBodies[g_bodiesPerPass];

template<typename T>
__global__ void
ComputeNBodyGravitation_GPU_AOS_const(
    T *force,
    T *posMass,
    T softeningSquared,
```

7. www.ncbi.nlm.nih.gov/pubmed/17894371

```
              size_t n,
              size_t N )
{
     for ( int i = blockIdx.x*blockDim.x + threadIdx.x;
               i < N;
               i += blockDim.x*gridDim.x )
     {
         T acc[3] = {0};
         float4 me = ((float4 *) posMass)[i];
         T myX = me.x;
         T myY = me.y;
         T myZ = me.z;
         for ( int j = 0; j < n; j++ ) {
             float4 body = g_constantBodies[j];
             float fx, fy, fz;
             bodyBodyInteraction(
                 &fx, &fy, &fz,
                 myX, myY, myZ,
                 body.x, body.y, body.z, body.w,
                 softeningSquared);
             acc[0] += fx;
             acc[1] += fy;
             acc[2] += fz;
         }
         force[3*i+0] += acc[0];
         force[3*i+1] += acc[1];
         force[3*i+2] += acc[2];
     }
}
```

As shown in Listing 14.6, the host code must loop over the bodies, calling `cudaMemcpyToSymbolAsync()` to load the constant memory before each kernel invocation.

Listing 14.6 Host code (constant memory N-Body).

```
float
ComputeNBodyGravitation_GPU_AOS_const(
    float *force,
    float *posMass,
    float softeningSquared,
    size_t N
)
{
    cudaError_t status;
    cudaEvent_t evStart = 0, evStop = 0;
    float ms = 0.0;
    size_t bodiesLeft = N;

    void *p;
    CUDART_CHECK( cudaGetSymbolAddress( &p, g_constantBodies ) );
```

```
CUDART_CHECK( cudaEventCreate( &evStart ) );
CUDART_CHECK( cudaEventCreate( &evStop ) );
CUDART_CHECK( cudaEventRecord( evStart, NULL ) );
for ( size_t i = 0; i < N; i += g_bodiesPerPass ) {
    // bodiesThisPass = max(bodiesLeft, g_bodiesPerPass);
    size_t bodiesThisPass = bodiesLeft;
    if ( bodiesThisPass > g_bodiesPerPass ) {
        bodiesThisPass = g_bodiesPerPass;
    }
    CUDART_CHECK( cudaMemcpyToSymbolAsync(
        g_constantBodies,
        ((float4 *) posMass)+i,
        bodiesThisPass*sizeof(float4),
        0,
        cudaMemcpyDeviceToDevice,
        NULL ) );
    ComputeNBodyGravitation_GPU_AOS_const<float> <<<300,256>>>(
        force, posMass, softeningSquared, bodiesThisPass, N );
    bodiesLeft -= bodiesThisPass;
}
CUDART_CHECK( cudaEventRecord( evStop, NULL ) );
CUDART_CHECK( cudaDeviceSynchronize() );
CUDART_CHECK( cudaEventElapsedTime( &ms, evStart, evStop ) );
Error:
    cudaEventDestroy( evStop );
    cudaEventDestroy( evStart );
    return ms;
}
```

14.5 Warp Shuffle

SM 3.x added a warp shuffle instruction (described in Section 8.6.1) that enables
threads to interchange data between registers without writing the data to
shared memory. The __shfl() intrinsic can be used to broadcast one thread's
register value to all other threads in the warp. As shown in Listing 14.4, instead
of using tiles sized to the threadblock and using shared memory, we can use
tiles of size 32 (corresponding to the warp size) and broadcast the body description read by each thread to the other threads within the warp.

Interestingly, this strategy has 25% lower performance than the shared memory implementation (34 billion as opposed to 45.2 billion interactions per second). The warp shuffle instruction takes about as long as a read from shared
memory, and the computation is tiled at the warp size (32 threads) rather than
a thread block size. So it seems the benefits of warp shuffle are best realized
when replacing both a write and a read to shared memory, not just a read.

Warp shuffle should only be used if the kernel needs shared memory for other purposes.

Listing 14.7 `ComputeNBodyGravitation_Shuffle`.

```
__global__ void
ComputeNBodyGravitation_Shuffle(
    float *force,
    float *posMass,
    float softeningSquared,
    size_t N )
{
    const int laneid = threadIdx.x & 31;
    for ( int i = blockIdx.x*blockDim.x + threadIdx.x;
                i < N;
                i += blockDim.x*gridDim.x )
    {
        float acc[3] = {0};
        float4 myPosMass = ((float4 *) posMass)[i];

        for ( int j = 0; j < N; j += 32 ) {
            float4 shufSrcPosMass = ((float4 *) posMass)[j+laneid];
#pragma unroll 32
            for ( int k = 0; k < 32; k++ ) {
                float fx, fy, fz;
                float4 shufDstPosMass;

                shufDstPosMass.x = __shfl( shufSrcPosMass.x, k );
                shufDstPosMass.y = __shfl( shufSrcPosMass.y, k );
                shufDstPosMass.z = __shfl( shufSrcPosMass.z, k );
                shufDstPosMass.w = __shfl( shufSrcPosMass.w, k );

                bodyBodyInteraction(
                    &fx, &fy, &fz,
                    myPosMass.x, myPosMass.y, myPosMass.z,
                    shufDstPosMass.x,
                    shufDstPosMass.y,
                    shufDstPosMass.z,
                    shufDstPosMass.w,
                    softeningSquared);
                acc[0] += fx;
                acc[1] += fy;
                acc[2] += fz;
            }
        }

        force[3*i+0] = acc[0];
        force[3*i+1] = acc[1];
        force[3*i+2] = acc[2];
    }
}
```

14.6 Multiple GPUs and Scalability

Because the computational density is so high, N-Body scales well across multiple GPUs. Portable pinned memory is used to hold the body descriptions so they can easily be referenced by all GPUs in the system. For a system containing k GPUs, each GPU is assigned N/k forces to compute.[8] Our multi-GPU implementation of N-Body is featured in Chapter 9. The rows are evenly divided among GPUs, the input data is broadcast to all GPUs via portable pinned memory, and each GPU computes its output independently. CUDA applications that use multiple GPUs can be multithreaded or single-threaded. Chapter 9 includes optimized N-Body implementations that illustrate both approaches.

For N-Body, the single- and multithreaded implementations have the same performance, since there is little work for the CPU to do. Table 14.3 summarizes the scalability of the multithreaded implementation for a problem size of 96K bodies and up to 4 GPUs. The efficiency is the percentage of measured performance as compared to perfect scaling. There is room for improvement over this result, since the performance results reported here include allocation and freeing of device memory on each GPU for each timestep.

Table 14.3 N-Body Scalability

NUMBER OF GPUS	PERFORMANCE (BILLIONS OF BODY-BODY INTERACTIONS PER SECOND)	EFFICIENCY
1	44.1	100%
2	85.6	97.0%
3	124.2	93.4%
4	161.5	91.6%

---

8. Our implementation requires that N be evenly divisible by k.

14.7 CPU Optimizations

Papers on CUDA ports often compare against CPU implementations that are not optimized for highest performance. Although CUDA hardware generally is faster than CPUs at the workloads described in these papers, the reported speedup is often higher than it would be if the CPU implementation had been optimized properly.

To gain some insight into the tradeoffs between CUDA and modern CPU optimizations, we optimized the N-Body computation using two key strategies that are necessary for multicore CPUs to achieve peak performance.

- SIMD ("single instruction multiple data") instructions can perform multiple single-precision floating-point operations in a single instruction.

- Multithreading achieves near-linear speedups in the number of execution cores available in the CPU. Multicore CPUs have been widely available since 2006, and N-Body computations are expected to scale almost linearly in the number of cores.

Since N-Body computations have such high computational density, we will not concern ourselves with affinity (for example, trying to use NUMA APIs to associate memory buffers with certain CPUs). There is so much reuse in this computation that caches in the CPU keep external memory traffic to a trickle.

The Streaming SIMD Extensions (SSE) instructions were added to Intel's x86 architecture in the late 1990s, starting with the Pentium III. They added a set of eight 128-bit XMM registers that could operate on four packed 32-bit floating-point values.[9] For example, the ADDPS instruction performs four floating-point additions in parallel on corresponding packed floats in XMM registers.

When porting N-Body to the SSE instruction set, the AOS (array of structures) memory layout that we have been using becomes problematic. Although the body descriptions are 16 bytes, just like XMM registers, the instruction set requires us to rearrange the data such that the X, Y, Z, and Mass components are packed into separate registers. Rather than perform this operation when

---

9. Intel later added instructions that could consider the XMM registers as packed integers (up to 16 bytes) or two packed double-precision floating-point values, but we do not use any of those features. We also do not use the AVX ("Advanced Vector Extensions") instruction set. AVX features registers and instructions that support SIMD operations that are twice as wide (256-bit), so it potentially could double performance.

computing the body-body interactions, we rearrange the memory layout as structure of arrays: Instead of a single array of `float4` (each element being the X, Y, Z, and Mass values for a given body), we use four arrays of `float`, with an array of X values, an array of Y values, and so on. With the data rearranged in this way, four bodies' descriptions can be loaded into XMM registers with just 4 machine instructions; the difference vectors between four bodies' positions can be computed with just 3 SUBPS instructions; and so on.

To simplify SSE coding, Intel has worked with compiler vendors to add cross-platform support for the SSE instruction set. A special data type `__m128` corresponds to the 128-bit register and operand size and intrinsic functions such as `_mm_sub_ps()` that correspond to the SUBPS instruction.

For purposes of our N-Body implementation, we also need a full-precision reciprocal square root implementation. The SSE instruction set has an instruction RSQRTPS that computes an approximation of the reciprocal square root, but its 12-bit estimate must be refined by a Newton-Raphson iteration to achieve full float precision.[10]

$$x_0 = RSQRTSS\left(a\right)$$

$$x_1 = \frac{x_0\left(3 - ax_0^2\right)}{2}$$

Listing 14.8 gives an SSE implementation of the body-body computation that takes the 2 bodies' descriptions as `__m128` variables, computes the 4 body-body forces in parallel, and passes back the 3 resulting force vectors. Listing 14.8 is functionally equivalent to Listings 14.1 and 14.2, though markedly less readable. Note that the x0, y0, and z0 variables contain descriptions of the same body, replicated across the `__m128` variable four times.

Listing 14.8 Body-body interaction (SSE version).

```
static inline __m128
rcp_sqrt_nr_ps(const __m128 x)
{
    const __m128
            nr      = _mm_rsqrt_ps(x),
            muls    = _mm_mul_ps(_mm_mul_ps(nr, nr), x),
            beta    = _mm_mul_ps(_mm_set_ps1(0.5f), nr),
            gamma   = _mm_sub_ps(_mm_set_ps1(3.0f), muls);
```

10. This code is not present in the SSE compiler support and is surprisingly difficult to find. Our implementation is from http://nume.googlecode.com/svn/trunk/fosh/src/sse_approx.h.

```
        return _mm_mul_ps(beta, gamma);
}

static inline __m128
horizontal_sum_ps( const __m128 x )
{
    const __m128 t = _mm_add_ps(x, _mm_movehl_ps(x, x));
    return _mm_add_ss(t, _mm_shuffle_ps(t, t, 1));
}

inline void
bodyBodyInteraction(
    __m128& f0,
    __m128& f1,
    __m128& f2,

    const __m128& x0,
    const __m128& y0,
    const __m128& z0,

    const __m128& x1,
    const __m128& y1,
    const __m128& z1,
    const __m128& mass1,

    const __m128& softeningSquared )
{
    __m128 dx = _mm_sub_ps( x1, x0 );
    __m128 dy = _mm_sub_ps( y1, y0 );
    __m128 dz = _mm_sub_ps( z1, z0 );

    __m128 distSq =
        _mm_add_ps(
            _mm_add_ps(
                _mm_mul_ps( dx, dx ),
                _mm_mul_ps( dy, dy )
            ),
            _mm_mul_ps( dz, dz )
        );
    distSq = _mm_add_ps( distSq, softeningSquared );

    __m128 invDist = rcp_sqrt_nr_ps( distSq );
    __m128 invDistCube =
        _mm_mul_ps(
            invDist,
            _mm_mul_ps(
                invDist, invDist )
        );

    __m128 s = _mm_mul_ps( mass1, invDistCube );

    f0 = _mm_add_ps( a0, _mm_mul_ps( dx, s ) );
    f1 = _mm_add_ps( a1, _mm_mul_ps( dy, s ) );
    f2 = _mm_add_ps( a2, _mm_mul_ps( dz, s ) );
}
```

To take advantage of multiple cores, we must spawn multiple threads and have each thread perform part of the computation. The same strategy is used for multiple CPU cores as for multiple GPUs:[11] Just evenly divide the output rows among threads (one per CPU core) and, for each timestep, have the "parent" thread signal the worker threads to perform their work and then wait for them to finish. Since thread creation can be expensive and can fail, our application creates a pool of CPU threads at initialization time and uses thread synchronization to make the worker threads wait for work and signal completion.

The portable CUDA handbook threading library, described in Section A.2, implements a function `processorCount()` that returns the number of CPU cores on the system and a C++ class `workerThread` with methods to create and destroy CPU threads and delegate work synchronously or asynchronously. After delegating asynchronous work with the `delegateAsynchronous()` member function, the static function `waitAll()` is used to wait until the worker threads are finished.

Listing 14.9 gives the code that dispatches the N-Body calculation to worker CPU threads. The `sseDelegation` structures are used to communicate the delegation to each worker CPU thread; the `delegateSynchronous` function takes a pointer-to-function to execute and a `void *` that will be passed to that function (in this case, the `void *` points to the corresponding CPU thread's `sseDelegation` structure).

Listing 14.9 Multithreaded SSE (master thread code).

```
float
ComputeGravitation_SSE_threaded(
    float *force[3],
    float *pos[4],
    float *mass,
    float softeningSquared,
    size_t N
)
{
    chTimerTimestamp start, end;
    chTimerGetTime( &start );

    {
        sseDelegation *psse = new sseDelegation[g_numCPUCores];
        size_t bodiesPerCore = N / g_numCPUCores;
        if ( N % g_numCPUCores ) {
            return 0.0f;
        }
```

---

11. In fact, we used the same platform-independent threading library to implement the multi-threaded multi-GPU support in Chapter 9.

```
        for ( size_t i = 0; i < g_numCPUCores; i++ ) {
            psse[i].hostPosSOA[0] = pos[0];
            psse[i].hostPosSOA[1] = pos[1];
            psse[i].hostPosSOA[2] = pos[2];
            psse[i].hostMassSOA = mass;
            psse[i].hostForceSOA[0] = force[0];
            psse[i].hostForceSOA[1] = force[1];
            psse[i].hostForceSOA[2] = force[2];
            psse[i].softeningSquared = softeningSquared;

            psse[i].i = bodiesPerCore*i;
            psse[i].n = bodiesPerCore;
            psse[i].N = N;

            g_CPUThreadPool[i].delegateAsynchronous(
                sseWorkerThread,
                &psse[i] );
        }
        workerThread::waitAll( g_CPUThreadPool, g_numCPUCores );
        delete[] psse;
    }

    chTimerGetTime( &end );

    return (float) chTimerElapsedTime( &start, &end ) * 1000.0f;
}
```

Finally, Listing 14.10 gives the sseDelegation structure and the delegation function invoked by ComputeGravitation_SSE_threaded in Listing 14.9. It performs the body-body calculations four at a time, accumulating four partial sums that are added together with horizontal_sum_ps() before storing the final output forces. This function, along with all the functions that it calls, uses the SOA memory layout for all inputs and outputs.

Listing 14.10 sseWorkerThread.

```
struct sseDelegation {
    size_t i;    // base offset for this thread to process
    size_t n;    // size of this thread's problem
    size_t N;    // total number of bodies

    float *hostPosSOA[3];
    float *hostMassSOA;
    float *hostForceSOA[3];
    float softeningSquared;

};

void
sseWorkerThread( void *_p )
{
```

```
sseDelegation *p = (sseDelegation *) _p;
for (int k = 0; k < p->n; k++)
{
    int i = p->i + k;
    __m128 ax = _mm_setzero_ps();
    __m128 ay = _mm_setzero_ps();
    __m128 az = _mm_setzero_ps();
    __m128 *px = (__m128 *) p->hostPosSOA[0];
    __m128 *py = (__m128 *) p->hostPosSOA[1];
    __m128 *pz = (__m128 *) p->hostPosSOA[2];
    __m128 *pmass = (__m128 *) p->hostMassSOA;
    __m128 x0 = _mm_set_ps1( p->hostPosSOA[0][i] );
    __m128 y0 = _mm_set_ps1( p->hostPosSOA[1][i] );
    __m128 z0 = _mm_set_ps1( p->hostPosSOA[2][i] );

    for ( int j = 0; j < p->N/4; j++ ) {

        bodyBodyInteraction(
            ax, ay, az,
            x0, y0, z0,
            px[j], py[j], pz[j], pmass[j],
            _mm_set_ps1( p->softeningSquared ) );

    }
    // Accumulate sum of four floats in the SSE register
    ax = horizontal_sum_ps( ax );
    ay = horizontal_sum_ps( ay );
    az = horizontal_sum_ps( az );

    _mm_store_ss( (float *) &p->hostForceSOA[0][i], ax );
    _mm_store_ss( (float *) &p->hostForceSOA[1][i], ay );
    _mm_store_ss( (float *) &p->hostForceSOA[2][i], az );
}
}
```

14.8 Conclusion

Since instruction sets and architectures differ, performance is measured in
body-body interactions per second rather than GFLOPS. Performance was measured on a dual-socket Sandy Bridge system with two E5-2670 CPUs (similar to
Amazon's cc2.8xlarge instance type), 64GB of RAM, and four (4) GK104 GPUs
clocked at about 800MHz. The GK104s are on two dual-GPU boards plugged into
16-lane PCI Express 3.0 slots.

Table 14.4 summarizes the speedups due to CPU optimizations. All measurements were performed on a server with dual Xeon E2670 CPUs (2.6GHz). On this
system, the generic CPU code in Listing 14.2 performs 17.2M interactions per

Table 14.4 Speedups Due to CPU Optimizations

IMPLEMENTATION	BODY-BODY INTERACTIONS PER SECOND (IN BILLIONS)	SPEEDUP OVER SCALAR CPU
Scalar CPU	0.017	1x
SSE	0.307	17.8x
Multithreaded SSE	5.650	332x

second; the single-threaded SSE code performs 307M interactions per second, some 17.8x faster! As expected, multithreading the SSE code achieves good speedups, with 32 CPU threads delivering 5650M interactions per second, about 18x as fast as one thread. Between porting to SSE and multithreading, the total speedup on this platform for CPUs is more than 300x.

Because we got such a huge performance improvement from our CPU optimizations, the performance comparisons aren't as pronounced in favor of GPUs as most.[12] The highest-performing kernel in our testing (the shared memory implementation in Listing 14.4, with a loop unroll factor of 4) delivered 45.2 billion body-body interactions per second, exactly 8x faster than the fastest multithreaded SSE implementation. This result understates the performance advantages of CUDA in some ways, since the server used for testing had two high-end CPUs, and the GPUs are derated to reduce power consumption and heat dissipation.

Furthermore, future improvements can be had for both technologies: For CPUs, porting this workload to the AVX ("Advanced Vector eXtensions") instruction set would potentially double performance, but it would run only on Sandy Bridge and later chips, and the optimized CPU implementation does not exploit symmetry. For GPUs, NVIDIA's GK110 is about twice as big (and presumably about twice as fast) as the GK104. Comparing the source code for Listings 14.1 and 14.9 (the GPU and SSE implementations of the core body-body interaction code), though, it becomes clear that performance isn't the only reason to favor CUDA over

---

12. In fairness, that would be true of many other workloads in this book, like the SAXPY implementation in Chapter 11 and the normalized cross-correlation implementation in Chapter 15. Porting those workloads to multithreaded SIMD would proffer similar tradeoffs in performance versus engineering investment, readability, and maintainability as compared to the CUDA version.

optimizing CPU code. Dr. Vincent Natoli alluded to this tradeoff in his June 2010 article "Kudos for CUDA."[13]

> Similarly, we have found in many cases that the expression of algorithmic parallelism in CUDA in fields as diverse as oil and gas, bioinformatics, and finance is more elegant, compact, and readable than equivalently optimized CPU code, preserving and more clearly presenting the underlying algorithm. In a recent project we reduced 3500 lines of highly optimized C code to a CUDA kernel of about 800 lines. The optimized C was peppered with inline assembly, SSE macros, unrolled loops, and special cases, making it difficult to read, extract algorithmic meaning, and extend in the future. By comparison, the CUDA code was cleaner and more readable. Ultimately it will be easier to maintain.

Although it was feasible to develop an SSE implementation of this application, with a core body-body computation that takes about 50 lines of code to express (Listing 14.8), it's hard to imagine what the source code would look like for an SSE-optimized implementation of something like Boids, where each body must evaluate conditions and, when running on CUDA hardware, the code winds up being divergent. SSE supports divergence both in the form of predication (using masks and Boolean instruction sequences such as ANDPS/ANDNOTPS/ORPS to construct the result) and branching (often using MOVMSKPS to extract evaluated conditions), but getting the theoretical speedups on such workloads would require large engineering investments unless they can be extracted automatically by a vectorizing compiler.

14.9 References and Further Reading

N-Body and algorithms with similarly high computational density are a source of many high-profile speedups, since they can approach the theoretical limits of the GPU's computing capabilities. The following are just a sample of the numerous papers on compute-intensive methods such as N-Body.

Gravitational Simulation

Burtscher, Martin, and Keshav Pingali. An efficient CUDA implementation of the tree-based Barnes-Hut n-body algorithm. In *GPU Gems Emerald Edition*, Wen-Mei Hwu, ed., Morgan-Kaufmann, 2011, Burlington, MA, pp. 75–92.

http://cs.txstate.edu/~burtscher/papers/gcg11.pdf

---

13. www.hpcwire.com/hpcwire/2010-07-06/kudos_for_cuda.html

Harris, Mark, Lars Nyland, and Jan Prins. Fast n-body simulation with CUDA. In *GPU Gems 3*, Addison-Wesley, Boston, MA, 2007, pp. 677–695.
http.developer.nvidia.com/GPUGems3/gpugems3_ch31.html

Molecular Modeling

Götz, Andreas, Mark J. Williamson, Dong Xu, Duncan Poole, Scott Le Grand, and Ross C. Walker. Routine microsecond molecular dynamics simulations with AMBER on GPUs—Part I: Generalized Born, *J. Chem. Theory Comput.* 8 (5), 2012, pp. 1542–1555.

Hwu, Wen-Mei, and David Kirk. *Programming Massively Parallel Processors*. Morgan-Kaufmann, 2010, pp. 173–188.

Hardy, David J., John E. Stone, Kirby L. Vandivort, David Gohara, Christopher Rodrigues, and Klaus Schulten. Fast molecular electrostatics algorithms on GPUs. In *GPU Computing Gems*, Elsevier, Burlington, MA, 2011, pp. 43–58.

Stone, John E., James C. Phillips, Peter L. Freddolino, David J. Hardy, Leonardo G. Trabuco, and Klaus Schulten. Accelerating molecular modeling applications with graphics processors. *Journal of Computational Chemistry* 28 (2007), pp. 2618–2640.

http://cacs.usc.edu/education/cs653/Stone-MDGPU-JCC07.pdf

Stone, John E., David J. Hardy, Barry Isralewitz, and Klaus Schulten. GPU algorithms for molecular modeling. In *Scientific Computing with Multicore and Accelerators*, Jack Dongarra, David A. Bader, and Jakob Kurzak, eds. Chapman & Hall/CRC Press, London, UK, 2010, pp. 351–371.

Boids

da Silva, A.R., W.S. Lages, and L. Chaimowicz. Boids that see: Using self-occlusion for simulating large groups on GPUs. *ACM Comput. Entertain.* 7 (4), 2009.
http://doi.acm.org/10.1145/1658866.1658870

Chapter 15

Image Processing: Normalized Correlation

Normalized cross-correlation is a popular template-matching algorithm in image processing and computer vision. The template typically is an image that depicts a sought-after feature; by repeatedly computing a statistic between the template image and corresponding pixels of a subset of an input image, a search algorithm can locate instances of the template that are present in the input image.

The popularity of normalized cross-correlation for this application stems from its *amplitude independence*, which, in the context of image processing, essentially means that the statistic is robust in the face of lighting changes between the image and the template. Normalized correlation is popular enough, and sufficiently compute-intensive enough, that it has prompted companies to build custom hardware. This chapter develops an optimized implementation of normalized cross-correlation for 8-bit grayscale images, but many of the concepts can be extended to other types of image processing or computer vision algorithms.

15.1 Overview

Two 2D images, the image and the template, are compared by computing a correlation coefficient as follows.

$$\gamma(s,t)=\frac{\sum_x\sum_y\left[I(x,y)-\bar{I}(x,y)\right]\left[T(x-s,y-t)-\bar{T}\right]}{\sqrt{\sum_x\sum_y\left[I(x,y)-\bar{I}(x,y)\right]^2\sum_x\sum_y\left[T(x-s,y-t)-\bar{T}\right]^2}}$$

where I and T are the image and template, respectively; $\bar{T}$ is the average value of the template; and $\bar{I}$ is the average value of the image pixels corresponding to the template.

The value of this coefficient falls into the range [–1.0, 1.0]; a value of 1.0 corresponds to a perfect match. An optimized implementation of normalized correlation factors out the statistics that may be precomputed and computes sums instead of averages to avoid a separate pass over the input data. If N pixels are being compared, replacing $\bar{I}$ with $\dfrac{\sum_x\sum_y\left[t(x,y)\right]}{N}$ and multiplying the numerator and denominator by N yields a coefficient that can be expressed entirely in terms of sums. Rewriting without the coordinate notation:

$$\frac{N\Sigma IT-\Sigma I\Sigma T}{\sqrt{\left(N\Sigma I^2-\left(\Sigma I\right)^2\right)\left(N\Sigma T^2-\left(\Sigma T\right)^2\right)}}$$

Assuming the template will be the same for many correlation computations, the statistics on the template $\sum T$ and $\sum T^2$ can be precomputed, as can the subexpression $\left(N\Sigma T^2-\left(\Sigma T\right)^2\right)$ in the denominator. Translating this notation to C variable names gives the following.

STATISTIC	C VARIABLE NAME
$\sum I$	SumI
$\sum T$	SumT
$\sum IT$	SumIT
$\sum I^2$	SumSqI
$\sum T^2$	SumSqT

Then a normalized correlation value may be computed using this function.

```
float
CorrelationValue( float SumI, float SumISq,
float SumT, float SumTSq, float SumIT,
float N )
{
    float Numerator = N*SumIT - SumI*SumT;
    float Denominator = (N*SumISq - SumI*SumI)*
(N*SumTSq - SumT*SumT);
    return Numerator / sqrtf(Denominator);
}
```

In practical applications for this algorithm, the template is kept fixed across many invocations, matching against different offsets into an image. Then it makes sense to precompute the template statistics and the denominator subexpression

```
float fDenomExp = N*SumSqT - SumT*SumT;
```

In practice, it's best to use double precision to compute `fDenomExp`.

```
float fDenomExp = (float) ((double) N*SumSqT - (double) SumT*SumT);
```

Note: This computation is done on the CPU, once per template.

It is faster to multiply by the reciprocal square root than to divide by the square root, which results in the following `CorrelationValue()` function.

```
float
CorrelationValue( float SumI, float SumISq, float SumIT,
float N, float fDenomExp )
{
    float Numerator = cPixels*SumIT - SumI*SumT;
    float Denominator = fDenomExp*(cPixels*SumISq - SumI*SumI);
    return Numerator * rsqrtf(Denominator);
}
```

Hence, an optimized implementation of this algorithm need only compute three sums over the pixels to compute a given correlation coefficient: $\sum I$, $\sum I^2$, and $\sum IT$. Since the SMs include hardware support for integer multiply-add, NVIDIA GPUs are able to perform this computation extremely fast.

CUDA offers a number of paths that could be used to deliver the data to the streaming multiprocessors.

- Global memory or texture memory for the image, the template, or both

- Constant memory for the template and possibly other template-specific parameters (up to 64K)

- Shared memory to hold image and/or template values for reuse

This chapter assumes the pixels are 8-bit grayscale. The hardware works very well on images with higher precision, but if anything, that simplifies the problem by making it easier to efficiently address global and shared memory.

All of the CUDA implementations in this chapter use texture for the image that is being compared with the template. There are several reasons for this.

- The texture units deal with boundary conditions gracefully and efficiently.

- The texture cache aggregates external bandwidth on reuse, which will occur as nearby correlation values are computed.

- The 2D locality of the texture cache is a good fit with the access patterns exhibited by correlation search algorithms.

We'll explore the tradeoffs of using texture versus constant memory for the template.

15.2 Naïve Texture-Texture Implementation

Our first implementation of normalized cross-correlation uses the texture unit to read both image and template values. This implementation is not optimized; it does not even include the optimization to precompute the template statistics. But it is simple to understand and will serve as a good basis for more highly optimized (but more byzantine) implementations.

Listing 15.1 gives the kernel that performs this computation. It computes the five sums, then uses the `CorrelationValue()` utility function given earlier to write the `float`-valued correlation coefficients into the output array. Note that the expression computing `fDenomExp` will issue a warning on pre–SM 1.3 architectures, which do not include double precision support. The kernel will still work as long as the number of pixels in the template is not too large.

The upper left corner of the image is given by (`xUL`, `yUL`); the width and height of the search window, and thus the output array of coefficients, is given by `w` and `h`. If the template is in a texture, the upper left corner of the template in the texture image is given by (`xTemplate`, `yTemplate`).

Finally, an offset (`xOffset`, `yOffset`) specifies how the template will be overlaid with the image for comparison purposes. When fetching image pixels, this offset is added to the coordinates of the search rectangle whose upper left corner is (xUL, yUL).

It's instructive to look at how the correlation function "falls off" in the neighborhood of the image from which a template is extracted. The sample program normalizedCrossCorrelation.cu writes out the neighborhood around the template:

```
Neighborhood around template:
 0.71 0.75 0.79 0.81 0.82 0.81 0.81 0.80 0.78
 0.72 0.77 0.81 0.84 0.84 0.84 0.83 0.81 0.79
 0.74 0.79 0.84 0.88 0.88 0.87 0.85 0.82 0.79
 0.75 0.80 0.86 0.93 0.95 0.91 0.86 0.83 0.80
 0.75 0.80 0.87 0.95 1.00 0.95 0.88 0.83 0.81
 0.75 0.80 0.86 0.91 0.95 0.93 0.87 0.82 0.80
 0.75 0.80 0.84 0.87 0.89 0.88 0.85 0.81 0.78
 0.73 0.78 0.81 0.83 0.85 0.85 0.82 0.79 0.76
 0.71 0.75 0.78 0.81 0.82 0.82 0.80 0.77 0.75
```

In the coins image included in the book, the default template is a 52x52 subimage around the dime in the lower right corner (Figure 15.1). The default program optionally can write a PGM file as output, with the correlation values converted to pixel values in the range 0..255. For the template highlighted in Figure 15.1, the resulting image is given in Figure 15.2. The other dimes are very bright, with strong matches, while the other coins get less intense responses.

Figure 15.1 Coins.pgm (with default template highlighted).

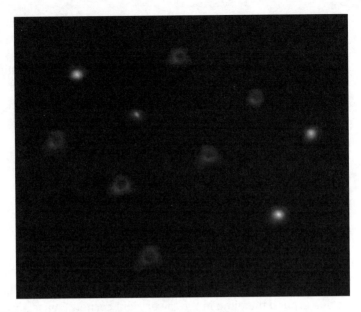

Figure 15.2 Correlation image with default template.

Listing 15.1 `corrTexTex2D_kernel`.

```
__global__ void
corrTexTex2D_kernel(
    float *pCorr, size_t CorrPitch,
    float cPixels,
    int xOffset, int yOffset,
    int xTemplate, int yTemplate,
    int wTemplate, int hTemplate,
    float xUL, float yUL, int w, int h )
{
    size_t row = blockIdx.y*blockDim.y + threadIdx.y;
    size_t col = blockIdx.x*blockDim.x + threadIdx.x;

    // adjust pCorr to point to row
    pCorr = (float *) ((char *) pCorr+row*CorrPitch);

    // No __syncthreads in this kernel, so we can early-out
    // without worrying about the effects of divergence.
    if ( col >= w || row >= h )
        return;

    int SumI = 0;
    int SumT = 0;
    int SumISq = 0;
    int SumTSq = 0;
```

```
        int SumIT = 0;
        for ( int y = 0; y < hTemplate; y++ ) {
            for ( int x = 0; x < wTemplate; x++ ) {
                unsigned char I = tex2D( texImage,
                    (float) col+xUL+xOffset+x, (float) row+yUL+yOffset+y );
                unsigned char T = tex2D( texTemplate,
                    (float) xTemplate+x, (float) yTemplate+y);
                SumI += I;
                SumT += T;
                SumISq += I*I;
                SumTSq += T*T;
                SumIT += I*T;
            }
            float fDenomExp = (float) ( (double) cPixels*SumTSq -
                (double) SumT*SumT);
            pCorr[col] = CorrelationValue(
                SumI, SumISq, SumIT, SumT, cPixels, fDenomExp );

        }
    }
```

Listing 15.2 gives the host code to invoke `corrTexTex2D_kernel()`. It is designed to work with the testing and performance measurement code in the sample source file `normalizedCrossCorrelation.cu`, which is why it has so many parameters. This host function just turns around and launches the kernel with the needed parameters, but later implementations of this function will check the device properties and launch different kernels, depending on what it finds. For images of a useful size, the cost of doing such checks is negligible compared to the GPU runtime.

Listing 15.2 `corrTexTex2D()` (host code).

```
void
corrTexTex2D(
    float *dCorr, int CorrPitch,
    int wTile,
    int wTemplate, int hTemplate,
    float cPixels,
    float fDenomExp,
    int sharedPitch,
    int xOffset, int yOffset,
    int xTemplate, int yTemplate,
    int xUL, int yUL, int w, int h,
    dim3 threads, dim3 blocks,
    int sharedMem )
{
    corrTexTex2D_kernel<<<blocks, threads>>>(
        dCorr, CorrPitch,
        cPixels,
        xOffset, yOffset,
```

```
        xTemplate+xOffset, yTemplate+yOffset,
        wTemplate, hTemplate,
        (float) xUL, (float) yUL, w, h );
}
```

A texture-texture formulation is a very good fit if the application is choosing different templates as well as different images during its search—for example, applying transformations to the template data while comparing to the image. But for most applications, the template is chosen once and compared against many different offsets within the image. The remainder of the chapter will examine implementations that are optimized for that case.

15.3 Template in Constant Memory

Most template-matching applications perform many correlation computations with the same template at different offsets of the input image. In that case, the template statistics (SumT and fDenomExp) can be precomputed, and the template data can be moved to special memory or otherwise premassaged. For CUDA, the obvious place to put the template data is in constant memory so each template pixel can be broadcast to the threads computing correlation values for different image locations.

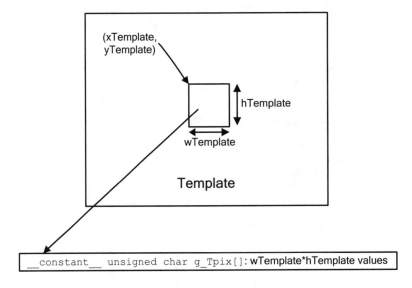

Figure 15.3 Template in __constant__ memory.

The CopyToTemplate function given in Listing 15.3 pulls a rectangular area of pixels out of the input image, computes the statistics, and copies the data and statistics to __constant__ memory.

Listing 15.3 CopyToTemplate function (error handling removed).

```
cudaError_t
CopyToTemplate(
    unsigned char *img, size_t imgPitch,
    int xTemplate, int yTemplate,
    int wTemplate, int hTemplate,
    int OffsetX, int OffsetY
)
{
    cudaError_t status;
    unsigned char pixels[maxTemplatePixels];

    int inx = 0;
    int SumT = 0;
    int SumTSq = 0;
    int cPixels = wTemplate*hTemplate;
    size_t sizeOffsets = cPixels*sizeof(int);
    float fSumT, fDenomExp, fcPixels;

    cudaMemcpy2D(
        pixels, wTemplate,
        img+yTemplate*imgPitch+xTemplate, imgPitch,
        wTemplate, hTemplate,
        cudaMemcpyDeviceToHost );

    cudaMemcpyToSymbol( g_Tpix, pixels, cPixels );

    for ( int i = OffsetY; i < OffsetY+hTemplate; i++ ) {
        for ( int j = OffsetX; j < OffsetX+wTemplate; j++) {
            SumT += pixels[inx];
            SumTSq += pixels[inx]*pixels[inx];
            poffsetx[inx] = j;
            poffsety[inx] = i;
            inx += 1;
        }
    }
    g_cpuSumT = SumT;
    g_cpuSumTSq = SumTSq;

    cudaMemcpyToSymbol(g_xOffset, poffsetx, sizeOffsets);
    cudaMemcpyToSymbol(g_yOffset, poffsety, sizeOffsets);

    fSumT = (float) SumT;
    cudaMemcpyToSymbol(g_SumT, &fSumT, sizeof(float));

    fDenomExp = float( (double)cPixels*SumTSq - (double) SumT*SumT);
    cudaMemcpyToSymbol(g_fDenomExp, &fDenomExp, sizeof(float));
```

```
    fcPixels = (float) cPixels;
    cudaMemcpyToSymbol(g_cPixels, &fcPixels, sizeof(float));
Error:
    return status;
}
```

The `corrTemplate2D()` kernel given in Listing 15.4 then can read the template values from `g_TPix[]`, which resides in constant memory. `corrTemplate2D()` is even simpler and shorter than `corrTexTex2D()`, since it does not have to compute the template statistics.

Listing 15.4 `corrTemplate2D` kernel.

```
__global__ void
corrTemplate2D_kernel(
    float *pCorr, size_t CorrPitch,
    float cPixels, float fDenomExp,
    float xUL, float yUL, int w, int h,
    int xOffset, int yOffset,
    int wTemplate, int hTemplate )
{
    size_t row = blockIdx.y*blockDim.y + threadIdx.y;
    size_t col = blockIdx.x*blockDim.x + threadIdx.x;

    // adjust pointers to row
    pCorr = (float *) ((char *) pCorr+row*CorrPitch);

    // No __syncthreads in this kernel, so we can early-out
    // without worrying about the effects of divergence.
    if ( col >= w || row >= h )
        return;

    int SumI = 0;
    int SumISq = 0;
    int SumIT = 0;
    int inx = 0;

    for ( int j = 0; j < hTemplate; j++ ) {
        for ( int i = 0; i < wTemplate; i++ ) {
            unsigned char I = tex2D( texImage,
                                (float) col+xUL+xOffset+i,
                                (float) row+yUL+yOffset+j );
            unsigned char T = g_Tpix[inx++];
            SumI += I;
            SumISq += I*I;
            SumIT += I*T;
        }
    }
```

```
        pCorr[col] =
            CorrelationValue(
                SumI, SumISq, SumIT, g_SumT, cPixels, fDenomExp );
}
```

15.4 Image in Shared Memory

For rectangles of correlation values such as the ones computed by our sample program, the CUDA kernel exhibits a tremendous amount of reuse of the image data as the template matches are swept across the image. So far, our code has relied on the texture caches to service these redundant reads without going to external memory. For smaller templates, however, shared memory can be used to further increase performance by making the image data available with lower latency.

The kernels in Listings 15.1 and 15.3 implicitly divided the input image into tiles that were the same size as the threadblocks. For our shared memory implementation shown in Listing 15.5, we'll use the height of the threadblock (blockDim.y) but specify an explicit tile width of wTile. In our sample program, wTile is 32. Figure 15.4 shows how the kernel "overfetches" a rectangle of wTemplate×hTemplate pixels outside the tile; boundary conditions are handled by the texture addressing mode. Once the shared memory has been populated with image data, the kernel does __syncthreads() and computes and writes out the tile's correlation coefficients.

Listing 15.5 corrShared_kernel().

```
__global__ void
corrShared_kernel(
    float *pCorr, size_t CorrPitch,
    int wTile,
    int wTemplate, int hTemplate,
    float xOffset, float yOffset,
    float cPixels, float fDenomExp, int SharedPitch,
    float xUL, float yUL, int w, int h )
{
    int uTile = blockIdx.x*wTile;
    int vTile = blockIdx.y*blockDim.y;
    int v = vTile + threadIdx.y;

    float *pOut = (float *) (((char *) pCorr)+v*CorrPitch);
```

```
for ( int row = threadIdx.y;
          row < blockDim.y+hTemplate;
          row += blockDim.y ) {
    int SharedIdx = row * SharedPitch;
    for ( int col = threadIdx.x;
              col < wTile+wTemplate;
              col += blockDim.x ) {

        LocalBlock[SharedIdx+col] =
            tex2D( texImage,
                    (float) (uTile+col+xUL+xOffset),
                    (float) (vTile+row+yUL+yOffset) );

    }
}

__syncthreads();

for ( int col = threadIdx.x;
          col < wTile;
          col += blockDim.x ) {

    int SumI = 0;
    int SumISq = 0;
    int SumIT = 0;
    int idx = 0;
    int SharedIdx = threadIdx.y * SharedPitch + col;
    for ( int j = 0; j < hTemplate; j++ ) {
        for ( int i = 0; i < wTemplate; i++) {
            unsigned char I = LocalBlock[SharedIdx+i];
            unsigned char T = g_Tpix[idx++];
            SumI += I;
            SumISq += I*I;
            SumIT += I*T;
        }
        SharedIdx += SharedPitch;
    }
    if ( uTile+col < w && v < h ) {
        pOut[uTile+col] =
            CorrelationValue( SumI, SumISq, SumIT, g_SumT,
                                cPixels, fDenomExp );
    }
}
__syncthreads();
}
```

To ensure that shared memory references will avoid bank conflicts from one row to the next, the amount of shared memory per row is padded to the next multiple of 64.

```
sharedPitch = ~63&(((wTile+wTemplate)+63));
```

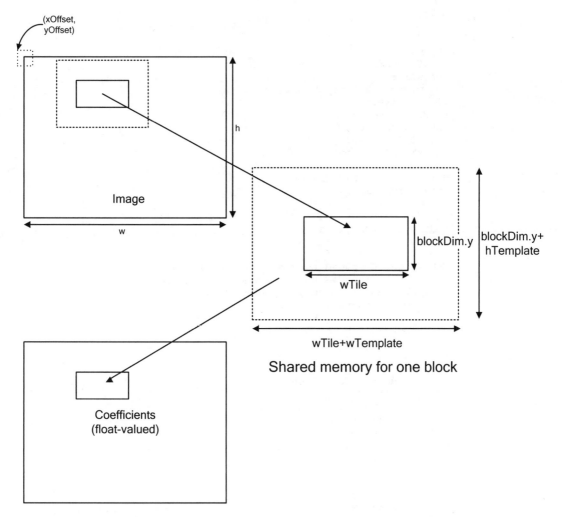

Figure 15.4 Image in shared memory.

The total amount of shared memory needed per block is then the pitch multiplied by the number of rows (block height plus template height).

```
sharedMem = sharedPitch*(threads.y+hTemplate);
```

The host code to launch `corrShared_kernel()`, shown in Listing 15.6, detects whether the kernel launch will require more shared memory than is available. If that is the case, it calls `corrTexTex2D()`, which will work for any template size.

Listing 15.6 `corrShared()` (host code).

```
void
corrShared(
    float *dCorr, int CorrPitch,
    int wTile,
    int wTemplate, int hTemplate,
    float cPixels,
    float fDenomExp,
    int sharedPitch,
    int xOffset, int yOffset,
    int xTemplate, int yTemplate,
    int xUL, int yUL, int w, int h,
    dim3 threads, dim3 blocks,
    int sharedMem )
{
    int device;
    cudaDeviceProp props;
    cudaError_t status;

    CUDART_CHECK( cudaGetDevice( &device ) );
    CUDART_CHECK( cudaGetDeviceProperties( &props, device ) );
    if ( sharedMem > props.sharedMemPerBlock ) {
        dim3 threads88(8, 8, 1);
        dim3 blocks88;
        blocks88.x = INTCEIL(w,8);
        blocks88.y = INTCEIL(h,8);
        blocks88.z = 1;
        return corrTexTex2D(
            dCorr, CorrPitch,
            wTile,
            wTemplate, hTemplate,
            cPixels,
            fDenomExp,
            sharedPitch,
            xOffset, yOffset,
            xTemplate, yTemplate,
            xUL, yUL, w, h,
            threads88, blocks88,
            sharedMem );
    }
    corrShared_kernel<<<blocks, threads, sharedMem>>>(
        dCorr, CorrPitch,
        wTile,
        wTemplate, hTemplate,
        (float) xOffset, (float) yOffset,
        cPixels, fDenomExp,
        sharedPitch,
        (float) xUL, (float) yUL, w, h );
Error:
    return;
}
```

15.5 Further Optimizations

Two more optimizations are implemented in the sample source code: SM-aware kernel invocation (since SM 1.x has different instruction set support for multiplication, which is in the innermost loop of this computation) and an unrolled inner loop of the kernel.

15.5.1 SM-AWARE CODING

SM 1.x hardware uses a 24-bit multiplier (plenty wide enough to do the multiplications in the inner loop of this computation), yet SM 2.x and SM 3.x hardware use 32-bit multipliers. Sometimes the compiler can detect when the participating integers are narrow enough that it can use the 24-bit multiply on SM 1.x–class hardware, but that does not seem to be the case for corrShared_ kernel(). To work around the issue, we can use a template on the kernel declaration.

```
template<bool bSM1>
__global__ void
corrSharedSM_kernel( ... )
```

The inner loop of the kernel then becomes

```
for ( int j = 0; j < hTemplate; j++ ) {
    for ( int i = 0; i < wTemplate; i++) {
        unsigned char I = LocalBlock[SharedIdx+i];
        unsigned char T = g_Tpix[idx++];
        SumI += I;
        if ( bSM1 ) {
            SumISq += __umul24(I, I);
            SumIT += __umul24(I, T);
        }
        else {
            SumISq += I*I;
            SumIT += I*T;
        }
    }
    SharedIdx += SharedPitch;
}
```

And the host function that invokes the kernel must detect whether the device is SM 1.x and, if so, invoke the kernel with bSM1=true. In the sample source code, this implementation is given in the corrSharedSM.cuh and corrSharedSMSums.cuh header files.

15.5.2. LOOP UNROLLING

Since each thread is accessing adjacent bytes in shared memory, the innermost loop of these kernels generates 4-way bank conflicts on SM 1.x-class hardware. If we rewrite

```
for ( int j = 0; j < hTemplate; j++ ) {
    for ( int i = 0; i < wTemplate; i++) {
        unsigned char I = LocalBlock[SharedIdx+i];
        unsigned char T = g_Tpix[idx++];
        SumI += I;
        SumISq += I*I;
        SumIT += I*T;
    }
    SharedIdx += SharedPitch;
}
```

as follows

```
for ( int j = 0; j < hTemplate; j++ ) {
    for ( int i = 0; i < wTemplate/4; i++) {
        corrSharedAccumulate<bSM1>( ... LocalBlock[SharedIdx+i*4+0], );
        corrSharedAccumulate<bSM1>( ... LocalBlock[SharedIdx+i*4+1], );
        corrSharedAccumulate<bSM1>( ... LocalBlock[SharedIdx+i*4+2], );
        corrSharedAccumulate<bSM1>( ... LocalBlock[SharedIdx+i*4+3], );
    }
    SharedIdx += SharedPitch;
}
```

where the corrSharedAccumulate() function encapsulates the template parameter bSM1

```
template<bool bSM1>
__device__ void
corrSharedAccumulate(
 int& SumI, int& SumISq, int& SumIT,
 unsigned char I, unsigned char T )
{
 SumI += I;
 if ( bSM1 ) {
 SumISq += __umul24(I,I);
 SumIT += __umul24(I,T);
 }
 else {
 SumISq += I*I;
 SumIT += I*T;
 }
}
```

Although the primary motivation is to decrease bank conflicts due to byte reads—an effect that only occurs on SM 1.x hardware—the resulting kernel is faster on all CUDA hardware.

15.6 Source Code

When working on optimized normalized cross-correlation code, it does not take long to realize that it's surprisingly difficult and error-prone. Converting the sums to correlation coefficients, as described in Section 15.1, must be done carefully due to the precision characteristics of float versus int (float has a greater dynamic range, but only 24 bits of precision). It is good practice to develop separate subroutines that report the computed sums to root cause whether a given implementation is reporting incorrect coefficients due to incorrect sums or an incorrect coefficient computation. Also, the sums can be bitwise-compared with CPU results, while the float-valued coefficients must be fuzzily compared against an epsilon value.

The different implementations of correlation are broken out into separate header (.cuh) files, and the kernels that emit sums as well as correlation coefficients are separate.

FILE	DESCRIPTION
corrShared.cuh	Loads shared memory with texture, then reads image from shared memory
corrSharedSums.cuh	
corrShared4.cuh	corrSharedSM, with innermost loop unrolledx4
corrShared4Sums.cuh	
corrSharedSM.cuh	corrShared, with SM-aware kernel launches
corrSharedSMSums.cuh	
corrTexConstant.cuh	Reads image from texture and template from constant memory
corrTexConstantSums.cuh	
corrTexTex.cuh	Reads image and template from texture
corrTexTexSums.cuh	
normalizedCrossCorrelation.cu	Test program

The `normalizedCrossCorrelation.cu` program tests both the functionality and the performance of the kernels. By default, it loads `coins.pgm` and detects the dime in the lower right corner. The dime is located at (210,148) and is 52×52 pixels in size. The program also writes the performance measurements to `stdout`—for example:

```
$ normalizedCrossCorrelation --padWidth 1024 --padHeight 1024
-wTemplate 16 -hTemplate 16
corrTexTex2D: 54.86 Mpix/s 14.05Gtpix/s
corrTemplate2D: 72.87 Mpix/s 18.65Gtpix/s
corrShared: 69.66 Mpix/s 17.83Gtpix/s
corrSharedSM: 78.66 Mpix/s 20.14Gtpix/s
corrShared4: 97.02 Mpix/s 24.84Gtpix/s
```

The program supports the following command line options.

> `--input <filename>`:   specify the input filename (default: `coins.pgm`).
>
> `--output <filename>`:   optionally specify the output filename. If specified, the program will write a PGM file containing an intensity map (like Figure 15.3) to this filename.
>
> `--padWidth <width>`:   pad the width of the image.
>
> `--padHeight <height>`:   pad the height of the image.
>
> `--xTemplate <value>`:   specify the X coordinate of the upper left corner of the template.
>
> `--yTemplate <value>`:   specify the Y coordinate of the upper left corner of the template.
>
> `--wTemplate <value>`:   specify the width of the template.
>
> `--hTemplate <value>`:   specify the height of the template.

15.7 Performance and Further Reading

Our sample program uses CUDA events to report the performance of some number of consecutive kernel launches (default 100) and reports the rates of both output coefficients (which varies with the template size) and the "template-pixel" rate, or the number of inner loop iterations per unit time.

The raw performance of GPUs at performing this computation is astonishing. A GeForce GTX 280 (GT200) can perform almost 25 billion template-pixel calculations per second (Gtpix/s), and the GeForce 680 GTX (GK104) delivers well over 100 Gtpix/s.

The default parameters of the program are not ideal for performance measurement. They are set to detect the dime in the lower right corner and optionally write out the image in Figure 15.3. In particular, the image is too small to keep the GPU fully busy. The image is only 300×246 pixels (74K in size), so only 310 blocks are needed by the shared memory implementation to perform the computation. The --padWidth and --padHeight command-line options can be used in the sample program to increase the size of the image and thus the number of correlation coefficients computed (there are no data dependencies in the code, so the padding can be filled with arbitrary data); a 1024×1024 image is both more realistic and gets best utilization out of all GPUs tested.

Figure 15.5 summarizes the relative performance of our 5 implementations.

- corrTexTex: template and image both in texture memory

- corrTexConstant: template in constant memory

- corrShared: template in constant memory and image in shared memory

- corrSharedSM: corrShared with SM-aware kernel invocations

- corrShared4: corrSharedSM with the inner loop unrolled 4x

The various optimizations did improve performance, to varying degrees, as shown in Figure 15.6. Moving the template to constant memory had the biggest impact on GK104, increasing performance by 80%; moving the image to shared memory had the biggest impact on GF100, increasing performance by 70%. The SM-aware kernel launches had the most muted impact, increasing performance on GT200 by 14% (it does not affect performance on the other architectures, since using the built-in multiplication operator is also fastest).

On GT200, corrShared suffered from bank conflicts in shared memory, so much so that corrShared is slower than corrTexConstant; corrShared4 alleviates these bank conflicts, increasing performance by 23%.

The size of the template also has a bearing on the efficiency of this algorithm: The larger the template, the more efficient the computation on a per-template-pixel basis. Figure 15.6 illustrates how the template size affects performance of the corrShared4 formulation.

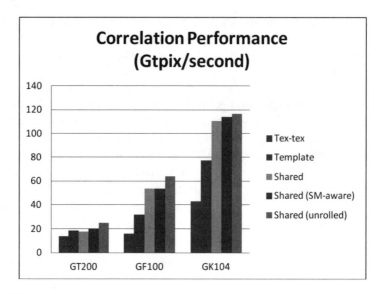

Figure 15.5 Performance comparison.

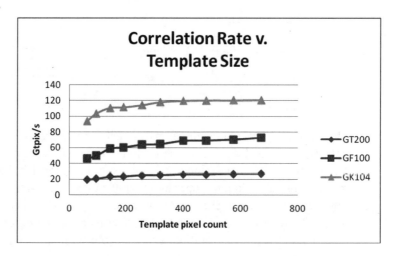

Figure 15.6 Correlation rate versus template size.

As the template grows from 8×8 to 28×28, GT200 performance improves 36% (19.6 Gtpix/s to 26.8 Gtpix/s), GF100 improves 57% (46.5 Gtpix/s to 72.9 Gtpix/s), and GK104 improves 30% (93.9 Gtpix/s to 120.72 Gtpix/s).

For small templates, the compiler generates faster code if the template size is known at compile time. Moving `wTemplate` and `hTemplate` to be template parameters and specializing for an 8×8 template improved performance as follows.

| PART | RATE (GTPIX/S) | | IMPROVEMENT |
	CORRSHARED4	CORRSHARED4 (SPECIALIZED)	
GT200	19.63	24.37	24%
GF100	46.49	65.08	40%
GK104	93.88	97.95	4%

15.8 Further Reading

Digital Image Processing includes both a discussion of normalized correlation (pp. 583–586) and the logarithmic transform used to compute the output pixels in our sample program (pp. 168–169).

Gonzalez, Rafael C., and Richard E. Woods. *Digital image processing.* Addison-Wesley, Reading, MA, 1992.

www.imageprocessingplace.com/root_files_V3/publications.htm

J.P. Lewis has an excellent discussion, including a more asymptotically efficient way to accelerate the type of correlation operation implemented by our sample program, where a template match against every pixel in the input image is desired. Lewis uses FFTs to compute the numerators and summed area tables to compute the denominators of the coefficients.

Lewis, J.P. Fast template matching. *Vision Interface 10*, 1995, pp. 120–123. An expanded version entitled "Fast Normalized Correlation" may be found online at http://bit.ly/NJnZPI.

Appendix A

The CUDA Handbook Library

As mentioned in Chapter 1, the source code accompanying this book is open source under the two-paragraph BSD license. A pointer to the source code is available on www.cudahandbook.com, and developers can find the Git repository at https://github.com/ArchaeaSoftware/cudahandbook.

This Appendix briefly describes the features of the CUDA Handbook Library (chLib), a set of portable header files located in the chLib/ subdirectory of the source code project. chLib is not intended to be reused in production software. It provides the minimum functionality, in the smallest possible amount of source code, needed to illustrate the concepts covered in this book. chLib is portable to all target operating systems for CUDA, so it often must expose support for the intersection of those operating systems' features.

A.1 Timing

The CUDA Handbook library includes a portable timing library that uses QueryPerformanceCounter() on Windows and gettimeofday() on non-Windows platforms. An example usage is as follows.

```
float
TimeNULLKernelLaunches(int cIterations = 1000000 )
{
    chTimerTimestamp start, stop;
```

```
        chTimerGetTime ( &start );
        for ( int i = 0; i < cIterations; i++ ) {
            NullKernel<<<1,1>>>();
        }
        cudaThreadSynchronize();
        chTimerGetTime ( &stop );
        return 1e6*chTimerElapsedTime ( &start, &stop ) /
            (float) cIterations;
}
```

This function times the specified number of kernel launches and returns the microseconds per launch. `chTimerTimestamp` is a high-resolution timestamp. Usually it is a 64-bit counter that increases monotonically over time, so two timestamps are needed to compute a time interval.

The `chTimerGetTime()` function takes a snapshot of the current time. The `chTimerElapsedTime()` function returns the number of seconds that elapsed between two timestamps. The resolution of these timers is very fine (perhaps a microsecond), so `chTimerElapsedTime()` returns double.

```
#ifdef _WIN32
#include <windows.h>
typedef LARGE_INTEGER chTimerTimestamp;
#else
typedef struct timeval chTimerTimestamp;
#endif

void chTimerGetTime(chTimerTimestamp *p);
double chTimerElapsedTime ( chTimerTimestamp *pStart, chTimerTimestamp
*pEnd );
double chTimerBandwidth ( chTimerTimestamp *pStart, chTimerTimestamp
*pEnd, double cBytes );
```

We may use CUDA events when measuring performance in isolation on the CUDA-capable GPU, such as when measuring device memory bandwidth of a kernel. Using CUDA events for timing is a two-edged sword: They are less affected by spurious system-level events, such as network traffic, but that sometimes can lead to overly optimistic timing results.

A.2 Threading

chLib includes a minimalist threading library that enables the creation of a pool of "worker" CPU threads, plus facilities that enable a parent thread to "delegate" work onto worker threads. Threading is a particularly difficult feature to abstract, since different operating systems have such different facilities to enable it. Some operating systems even have "thread pools" that enable threads to be easily recycled, so applications don't have to keep threads suspended waiting for a synchronization event that will be signaled when some work comes along.

Listing A.1 gives the abstract threading support from chLib/chThread.h. It includes a processorCount() function that returns the number of CPU cores available (many applications that use multiple threads to take advantage of multiple CPU cores, such as our multithreaded N-body implementation in Chapter 14, want to spawn one thread per core) and a C++ class workerThread that enables a few simple threading operations.

Creation and destruction

- delegateSynchronous(): the parent thread specifies a pointer to function for the worker to execute, and the function does not return until the worker thread is done.

- delegateAsynchronous(): the parent thread specifies a pointer to function for the worker to run asynchronously; workerThread::waitAll must be called in order to synchronize the parent with its children.

- The member function waitAll() waits until all specified worker threads have completed their delegated work.

Listing A.1 workerThread class.

```
//
// Return the number of execution cores on the platform.
//
unsigned int processorCount();

//
// workerThread class - includes a thread ID (specified to constructor)
//
class workerThread
{
public:
    workerThread( int cpuThreadId = 0 );
    virtual ~workerThread();
    bool initialize( );

    // thread routine (platform specific)
    static void threadRoutine( LPVOID );

    //
    // call this from your app thread to delegate to the worker.
    // it will not return until your pointer-to-function has been
    // called with the given parameter.
    //
```

```
    bool delegateSynchronous( void (*pfn)(void *), void *parameter );

    //
    // call this from your app thread to delegate to the worker
    // asynchronously. Since it returns immediately, you must call
    // waitAll later

    bool delegateAsynchronous( void (*pfn)(void *), void *parameter );

    static bool waitAll( workerThread *p, size_t N );

};
```

A.3 Driver API Facilities

chDrv.h contains some useful facilities for driver API developers: The chCU-DADevice class, shown in Listing A.2, simplifies management of devices and contexts. Its loadModuleFromFile method simplifies the creation of a module from a .cubin or .ptx file.

In addition, the chGetErrorString() function passes back a read-only string corresponding to an error value. Besides implementing this function declared in chDrv.h for the driver API's CUresult type, a specialization of chGetError-String() also wraps the CUDA runtime's cudaGetErrorString() function.

Listing A.2 chCUDADevice class.

```
class chCUDADevice
{
public:
    chCUDADevice();
    virtual ~chCUDADevice();

    CUresult Initialize(
        int ordinal,
        list<string>& moduleList,
        unsigned int Flags = 0,
        unsigned int numOptions = 0,
        CUjit_option *options = NULL,
        void **optionValues = NULL );
    CUresult loadModuleFromFile(
        CUmodule *pModule,
        string fileName,
        unsigned int numOptions = 0,
        CUjit_option *options = NULL,
        void **optionValues = NULL );
```

```
    CUdevice device() const { return m_device; }
    CUcontext context() const { return m_context; }
    CUmodule module( string s ) const { return (*m_modules.find(s)).
second; }

private:
    CUdevice m_device;
    CUcontext m_context;
    map<string, CUmodule> m_modules;
};
```

A.4 Shmoos

A "shmoo plot" refers to a graphical display of test circuit patterns as two inputs (such as voltage and clock rate) vary. When writing code to identify the optimal blocking parameters for various kernels, it is useful to do similar tests by varying inputs such as the threadblock size and loop unroll factor. Listing A.3 shows the chShmooRange class, which encapsulates a parameter range, and the chShmooIterator class, which enables for loops to easily iterate over a given range.

Listing A.3 chShmooRange and chShmooIterator classes.

```
class chShmooRange {
public:
    chShmooRange( ) { }
    void Initialize( int value );
    bool Initialize( int min, int max, int step );
    bool isStatic() const { return m_min==m_max; }

    friend class chShmooIterator;

    int min() const { return m_min; }
    int max() const { return m_max; }

private:
    bool m_initialized;
    int m_min, m_max, m_step;
};

class chShmooIterator
{
public:
    chShmooIterator( const chShmooRange& range );
```

```
        int operator *() const { return m_i; }
        operator bool() const { return m_i <= m_max; }
        void operator++(int) { m_i += m_step; };
private:
        int m_i;
        int m_max;
        int m_step;
};
```

The command line parser also includes a specialization that creates a
chShmooRange based on command-line parameters: Prepend "min,"
"max," and "step" onto the keyword, and the corresponding range will be
passed back. If any of the three are missing, the function returns false. The
concurrencyKernelKernel sample (in the concurrency/subdirectory),
for example, takes measurements over ranges of stream count and clock cycle
count. The code to extract these values from the command line is as follows.

```
chShmooRange streamsRange;
const int numStreams = 8;
if ( ! chCommandLineGet(&streamsRange, "Streams", argc, argv) ) {
    streamsRange.Initialize( numStreams );
}
chShmooRange cyclesRange;
{
    const int minCycles = 8;
    const int maxCycles = 512;
    const int stepCycles = 8;
    cyclesRange.Initialize( minCycles, maxCycles, stepCycles );
    chCommandLineGet( &cyclesRange, "Cycles", argc, argv );
}
```

And users can specify the parameters to the application as follows.

```
concurrencyKernelKernel -- minStreams 2 --maxStreams 16 stepStreams 2
```

A.5 Command Line Parsing

A portable command line parsing library (only about 100 lines of C++) is in
chCommandLine.h. It includes the templated function chCommandLineGet(),
which passes back a variable of a given type, and chCommandLineGetBool(),
which returns whether a given keyword was given in the command line.

```
template<typename T> T
chCommandLineGet( T *p, const char *keyword, int argc, char *argv[] );
```

As described in the previous section, a specialization of chCommandLineGet()
will pass back an instance of chShmooRange. In order for this specialization to
be compiled, chShmoo.h must be included before chCommandLine.h.

A.6 Error Handling

chError.h implements a set of macros that implement the goto-based error
handling mechanism described in Section 1.2.3. These macros do the following.

- Assign the return value to a variable called status

- Check status for success and, if in debug mode, report the error to stderr

- If status contains an error, goto a label called Error

The CUDA runtime version is as follows.

```
#ifdef DEBUG
#define CUDART_CHECK( fn ) do { \
  (status) = (fn); \
  if ( cudaSuccess != (status) ) { \
  fprintf( stderr, "CUDA Runtime Failure (line %d of file %s):\n\t" \
  "%s returned 0x%x (%s)\n", \
  __LINE__, __FILE__, #fn, status, cudaGetErrorString(status) ); \
  goto Error; \
  } \
  } while (0);
#else

#define CUDART_CHECK( fn ) do { \
  status = (fn); \
  if ( cudaSuccess != (status) ) { \
  goto Error; \
  } \
} while (0);
#endif
```

The do..while is a C programming idiom, commonly used in macros, that
causes the macro invocation to evaluate to a single statement. Using these
macros will generate compile errors if either the variable status or the label
Error: is not defined.

One implication of using goto is that all variables must be declared at the top
of the block. Otherwise, some compilers generate errors because the goto
statements can bypass initialization. When that happens, the variables being

initialized must be moved above the first `goto` or moved into a basic block so the `goto` is outside their scope.

Listing A.4 gives an example function that follows the idiom. The return value and intermediate resources are initialized to values that can be dealt with by the cleanup code. In this case, all of the resources allocated by the function also are freed by the function, so the cleanup code and error handling code are the same. Functions that will only free some of the resources they allocate must implement the success and failure cases in separate blocks of code.

Listing A.4 Example of `goto`-based error handling.

```
double
TimedReduction(
    int *answer, const int *deviceIn, size_t N,
    int cBlocks, int cThreads,
    pfnReduction hostReduction
)
{
    double ret = 0.0;
    int *deviceAnswer = 0;
    int *partialSums = 0;
    cudaEvent_t start = 0;
    cudaEvent_t stop = 0;
    cudaError_t status;

    CUDART_CHECK( cudaMalloc( &deviceAnswer, sizeof(int) ) );
    CUDART_CHECK( cudaMalloc( &partialSums, cBlocks*sizeof(int) ) );
    CUDART_CHECK( cudaEventCreate( &start ) );
    CUDART_CHECK( cudaEventCreate( &stop ) );
    CUDART_CHECK( cudaThreadSynchronize() );

    CUDART_CHECK( cudaEventRecord( start, 0 ) );
    hostReduction(
        deviceAnswer,
        partialSums,
        deviceIn,
        N,
        cBlocks,
        cThreads );
    CUDART_CHECK( cudaEventRecord( stop, 0 ) );
    CUDART_CHECK( cudaMemcpy(
        answer,
        deviceAnswer,
        sizeof(int),
        cudaMemcpyDeviceToHost ) );

    ret = chEventBandwidth( start, stop, N*sizeof(int) ) /
        powf(2.0f,30.0f);
```

```
        // fall through to free resources before returning
Error:
    cudaFree( deviceAnswer );
    cudaFree( partialSums );
    cudaEventDestroy( start );
    cudaEventDestroy( stop );
    return ret;
}
```

Glossary / TLA Decoder

aliasing – Creating more than one way to access the same memory. Examples: A mapped pinned buffer in CUDA is aliased by a host pointer and a device pointer; a texture reference bound to device memory aliases the device memory.

AOS – *See* array of structures.

API – Application programming interface.

array of structures – Memory layout in which the elements that describe an object are contiguous in memory (as if declared in a structure). Contrast with *structure of arrays*.

asynchronous – Function calls that return before the requested operation has been performed. For correct results, CUDA applications using asynchronous operations subsequently must perform CPU/GPU synchronization using CUDA streams or events.

computational density – Amount of computation relative to external memory traffic.

constant memory – Read-only memory, optimized for broadcast when a single memory location is read.

CPU – Central processing unit. The conductor of the orchestra that is a modern computer these days, be it x86, x86-64, or ARM.

CUDA array – 1D, 2D, or 3D array whose layout is opaque to developers. Applications can read or write CUDA arrays using memcpy functions. CUDA kernels can read CUDA arrays via texture fetch, or read or write them using surface load/store intrinsics.

CUDART – CUDA runtime. The "high-level" API that comes with language integration.

DDI – Device driver interface. Examples of DDIs include XPDDM and WDDM.

demand paging – A system where the operating system can mark pages non-resident such that when an application tries to access a nonresident page, the hardware can signal an interrupt. The operating system can use this facility to mark pages nonresident that have not been accessed "in a while" according to some heuristic, writing their contents to disk to free up more physical memory for more active virtual pages.[1] If an application accesses the page again, the page is reloaded "on demand" (possibly to a different physical page). To date, GPUs implement a reasonably competent virtual memory system that decouples virtual and physical addresses, but they do not implement hardware for demand paging.

device memory – Memory that is readily accessible to the GPU. CUDA arrays, global memory, constant memory, and local memory are all different ways to manipulate device memory.

DMA – Direct memory access. When peripherals read or write CPU memory asynchronously and independently of the CPU.

driver – Software that uses OS facilities to expose a peripheral's hardware capabilities.

Driver API – The "low-level" API that enables full access to CUDA's facilities.

dynamic instruction count – The number of machine instructions actually executed by a program. Contrast with *static instruction count*.

ECC – Error correction code. Some CUDA hardware protects the external memory interface of the GPU by setting aside 12.5% of video memory (1 bit per 8 bits of accessible memory) and using it to detect and sometimes to correct errors in the memory transactions. nvidia-smi or the NVIDIA Management Library can be used to query whether correctable (single-bit) or uncorrectable (double-bit) errors have occurred.

front side bus (FSB) – Chipset interface to memory on non-NUMA system configurations.

global memory – Device memory that is read or written by CUDA kernels using pointers.

---

1. Demand paging hardware can be used to implement many other features, like copy-on-write and mapped file I/O. For more information, consult a textbook on operating systems.

GPU – Graphics processing unit.

GPU time – Time as measured by CUDA events, as opposed to the system timer. Such times can be used to direct optimization, but they do not give an accurate picture of overall performance. Contrast with *wall clock time*.

HPC – High performance computing.

ILP – See instruction level parallelism.

instruction level parallelism – The fine-grained parallelism between operations during program execution.

intrinsic function – A function that directly corresponds to a low-level machine instruction.

JIT – Just-in-time compilation. See also *online compilation*.

kernel mode – Privileged execution mode that can perform sensitive operations such as editing page tables.

kernel thunk – The transition from user mode to kernel mode. This operation takes several thousand clock cycles, so drivers running on operating systems that require kernel thunks in order to submit commands to the hardware must queue up hardware commands in user mode before performing the kernel thunk in order to submit them.

lane – Thread within a warp. The lane ID may be computed as `threadIdx.x&31`.

MMU – Memory management unit. The hardware in the CPU or GPU that translates virtual addresses to physical addresses and signals a problem when invalid addresses are specified.

node – A unit of memory bandwidth in NUMA systems. In inexpensive NUMA systems, nodes typically correspond to physical CPUs.

NUMA – Nonuniform memory access. Refers to the memory architecture of AMD Opteron or Intel Nehalem processors, where the memory controller is integrated into the CPU for lower latency and higher performance.

occupancy – The ratio of the number of warps executing in an SM as compared to the theoretical maximum.

online compilation – Compilation done at runtime, not when the developer builds the application.

opt-in – An API provision where the developer must request a behavior change at the interface level. For example, creating a blocking event is an "opt-in" because the developer must pass a special flag to the event creation APIs. Opt-ins are a way to expose new functionality without running the risk of regressions due to existing applications relying on the old behavior.

opt-out – An API provision to suppress a legacy behavior—for example, creating an event with timing disabled.

pageable memory – Memory that is eligible for eviction by the VMM. Operating system designers prefer memory to be pageable because it enables the operating system to "swap out" pages to disk and make the physical memory available for some other purpose.

page fault – The execution fault that happens when an application accesses virtual memory that is marked nonresident by the operating system. If the access was valid, the operating system updates its data structures (perhaps by pulling the page into physical memory and updating the physical address to point there) and resumes execution. If the access was not valid, the operating system signals an exception in the application.

page-locked memory – Memory that has been physically allocated and marked as nonpageable by the operating system. Usually this is to enable hardware to access the memory via DMA.

PCIe – PCI Express bus, used by CUDA for data interchange between host and device memory.

pinned memory; see *page-locked memory*.

pitched memory allocation – An allocation where the number of bytes per row is specified separately from the row elements multiplied by the element size. Used to accommodate alignment constraints that must stay the same from one row of the array to the next.

pitch-linear layout – The memory layout used for a pitched memory allocation, specified by a "tuple" of a base address and the number of bytes per row (the "pitch").

predicate – A single bit or Boolean true/false value. In C, an integer may be converted to a predicate by evaluating whether it is nonzero (true) or zero (false).

process – Unit of execution in multitasking operating systems, with its own address space and lifetime management of resources (such as file handles).

When the process exits, all resources associated with it are "cleaned up" by the operating system.

PTE – Page table entry.

PTX - Parallel Thread eXecution, the intermediate assembly language and bytecode used as input to the driver's JIT process when compiling onto a specific GPU architecture.

SASS – The assembly-level, native instruction set for CUDA GPUs. The meaning of the acronym has been lost in the mists of time, but Shader ASSembly language seems like a plausible guess!

SBIOS – System BIOS ("basic input/output system"). The firmware that controls the most basic aspects of a computer system's I/O subsystem, such as whether to enable CPU or chipset features that may not be supported by certain operating systems. The SBIOS is lower-level than the operating system.

shared memory – Onboard GPU memory used by CUDA kernels as a fast "scratchpad" to hold temporary results.

SIMD – Single instruction, multiple data—a primitive for parallel programming that involves performing a uniform operation across different data in parallel. The streaming multiprocessors in CUDA hardware operate in SIMD manner across 32 threads. SSE instructions in x86 hardware operate in SIMD manner on packed data across wide registers.

SM – Streaming multiprocessor—one of the core execution units of the GPU. The number of SMs in a GPU may range from 2 to dozens. Additionally, the instruction set of a GPU may be designated with a version number—for example, "SM 2.0."

SMX – Streaming multiprocessor, as implemented in Kepler-class (SM 3.x) hardware.

SSE – Streaming SIMD extensions. An instruction set extension added to x86 in the late 1990s that could perform four single-precision floating point operations in a single instruction. Later additions have enabled SIMD operations on integers and have widened the operations from 128 bits to 256 bits.

static instruction count – The number of machine instructions in a program; the amount of data occupied by the program increases with the static instruction count. Contrast with *dynamic instruction count*.

structure of arrays (SOA) – Memory layout that uses an array for each data element that describes an object. Contrast with *array of structures (AOS)*.

synchronous – An adjective used to describe functions that do not return until the requested operation has completed.

TCC – Tesla Compute Cluster driver, an XPDDM class driver that can run on Windows Vista and later. It does not get the benefits of WDDM (Windows Desktop Manager acceleration, graphics interoperability, emulated paging), but can submit commands to the hardware without performing a kernel thunk and implement the 64-bit unified address space.

Thrust – C++-based productivity library for CUDA, loosely based on the STL.

TLA – Three-letter acronym.

TLS – Thread local storage.

ulp – Unit of last precision—the least significant digit in the mantissa of a floating point value.

user mode – The unprivileged execution mode, where memory is generally pageable and hardware resources can only be accessed through APIs that interact with the operating system's kernel mode software.

UVA – Unified virtual addressing.

VMM – Virtual memory manager. The part of the operating system that manages memory: allocation, page-locking, managing page faults, and so on.

wall clock time – Time as measured by reading a system clock before and after performing a set of operations. The wall clock time includes all system effects and gives the most accurate measure of overall performance. Contrast with *GPU time*.

warp – The basic unit of execution for streaming multiprocessors. For the first three generations of CUDA hardware, warps have had exactly 32 threads, so the warp ID in a 1D threadblock may be computed as `threadIdx.x>>5`. Also see *lane*.

WDDM – Windows Display Driver Model. This driver model, new with Windows Vista, moved most of the display driver logic from kernel mode into user mode.

XPDDM – Windows XP Display Driver Model. Architecturally, this driver model actually dates back to Windows NT 4.0 (c. 1996). This acronym was invented at the same time as "WDDM" for contrast.

Index

    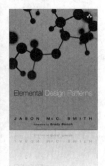

FREE
Online Edition

Your purchase of **The CUDA Handbook** includes access to a free online edition for 45 days through the **Safari Books Online** subscription service. Nearly every Addison-Wesley Professional book is available online through **Safari Books Online**, along with thousands of books and videos from publishers such as Cisco Press, Exam Cram, IBM Press, O'Reilly Media, Prentice Hall, Que, Sams, and VMware Press.

Safari Books Online is a digital library providing searchable, on-demand access to thousands of technology, digital media, and professional development books and videos from leading publishers. With one monthly or yearly subscription price, you get unlimited access to learning tools and information on topics including mobile app and software development, tips and tricks on using your favorite gadgets, networking, project management, graphic design, and much more.

Activate your FREE Online Edition at
informit.com/safarifree

STEP 1: Enter the coupon code: XNFBNXA.

STEP 2: New Safari users, complete the brief registration form.
Safari subscribers, just log in.

If you have difficulty registering on Safari or accessing the online edition,
please e-mail customer-service@safaribooksonline.com